D0350228

DIET FOR A DEAD PLANET

DIET FOR A DEAD PLANET

How the Food Industry Is Killing Us

CHRISTOPHER D. COOK

THE NEW PRESS

NEW YORK
LONDON

Requests for permission to reproduce selections from this book should be mailed to:
Permissions Department, The New Press, 38 Greene Street, New York, NY 10013

Published in the United States by The New Press, New York, 2004
Distributed by W. W. Norton & Company, Inc., New York

Library of Congress Cataloging-in-Publication Data

Cook, Christopher D., 1967–
    Diet for a dead planet: how the food industry is killing us / Christopher D. Cook.
    p. cm.
    Includes bibliographical references and index.
    ISBN 1-56584-864-0
    1. Food industry and trade—Health aspects. 2. Food adulteration and inspection.
3. Convenience foods—Health aspects. 4. Genetically modified foods. 5. Food
contamination. 6. Agricultural pollution. 7. Food industry and trade—Government
policy—United States. 8. Agriculture and state—United States. 9. Nutrition
policy—United States. I. Title.

HD9000.9.A1C65 2004
363.19'2—dc22   2004040324

The New Press was established in 1990 as a not-for-profit alternative to the large,
commercial publishing houses currently dominating the book publishing industry.
The New Press operates in the public interest rather than for private gain, and is
committed to publishing, in innovative ways, works of educational, cultural,
and community value that are often deemed insufficiently profitable.

www.thenewpress.com

Composition by Westchester Book Composition

Printed in the United States of America

2   4   6   8   10   9   7   5   3   1

CONTENTS

Acknowledgments   ix

Part I. Consumed
1. Agricultural Apocalypse   3
2. One Big Supermarket   12
3. Food Gone Mad   27
4. Dying from Consumption   44

Part II. The Rise of the Corporate Cornucopia
   Introduction   77
5. "Get Big or Get Out"   79
6. Agribusiness Takes Over   98
7. Almost Nothing Left: The 1980s   110
8. Hostile Takeover: The New Farm Crisis   125

Part III. Recipes for Disaster
   Introduction   155
9. Killing Fields: The Spraying of America   160
10. The Age of Effluents   174
11. Sliced and Diced: The Labor You Eat   187
12. Subsidizing Madness, Exporting Misery   217
13. The Good News: A Menu for Change   243

   Appendix: Resources   261
   Notes   283
   Index   317

This book is dedicated to my dear grandmother Ruth Brechner, 1915–2004, who always believed in me (and told me to eat well). This one is for you.

And for the farmers and workers.

ACKNOWLEDGMENTS

The making of a book entails accumulating years of thinking, knowledge, and favors. This book would be either nonexistent or vastly inferior to its present imperfect form were it not for many helping hands. Colin Robinson has been an outstanding publisher, providing astute guidance that has made this a better book than it otherwise would have been. The New Press staff, particularly Abigail Aguirre, Sarah Fan, and Lizzie Seidlin-Bernstein, has been blessedly patient and attentive. Katherine Scott provided sharp editing. Claudia Eyzaguirre and Brynn Saito, both up-and-coming writers, helped bolster my case with excellent research assistance.

My dear friend and colleague John Rodgers, with whom I co-wrote stories on community food security that are quoted within, critiqued the entire manuscript and gave incisive feedback that always kept me on my toes. Christian Parenti, lifelong comrade-in-arms, helped me develop the ideas and overall frame for the book and gave valuable critiques (and invaluable encouragement) along the way. Rachel Brahinsky, friend and literary comet, generously provided her finely tuned ear for sharpening prose and clarifying concepts, and was generally a big help. Heather Rogers, filmmaker and writer and comrade, doled out very helpful insights on several chapters. Camille Taiara and A.C. Thompson also gave sharp critiques that helped the book.

Eric Bates, a great magazine editor, critiqued portions of the manuscript and has been a source of inspiration and support. Matthew Rothschild and Anne-Marie Cusac of *The Progressive* published much of my work on labor in the food industry, and encouraged me to stay on the story. I am extremely grateful for the guidance, support, and friendship of Ross Gelbspan, as well as Donald Barlett and James B. Steele—all shining exemplars of the craft. I would also like to thank my original mentor, Diana Hembree, then of the Center for Investigative Reporting, who cultivated my instinct to dig deeper. I am, too, immensely thankful for the immeasurable gift of time and space generously provided by Peter Barnes and the Mesa Refuge, and the Blue Mountain Center in upstate New York—without these treasures, I, and many other writers and artists, would be much poorer. My appreciation also goes out to my fine office mates and colleagues at the San Francisco Writers' Grotto.

John Gulick and Joshua Bloom provided useful general feedback and intellectual booster shots, as did Erica Etelson and Kathleen McClung. For all their undying friendship and support, I give great thanks to my extended "family": Chris, Shannon, Noah, Laurie and Andy, Will, Kim, Leslie, and Greg. I am, above all, deeply grateful for the loving support (and laughter) of Ginger Williamson, who has taught me much and without whom I would be a lesser person. And finally, thanks to my mother and father, Jane and Bob, who encouraged me to think and care about the world.

Part I

Consumed

AGRICULTURAL APOCALYPSE

"The food business is far and away the most important business in the world. Everything else is a luxury. Food is what you need to sustain life every day. Food is fuel. You can't run a tractor without fuel, and you can't run a human being without it either. Food is the absolute beginning."

—Dwayne Andreas, former chairman,
Archer Daniels Midland

AISLE 5: BROWSING THE GLOBAL GARDEN

You are in the supermarket, exhausted after another long day at the office (or perhaps the factory). You just want to get home and eat, and now your senses are pummeled by the brightly packaged bounty all around you. You are at once awakened and overwhelmed. What will you pick from this vast corporate garden?

It's an astounding selection, a global cornucopia that appears—at first glance—to be relatively affordable (at least for the economically comfortable). Shiny, freshly waxed fruits and vegetables, radiantly colored, beckon from overflowing bins; there's nary a bruise or nonconforming shape in sight. Broccoli, oranges, bananas, asparagus, melons, and pineapples are piled high in the middle of winter. Crops hailing from Mexico, Guatemala, Honduras, Chile, Argentina, every productive corner of America, and elsewhere display the terrific powers of industrial agriculture, seemingly boundless international trade, and rapid long-distance transport of perishable foods.

A short stroll away, past a rainbow of fruit cocktails and juices and columns of dairy products, lie coolers stuffed with all kinds of meat, chicken, and fish—sliced and diced, "lean" and "choice cut," marinated and filleted. A few more swivels of the shopping cart reveal long fluorescent boulevards of packages and cans, each promising to save you time and enliven your taste buds. There are precut and flavored fruits and vegetables (produce with "value added"), fully prepared kids' lunches, multicolored chips, soups and stews, frozen dinners, a whole kingdom of precision-flavored cereals, sauces, and powdered meals. Just add water and plug in the microwave. It's a bachelor's or working parent's paradise.

In today's American supermarket, there are no seasons, no limits. The world's harvests and manufactured meals are at your fingertips. It's like a miraculous gastronomic democracy—Roman Empire–style excess readily available to the common man and woman. The supermarket appears to symbolize the best of democratic capitalism, offering consumer choice and a bounty born of amazing productivity. But what makes this unprecedented harvest possible? How does all this food actually get here? Is it really as cheap and convenient as it seems? On this side of the balance sheet, things look too good to be true.

In fact, this veneer of epicurean egalitarianism conceals a less glamorous set of realities. Food, our most basic necessity, has become a force behind a staggering array of social, economic, and environmental epidemics—a toxic cornucopia of poison-laminated harvests, extreme labor abuse, and treacherous and secretive science. At the reins of the food combine are a few increasingly monopolistic corporations controlling nearly every aspect of human sustenance. The way we make, market, and eat food today creates rampant illness, hunger, poverty, community disintegration, and ecological degradation—and threatens our future food supply. Welcome to what I'd call Silent Autumn.

Consider for a moment the other side of the ledger:

- The way this extraordinary bounty is produced is putting our future at risk: eroding topsoil and water supplies, poisoning the ground, and polluting rivers and streams with millions of gallons of pesticide and literally tons of toxic manure runoff from huge animal factory farms.

- The meat and chicken in your cart are filled with growth hormones and pesticides—nothing likely to *kill* anyone but enough to pose possible long-term health risks. What can—and does—kill is all the bacteria in the meat, a plague exacerbated by the way animals are "farmed" in enormous warehouses and processed on lightning-fast assembly lines. Thousands of people die each year from food-borne illnesses, and hundreds of thousands more require hospital care.

- Thanks in part to all that meat and dairy, and the proliferation of fats and sugars in processed foods, close to two thirds of Americans are overweight, and nearly one third are obese.

- Meat-packing and poultry plants, by virtue of the intense speed and volume of their output, maim and cripple tens of thousands of workers each year. Many of them are immigrants shipped up from Mexico and Central America, and are discarded and replaced every few months. Our meat supply and a large portion of our fruit and vegetable harvests rely on this steady flow of cheap, highly exploited, disposable labor.

- The system that produces and transports this superabundance runs on oil and diesel. The average food item on your supermarket shelf has traveled roughly 1,500 miles, and all that long-distance transport requires millions of gallons of diesel fuel. On today's industrial farm, giant tractors and combines spew diesel fumes and kick up dust pollution, while huge single-crop harvests are coaxed by 15 million tons of petroleum-based fertilizers each year.[1] Experts such as Cornell University's Dr. David Pimentel have found that U.S. agriculture—largely through its reliance on petrochemical-based pesticides and fertilizers—uses some 400 gallons of fossil fuels a year to feed every American. That's more than 100 *billion* gallons of oil and oil equivalents used in the United States each year just to manufacture food.[2]

- The bulk of the food items in your shopping cart—especially the meat, dairy, and packaged products—are produced by a handful of exceedingly powerful corporations that exercise increasing

control over what we eat, how it is made, how much it costs, and who produces and profits from it.
- Due largely to this intensifying corporate takeover, nearly 20,000 farmers go under each year—more than 300 farm closures a week, about 50 every day. America loses one farm every half-hour.[3] When farms shut down, the social and economic fabric of rural communities and small towns is shattered. And whole generations of highly skilled producers of food are lost.

These are just some of the immense costs we never see itemized on our grocery bill. But we pay them nonetheless, in the form of taxes and public spending: in excess of $10 billion a year in public health costs to treat food-related illnesses, not to mention diabetes, obesity, and heart disease;[4] environmental expenses for monitoring and cleaning up factory-farm-runoff spills that have discharged millions of tons of animal manure into rivers and streams; workers' compensation costs and public medical bills for injured farmworkers and meat factory employees, who typically have no insurance; unemployment and welfare payments to foreclosed farmers and often to employees of many of the surrounding businesses that rely on those farmers. The list goes on. It is part of the hidden price we all pay for subsidizing a few powerful corporations and a system that is at its core unsustainable.

THE BAD MIRACLE

How is it that providing humanity's food has become a force of such destructive magnitude? Since the 1950s we have heard agribusiness feverishly boasting of its triumphs: giant new machines raking in phenomenally massive harvests; the miraculous ever-increasing productivity of the American farm, breadbasket and supermarket to the world; an array of high-tech über-plants. No one can deny that the modern industrial superfarm produces unprecedented bounty. But until lately we have heard little about the severe consequences, what a recent anthology calls "the tragedy of industrial agriculture."[5] There is growing awareness of the links between our system of food production and seemingly isolated issues like obesity, poisonous hamburgers, and the many other perils of a "fast-food nation."[6] But most of the by-products of big agriculture are far removed from supermarket shelves. "The present land economy rests on a foundation of general ignorance," argues the famed writer-farmer Wendell Berry. "Most of us don't know how we live and at what costs, either ecologically or human. . . . For how long can we maintain an industrial superstition that we can beat the world by destroying the world's capacity to produce food?"[7]

Our ignorance is nurtured by and also strengthens the growing corporate stranglehold on our food system. In recent years, leading firms like Tyson Foods, Safeway, Archer Daniels Midland (ADM), and Cargill have gobbled up competitors and consolidated their near-monopoly control over the entire food chain. In just three years, between 1997 and 2000, the top five food retailers in America (Kroger, Albertson's, Wal-Mart, Safeway, and Ahold USA) nearly doubled their market share, growing from 24 percent of all retail food sales to an amazing 42 percent.[8] The top four beef producers account for an almost unprecedented 80 percent of the U.S. meat market.[9] Each time the Justice Department approves another merger or takeover, both farmers and consumers lose more control over what we grow and eat, how it is grown, and how much it costs.

Every day agribusiness claims new victims: farmers are erased from the landscape, never to return; local and regional brand-name food companies and supermarkets are sucked up by ever-larger corporations; wind-borne corporate-patented seeds from genetically engineered crops descend on neighboring fields, effectively destroying sustainable organic alternatives. We are losing control over "the absolute beginning" of life.

THIS BOOK IS GMO-FREE

In this book you will find virtually nothing about the latest grave assault on our food system, genetically modified crops. Reams of books and studies debate the real purpose and impact of genetically modified organisms (GMOs) on our health and the environment. There is evidence suggesting that these corporate-patented superplants pose a real ecological threat and endanger future biodiversity. They may also be a significant hazard to people with allergies, by blending together different foods that are marketed ubiquitously, without labeling. One example: Brazil nut proteins are inserted into soybeans; one study found this particular concoction caused reactions in people allergic to Brazil nuts. Most genetically modified foods, according to the Union of Concerned Scientists, "carry fully functioning antibiotic-resistance genes"—which could potentially "reduce the effectiveness of antibiotics to fight disease when these antibiotics are taken with meals."[10]

The truth is, much of the time we don't really know what we're eating. Critics acknowledge that the science on GM hazards is not conclusive. Indeed, that's the problem: with our government's blessing, a few politically influential firms (most famously Monsanto) have almost overnight turned our corn and soybean harvests into genetically engineered experiments. We consumers are the guinea pigs. The U.S. Food and Drug Administration accepts the results of Monsanto's Roundup Ready field tests at face value, without verification, and gives the company the green light to continue growing. So much for the precautionary principle, which also seems to have been modified: First, do no harm—to profits.[11]

Genetically modified food is billed by industry (and the government) as the next great thing to eliminate world hunger, a technological marvel that, for instance, infuses staple foods like rice with extra vitamins. But research shows demonstratively that hunger and malnutrition are caused not by any global food shortage, but instead by severe economic inequalities and lack of distribution and access.[12] There is, without any need of new-fangled food technologies, more than enough food to feed the world. According to the UN Food and Agriculture Organization, the world's total food supply as of 2001 contained 2,800 calories and 76 grams of protein per person, per day—plenty to sustain a burgeoning population and stamp out hunger, if distributed equitably.[13] Yet despite this global abundance, some 842 million people—798 million of them in poor "developing" countries—are undernourished.[14] The real problem is not a food shortage but the fact that the same miraculous productivity that stuffs our supermarkets and fattens our waistlines dumps its excesses onto developing countries, often destroying their internal markets and burying poor Third World farmers in an avalanche of cheap American food, exacerbating hunger and dependency. This is a problem of economics and policy, not science.

Headlines register the raging skirmishes over bizarre and scary new laboratory-arranged marriages between animals and plants. It's clearly the hottest food topic today. But the gene revolution is part of a far broader, long-developing war between corporate agribusiness and, well, the rest of us—those who farm food and those who eat it. The increasing alienation, via processing technologies, of food from its essence—from powdered potatoes and frozen dinners to self-sterilizing seeds and flounder-infused tomatoes—diminishes both the diet and the market for fresh, unaltered produce. With so much attention focused now on fast food and GM crops, one might easily conclude these are the only urgent food-industry problems to be remedied. But even if we strip away these much-discussed crises, even if they were somehow resolved overnight, we are still left with an overall food system that causes phenomenal harm to society and the planet. My focus in this book is on these other, more systemic problems.

VALUE *SUBTRACTED*

Nearly everything in the supermarket outside the produce aisle has, as consumer economists put it, "value added." Usually that "value" adds up to a long list of undecipherable chemicals and "flavors," processing in one or more factories, and a lot of packaging. Then there's all the hidden "value" that's "added" by a host of intermediaries, such as grain elevators, wholesalers, and long-distance distributors who stand between the producers and consumers of food. This "value" is actually added cost to the consumer—and profit to the intermediaries. Every time value is added off the farm, both farmers and consumers lose a little bit more money and control in the marketplace—and farmers' role in the food web gets smaller and smaller, their prospects for survival dimmer. Call it value subtracted.

But: Does it really matter who makes our food, so long as we have it? Why should I or anyone else who buys and eats food care? The very way we eat—not just *what* we eat, but *how* we eat—affects the future of food. Our buying and dining choices today affect our food options tomorrow. It's not so simple as big farm versus small farm, pesticides against organics, natural versus genetically modified. The food we eat is the product of a whole system that is in the process of destroying itself—poisoning our air and water, grinding topsoil into useless dust, and putting farmers out to pasture. If we are to have a truly healthy cornucopia that sustains society, the entire system of making, distributing, and marketing food must be sustainable.

What does that mean? Banning all pesticides is not, by itself, the solution (though, as I document in chapter 6, doing so would save the lives of millions of birds and fish and, quite possibly, of tens of thousands of people). Nor is it enough to limit farm size and curtail factory farms and corporate food oligopolies. Niche markets promoting small farms and organic produce are very promising, yet often fall prey to elite, upscale pricing and corporate takeover. Any approach that focuses on one part of the system—such as helping farmers, consumers, or the environment—will indeed produce some benefits but will fail to deal with the deeper fundamental problem underlying the entire food system. Today's food fight is not merely a struggle between small farms and big farms, nor one over whether our tacos and corn dogs will be tainted with genetically engineered corn. It is about power and control over food: how it is produced, by whom, and for whom.

What's needed, I argue in the end, is a whole new way of thinking about food, one that encompasses health, affordability, accessibility, ecological sustainability, and an economics that enables farmers to keep farming. We need a new economics of farming and food that sustains the whole system, not just one group or another. The way we currently are meeting our essential life need for food is eroding our ability to feed future generations. Farmers, so distantly romantic to the urban and suburban consumer, are as crucial as ever to our future survival, yet they have all but vanished from the public consciousness and the pastoral landscape. Once a nation of farmers, America has become profoundly detached from the source of its food.

Every five years Congress wages war over something called the Farm Bill, whose provisions determine much about our nation's (and the world's) food supply. Yet, tellingly, the debate surrounding the bill is framed as if the issue affected only rural farm states rather than as one that affects us all. What if, as the writer Michael Pollan has suggested, we called it the Food Bill?[15] Perhaps this would help stitch together in the public mind the no longer obvious connection between farming and food. If there is one underlying purpose to this book, it is to lay bare these connections—to stimulate thinking, and encourage action, that goes beyond single-topic pursuits and makes the broader food crisis a central aspect of our social and economic priorities, and public policy.

Because ultimately, we all suffer: some quickly, from tainted meat and foreclosed farms, others gradually, from pesticide sprayings and sugar- and fat-laden carcinogenic diets. The only winners are large-scale subsidized farmers and agribusiness executives and shareholders. But even they must eat.

ONE BIG SUPERMARKET

"Attractively priced specials lure customers through the doors; the store cheerfully takes the loss it suffers on the item and compensates by markups on other merchandise, often strategically shelved near the alluring loss leader. Carefully calculated store arrangements place high-profit items along the most heavily traversed aisles."
—John L. Shover, *First Majority, Last Minority: The Transforming of Rural Life in America* (1976)

"Wal-Mart coming to your village is like the black plague of death arriving."
—Mark Husson, senior food and drug analyst, Merrill Lynch (1999)

As witness A and witness B entered the room with black hoods draped over their heads, the chairman of the Senate Small Business Committee commanded the television camera crews to avert their lenses. With the help of guards, the witnesses were led down the aisle and escorted to their seats concealed behind a wall of smoked glass. "My family's American dream is collapsing," said witness B, her voice electronically altered to keep her identity secret. "It's scary to think I might not be in business tomorrow."[1]

The witnesses weren't hiding from Mafia death threats. They were, one report described, "small manufacturers who say they're losing sales because they can't afford the high fees that retailers demand for putting their products on the shelves."[2] They were the brave ones: of eighty potential witnesses contacted by the committee, only six agreed to testify, even anonymously; three of these backed out. Many of them feared economic retribution from supermarket companies' purchasing agents.

Grocery purchasing agents seem an unlikely group to instill such fear, but food producers who complain about the fees they must pay for shelf access—known as "slotting fees," or "vendor allowances," or "hello payments"—can quickly find themselves shut out of business. "We have heard too many instances where someone complaining about slotting fees has been totally excluded from the market," said Senator Christopher S. Bond, a Missouri Republican. "Anybody who complains about the fees publicly, even anonymously, if they're discovered, gets dealt with."[3]

Welcome to the cutthroat shadowy world of supermarket pricing, where coveted shelf space is "the most expensive real estate in America," as Bond put it.[4] Store shelves, which appear as neatly, logically arranged displays of food for consumer convenience, are actually a secretive battleground in which increasingly powerful supermarkets use their economic leverage to exact a whole host of fees and payments—often off the books, sometimes legally dubious—from food companies and farmers.

Witness B, owner of a small yet successful food manufacturer in operation since the 1950s, said exorbitant grocery-store shelving fees have knocked many of her colleagues out of business: "Over a period of several years I have watched other family-owned businesses in my industry be destroyed by a combination of the large predatory competitor and through the consolidation of retail grocers with the ever increasing demand for slotting fees." Small family-run businesses, muscled out by corporations that can afford the fees, are not the only victims. "Those manufacturers who cannot pay the slotting fees are squeezed literally out of the competitive marketplace," she told the committee. And firms that do pay "are forced to recoup the fees by charging higher prices for their products, which ultimately harms the consumer."[5]

This growing problem, she noted, is "exacerbated by the trend toward consolidation of the grocery retailers into ever-larger, national supermarket conglomerates, with commensurately more power over manufacturers and fewer shopping outlets for consumers." As today's corporate supermarket chains attain intense economic power and market share, they not only have shunted aside innumerable local and regional businesses but also have gained control of the public marketplace for food, defining what is available for consumption, to whom, and at what price. Certainly consumers help shape this demand and supply, and ultimately decide what sells, but only after supermarkets have narrowed down the field of choices and set the going price. And these choices dictate to a large extent what we eat and who supplies it.

A detailed report by a team of researchers at the University of Missouri, released in 2001, spells out some of the consequences of the growing mega-supermarket. Corporate retailers, they wrote, "are now in a position to dictate terms to food manufacturers who then force changes back through the system to the farm level." The researchers estimated that between 50 and 75 percent of total net profit for the large supermarkets comes from the fees—slotting allowances, display fees, presentation fees, "pay-to-stay" fees—they are able to impose on manufacturers and wholesalers.[6]

MORE THAN THE MARKET CAN BEAR

For the distinct privilege of selling food in today's supermarket, a company must fork over anywhere from $1,000 to $20,000 for each product, witness A testified. "When a new product is introduced, one can expect at least one hundred thousand dollars in fees just to call on fifteen accounts before you do any selling of any kind." Small firms, he said, are hard-pressed to foot the bill: the number of businesses "with products on the shelves of the national chains," with annual sales under $15 million "can be counted on one hand." Sometimes even paying the bill and signing a contract isn't enough. Agreements guaranteeing shelf space for a period of one to two years, said witness B, "are often broken because the buyer will receive a new and more financially rewarding program from the dominant competitor."

Supermarket executives insist they need the money to cover losses from the many new products that fail to sell. Since they purchase items up-front, they need some protection. But the fees—and numerous other "pay-to-play" schemes—extend to such "new products" as fruits and vegetables. Farmers large and small are "battling like never before to remain economically viable," said David Moore, president of the Western Growers Association, in hearings about slotting fees before the same Senate committee a year later. "The proliferation of slotting fees and other anticompetitive business practices by the large supermarkets is a very real threat to family farmers."[7] When growers "are also required to pay up-front fees or provide free merchandise to retailers to stock their produce," Senator Bond noted, "it becomes significantly more difficult for farmers to make a profit and continue to farm."

Such threats, added Thomas E. Stenzel, the president and CEO of the United Fresh Fruit and Vegetable Association, include a "seemingly growing appetite for side deals, slotting fees, rebates, allowances, promotional fees, and all sorts of charges ranging from warehouse construction to store remodeling that are not contained in contracts, do not appear on invoices, and are otherwise unaccounted for in transactions." Secret off-the-books charges are frequent. So powerful are the supermarkets that "even the very largest produce companies are concerned about these practices," said Stenzel.

In one case recounted by Moore in Senate hearings, Ralph's/Food 4 Less Warehouse Stores, a giant corporate retailer, required produce farmers and shippers to pay a "new distributing facility opening fee" to defray its expansion costs. Growers were in effect required to pay Ralph's, either in money or free product, "to help underwrite the cost of construction of [a] new warehouse," built to "benefit the efficiency of the retailer," explained Moore.[8] According to a policy paper by the Arizona-based National Food and Agriculture Policy Project, one produce shipper "even disclosed that his firm was required to make a substantial contribution to a particular charity at the behest of a retail buyer."[9]

Some food companies allege they are victims of outright shakedowns. One food manufacturer reportedly told CBS News, "When I went in, that particular buyer in that particular case asked for ten thousand dollars personally and between one hundred and two hundred thousand for his stores."[10] In another instance, according to testimony by Robert N. Pyle, president of the Independent Bakers Association, a supermarket chain in the New York area "regularly charges twenty

thousand dollars for each new item introduced by a food manufacturer, as well as 'requesting' annual contributions to the purchasing
manager's Christmas party."[11]

Even without these extralegal payments, "legitimate" slotting fees
have become a lucrative income source for supermarkets, netting them
up to $9 billion a year, according to the Federal Trade Commission. In
a 2003 report, the commission said that shelf payments can represent
"a large fraction of the revenues earned by some products in their first
year"; the study estimated it could cost a firm upward of $2 million in
slotting fees alone to introduce a product nationwide.

Such information can be hard to come by: supermarket chains,
claiming to be protecting proprietary information, have repeatedly
stonewalled government inquiries. When the U.S. Department of Agriculture (USDA) tried to gather data on the fees, the industry refused to
cooperate.[12] The supermarkets also stymied an investigation by the
General Accounting Office, known for its dogged pursuit of information. "Despite repeated attempts over the last eight months, we have
been unsuccessful in gaining the cooperation needed from the industry to conduct this study," the GAO's Lawrence J. Dyckman told the
Senate Small Business Committee in 2000. He said it was the only time
in more than thirty years with the agency that he couldn't complete a
study.[13] All of this prompted Senator Bond to call slotting fees "the
'dirty little secret' in retailing. Often nothing is in writing between the
manufacturer and the retailer, and the amount of money paid in slotting fees is usually known only to supermarkets, their brokers and distributors."

A NICE SPREAD

The industry claims shelf-access charges enrich competition and innovation, providing consumers with only the best products, the ones
worth paying hundreds of thousands of dollars to get on the shelves.
"Slotting fees, if properly structured, are a legal and rational approach
to allocating the cost of new product introductions in a way that can

benefit consumers," insists Tim Hammonds, president of the Food Marketing Institute, which represents more than 20,000 retail food stores. "Entrepreneurs with good ideas that meet consumer needs can succeed."[14]

Among economists and antitrust experts, there is considerable debate about the impact these fees have on consumer prices. Some claim the charges enable supermarkets to offer competitive prices for shoppers. But there is a good deal of anecdotal evidence to suggest supermarkets are using their power to inflate food prices. "As buying power concentrates within the retail grocery industry, fresh produce growers have fewer customers to whom they can sell their products," says Michael J. Stuart, the president of the Florida Fruit and Vegetable Association. "The net result is continued pressure to reduce prices paid to growers." Yet consumers, Stuart notes, "rarely see the benefit of these lower prices at the supermarket. . . . Consumers get no relief at the marketplace and growers see no increased sales of their products."[15] (Related research suggests consolidation in the food-processing business, including products such as processed meat and canned foods, often leads to higher prices. A 2002 study by agricultural economist Azzeddine Azzam at the University of Nebraska found that increased concentration led to higher consumer prices in twenty-four of thirty-three food-processing industries.)[16]

According to Moore of the Western Growers Association, wholesale produce prices frequently "have dropped without any corresponding decrease in the retail price. This is strong evidence that consumers are being adversely impacted when large retailers have the market power to keep prices high when wholesale prices paid to growers are declining." This "price spread," the often huge gap between what supermarkets pay and what consumers are charged, amounts to lower incomes for farmers, greater profits for supermarkets, and higher food costs for shoppers. The gulf between wholesale and retail prices can be quite enormous—retail may be 400 percent to as high as 1000 percent higher than wholesale prices, Moore told Congress. And these already profitable spreads for supermarkets "do not include any additional

payments by the growers to retailers in the form of slotting fees, rebates, promotional allowances or other off-invoice fees."[17]

A detailed database maintained by the produce growers group
provides a glimpse into this profit divide. In February 2004, while
farmers were getting just $.19 for a pound of red-leaf lettuce, markets
in Chicago were charging $1.57, a 726 percent markup, and stores in
New York asked $1.92, a markup of more than 900 percent. For a ten-
pound bag of potatoes the markup was smaller, yet still quite high:
farmers got $.58 whereas markets across the country were getting be-
tween $3 and $4. Tomatoes and other basic produce offered similar low
returns for farmers and nifty markups for supermarkets.[18]

ONE BIG SUPERMARKET

What gives supermarkets such free rein to, in the great American tradition, buy low and sell high? Sheer economic might seems to be the primary ingredient. Over the past ten years, the supermarket business has
undergone phenomenal consolidation, with giant retail chains corner-
ing more and more of this hotly contested market. Even the USDA's
Economic Research Service acknowledged, "The spread of slotting fees
and other trade practices and consolidation among grocery retailers
and wholesalers has raised concerns that such practices may reflect increased buyer power" on the part of supermarkets. The nation's largest
twenty retailers have dramatically increased their share of total grocery
sales, expanding from 40.4 percent in 1987 to 58.9 percent by 2001.[19]

The exuberant go-go nineties spurred retail consolidation into high
gear. Between 1996 and 2000, ever-larger competitors bought out
nearly 3,500 supermarkets representing annual sales of $67 billion. In
1998, corporate executives announced two of the "largest food retailing
combinations in history": the merger of fourth-ranked Albertson's
with American Stores, number two at the time, and the acquisition by
top-ranked Kroger Company of Fred Meyer, then the country's sixth-
largest food retailer. As these leading firms culled their competitors,
their market share ballooned. Between 1992 and 1998, the top four
supermarket chains nearly doubled their portion of national grocery

sales, from 15.9 percent to 28.8 percent;[20] by 2001 the top five grocers gobbled up 42 percent of all retail food sales in America.[21] What is perhaps equally startling is that economists consider these levels of concentrated corporate power to be low, noting there is still plenty of room for more takeovers.

The thunderous arrival of Wal-Mart, by far the world's largest retailer, on the food scene has intensified the rush by Kroger, Safeway, and others to expand in order to protect their backyard from the Arkansas-based behemoth. Wal-Mart, which "had virtually nonexistent food sales in 1993," now sits atop America's supermarket food pyramid, boasting $65 billion in annual grocery sales in 2002—far exceeding the $50 billion sales of Kroger, the onetime supermarket king, according to *Supermarket News*.[22] "Wal-Mart coming to your village is like the black plague of death arriving," a Merrill Lynch food and drug analyst, Mark Husson, told a 1999 shopping-center-industry convention. Mom-and-pop stores are not the only ones endangered: According to the *Wall Street Journal*, when Wal-Mart plunked down two Supercenters near a Kroger supermarket in Houston, "the Kroger's sales dropped 10%."[23] And analysts observe, "More consolidation in the grocery sector, due to factors such as the emergence of superstores . . . is inevitable."[24] As of 2002, Wal-Mart and its subsidiaries, including 517 Sam's Club warehouse stores and its new forty-nine-store chain called Neighborhood Market, occupied a robust 10 percent of the $682 billion U.S. grocery market.[25]

Ironically, the intense supermarket consolidations of the late 1980s and early 1990s enabled Wal-Mart to crack the food retail business. "With less competition, the price of food sold at supermarkets nationwide grew at twice the rate of the producer-price index from 1991 through 2001, fattening profits," the *Wall Street Journal* explained. Wal-Mart "could come in, cut prices 10 to 15% and still make a profit." Wal-Mart's burgeoning success left a long trail of economic carcasses in its wake: of twenty-nine supermarket chains that filed for bankruptcy in the past decade, Wal-Mart was "a catalyst in 25 of those cases."[26]

The Wal-Mart formula for success includes its everything-under-one-roof strategy, luring shoppers through scale and convenience. Its potent high-volume buying power enables huge discounts that under-cut the competition: "Studies show that items at Wal-Mart cost 8% to 27% less than at Kroger, Albertson's or Safeway, including discounts from these competitors' loyalty cards and specials," the *Journal* reported. Labor-cost cutting and union busting are other key strategies in the megastore's repertoire. America's top employer, with more than 1 million hourly workers punching in each day, Wal-Mart pays an average wage of $18,000 a year (often as low as $14,000), but deducts payments for a voluntary health plan that costs up to $2,800. As one employee, Jennifer McLaughlin, told *Mother Jones*, "They're on top of the Fortune 500, and I can't get health insurance for my kid."[27] As the undisputed market leader, Wal-Mart's purchasing and labor efficiencies set the industry standard, pressuring competitors like Safeway—embroiled in a long strike in 2003–4 over increased employee health-care costs and other issues—to follow suit. A *New York Times* story reported that California supermarkets' "fears of fierce competition from Wal-Mart and their related drive to cut costs are widely seen as the main reason" behind the huge strike involving 70,000 unionized supermarket workers in Southern California in early 2004. Those unionized workers make 50 percent more than Wal-Mart employees in wages and benefits, and Wal-Mart saves considerably by paying 30 percent less for health coverage per insured worker than the industry average.[28]

NOT COMING TO A NEIGHBORHOOD NEAR YOU

The seemingly boundless economic ambitions of Safeway, Wal-Mart, Kroger, and their cohorts, however, often fail to cross to the poorer side of the railroad tracks. Access to food markets has long been a problem for lower-income communities, and now there is increasing evidence that the era of supermarket concentration has come particularly at the expense of the poor, thus exacerbating the situation. The more intensely competitive the business gets, the more supermarket firms eye poor neighborhoods warily as potentially risky investments. As retail power consolidates, explains a team of University of Missouri researchers, "smaller entities in all parts of the food system are being left out. The retailer fees in place at most of the larger retail stores present barriers to smaller processors and/or farmers wishing to place products on the retail shelf. Such restructuring presents critical problems for consumers and communities in inner urban and rural areas that are no longer profitable for global food clusters."[29]

The "white flight" to the suburbs in the 1950s and 1960s, when much of the white middle class fled inner-city neighborhoods, pulled supermarkets with it. Crime and poverty, both real and perceived, were seen as bad for business. Increasingly, access to decent food became not solely an issue of affordability but of one's race and geographic location. For the inner-city poor, particularly African Americans, healthy food was getting harder to find, as a combination of social and economic forces, including supermarket industry relocations, created a type of dietary segregation. And out of this arose a host of serious public health concerns, as whole generations of low-income urban residents grew up on food that was, as it turned out, neither nutritious nor cheap.

The trend of pulling out of poorer neighborhoods became known as supermarket redlining, analogous to bank and insurance industry redlining, a pattern of businesses' refusal to invest and locate in poor urban neighborhoods. "Various studies suggest that low-income households, particularly those in rural areas and poor central cities, have less access to reasonably priced, high-quality food than other households," said a 2001 article published by the USDA's Economic Research Service.[30] That may be putting it cautiously. A 1995 study by the University of Connecticut's Food Marketing Policy Center examined twenty-one major metropolitan areas in the United States and found that there were "30% fewer supermarkets in low-income areas than in higher-income areas."[31] Mark Winne, director of the nonprofit Hartford Food System, remarked, "There are two ways to buy food in Connecticut, one for the poor and one for everybody else."[32] This "grocery gap" has hit numerous major American cities. Exacerbated by the rash of supermarket mergers and buyouts in the 1980s, several metro areas were left with fewer shopping options. In much-maligned Detroit, a city of roughly 1 million, just eight major supermarkets can be found, even as its suburbs offer large grocery stores on most major street corners.[33] Between 1970 and 1992, thirty-four of Boston's fifty supermarkets closed their doors. In Chicago during the same period, more than half of the city's one thousand-plus super-markets shut down. Los Angeles, too, lost more than three hundred large food stores.[34]

In the wake of Los Angeles' fiery urban riots of 1992, city officials, academics, and even industry executives "recognized the need to over-come the unequal distribution of supermarkets . . . that left low-income communities underserved by full-service grocery stores." A 1995 study, titled "The Urban Grocery Store Gap," revealed that while metropolitan Los Angeles as a whole offered one supermarket for every 7,795 people, in lower-income areas the ratio was half that, with just one full-service grocery store for every 16,571 residents. Super-market CEOs lined up to confess they had badly underestimated the needs—and potential value—of inner-city neighborhoods. "Change, it seemed, was in the air," said a report issued by Occidental College's Urban and Environmental Policy Institute in 2002. "Yet ten years later low-income, predominantly minority communities in Los Angeles still have significantly fewer supermarkets than do suburban, white, mid-dle and upper class neighborhoods."[35]

The disappearance of urban supermarkets was ushered in largely by structural changes in the business as well as demographics, reports sug-gest. Although pursuing suburban purchasing power was the key incen-tive behind this urban exodus, the industry's consolidation into massive shopping centers featuring a broadening array of services was also a major driver of the restructuring, according to a report by California Food Policy Advocates. "The new supermarkets—and their requisite large parking lots—necessitated both expansive land parcels that often are not available in inner-city neighborhoods and easy automobile ac-cess for a significant portion of their customers." The trend sped up through the 1990s, as supermarket chains, "faced with low profit mar-gins, expanded the size and format of their suburban stores to increase sales volume and developed new profit centers within their stores, such as banks, pharmacies, bakeries, deli counters, and prepared meals, that typically generate higher profit margins than conventional groceries."[36]

LESS FOR MORE

Still, the largely untapped "inner-city market" is grossly underestimated, and underserved. Poor people spend money, of course—including billions of dollars in food stamps. The nationwide inner-city grocery market, according to Price Waterhouse Coopers LLC, is worth $85 billion, and $21 billion of that potential commerce "has yet to be realized by retailers."[37] Some 77 percent of the nation's $20 billion worth of food stamps are spent in supermarkets, but this percentage declines significantly in low-income urban and rural communities, because of the absence of supermarkets.[38] The poor therefore are often shopping in more expensive convenience stores. A 1997 study by the USDA found that prices at supermarkets were roughly 10 percent lower than in neighborhood stores, convenience stores, and grocery-gas combinations, which predominate "in rural areas and central cities where a greater proportion of the poor live."[39]

Actually, the government's discouraging figures once again understate the problem. In a survey of grocery shopping options in inner-city San Francisco, California Food Policy Advocates found dramatic price differences between immediately accessible corner stores and discount supermarkets in other parts of the city. Residents in one poor neighborhood paid 42 percent more "for the same food items at a neighborhood corner store than they would at a discount supermarket"; in another low-income area residents paid 64 percent more for their food.[40]

Even among inner-city and suburban supermarkets there are troubling price disparities. A survey by the *Detroit News* found that the cheapest brand of chicken legs and thighs in inner-city supermarkets cost twice as much as the lowest-priced brand in suburban supermarkets, and potatoes cost 25 percent more. Likewise, when Ralph's announced a company merger in 1995, the firm reportedly acknowledged that prices in its south-central Los Angeles stores "have traditionally been higher" than those in its suburban outlets.[41]

But the most disturbing impact of the grocery gap is the severe lack of nutritious food in poor neighborhoods. Not only do the poor pay more at the corner store, they also get less nutrition for their dollar. Because many low-income residents live far from a supermarket and are hampered by inadequate public transit, one report explained, "the absence of nearby supermarkets often represents an inability to purchase nutritious, affordable food, particularly fresh fruit and vegetables and other perishables. Healthy diets therefore are compromised, contributing to a high prevalence of hunger, food insecurity, and obesity. . . . While poverty is the main cause of malnutrition in California, lack of access to nutritious, affordable food is also a critical element."[42] This issue has not escaped the notice of the EPA, which observed that the dearth of supermarkets in "low-wealth and predominantly black neighborhoods suggests that residents of these neighborhoods may be at a disadvantage when attempting to achieve a healthy diet."[43]

These "disadvantages" can be quite severe. A host of serious life-threatening illnesses plague poor people of color, and poor nutrition is a major factor. According to a USDA report, "A disproportionate number of diet-related disease is borne by minority, low-income and educationally disadvantaged persons [with] such populations having higher rates of high blood pressure, stroke and diabetes mellitus than the general population."[44] Among the causes—in addition to a toxic combination of fattening fast food and convenience-store junk food—is almost certainly a lack of fresh fruits and vegetables. In a 2003 article for *Environmental Health Perspectives*, the journal of the National Institutes of Health, a team of health writers linked poor supermarket access to "increased exposure to high-calorie fast foods, 'junk' foods, and refined sugars." Researchers have found that "the presence of a single supermarket within a census tract was associated with a 32 percent increase in fruit and vegetable intake compared with neighborhoods without supermarkets." White neighborhoods are four times more likely than black neighborhoods to have a supermarket.[45]

A WAL-MART ON EVERY BLOCK?

Placing a Wal-Mart or Kroger on every inner-city corner might seem like a step up from the increasing ubiquity of McDonald's and Burger King, but it is not the answer to these public health problems. As I argue throughout this book, the bulk of the food in mainstream American supermarkets is deeply problematic: fruits and vegetables are covered in pesticide residues; factory-farmed meat and poultry are filled with powerful hormones and often are teeming with dangerous bacteria; heavily packaged processed foods laden with fatty oils, cholesterol, and excessive doses of sugar and salt lure consumers to spend their food dollars on empty calories and harmful additives.

Ending supermarket segregation and expanding access to their bounty is critical in the short term from a social equity and public health standpoint and is a worthy goal. But the more vital long-term project is to break up the growing corporate monopoly on food. Eric Schlosser, in *Fast Food Nation,* potently demonstrated the need to escape the fast-food industry's toxic grip; now we must understand how the supermarket industry feeds and thrives on the many destructive practices of agribusiness.[46]

There are many promising alternatives. Farmers' markets and community-supported agriculture projects, which give consumers a better and often healthier bang for their buck while paying small farmers directly, are dramatically on the rise. Public-financed "community food security" programs to create new accessible markets for small growers and lower-income consumers are sprouting up around the country.

But these initiatives are small potatoes indeed. As long as our public policies continue to enable supermarket mergers and takeovers and ever-concentrating market share, the alternatives necessary to make our food system humane, healthy, and sustainable from top to bottom will be on precarious footing.

The supermarket empires of today have purchased phenomenal and intensifying power over our food supply. Their clout can be seen most clearly not just in the demise of small local and regional grocery retailers, but even more so by these corporations' ability to push around very large wholesalers and food-processing firms—to dictate the terms of supply and demand throughout the food web. This has profound ramifications for farmers and the rest of the food industry, and not least for consumers.

These sprawling food bazaars appear to offer everything under the sun, at relatively reasonable (though arguably inflated) prices. Many of them even feature organic and "health food" sections. It would appear that supermarkets are listening to consumers, giving us what we want. Yet what choice do we really have over the corporate supermarket menu? The chicken-or-the-egg debate as to whether consumers drive the market or vice versa clouds a more fundamental issue—that of power and control. For the majority of people in America—those who are "fortunate" enough to have ready access to Kroger, Safeway, and the like—alternatives are few and far between. Organics tend to be featured in a smattering of major metropolitan supermarkets and local health-food stores, with little availability elsewhere. But what if we want to purchase food that is truly healthy—not only for our bodies but also for local farmers, for our communities, for farm workers, and for the environment? What if we want our food purchases to sustain diversified family farms, small businesses, well-paid employees, and independent local economies? No supermarket chain offers that option. It's not in their business plan.

A University of Missouri sociologist, William Heffernan, and his colleagues helped break important ground with their research on the escalating monopolization of supermarkets. Their findings compelled these academics to raise a bigger question worth serious consideration: "At some point, citizens must ask what kind of a food system they want and then design our food and farm policies to create and encourage that system. Even though the food system is becoming more like—and not different from—other economic sectors, such a question will probably force us to grapple with the question: is it possible that food is so unique that it requires special public policies?"[47]

FOOD GONE MAD

The warning signs are getting harder to ignore. In late January 2004, a column of men clad in white space-age suits, their bodies completely sealed, marched down a dirt road in South Korea. It looked like a counterterrorism exercise, but the dozen or so soldiers and veterinary officials were stalking a different sort of weapon of mass destruction: a duck farm.

The poultry farm was infected with avian flu, a deadly epidemic raging across much of Asia and, ominously, spilling over to the human population. The bird flu "appears to have jumped the species barrier," reported *Time Asia*, "killing at least four people, and . . . suspected of causing another 10 deaths."[1] The World Health Organization dispatched dire warnings of a "threat to human health and a disaster for agricultural production," urging farmers to slaughter at-risk birds immediately. "This is a serious global threat to human health," said WHO's Dr. Lee Jong-wook.[2]

In the first weeks of the deadly virus, an astounding 1 million poultry farm birds died in Vietnam, and another 800,000 were slaughtered as a precautionary measure. By mid-March, the bird flu in Vietnam (and further precautionary killings) had ravaged 38 million fowl; and in ten countries throughout Asia hit by the bug, farmers destroyed some 100 million birds. The United States, home to giant chicken factory farms that pack thousands of birds under one roof, was not immune: when birds at a few huge poultry farms in Delaware and Maryland caught the virus, farmers quickly slaughtered flocks totaling more than 400,000 chickens. Just six years earlier, in Hong Kong, government officials "culled" some 1.4 million chickens to prevent a similar virus from spreading. In the early 1980s in the United States more than 17 million birds were destroyed—at a cost of $65 million— to control a similar outbreak. According to *Time Asia,* "The disease manifests itself [among chickens] as a hemorrhagic fever, turning a pen of healthy birds into a bloody mass of goop and feathers within 24 hours."[3]

Even more disconcerting, it was soon revealed that the Vietnamese government, wary of bad publicity, had kept the spreading plague secret for months. The epidemic was already apparent in July 2003, a government veterinarian revealed. "At the time, Vietnam was preparing actively for the Twenty-second Southeast Asian games," he explained, "and we thought we could control the disease, so we did not announce it for political and economic reasons." By March 2004, twenty-three people were dead from the avian virus.[4]

Half a planet away, in the beef capital of the world, one mad cow stumbled into a Mabton, Washington, slaughterhouse in December 2003 and set off equally dramatic tremors. For years the meat industry had made heady assurances to domestic and foreign consumers that the United States was immune to the deadly cow ailment—bovine spongiform encephalopathy (BSE), thought to be induced by feeding animal meat by-products to these naturally vegetarian ruminant beasts. Now, the disease that ravaged Britain's beef industry and led to the apocalyptic wholesale slaughter of nearly 5 million cattle had jumped over the pond.

First reported in the United Kingdom in 1986, BSE attacks a cow's central nervous system, forming spongelike holes in the brain and leading to "nervousness or aggression; abnormal posture; incoordination and difficulty in rising," and other symptoms, according to the U.S. Department of Agriculture. It is incurable and fatal. The infection can take up to eight years to present; once it does, "the animal's condition deteriorates until it dies or is destroyed."[5] The disease, thought to be derived from an infection in sheep known as scrapie, killed some 200,000 cows in the UK, and the government slaughtered millions more to prevent its spread. Mad cow disease also nearly killed Britain's beef industry, costing the country an astounding $6.7 billion.[6]

What especially energized those outside of the farming and animal-rights sectors was the parallel arrival of a new strain of a rare degenerative human disease, also incurable and fatal, called Creutzfeldt-Jakob. The Centers for Disease Control (CDC), echoing widespread scientific opinion, said the new variant Creutzfeldt-Jakob was "most probably" caused by "the consumption of beef products contaminated by central nervous system tissue" containing BSE infection. A few years after mad cow overtook the English countryside, in the early 1990s, meat-eating Britons began to die from variant Creutzfeldt-Jakob in small numbers. By 2004 a total of 139 people had died from the brain-wasting neurological disorder.[7]

Fish lovers were not immune to bad news in that first month of 2004 either. Suddenly, salmon, particularly the industrial farm-raised variety, had "joined the lengthening list of suspect foods—right after disease-prone cows and Mercury-laden tuna."[8] Citing elevated levels of PCBs and other toxins, a team of scientists concluded that, "consumption of farmed Atlantic salmon may pose health risks that detract from the beneficial effects of fish consumption."[9] Analyzing more than two tons of farmed and wild salmon from around the globe, the scientists found the farm-raised fish contained "significantly higher" (about ten times as high) amounts of carcinogens such as PCBs, dioxins, dieldrin, and other pesticides. Because industrial salmon dine on manufactured pellets of smaller contaminated fish, they accumulate more cancer-causing toxins, leading the researchers to recommend no more than one serving of farm-raised salmon every two months.[10] That March, after months of debate and delays, the EPA and FDA urged consumers—particularly children and pregnant women—to limit their intake of canned alba-core tuna to just one can a week, due to high levels of mercury in that most popular fish. But even one can of albacore per week is "dangerous to the health of 99 percent of U.S. pregnant women and their unborn children," said nationally recognized mercury expert Vas Aposhian, who resigned from the FDA's Food Advisory Committee, believing the government's warnings were too cautious.[11]

Indeed, the list of risky or questionable food keeps growing. Numerous fish, most notably tuna, carry mercury and other toxins. Poultry influenza is back with a vengeance, propelled astronomically by large-scale confinement farming. The vast bulk of fruits and vegetables—73 percent of conventional, and a disturbing 23 percent of organics—are coated with pesticide residue, often containing at least trace amounts of carcinogens.[12] Mad cow disease, with the potential to kill humans, has ravaged Britain and now has landed in America. More immediately palpable, illnesses from food-borne bacterial pathogens such as salmonella and E. coli 0157:H7 have increased dramatically over the past twenty-five years. Millions of Americans get sick, and thousands die, from food-related illnesses each year. Feasting on a truly supersized diet, more Americans than ever are overweight and obese. What's going on here?

Today's looming crisis in food safety, which will be explored at length in the next chapter, provides a revealing window into our whole food system. We are increasingly eating at our own risk, not because it is the natural way of things, but largely because of a highly centralized food industry that tends to put its bottom-line concerns above matters such as consumers' safety and health, not to mention the well-being of workers and the environment. And government, despite its charge to protect the public good, frequently aids agribusiness in its quest to protect and pad profits. The frightening arrival of mad cow disease, spurred in part by profit concerns and intense corporate resistance to regulation, offers a chilling case study of this modern food system gone awry.

TURNING COWS INTO CANNIBALS

The trouble started in cattle feed. Looking to speed cow growth and cut costs, the British beef industry in the 1980s began the ultimately perilous practice of using high-protein feed bulked up with sheep and cow remains. Scientists believe BSE "originated when scrapie-infected sheep were rendered [melted down] and fed to cows," explain Sheldon Rampton and John Stauber in their acclaimed 1997 book *Mad Cow U.S.A.* Following the initial infection, "the practice of cow cannibalism through the rendering process became the decisive factor in enabling the disease to multiply."[13] The U.S. cattle business followed suit, adding rendered cow remnants to a decidedly unnatural blend that included (until 2004) other goodies such as chicken litter, defined as "bedding, spilled feed, feathers, and fecal matter that are collected from living quarters where poultry is raised."[14]

A 2001 paper by the Centers for Disease Control vividly describes how excess animal parts are churned into feed: "During rendering, carcasses from which all conceivable parts had been removed were milled and then decomposed in large vats by boiling at atmospheric or higher pressures, producing an aqueous slurry of protein under a layer of fat (tallow). After the fat was removed, the slurry was desiccated into a meat and bone meal product that was packaged by the animal food industry and distributed to owners of livestock and other captive animals (e.g., zoo and laboratory animals, breeding species, pets)."[15]

Originally, rendering was "a small-scale activity carried on by frugal farmers and local butchers," write Rampton and Stauber. But over the past century, "Capitalism and industrialization concentrated these activities in mechanized factories where thousands of tons of waste animal parts were dumped by the truckload to be ground together and blended in huge cooking machines. Rendering plants had become central collection points for any diseases or persistent toxins that these animals carry. Infected tissue from a single animal had the potential to mingle with tissues from thousands of others, and then to be distributed widely in feeds." Diseases like BSE "were naturally rare, but when large quantities of animal tissue are pooled, even a rare disease can pose significant dangers."[16]

Increasingly, scientists and historians agree with this view. An analysis by the CDC undertaken in 2001 said it was "likely that changes in the rendering process that had taken place around 1980" allowed BSE in infected carcasses "to survive, contaminate the protein supplement, and infect cattle." The animals' carcasses and wastes "were then recycled through the rendering plants, increasing levels of the now cattle-adapted pathogen in the protein supplement and eventually causing a full-scale BSE epidemic."[17]

But as Rampton and Stauber explain, modern rendering had become big business: "Rendering had become so entrenched within the meat industry that ending it would have serious economic implications all by itself—a cost of $600 million in England alone, according to industry representatives. Rendered animal protein wasn't simply a cheap food supplement. It helped solve a nasty waste disposal problem. Eliminate it as an option, and you had to pass the additional cost on to consumers."[18]

Nonetheless, in July 1988, as the mad cow body count began to pile up, the UK banned cattle cannibalism. It would be nine years before the United States would impose a similar measure. Seven years after that, in 2004, a six-year-old Canadian-born dairy cow being prepared for slaughter in a U.S. feedlot was carrying the disease.

DEAD COW WALKING

The hobbled Washington dairy cow couldn't even walk to meet its maker. The Holstein was dispatched to the slaughterhouse on December 9, but, the *Washington Post* reported, "since it was unable to move on its own and believed to be at higher risk for illnesses like BSE, tissue samples were taken after it was slaughtered." Yet even as samples went to the lab, meat from the animal "traveled through three separate processing plants before a test first revealed the problem 12 days later."[19]

The infected brain and spinal tissues of the cow were sent to a rendering plant, "heated and ground up," and possibly turned into chicken feed or a cosmetics product. Agriculture Department officials, the

Washington Post said, acknowledged that, "chickens that ate the infected meat could have been slaughtered in turn and ended up as cattle feed," but they insisted the disease could not be transmitted that way.

The USDA quickly quarantined the dairy farm, near Yakima, Washington, where the cow originated. The slaughterhouse recalled more than 10,000 pounds of beef that could have been tainted by some part of the infected cow. By late January, six herds of cattle in Washington state were under quarantine, and the USDA's investigation expanded to Oregon after discovering that a cow there was linked to the infected Holstein.[20] As an added precaution the USDA killed 620 cows—none of which tested positive for BSE—in three of the quarantined herds.

On January 8 the USDA proudly unveiled new regulations, most notably banning "downer" cows (those too sick to stand or walk) from human food. The agency also promised to double the number of annual BSE tests to 40,000, still a tiny sampling of the 35 million beef cows led to slaughter each year (after much domestic and international criticism, the agency later announced it would expand testing to 268,000 cows).[21] But huge loopholes remained. "Even now, federal law permits calves to be fed a formula made with cow's blood in place of their mother's milk, a cost-cutting practice that could spread BSE," explained the Physicians Committee for Responsible Medicine.[22] Also untouched was the practice of serving rendered cattle remains to hogs and chickens, which could in turn be rendered and fed back to cattle, potentially spreading BSE infection.

At Senate hearings in late January, some questioned why the non-ambulatory Washington Holstein, considered a "downer" in trade parlance, was allowed into the food system at all. Senator Richard Durbin of Illinois asked President George W. Bush's agriculture secretary, Ann Veneman: "The inspectors at the Washington plant were correct in singling out this animal for BSE sampling, but why was the carcass not held until the results were known? If the inspectors recognized that the animal was uncoordinated or unable to rise on her own, why was she allowed into the human food chain at all?"[23]

The answer, of course, was that it was perfectly legal. Only after mad cow hit the headlines did the USDA announce its complete ban of all "downer" cattle from human food. Although these cows, which represent a tiny fraction of the beef supply, are at greater risk of having BSE since many of them display neurological disorders, the beef industry and its allies in Congress repeatedly stymied efforts to remove them from the food supply—until the country's first mad cow case made such a rule politically inevitable.[24] The day the mad cow story broke, Karen Taylor Mitchell, of the feisty food-safety group Safe Tables Our Priority, said, "We shouldn't be using downer cows in our food supply at all. There is a USDA regulation about not using them for the school lunch program. Yet it's OK for the same children who are protected at school to go home and be served sick cows." [25]

Senator Durbin also testified that because test results were not released for nearly two weeks—BSE tests can be conducted in five to seven days—the infected animal "was processed, according to Dr. Steven Solomon from FDA, into 2.8 million pounds of consumer products, all of which were potentially contaminated with BSE." But even as that potentially infected meat made its way into the supermarkets and restaurants of America, the USDA was powerless to require the product to be recalled, or the retailers who carried it to be identified. Such information is considered proprietary and left to the discretion of business.

Secretary Veneman, some of whose top staffers were reportedly once in the employ of the National Cattlemen's Beef Association (NCBA),[26] moved swiftly to instill public confidence in beef, assuring the public, "We believe the risk of any human health effects is very low. I plan to serve beef for my holiday dinner."[27] It was Christmas Eve, after all. On New Year's Day President Bush chimed in, "I ate beef today, and will continue to eat beef."[28]

"EXTRAORDINARY EMERGENCY"

But if industry and government officials weren't losing sleep over potential health risks, they were more than a little worried about economic fallout. In a notice quietly disseminated through the *Federal Register,* the USDA declared mad cow an "extraordinary emergency," calling the disease "a significant danger to the national economy and a potential serious burden to interstate and foreign commerce."[29] The emergency designation gave officials added authority to quarantine herds.

America's beef exports, worth $2.6 billion annually, about 10 percent of production, were immediately stifled by international sanctions. Within hours of the revelation, imports of U.S. beef were banned by Japan, Mexico, Chile, South Korea, Singapore, Malaysia, Thailand, Taiwan, and Australia.[30] In all, more than forty countries cut off imports of U.S. beef. While U.S. officials would argue strenuously against the ban on American beef and insist that one mad cow did not constitute a crisis, they were on shaky ground: seven months earlier the United States and other countries rejected Canadian beef exports after that country's first reported mad cow. There was also simmering resentment over previous American tariffs and other trade bullying. "We've made a lot of enemies around the world with our own arbitrary tariffs," remarked Dean Cliver, professor of food safety at UC Davis. "I think they will take great pleasure in embargoing U.S. beef."

The New York–based Insurance Information Institute estimated that the economic costs in lost trade and domestic consumption from this one mad cow "could easily be in the billions." There was also the prospect of litigation mayhem, with negligence lawsuits flying back and forth between economically aggrieved farmers, meat packers, processors, feed suppliers, retailers, and restaurants, all pointing the finger at one party or another.[31]

The hemorrhaging exports inspired gloomy projections by the USDA of more than $3 billion in lost sales, and tens of thousands of layoffs in the beef industry.[32] Prices for slaughter cattle plummeted by nearly 20 percent. Across the heartland and the Great Plains, meatpacking companies laid off workers, since "some of the 'secondary' meats they produce—such as beef tongues and intestines—primarily go to international markets." Excel Corp., citing lost exports, laid off 700 workers at plants in Texas, Kansas, Colorado, and Nebraska. Swift & Co. eliminated 140 jobs in several states. Experts said an extended ban on American beef could lead to tens of thousands of layoffs.[33] Tyson Foods, the biggest meat corporation in the world, reported by late January that it had lost $61 million owing to the mad cow outbreak.[34]

All this because the U.S. meat industry, at least until 1997, insisted on feeding risky high-protein formula containing cattle and sheep remains to cows. All this despite nearly a decade of mad cow disaster in Britain, Japan, and elsewhere caused by this very practice.

PR: IT'S WHAT'S FOR DINNER

Yet, five weeks after the BSE discovery, Agriculture Secretary Veneman told reporters at the annual National Cattlemen's Beef Association convention, "Our worst fears have not played out—consumer confidence in U.S. beef remains strong."[35] Veneman's own confidence was no doubt stoked by a survey, funded by cattle producers, registering 90 percent consumer confidence in the safety of U.S. beef. In a press release, the NCBA celebrated this apparent public-relations success, and uttered hardly a word about any concrete measures to prevent future BSE cases. "From the beginning, consumer messages focused on two key points," the association said in a press release in January. "1. The US beef supply is safe. 2. The system worked—the one infected animal was identified and the public was assured that risk material from that animal never entered the food supply."[36]

"This is all really a nonissue," a spokesman for the American Meat Institute, Dan Murphy, told *LA Weekly,* exhibiting more than a little hubris. "There is no threat to public health. Beef is safe. The flames have been fanned by misguided media coverage, and by activists with agendas—the kind of people who want to turn us all into vegetarians or denounce corporate globalization and the WTO or whatever."[37]

The industry's "crisis-management reserve fund" was tapped to produce radio ads "designed to increase beef consumption around the Super Bowl and to conduct periodic consumer attitude tracking research." One prominent Florida beef producer and association member remarked, "The industry has been working on a BSE response plan for several years in the event that this may happen. The fact that a majority of consumers are aware of BSE and are still confident in the safety of beef is a testament that the plan is working."[38]

But if the industry's PR plan was working, the system certainly wasn't. For in fact, since the human effects of BSE take years to manifest, there was no way of knowing whether the lone-mad-cow theory was right; and given the rampant and serious regulatory and enforcement loopholes, there was plenty of cause to wonder if there weren't more mad cows in our midst. While BSE in America made big headlines, what was perhaps most surprising was that it took so long for the fatal and incurable disease to breach the porous regulatory system of the U.S. beef industry.

MAD COW ROULETTE

The government's own monitoring of BSE-related enforcement is not reassuring. Under rules laid out by the August 1997 federal ban on feeding animal-meat proteins to cows, the FDA is charged with inspecting all the nation's renderers and feed mills. (The FDA regulates animal feed, while the USDA monitors live animals.) In a July 6, 2001, update by the FDA's Center for Veterinary Medicine, it was disclosed with little fanfare that a startling number of these operations were using materials "prohibited for use in ruminant feed." More than 75 percent of the rendering firms and nearly 40 percent of feedmills inspected were found with prohibited materials.[39] Although these materials are designated only for nonruminant feed, such as pet food, if ingredients are inadvertently mixed or equipment cleaned improperly, there is risk of these banned materials finding their way into cattle feed. There is anecdotal evidence to suggest this sort of toxic cross-polluting is occurring—and this could be just the tip of the iceberg.

One company in Washington state, X-Cel Feeds Inc., committed repeated violations for more than a decade before a July 2003 Justice Department action forced the firm to clean up its act, literally. The feed manufacturer, which produced meal for both cattle and nonruminants, did not adequately clean its machinery and thus could not assure that its cattle feed was free of prohibited ruminant material. Also worrying,

X-Cel had "failed to properly label animal feeds that contained meat and bone meal from ruminants with the statement, 'Do not feed to cattle or other ruminants,' as required by law," reported the *Seattle Post-Intelligencer,* citing the results of a 2002 FDA inspection.[40] In the Justice Department consent decree, according to the FDA, the company "admitted liability for introducing adulterated and misbranded animal feeds into interstate commerce."[41]

In January 2001, FDA inspectors found "a very low level of prohibited material" fed to cattle in a Texas feedlot, in violation of the 1997 feed ban. The amount of ruminant material in the feed was small, the FDA said, amounting to about a quarter of an ounce consumed by each cow. "The potential risk of BSE to such cattle is therefore exceedingly low, even if feed were contaminated," the agency said. Nonetheless, Purina Mills Inc. purchased more than 1,200 of the cattle to remove them from the human food supply.[42]

One could argue the above case shows that the system works—the tainted feed was identified and the cows removed from human consumption. But it also shows, disturbingly, that despite all the evidence of risk and all the talk of stringent enforcement, some cows in America are still eating their own. And perhaps more frightening, the state of testing and inspection today is dismally inadequate. The truth is we don't really know if our meat supply is free of this deadly infection.

About three weeks after the mad cow story broke, an investigation by United Press International revealed that USDA tests for BSE in live animals were in fact few and far between. In Washington state, where the nation's first mad cow was discovered, officials hadn't conducted a single test for BSE in the first seven months of 2003, records showed. At Vern's Moses Lake Meats, the slaughterhouse where the mad cow case was discovered, the USDA hadn't tested animals for two years.[43]

Nationwide, UPI found, "Tests were conducted at fewer than 100 of the 700 plants known to slaughter cattle. Some of the biggest slaughterhouses were not tested at all." Equally troubling, the report found, states with the most cows were tested the least: only 11 percent of the plants tested were from the top four beef-producing states, which account for 70 percent of the nation's annual cattle slaughter.

"It's really significant that they're focusing all of their attention on the very smallest plants," remarked Felicia Nestor, the food-safety program director for the Government Accountability Project, a whistleblower group in Washington, D.C. "It's almost like the USDA wants to protect the big plants from a finding because the implications would be too scary. If they find a case at a small plant, the USDA can then say it's an isolated problem."

This was by no means the first revelation of major gaps in government testing and enforcement of BSE regulations. In January 2002 the General Accounting Office issued a stinging critique of the FDA and the USDA, concluding rather prophetically, "The continuing absence of BSE in the United States cannot be sufficiently ensured by current federal prevention efforts."

Government investigators found some recalcitrant firms "had not been reinspected for 2 or more years," and other cases in which "no enforcement action had occurred even though the firms had been found noncompliant on multiple inspections." More broadly, the report concluded, the FDA "has not acted promptly to compel firms to keep prohibited proteins out of cattle feed and to label animal feed that cannot be fed to cattle."[44] The X-Cel case was clearly no isolated instance. In a September 2000 report, the General Accounting Office found that of 9,100 firms visited by FDA inspectors to gauge cooperation with the 1997 feed ban, nearly 1,700 "were not aware of the regulation and thus could produce or use animal feed that was not in compliance." A full 20 percent of feed and rendering companies that handled prohibited materials "did not have a system in place to prevent commingling and cross-contamination."[45]

As of October 2001, the FDA had identified 364 companies, including renderers and feed manufacturers, that were not following federal rules to prevent ruminant proteins from getting into cattle feed. Worse, the FDA admitted that at least 1,200 companies supposed to be covered by the ban had not even been identified and inspected. And the agency's databases were so "severely flawed," congressional investigators found, that the FDA "does not know the full extent of industry compliance." There was no way of knowing how many renderers and feed companies were either purposefully or inadvertently breaking rules designed to prevent the spread of mad cow disease.

The FDA insists enforcement has improved, and that 99 percent of firms now comply with cattle-feed rules. But even if that is the case, there is no assurance that BSE-infected cow feed was not disseminated in earlier years when enforcement was more lax. And since the disease normally incubates within the body for several years, it would be possible for many mad cows' carcasses to have entered the food supply. Unless, of course, there was universal testing for BSE.

Given the tremendous economic fallout from a single mad cow, consumer advocates could argue credibly that the industry might have saved money by allowing more testing and prevention. Said Carol Tucker Foreman, who directed food-safety programs for the USDA during the Carter administration, "I think the damage to the American meat industry costs infinitely more than anything U.S. cattlemen would have had to pay to do this thing right."[46]

But the industry, led by the National Cattlemen's Beef Association, has vigorously and repeatedly fought off this basic reform.

THE POWER OF BEEF

Representing a $70-billion-a-year business, the beef lobby exerts legendary clout on Capitol Hill. Between 1990 and 2003, the livestock and meat-processing industries donated nearly $28 million to congressional and presidential candidates.[47] During the 2002 election cycle the NCBA alone generously distributed nearly $500,000 to congressional candidates, 83 percent of it to Republicans.[48]

The infamous revolving door between the meat business and government is well greased. According to Eric Schlosser and other writers, some of Agriculture Secretary Veneman's top aides are hired hands from the National Cattlemen's Beef Association. Veneman's spokeswoman, Alisa Harrison, in her prior capacity as the organization's director of public relations, "battled government food safety efforts, criticized Oprah Winfrey for raising health questions about American hamburgers, and sent out press releases with titles like 'Mad

Cow Disease Not a Problem in the U.S.,' " writes Schlosser. Veneman's chief of staff, Dale Moore, was formerly the beef trade group's top lobbyist.[49]

As journalist Vince Beiser found, the cattle business has cultivated good friends on both sides of the congressional aisle. In July 2003, a "nearly successful" measure prohibiting the sale of meat from "downer" cows was killed by Robert Goodlatte, Republican chairman of the House Agriculture Committee, with a powerful assist by the committee's top Democrat, Representative Charles Stenholm of Texas. "Both men have received tens of thousands of dollars from cattle interests in recent years," writes Beiser.[50]

That wasn't the first time the beef industry quashed the banning of downer cows from the food supply. According to the *New York Times,* Congress "came close three times to banning the sale of meat from downer cows, ones that are too sick or hurt to amble into slaughterhouses, only to see the industry's allies block each bill at the last moment."[51]

Chandler Keyes, the NCBA's Washington lobbyist, insisted that since some downed animals are hobbled by injury rather than disease, there should be no blanket rule—discretion should be entrusted to federal veterinarians working in the slaughterhouses. But some government inspectors aren't so confident. One inspector at a meatpacking company in the Midwest told the *New York Times,* "In his two years overseeing the killing of some 600 downed cows, the veterinarian at his plant tested the central nervous tissue of only one of the animals." The inspector stated, "All we tested downer cows for was antibiotic residue," not BSE.[52]

The veterinarian was hardly alone, as several signed affidavits from USDA inspectors, gathered by Public Citizen's Government Accountability Project, reveal. In January 2004 George J. Pauley III stated that after ten years as a USDA meat inspector, "To this very day I have not received formal training in the detection of BSE. . . . Since our mad cow scare a few weeks ago, I am still waiting for training in BSE inspection protocols." Since April 2003, only 2 to 3 percent of roughly a thousand downer cattle he saw slaughtered were tested for BSE.[53] In another signed affidavit, a USDA consumer safety inspector, Paul Carney, said, "There is no systematic testing for mad cow in the plants where I work. . . . We just trust the industry to pick out the most suspect cows from their own herds, then we test those, and tell the public there is no mad cow. We simply are not testing enough or with a process that has sufficient integrity to really know whether this disease is in U.S. meat."[54]

Equally frightening is the fact that, according to another veteran regulator, only a small fraction of all slaughter-bound cattle are inspected in some plants. Under the USDA's Alternate Ante Mortem Inspection Program, used by many beef-slaughtering plants, "only 10% of the live animals are required to be inspected by an FSIS [the USDA's Food Safety and Inspection Service] veterinarian," stated Trent J. Berhow, a USDA inspector with thirteen years' experience. "At very large slaughter plants, that slaughter 5,000 cattle per day, only 500 are required to have ante-mortem inspections performed on them."[55]

Despite years of warnings from scientists that mad cow "would eventually appear in the United States, cattle owners and meat packers repeatedly resisted calls for a more substantial program to test for the disease, and the Agriculture Department went along with them," the *New York Times* reported.[56] As early as 1991, six years before the cattle feed ban, a report by the USDA's Animal and Plant Health Inspection Service debated the policy option of prohibiting "the feeding of sheep and cattle-origin protein products to all ruminants, regardless of age," Rampton and Stauber revealed in their book. But the agency hedged its bets, stating, "The advantage of this option is that it minimizes the risk of BSE. The disadvantage is that the cost to the livestock and rendering industries would be substantial."[57]

It was in keeping with tradition, then, that the industry and the USDA resisted comprehensive BSE testing, even after mad cow disease set foot in the United States. Even under Secretary Veneman's plan to test 268,000 cows a year, the United States will only examine less than 1 percent of its slaughter-bound cattle for mad cow disease. Japan, having endured several cases of mad cow since 2001, tests every single cow bound for slaughter. Belgium conducts twenty times as many BSE tests each year as does the United States, despite its far smaller cattle population.[58] France tests half of all its cows, and Britain tests all cows over twenty-four months old.[59]

It is estimated that even a huge increase in testing would cost consumers just a nickel or so more per pound of beef, in return for greater safety and less likelihood of costly meat recalls.[60] One such test developed by Nobel Prize–winning biochemist Dr. Stanley Prusiner (whose work identified prions, the infectious proteins that cause BSE) costs six cents a pound—a tiny tax that the *Boston Globe* called "a reasonable price for protection against a disease that is invariably fatal in cows or human beings."[61] Yet Veneman and NCBA officials steadfastly rejected the concept of either universal or dramatically increased testing, claiming that the new levels were an adequate sample of the nation's herd. In a Reuters straw poll of more than 600 U.S. farmers at the American Farm Bureau Federation's 2004 convention in Honolulu, two thirds "said they oppose mandatory testing of all U.S. cattle for mad cow disease."[62]

Indeed, many leaders of mainstream American agriculture seem positively allergic to more sweeping measures to prevent BSE. When the Farm Bureau Federation's president, Bob Stallman, was asked whether he supported banning ruminant remains from feed for pigs and chickens, he told Reuters that such a reform would only be necessary if public confidence in food safety diminished further. "Right now," he said, "I think it might be too soon."[63]

4

DYING FROM CONSUMPTION

"Despite the great advances in public health during the twentieth century, the leading conditions related to diet—coronary heart disease, cancers at certain sites, diabetes, stroke, and liver cirrhosis, for example—could be reduced in prevalence or delayed until later in life if people ate less of dietary components that increased disease risk. Advice to eat less, however, runs counter to the interests of food producers."

—Marion Nestle, *Food Politics*[1]

PROFITS AND LOSSES

We are well acquainted with—and perhaps numb to—the fact that the food industry, like any business, exists to make profit. This fact is so obvious it seems redundant, so normalized it seems innocuous: of *course* it is for-profit, one might say, *every* industry attempts to turn a profit from *something*. Why should food be any different? There are hundreds of thousands of answers to this question turning up each year in America's hospitals, thousands in cemeteries.

This is not hyperbole. Each year, according to the Centers for Disease Control (CDC), more than 75 million Americans are made sick by the food they eat. Of these, some 325,000 require hospital care. At least 5,000—in some recent years as many as 9,000—die from that now-ubiquitous malady, "food-borne illness."[2] With a more watchful eye on food-industry practices, many of these deaths and illnesses might very well have been prevented.

Tainted food has a long history (recent reports suggest Mozart died from trichinosis after a lifelong love affair with pork), and food quality has improved in many respects since the ugly days depicted in Upton Sinclair's *The Jungle* a century ago. Nevertheless, food safety remains a serious problem with wide ramifications for public health, quality of life, and the nation's economy.

The term "food poisoning" implies something accidental, but these incidents, evidence suggests, are a by-product of a food system that prizes return on investment over health. Other than the industry's brutal mistreatment of its workers, there is arguably no expression of agribusiness's profit-driven impacts on society more direct than in the realm of food safety and public health.

Although food poisonings, obesity, and the health perils of pesticides may seem unrelated, a common underlying force links them: the corporate food industry's relentless push for maximum speed and volume. While we all must accept some responsibility for what we eat, our options for safe food and healthy diets are constrained, to say the least, by economic priorities and public policies that enable the food industry to produce vast quantities of food—and vast portions—that put our health at risk.

An array of growing public health epidemics can be linked, at least in part, to the food industry's unrelenting push to maintain sales of meat and dairy products and to expand markets for all manner of junk food, including soft drinks, candy, and fast foods that are typically high in salt, sugar, and fat. So-called "diseases of affluence," such as obesity, heart disease, and diabetes, are notably on the rise and can be traced in part to an American diet that is rich, indeed filled to overflowing, with fat and cholesterol.

Thanks to $25 billion to 30 billion a year spent by the food industry on advertising, Americans are partaking in deadly quantities of fat, sugar, and salt, even as nutritional awareness increases.[3] "The industries that produce the foods that are worst for us—including snacks, fast food, sugar beverages, and meat—have especially increased their promotional efforts," report Warren Leon and Caroline Smith DeWaal in their 2003 book, *Is Our Food Safe?* Between 1988 and 1999, the money spent on soft-drink advertising rose by 28 percent; that for candy and snacks, by 40 percent.

As a consequence, weight gain "has reached epidemic proportions, putting many people at risk for heart disease, diabetes, and other diseases." The proportion of overweight and obese adults ballooned to 64 percent by 2000—up from 25 percent in the 1970s. Nearly 59 million Americans, 30 percent of the adult population, are medically defined as obese. Most disturbingly, overweight among children and adolescents aged six to nineteen has risen to nearly 15 percent, compared with 4 percent in the early 1970s.[4]

With supersized portions on the rise until recently—one writer called it "portion creep"—total calorie intake has soared. Compared with twenty years ago, women today consume 300 more calories per day, while men ingest an extra 168. With all those added calories, diseases and deaths related to diet and overweight have increased sharply. According to the Centers for Disease Control, poor diet and physical inactivity are now the second-leading cause of preventable deaths in America (after tobacco)—responsible for at least 400,000 fatalities each year, up from 300,000 in 1990. "This is tragic," the Center's director, Dr. Julie Gerberding, said of the findings. "Our worst fears were confirmed." The economic costs of overweight and obesity (measured in direct medical treatment costs, lost work productivity, absenteeism, and premature death) are staggering. Medical expenses for these ailments alone reached an estimated $78 billion in 1998, accounting for nearly 10 percent of all U.S. medical expenditures.[5]

Marion Nestle, a nutritionist and author, documented in her exhaustively researched 2002 book, *Food Politics,* how agribusiness has left no stone unturned (and no electoral or lobbying dollar unspent) in its efforts to undermine government recommendations that Americans eat less meat and dairy products, and emphasizing the benefits of a more plant-based diet. It's not all industry bullying: the USDA, charged with promoting American agriculture, has often shied away from nutritional advice that could dampen markets, especially for the politically potent and connected meat and dairy industries. This coupled with aggressive food industry advertising has contributed to a national diet that many scientists, nutritionists, and health studies say is profoundly unhealthy.

At the heart of it, to stretch a pun, is the national dish—beef. Despite heightened attention to the perils of a diet heavy in red meat, such as high cholesterol and heart disease, Americans still devour mountains of the nation's gustatory icon. Even with slight declines in U.S. meat consumption over the past twenty-five years, the country ate *27 billion pounds of beef* in 2001, according to USDA statistics.[6]

"Americans and Europeans are literally eating themselves to death, gorging on marbled beef and other grain-fed animal products, taking into their bodies massive amounts of saturated fat and cholesterol," wrote Jeremy Rifkin, in his book *Beyond Beef.* "The fatty substances are building up in the bloodstream, clogging arteries, lining cell walls, blocking passages, triggering metabolic and hormonal changes, stimulating cell growth, and rupturing organs."[7]

Numerous studies suggest links between increased meat consumption and heart disease and cancer. A 2001 Italian study of gastric cancer, published in *Cancer Research,* examining 382 cancer patients and 561 control cases, concluded that the risk of tumors was "positively associated with high consumption of red meat and meat sauce and negatively associated with consumption of white meat." These risks were "strongly reduced by the frequent consumption of fresh fruit and vegetables." In 2003, a team of epidemiologists writing in the *American Journal of Epidemiology* likewise found that "intake of red meat was positively associated with colon cancer."[8]

The trouble with meat today is largely a result of how it is produced and consumed. Meat can be raised, slaughtered, and eaten healthfully: raised on grass and organic feed, slaughtered and processed with care and attention, and eaten in moderation. But such practices are, unfortunately, the exception; the great majority of meat is raised, processed, marketed, and consumed in ways that are damaging to public health, not to mention farmers, food industry workers, and the environment.

To speed production, increase lean profit margins, and induce the fatty taste Americans have grown to love, the meat and dairy industries "raise" ("manufacture" is probably a more accurate description) cattle on antibiotics, growth hormones, and corn feed that is laced with pesticide. These drugs and toxins, lodged deep in cattle meat and tissue, end up in our food and in our bodies. (It should be noted that modest portions of natural, organic, grass-fed beef can be quite nutritious and beneficial; this is a tiny yet growing sector of the industry, however, and this niche product is often pricey and difficult to obtain.)

And that's the better side of beef. Tainted meat, significantly on the rise over the past thirty years, has become a serious and pervasive health threat, one costing Americans at least $10 billion a year in health-care expenses, increased insurance premiums, and lost labor time.[9] Contaminated meat causes one third of all food-borne illnesses, afflicting nearly 10 percent of the population.[10]

Chicken, the "healthier" alternative to beef and pork for many Americans, is no less problematic. Although far lighter in cholesterol and fat, the birds are stuffed with hormones, antibiotics, and pesticides. Harvested, as all America's industrialized animals are, in enclosed cities that breed virulent bacterial strains, chickens are now commonly found to be infected with potentially lethal *Campylobacter jejuni* bacteria, responsible for millions of food-related illnesses every year.[11]

Most insidious of all are the hundreds of pesticides, many of them known to be carcinogenic and to damage nervous and reproductive systems—that is, after all, their job—resting invisibly on (and in) our food. In 1999 the Food and Drug Administration found that about 40 percent of food harvested in the United States contained pesticide residues, according to Leon and DeWaal. Most fell within the Environmental Protection Agency's "tolerance" levels considered safe for human consumption.[12] But as we shall see, those levels are no guarantee, and fail to protect us against the destructive health effects caused not only by traces of individual pesticides but even more so by the steady accumulation of numerous petrochemical toxins in our bodies. A 1987 study by the EPA estimated that pesticide residues on food may cause cancer for as many as 6,000 people every year.[13]

EAT MORE: THE FOOD PYRAMID SCHEME[14]

There is simply too much food in America, even with the substantial market relief provided by exports and subsidies. So overabundant is the U.S. food supply, according to Marion Nestle, "it contains enough to feed everyone in the country nearly twice over—even after exports are considered."[15] The nation's food system is built on an economy of surplus. From early efforts after the Revolutionary War to spur agricultural production in order to settle debts and sustain national independence, through the technological revolutions of the industrial and postwar eras, to the corporate consolidations and "efficiencies" of the present day, the U.S. food industry has been a pivotal tool in the ongoing project of building American economic might.

Like many other U.S. industries, the food business is structured on excess and overaccumulation. Especially since the petrochemical explosion and economic expansions after World War II, America has used surplus production and exports to balance trade accounts and penetrate international markets across the globe. These policies have served numerous, often dubious, economic and political purposes, but with a couple of brief exceptions, such as during the Soviet grain deals of the early 1970s, they have never relieved the country of its burden of surplus. To sustain and expand markets, agribusiness has devised an answer to its own excesses: convince the American public to eat more. As Nestle puts it: "To satisfy stockholders, food companies must convince people to *eat more* of their products or to eat their products instead of those of competitors" (Nestle's emphasis).[16]

The evidence is everywhere: from supermarkets that are "scientifically designed and carefully arranged to tempt us to increase our food purchases,"[17] to the billions of advertising dollars expended to lure us to consume fatty, nonnutritious foods, to the less visible yet tireless efforts by agribusiness to influence national nutritional advice to fit its marketing agendas.

Food corporations, Nestle writes, "use every means at their disposal—legal, regulatory, and societal—to create and protect an environment that is conducive to selling their products in a competitive marketplace." Like other industries, agribusiness lobbies government for "favorable" laws, regulations, and trade agreements, but it doesn't stop there: "Far less visible are the arrangements made with food and nutrition experts to obtain approving judgments about the nutritional quality or health benefits of food products."[18]

As Nestle and many others have documented (see also John Robbins, *Diet for a New America*), agribusiness, particularly the meat and dairy industries, has successfully marketed an American diet that prizes quantity over quality and that is truly punishing to our health.[19] And it has fought changes in government nutritional advice that recommend less meat and dairy every step of the way.

Since 1917, when the U.S. Department of Agriculture released its first dietary suggestions in a pamphlet titled *How to Select Foods,* government nutritional advice has emphasized broad food groups in an inclusive, politically inoffensive approach that, Nestle writes, "permits all foods to be recommended as part of healthful diets and precludes suggestions to restrict foods in one or another group." The USDA ignored "advice to limit intake of fat and sugar" and promoted vitamins and minerals "that are essential for life but are needed only in small amounts." The food industry "readily supported this emphasis because they grasped its marketing potential. They knew that the market for their products was limited. Food *already* was overabundant in the United States and *already* supplied more than enough calories for the population" (Nestle's emphasis).[20]

Through both the Depression and the Second World War, the government produced a chaotic collection of nutritional guides that frequently linked eating with patriotic duty. A 1942 guide advised Americans to "do your part in the national nutrition program," which meant, among other things, eating plenty of milk, meat, eggs, and butter, according to Nestle—"all sources of fat and cholesterol as well as of the essential vitamins and minerals." Another wartime nutrition pamphlet by the USDA counseled, "U.S. needs us strong: eat the Basic 7 every day."[21]

Over the years, government increasingly sought the food industry's advice, knowing, as the USDA once put it, that agribusiness "would have a vital interest in any food guide sponsored by the government." Though they did not always get their way, meat and dairy industry groups lobbied unhaltingly to maintain or increase serving suggestions and overall prioritization of their products—even when it came to matters such as the layout and design of government nutrition publications.[22]

This nutrition war intensified in the late 1960s and through the 1970s, as rising awareness of hunger and malnutrition in the United States spurred more public attention to chronic diseases caused by "overconsumption" of foods heavy in fat, cholesterol, salt, and sugar. Research since World War II had revealed an "epidemic" of coronary heart disease in America, and had begun to suggest "the contrasting absence of this disease among populations consuming largely plant-based diets."[23]

For the cholesterol-heavy sectors of the food industry, the writing appeared to be on the wall: nutrition experts within and outside government increasingly recommended less red meat, less milk, cheese, butter and eggs. Yet the meat industry, led then by the National Cattlemen's Association (now known as the National Cattlemen's Beef Association), successfully pressured Congress and federal agencies to blunt their criticism and to increase salt allowances, soften language about the hazards of cholesterol, and replace advice to "reduce" meat consumption with suggestions to instead choose meats lower in saturated fat.[24]

The upshot today, after numerous successive nutritional battles, is that meat, dairy, and other relatively high-cholesterol, fat-rich foods remain a central (if slightly less pivotal) feature of the American diet. As of the early 1990s, Jeremy Rifkin could write: "Just sixty-five years ago, over 40 percent of the protein in the American diet came from grain, bread, and cereal. Now just 17 percent comes from plant sources, while animal protein, which used to supply half of our protein intake, now supplies over two-thirds of all the protein we consume."[25] As of 1997, according to the Council for Agricultural Science and Technology, 70 percent of dietary protein and roughly 40 percent of dietary calories came from animal products. Meanwhile, the group said, "All dietary cholesterol and about 75 percent of saturated fatty acids come from animal-derived foods."[26]

America's obsession with animal protein—stoked by meat-industry advertising—may be both unnecessary and damaging to our health.

More than thirty years ago, in her classic *Diet for a Small Planet,*

Frances Moore Lappé demonstrated the potency of a plant-based diet. Grains, legumes, nuts, and vegetables provide more than enough protein and nutrients to sustain an active adult, with fewer calories, cholesterol, and fat than the meat-and-milk approach. She detailed specific menus, simple and easy to follow and not the least bit extravagant, with which one could meet or exceed government protein recommendations without any meat or dairy products.[27]

Lappé documented the tremendous ecological waste of resources devoted inefficiently to animal-protein production: half of all U.S. farmland at the time was devoted to feed crops, and 78 percent of the nation's grain was fed to animals, figures that remain roughly similar today. Her research also demonstrated that America's meat-centered diet led to excessive protein consumption and waste, whereas a plant-based diet (perhaps including milk, cheese, and eggs) could provide adequate high-quality protein without all the waste and inefficiency. On Lappé's food/protein continuum, soybeans, various nuts and other legumes, and cheeses ranked as high or higher than meat for protein quantity. In terms of quality—net protein utilization—meat was roughly on par with rice and cheese, and not far ahead of legumes and grains.[28]

Even as early as 1959, there was growing informed skepticism about the primacy of meat. An editorial in *Lancet*, a prominent medical journal, read: "Formerly, vegetable proteins were classified as second-class, and regarded as inferior to first-class proteins of animal origin, but this distinction has now been generally discarded."[29] Many scientists and nutrition experts argue that the typical meat-rich American diet only causes protein waste, filling our bodies with far more protein than necessary, which is then excreted and therefore squandered.[30] The average American, according to Rifkin, "consumes twice the amount of daily protein recommended by the [United Nations'] Food and Agricultural Organization, far more than the body can even absorb."[31] While there remains debate on this topic, it is clear at the very least that an animal-based diet is not the only way to meet one's protein needs.

In recent history there is anecdotal evidence suggesting a possible connection between decreased meat consumption and improved health. During World War I, Denmark, cut off from food imports by the Allied blockade, instituted an efficient food rationing system that virtually eliminated meat from the nation's diet. Grain was fed to people instead of to livestock. In this "mass experiment in vegetarianism," the mortality rate from disease was "by far the lowest in recorded history," plunging by 34 percent from the average for the previous eighteen years, according to Robbins, citing studies published in the *Journal of the American Medical Association*. As the study's author, Danish health official Dr. Mikkel Hindhede, explained in his 1920 article, the findings did not prove that meat was the culprit of higher disease rates in earlier years; but lack of meat certainly did not appear to have had a negative effect: "no one can dispute the fact that the people of Denmark have no cause to regret that during the war their diet consisted mostly of milk, vegetables and bran."[32]

Scientists discovered quite similar results in Norway during World War II. The nation's death rate from circulatory diseases plummeted and then rose again in episodes that corresponded to the elimination and subsequent reappearance of meat.[33] The *British Medical Journal* summarized: "During the second world war mortality from circulatory diseases in German occupied Norway fell by around 20% within 2–3 years. This accompanied dramatic enforced dietary changes—notably, a radical decrease in the consumption of meat, whole milk, cream, cheese, eggs, and margarine and a considerable increase in the consumption of fish and fresh vegetables."[34]

More contemporary research amplifies these findings. Many concern the phenomenal amount of fat in general and saturated fat in particular in the American diet, much of it from meat. Fat, according to Rifkin, "now makes up over 37 percent of daily caloric intake in North America." The 1987 report by the U.S. surgeon general concluded that 1.5 million of the 2.1 million deaths in America that year were diet-related and partially attributable to saturated fat and cholesterol, of which meat is a major source. In a major 1990 study of 8,000 people's diets and health in China, researchers found that "in counties where meat consumption increased, the rate of cardiovascular disease increased dramatically, in some cases an increase of fifty fold over the rate of heart disease in regions where animal fat still made up less than 15 percent of the average diet."[35]

There is also growing evidence of a possible relationship between excessive meat intake and cancer. A six-year study of more than 88,000 women between the ages of thirty and fifty-nine, published in the *New England Journal of Medicine* in 1990, found that women who ate red meat every day were "two and a half times more likely to have had colon cancer than the women who ate meat sparingly or not at all."[36] Other studies suggest a connection between excessive red meat consumption and breast cancer, noting that reducing fat-derived calories and saturated fat could reduce breast cancer significantly.[37]

For these and other compelling health reasons, the American Heart Association, the American Cancer Society, the National Academy of Sciences, and the American Academy of Pediatrics all "have urged a reduction in the consumption of animal fat and cholesterol and the shift to a more vegetarian diet high in protein," states Rifkin.[38]

But what if the well-documented nutritional case against industrial meat were somehow debunked? Even if meat were proved conclusively to be healthful and nutritionally essential, the way it (and chicken) is raised and processed today makes its regular consumption a high-risk affair, with consequences for consumers' immediate and long-term health, labor productivity, and public health care costs.

DISEASE CENTRAL

Although disease is a natural part of life—obviously, it predates factory farming—there is widespread expert opinion that the intensely confined quarters of industrial animal farms today are breeding grounds for virulent bacterial strains. "Industrialization of our meat supply opened up a conduit for salmonella, for campylobacter, for *E. coli* 0157:H7 infections," says Dr. Robert Tauxe, head of the food-borne illness division at the Centers for Disease Control.[39] There is strong evidence, both anecdotal and statistical, suggesting a relationship between the mass-scale farming and processing of meat and increases in food-borne illnesses and bacterial outbreaks.

It starts in the massive, densely packed feedlots and animal barns where the sources of our meat lead an existence that is increasingly nasty, brutish, and short. Since the meat industry began consolidating in the 1970s (poultry centralization began earlier, in the 1950s, and has recently intensified), the number and prevalence of bacterial diseases has grown dramatically. Food-borne salmonellosis (a.k.a. salmonella poisoning) "has risen significantly since the 1970s," states a USDA report using data from the Centers for Disease Control. During a thirty-year span, the annual number of *reported* salmonella illnesses from food doubled, rising from less than 20,000 in 1967 to more than 40,000 by 1995, a number that has remained fairly constant.[40] However, these figures actually "understate the total number of cases," the USDA report states, since many victims do not seek hospital care or report their illnesses. Based on this underreporting, government scientists estimate the actual number of food-borne salmonella cases to be more than 1.4 million. Food-related *Campylobacter* illnesses run in the neighborhood of 2.4 million a year.[41]

New bacterial strains have arrived on the scene with disturbing ferocity in the past fifteen to twenty years. In the mid-1990s, salmonella enteritidis was proving particularly virulent and prolific, especially in giant warehouses holding tens of thousands of chickens. The bacteria could be "passed from infected hen to eggs before shell formation occurs," and could easily "spread through the flock through chicken-to-chicken contact and through contact with contaminated feed, equipment, rodents, flies, animals, and human beings."[42] This strain represented just 6 percent of reported salmonella infections in 1980, but by 1994 it accounted for 26 percent, "an increase in which contaminated poultry play an important role," according to the journalist Nicols Fox.[43] The bacterial strain *E. coli* 0157:H7, now much dreaded for the many food-poisoning victims it has claimed, was "unheard-of before 1982."

In her 1997 exposé of food hazards, *Spoiled,* Fox wrote, "A quick look back into the literature of foodborne pathogens reveals that even 15 years ago none of the pathogens causing trouble today, with the exception of *Salmonella* and *V. cholerae,* was mentioned." She noted that "the new pathogens are coming not so much from the humans handling the foods, although that is still a factor, as from the foods themselves."[44]

Another particularly elusive pathogen, *Yersinia enterocolitica,* which can grow under refrigeration and inside vacuum-packed products, was emerging across the United States and Europe, as well as in the developing world. According to Fox, "the climb in *Yersinia* infections has precisely paralleled the trend in developing countries to raise swine intensively—in large numbers and in close quarters, conditions that favor the spread of any bacterial disease."[45]

Public-health officials argue that factory farms, through their sheer size and density, have opened these bacterial floodgates. So many animals packed tightly together, standing and sleeping in their own bacteria-laden feces: if one falls ill, a disease can quickly spread to the whole herd. "The new, highly industrialized way that we produce our food," says the CDC's Tauxe, "opened up new ecological homes for a number of bacteria, either on the farm, where animals might be together in much larger numbers than they used to be, or further down in the production chain." Dr. Glenn Morris of the University of Maryland concurs: "*E. coli* is an organism that has sort of taken advantage of, if you will, the modern farming techniques. . . . In larger feedlots, there's a greater chance for passing the microorganism back and forth. All of that contributes to spread of the microorganism such as *E. coli* 0157."[46]

As Tauxe suggests, the feedlots and factory barns are only half the problem: the miraculous speed and efficiency of the nation's meat and poultry processing factories is proving quite costly to human health. The very conditions that maim and disable so many workers inside the plants are, at the least, exacerbating disease outbreaks and food-related illnesses. The crisis in food safety is inextricably linked to the disregard for meat-industry workers' health which I examine in Chapter 11; the concerns of consumer health and labor are intimately connected. Consumers may benefit from the cheap prices made possible by poor factory wages and conditions, but those cost savings are quickly lost to the enormous public-health expenses incurred from food-borne illnesses.

It boils down to a question of volume and speed. These are the primary requisites for an industry with slim per-unit profit margins, where the only way to come out on top is to push through as much product as quickly as possible. Over the past twenty-five years the meatpacking and

poultry industries have, with the nodding acceptance of government regulators, boosted assembly-line speeds to astronomical levels perilous to
both employees and consumers. In the early 1980s, poultry lobbyists
convinced the USDA to allow processing line speeds to soar from an
already-blurry seventy birds per minute to the dizzying rate of ninety,
meaning that ninety chicken parts speed by workers and inspectors
every sixty seconds. Typically USDA inspectors working on the line eye-
ball about thirty birds per minute for signs of contamination.[47] In the
early 1980s the meatpacking business followed suit, ramping up its factory speeds. European plants run at slower speeds, in part to improve
food safety: the slower the line, the more likely inspectors are to catch
contaminated meat and remove it from the food supply.[48]

It is little wonder, then, that bacterial strains such as *E. coli* 0157:H7,
Salmonella, Listeria monocytogenes, and *Campylobacter* would become
epidemic by the 1990s and that tainted meat would emerge as a major
public-health hazard. Writes Nestle, "Whether we *should* worry more
about [bacterial microbes in food] is a matter of how we perceive risk.
For most of us as individuals, an occasional episode of stomach upset—
if not too severe—is tolerable. From a public health standpoint, however, the cost to society of such episodes is staggeringly high."[49]

High indeed. A 1996 USDA study concluded that six major bacterial pathogens were responsible for anywhere from 6.5 million to 33
million human illnesses a year and cost the public between three and
six *billion* dollars annually. And that wasn't counting the dozens of
other pathogens, as well as the human and economic costs of chronic
diseases: "The estimates of the annual costs to society of foodborne
illness would increase considerably if all foodborne pathogens were included in the analysis, all chronic illnesses that are triggered by food-
borne disease were considered, and less conservative estimates were
used to value premature death."[50]

A host of chronic ailments, including reactive arthritis, Reiter's syndrome, Miller-Fisher syndrome, and ulcers, have now been linked to
bacterial infections often caused by contaminated foods.[51] One ailment
caused by *Campylobacter* infection is Guillain-Barré syndrome, a potentially crippling autoimmune reaction that can lead to neuromuscular

paralysis. Each year, according to government estimates, between 526 and 3,830 people are afflicted by GBS through *Campylobacter* food poisoning. (This rather large range is due to varying estimates about the likelihood of the syndrome being caused by foodborne *Campylobacter* infection.) Altogether, the USDA found, "Reducing campylobacter in food could prevent up to $5.6 billion in costs annually."[52]

THE HIGHEST PRICE

The wakeup call came in December 1992. A decade after the arrival of *E. coli* 0157:H7, the bacterium was making headlines for poisoning hundreds of people who had consumed hamburgers at Jack in the Box restaurants in the Pacific Northwest. By the end of the outbreak in February 1993, 732 people had fallen ill and 195 had been hospitalized. Four children died.[53]

The case of five-year-old Lauren Rudolph was harrowing. A week before Christmas that year, after receiving good marks on her first-grade report card, Lauren and her brother Michael were treated to burgers at a Jack in the Box near San Diego. Two days later she was in bed with a bad headache. She was lethargic and weak. Then intense nausea set in. "She would double over with painful cramps and have frequent episodes of diarrhea," writes Nicols Fox. "In between she seemed almost lifeless, sleeping fitfully."[54]

By Christmas Eve, her stools were filled with blood and tissue, and she was admitted to San Diego Children's Hospital. There, despite constant monitoring, intravenous fluids, and painkillers, "the pain and diarrhea became uncontrollably worse." The next day, on Christmas, Lauren suffered a massive heart attack and fell into a coma. Three days later, after two more heart attacks, she was dead, a victim of hemolytic uremic syndrome from bacteria in the ground beef.[55]

The Jack in the Box scandal implicated feedlots and processors as much as the fast-food chain, and revived long-simmering attempts to revamp the meat-production system. As Nestle explains, regulators had been slowly playing catch-up with the industry for ten years. In the early 1980s, she writes, "Investigations by the General Accounting

Office (GAO) revealed that USDA inspectors were no longer able to keep up with the recently increased line speeds in meat-processing plants, but the department had failed to do anything to solve that problem." The GAO urged USDA to implement a more modern approach to combat microbial pathogens, a radical departure from traditional "poke and sniff" tactics. They proposed a science-based system called Hazard Analysis and Critical Control Point, or HACCP, to identify and monitor key stages in meat processing where microbial contamination could be prevented. It would require testing at these critical control points for hazardous pathogens such as *E. coli* 0157:H7. The lines wouldn't run any slower, but at least inspections would be smarter, more strategic. A 1985 report by the National Research Council, no liberal think tank, backed up the GAO's findings.[56]

Even after the Jack in the Box poisonings ignited national fear and outrage, it would take another three years of intense battling against industry resistance, and more deadly pathogen outbreaks, for HACCP to become official regulation. Full implementation had to wait another three years. It was, seemingly, the end of a twenty-year battle, beginning in the early 1970s, in which the meat industry fought off numerous crucial safety regulations, from limits on salmonella and other pathogens to simple labeling rules warning consumers of the hazards of undercooked meat.[57]

But HACCP, despite bringing some promising improvements, was soon better known derisively as "have a cup of coffee and pray." To consumer advocates and many government food-safety regulators, the new rules amounted to a privatization of meat inspection. Indeed, the new system struck a deal with agribusiness. In return for accepting more extensive regulation, industry was allowed to largely monitor itself, with government inspectors in the backdrop poring over assembly-line records to double-check that everything was on the up and up.[58]

Many former regulators familiar with the system said the new approach was dangerous. "Factory farms do their own testing of meats under USDA supervision," remarked a former USDA meat inspector, Albert Midoux, in 1998, not long after HACCP started up. "It's like the wolf guarding the henhouse. Their USDA stamp doesn't mean that food is safe, it means watch out."[59] A retired federal veterinarian, Dr. Theodore Bek, called HACCP a "disaster waiting to happen. The main thrust of the industry is profits. You can't add to profits by taking the time to run tests on a product."[60]

These regulators weren't alone in their apprehension. In January 1998, as the system was being launched, the Associated Press reported that some "federal inspectors on the front lines say relying on company workers to keep records on how well the systems operate places too much faith in the honesty of corporations out to make a profit. . . . No federal inspector will oversee the tests, and companies need only make available their own results."[61]

In September 2000, about a year after HACCP was fully implemented in most of the nation's meatpacking and poultry facilities, a report surveying hundreds of government food-safety regulators slammed the system for failing to lead to increased quality and credibility of meat inspection. "Inspectors are primarily limited to examining meat at an area that the Company designates as the 'critical control point,' and the Company is allowed to choose the location and number of these points," said the report, released by Public Citizen and the Government Accountability Project. "As a result, consumers are being allowed to eat meat that can be contaminated both with potentially infectious fecal matter and nonlethal substances—including tumors, pus, blisters, scabs, hair, feathers, rust, and bits of metal."[62]

The crux of the problem, regulators said, was the industry's overall control of the system. "Decreasing inspectors' authority to inspect all along the line means processing lines can operate faster—and that means more profits."[63] The industry was well aware of its newfound independence from pesky regulators: as Excel Corp. Vice President Dell Allen told the trade magazine *Meat & Poultry*, "the good news about the new rules is industry will be allowed to control its own destiny."[64]

A full two thirds of the inspectors surveyed said that since HACCP began, "There have been instances when they have not taken direct action against contamination (feces, vomit, metal shards, etc.) that they observed and would have taken action against under the old system." Almost all of these inspectors "responded that this occurs daily or weekly." A number of inspectors reported having been "personally threatened with a lawsuit by plant management for taking or preparing to take a regulatory action; and 20% said their USDA supervisors informed them that [they] could be sued as a result of regulatory enforcement." Eighty percent of 426 inspectors "felt they cannot, generally, enforce the law" as well as they could prior to HACCP.[65]

The comments of meatpacking inspectors, documented in the Public Citizen report, are troubling. A brief snapshot:

- "Instead of taking action immediately we are instructed to 'let the system work.'"
- "On a daily basis, when doing checks for fecal contamination, I find ingesta [vomit] on the inside of birds. Production doesn't have to take any corrective action for ingesta because it is not considered a safety hazard even though it is digestive tract content."
- "Before HACCP you could stop [the] slaughter line to report feces or ingesta. Now you must let [the] company handle [it]."
- "I was told by the IIC [inspector-in-charge] that I had to be cautious in my decisions to stop the line and make sure decisions are supported or the company could take legal actions against me."

Not only has inspectors' authority been diminished, their numbers have been dwindling. Through years of regulatory erosion, the USDA inspection squad had shriveled from 12,000 in 1978 to just 7,500 by 1997—a level that remained as of 2002.[66] As a consequence, the number of unannounced inspections of food and drug manufacturers' plants declined dramatically, from 22,189 in 1986 down to 15,104 a decade later.[67] Perhaps more grievous, the USDA had the meekest of enforcement powers: it lacked the authority to require companies to recall tainted meat and could not levy fines against food-safety violators. As an ultimate stopgap measure, USDA inspectors could, and sometimes did, walk out of a plant, which legally forced it to shut down.[68]

In the fall of 1997, President Clinton's agriculture secretary, Dan Glickman, pushed for broad new USDA enforcement powers. He complained, "We can use fines to protect farmers and ranchers from unfair trading practices. Abuse a circus elephant, sell a cat without a license, market a potato that's too small, keep bad records on watermelons, fail to report to the onion committee—fine, fine, fine, fine, fine. Yet if you produce unsafe food, the only one of these items that puts people's lives at stake, there is no civil penalty." Glickman proposed that food-safety violators be penalized $100,000 a day for every transgression, and that the USDA be given the authority to require recalls of tainted meat. The National Cattlemen's Beef Association, true to form, opposed the measure.[69] Glickman's proposal languished in congressional committee for months. Still, as of 2004, the agency lacked the basic power to require meat recalls, or to identify retailers who have sold tainted meat.[70]

Outside the marbled halls of Congress and the White House, in supermarkets and fast-food joints across America, the crisis of food safety had hardly been resolved. Throughout 1997 and 1998, a spate of massive tainted meat recalls involving hundreds of millions of pounds of contaminated meat and hundreds of illnesses kept the camera-shy industry in the spotlight. *Salmonella, E. coli* bacteria, and animal feces were the most common culprits.

In December 1998, the deadly bacterium *Listeria monocytogenes,* which causes a number of life-threatening diseases, reappeared on the scene after years of relative hibernation. It was found lingering inside 35 million pounds of hot dogs and processed luncheon meats produced by Bil Mar Foods, a subsidiary of Sara Lee. The bacteria, which can grow inside refrigerated packaged foods, are especially lethal to the elderly, people with weakened immune systems, pregnant women, and their unborn children. It can incubate inside the body for up to seventy days before striking; even with antibiotic treatment, the mortality rate is 30 percent. In the Sara Lee case, 100 people in twenty-two states fell ill, and 20 died.[71]

Yet when the USDA proposed mandatory microbial testing of ready-to-eat products, industry strenuously resisted. Food processors even found a way to blame their failings on the government. Jenny Scott, the senior food-safety program director for the National Food Processors Association, proclaimed: "The Federal government is standing in the way of doing testing. The problem is the zero-tolerance policy for *Listeria* in ready to eat products. Because you can't have any *Listeria* in a product, there is a potential legal and regulatory liability if you test the product and find *Listeria*."[72] In 2001 there were another 163 recalls totaling over 100 million pounds of contaminated meat.[73]

Fast-forward to July 2002: The costs of this loophole-riddled system keep piling up. ConAgra must recall 19 million pounds of beef— "enough to supply a tainted burger to at least one fourth of the US population"—potentially contaminated with *E. coli* 0157:H7. Inexplicably, USDA inspectors fail to tell ConAgra about the bacteria contamination for two weeks. Meanwhile, according to Eric Schlosser, "The bad meat continued to be sold at supermarkets, served at countless restaurants and grilled at outdoor barbecues nationwide." More than a month after the recall, health officials in states with recalled meat still can't get lists from ConAgra showing where the meat was. "I know it's here, but without knowing where it went, there's not a whole lot we can do," an Oklahoma public health official tells the *Denver Post*.[74] That summer there's another *Listeria* disaster: another 120 illnesses, and twenty people dead across the Northeast.[75] More scary headlines, outraged families, calls for reform. In between solemn apologies, the companies continue nudging blame onto consumers, advising that if people only washed their hands and cooked their meat better these accidents might not happen. People keep eating fecal-contaminated meat, and keep getting sick.

In a strident yet eloquent column for the *Denver Post*, Diane Carmen describes the ironies of blind trust in corporate food in an age of national security paranoia: "If 19 million pounds of meat distributed to half of this country had been contaminated with a deadly strain of *E. coli* bacteria by terrorists, we'd go nuts. But when it's done by a Fortune 100 corporation, we continue to buy it and feed it to our kids."[76] Meanwhile, she pointed out, each meat recall amounts to a phenomenal waste, of all the precious water and grain resources poured into cows, of years of hard work by the ranchers who raise the young cattle, of all the painstaking low-wage toil of immigrant workers, of all the dead cattle whose short, tortured lives have been thoroughly squandered. All, in large part, because the industry and its hamstrung (some argue compliant) regulators refuse to break up disease-plagued factory farms, and to slow down slaughterhouse assembly lines where one speck of contamination can quickly infect millions of burgers.

DRUGSTORE COW

Standing amid acres of filthy cattle, journalist Michael Pollan sees visions of fourteenth-century London. There is shit, massive piles of it, everywhere. It's a crowded, noxious scene packed tightly with "recent arrivals from who knows where, combined with a lack of modern sanitation," he writes. "This combination has always been a recipe for disease; the only reason contemporary animal cities aren't as plague-ridden as their medieval counterparts is a single historical anomaly: the modern antibiotic."[77]

Thanks to centralized meat and poultry production and the industrial quest for maximum efficiency, a veritable drug warehouse of antibiotics and growth-inducing hormones is a mainstay on today's animal farms. The "urbanization" of livestock, with its attendant risk of disease epidemics, is a financial boon to the pharmaceutical industry: most of the antibiotics sold in America are for animal feed. Each year, according to a 2001 report by the Union of Concerned Scientists, 25 million pounds of antibiotics "are fed to chickens, pigs, and cows for nontherapeutic purposes like growth promotion." This onslaught of pharmaceuticals, up from 16 million pounds in the mid-1980s, represents roughly 70 percent of total U.S. antibiotic production.[78]

As Pollan discovered in the process of raising his own steer for market, an arsenal of antibiotics is deployed to combat animal illnesses that are a direct result of modern industrial meat farming. First, there is the problem of corn. The raising of "corn-fed" beef, an industry convenience that has been marketed into the American gastronomic lexicon, creates a host of potential diseases, for which antibiotics have become a Band-Aid.

Cows are ruminants, natural grass eaters whose digestive systems are not designed for high-starch foods like corn. One of the more drastic ailments caused by a corn-based diet, according to Pollan, is feedlot bloat, in which "a layer of foamy slime that can trap gas forms in the rumen [a cow's large first stomach]. The rumen inflates like a balloon, pressing against the animal's lungs. Unless action is promptly taken to relieve the pressure, the cow suffocates." Corn also produces excessive acid in cows, causing "a kind of bovine heartburn" which can ultimately lead to diarrhea, ulcers, bloat, and liver disease among other problems. Antibiotics, intended strictly for illness, become an essential part of the cows' diet. As Nestle explains, "for reasons poorly understood, animals grow faster and need less feed when low-dose antibiotics are added to their food or drinking water."[79] The diet is bound to make cows ill: "The drugs are plainly being used to treat sick animals, yet the animals probably wouldn't be sick if not for what we feed them."[80] In other words, the meat industry's reliance on corn to produce high volumes of popular fat-marbled meat seems to create new health risks, which the industry seeks to repel with an army of antibiotics.

Corn-fed cows aren't particularly good for us, either, Pollan reports. He cites a study published in the *European Journal of Clinical Nutrition* showing that grass-fed meat is far less fatty than the more common grain-fed kind and contains more of the beneficial omega-3 fatty acids and fewer omega-6, which has been linked to heart disease. Corn "develops well-marbled flesh, giving it a taste and texture American consumers have learned to like. Yet this meat is demonstrably less healthy to eat, since it contains more saturated fat."[81]

Corn, however, produces slaughter-ready cows far more quickly than grass. Add corn's Band-Aid medication, antibiotics, along with growth hormones, and the time it takes to produce a steak-worthy cow has been whittled down from three years in the 1950s to just fourteen months today.[82]

Another product of the postwar petrochemical-induced surplus, cheap corn is the backbone of modern factory farming's consolidated animal feedlots. An economic symbiosis has evolved between cattle and corn, in which our meat supply has become dependent on this heavily subsidized grain. Just as antibiotics are dispensed in part to treat illnesses caused by a corn-based diet, pesticides are deployed in massive volumes—and at great expense to the environment and public health—to propel this carnivore's harvest (for more on this, see Chapter 9).

According to the National Corn Growers Association, the number-one use for corn worldwide is as feed for livestock. A remarkable 80 percent of America's corn harvest goes to feed livestock across the globe, 58 percent of it feeding the U.S. animal industries.[83] Since World War II, writes Pollan, "The USDA's policy has been to help farmers dispose of surplus corn by passing as much of it as possible through the digestive tracts of food animals, converting it into protein."[84] Scientists and agribusiness discovered the powers of hormones to boost growth rates in cattle and poultry as early as the 1930s. By the 1950s, a synthetic estrogen called diethylstilbestrol (DES) was used widely by the meat industry, "absorbed through the gastrointestinal tract after oral administration," described writer Orville Schell in his book *Modern Meat*. The hormone was popular with cattlemen because it increased weight gain by 15 to 19 percent. But in 1979, after years of legal battles, DES was banned, as doctors discovered it could "increase the risk of vaginal cancer in daughters of treated women," according to Cornell University's Institute for Comparative and Environmental Toxicology.[85]

Drugs on the farm are not new, but their proliferation is part and parcel of modern industrial animal farming. The "avalanche of drug usage" in the past thirty-five years, Robbins explains, is "coincidental with the shift in production methods from range grazing to feedlots. Before 1950, almost all the nation's cattle spent their lives grazing and foraging for their food." But by the early 1970s, three quarters of the cattle raised in America were warehoused in feedlots.[86]

The centrality of growth-enhancing drugs to contemporary meat production has inspired widespread opposition, including the European Union's ban in the mid-1990s of several major antibiotics. The EU has also banned synthetic estrogen pellets, implanted in cows' ears to speed growth, still used widely in the United States. These steroidal hormones make young animals gain weight faster and "help reduce the waiting time and the amount of feed eaten by an animal before slaughter," and can also increase milk production, according to the Cornell Institute. "Thus, hormones can increase the profitability of the meat and dairy industries."[87] Nonetheless, not all American ranchers are oblivious to the problems, not to mention the costs, of hormones. One rancher from South Dakota, Rich Blair, explained, "I'd love to give up hormones. If the consumer said, we don't want hormones, we'd stop in a second. The cattle could get along better without them. But the market signal's not there, and as long as my competitor's doing it, I've got to do it, too."[88] What is striking is the continued reliance on these drugs in the face of growing evidence of their potential harm to human health. Perhaps most disturbing is the fact that the drugging of meat animals is rendering many antibiotics ineffective for human use.

"Because of the large amounts of antibiotics we are using [in meat production], we are developing increasingly resistant microorganisms," says Dr. Glenn Morris Jr. of the University of Maryland. "And we are reducing our ability, as physicians, to treat patients who come in to us with infections."[89] Much as pesticides can breed superresistant bugs, antibiotics can, when abused prophylactically, help antibiotic-resistant bacteria to proliferate.

According to Marion Nestle, researchers were well aware of increased antibiotic resistance by the mid-1970s. In 1977, the FDA attempted to rein in the food industry's antibiotic abuse, but Congress "overruled this idea under pressure from farm-state lawmakers, livestock producers, and the makers of the drugs." By the early 1980s, even as research strengthened the case that animals could pass antibiotic-resistant bacteria along to humans, "the FDA stopped fighting this issue and instead proposed more relaxed standards." One congressman remarked that the FDA's main concern was "protection of the health of the animal drug industry."[90]

BACTERIA BLOWBACK

By the late 1990s, as food-borne illnesses and meat-factory recalls became regular front-page news, it was clear that antibiotic resistance had grown into a major problem. "The dangers of antibiotic-resistant foodborne bacteria were becoming more evident as more species acquired resistance to more and more antibiotics."[91] It was bacterial blowback: the crowded factory farming conditions that were spreading bacteria problems like wildfire were also creating new barriers to treating those foodborne illnesses.

Campylobacter, a virulent bacterial strain long overshadowed by its famous colleague *Salmonella,* had emerged as "the leading bacterial cause of foodborne illness in the country," according to the *New York Times.* Just six years earlier, researchers at the Centers for Disease Control had found anywhere from 30 to 70 percent of all chickens to be infected with *Campylobacter;* now the potentially lethal bacterium was in 70 to 90 percent of chickens. The bacterium was responsible for 2 million to 8 million food-related illnesses a year, and 200 to 800 deaths.[92]

Exacerbating this growing epidemic was the fact that *human* antibiotics treatment for campylobacteriosis was losing its effectiveness. Resistance in the birds was transferring to people: "the use of a group of antibiotics called fluoroquinolones to treat disease in chickens is creating strains of drug-resistant campylobacter in humans," the *New York Times* reported. Since the licensing of fluoroquinolones for chickens in 1995, said Dr. Michael Osterholm, an epidemiologist with the Minnesota Health Department, "levels of drug-resistant campylobacter in humans has gone up dramatically." Similar evidence was cropping up in the UK, the Netherlands, and Spain, where antibiotic resistance was over 80 percent. "The increase occurred immediately after the introduction of the use of fluoroquinolones in animals," said Osterholm.

Such disturbing findings were not confined to the laboratory. In a random sampling of chickens in Minnesota supermarkets, public health officials found 79 percent contaminated with *Campylobacter,* and 20 percent of them were strains resistant to antibiotics; of the 58 percent of turkeys with the bacterium, 84 percent carried an antibiotic-proof strain.[93] Four years later, in 2001, the situation was even worse, as resistance broadened. As much as 80 percent of meat (including pork, chicken, or beef) collected in supermarkets harbored antibiotic-resistant bacteria, according to the *New England Journal of Medicine.* "These bacteria survived a week or two in the intestines of people who ate them," Nestle described. "If these people became ill, the antibiotics would not help."[94]

EAT YOUR VEGETABLES

There is, of course one sort of "dairy" we all consume in our earliest years—but even mother's milk is not free from our toxic food chain. There is perhaps no greater indicator of pesticides' ubiquity in our food system than at the very beginning of human nourishment. The pesticides and chemicals we eat get deposited inside body fat, and the toxins are later drawn out of the fat and excreted during nursing. From the 1950s through the early 1980s, government and academic research scientists were finding almost universal contamination of breast milk, meaning that "breast-fed babies thereby may consume extraordinarily large amounts of the most toxic substances ever known to man," according to Robbins. Researchers found distressingly high concentrations of DDT, PCBs, dieldrin, heptachlor, dioxin, and other agricultural chemicals, and according to one study, breast milk was so full of these toxins that "it would be subject to confiscation and destruction by the FDA were it to be sold across state lines."[95] By 1976, according to Sandra Steingraber, "roughly 25 percent of all U.S. breast milk was too contaminated to be bottled and sold as a food commodity."[96]

One EPA analysis from 1976 was particularly telling. The breast milk of vegetarian women, researchers concluded, was far less toxic than that of women who ate meat. Robbins wrote, "The less meat, butter, eggs, cheese, milk, poultry, and fish in a woman's diet, the less toxic chemicals will be found in the milk that flows from her breast to her young." This is not just Robbins's own conclusion. In 1981 the *New England Journal of Medicine* published findings that "the highest levels of contamination in the breast milk of the vegetarians was lower than the lowest level of contamination . . . [in] non-vegetarian women."[97]

More recent research suggests some pesticide levels in breast milk may be slowly declining, at least in Europe. Long-term studies in Germany and Sweden, through the early 1990s, were showing modest declines of dioxins, PCBs, and pesticides in breast milk samples.[98] Nonetheless, evidence continues to point to disturbing toxic concentrations. Measuring pesticides in the amniotic fluid of pregnant women in the late 1990s, researchers with the Endocrine Society in the United

States and Canada found levels of a DDT breakdown product "sufficient to cause concern, since the levels measured are in the same range as some steroids [hormones] which occur naturally in the fetus at the same time of development."[99] (These disturbing facts don't necessarily outweigh the many benefits of breast-feeding. They instead make the case for eliminating—or at least dramatically reducing—pesticides all the more urgent.)

Despite the findings of reduced pesticide contamination among vegetarian women, fruits and vegetables are by no means a safe haven. For one thing, they are implicated in many bacterial food poisonings due to their regular and incidental contact with tainted meats and animal manure. For instance, cases of bacterial pathogens on lettuce have been traced to cattle excrement.[100]

Beyond the hazards of microbial intermingling, nonorganic fruits and vegetables are covered with residue from pesticides known to be carcinogenic and damaging to our neurologic and reproductive systems. Individually, none of these is likely to cause any immediate harm. Yet together, over a lifetime of eating, they can add up to serious trouble. What else should we expect from a diet filled with cancer-causing chemicals? The EPA has estimated that pesticide residues on food may be causing cancer in thousands of people every year. The estimated costs of pesticides to public health and the environment—including pesticide poisonings and chronic diseases such as cancer—mount up to over $8.3 billion a year.[101]

But as Leon and DeWaal point out, we're not even getting the full picture on the potential hazards of pesticide residues. Of the more than 4 million food shipments imported into the United States each year, only .5 percent are sampled by the FDA to ensure they fall within pesticide residue limits. Roughly 3 percent of tested domestic and imported food samples "contain pesticide residues for which the government agencies have no legal tolerance. That means we're eating a lot of food that simply should not be on the market."[102]

Owing to such vaporous regulation, illegal pesticide residues crop up in our food with regularity. A 1995 examination of FDA residue tests undertaken by the Washington, D.C.–based nonprofit watchdog organization Environmental Working Group found illegal levels of chlorpyrifos, a nerve agent that was then the most widely used insecticide in the United States, on sixteen of forty-two different foods.[103]

Children are especially at risk, both because their bodies and minds are in a vulnerable developmental stage and because many of their favorite foods are among the most likely to carry residues. Apples and strawberries, for instance, "contain one or more pesticide residues in over 95% of the samples" studied by USDA.[104] Children also consume far more (per body weight) apple juice, grape juice, mixed fruit juice, raisins, and applesauce than do adults, and all of these contain multiple pesticides.[105]

The immediate health impacts have not been conclusively determined, but are of considerable concern, for many pesticides are designed to disrupt hormonal and neurological systems in insects that also are key to children's physical and mental growth. "The data strongly suggest that exposure to neurotoxic compounds at levels believed to be safe for adults could result in permanent loss of brain function if it occurred during the prenatal and early childhood period of brain development" was the conclusion stated in an in-depth study by the National Research Council. "Policies that established safe levels of exposures to neurotoxic pesticides for adults could not be assumed to adequately protect a child less than 4 years of age."[106]

Even more worrying is the appearance of pesticides in baby food, even some that were banned long ago. In the late 1990s, according to the FDA, "elevated levels of lead" were found in processed vegetable baby food. "The source was traced to carrots grown in fields previously used as apple orchards that had been treated with lead arsenate." In another case, elevated levels of arsenic were discovered in a sample of peanut butter; the peanuts were grown in a field that had once been treated with a defoliant containing arsenic.[107] Another detailed analysis found sixteen different pesticides in eight baby food products. Three of those pesticides are "probable human carcinogens." More than half of the baby food items analyzed—and 78 percent of peaches and pears—contained detectable levels of pesticides.[108]

Here again, the concern is not so much with one particular pesticide but rather with children's ongoing exposure to a plethora of toxins. In a 1999 study based on USDA and FDA pesticide records, the Environmental Working Group documented that "multiple pesticides known or suspected to cause brain and nervous system damage, cancer, disruption of the endocrine and immune systems, and a host of other toxic effects are ubiquitous in foods children commonly consume at levels that present serious health risks." All told, more than 20 million children between one and five years old ingest at least eight pesticides every day, the study found. Over a single year children endure 2,900 pesticide exposures from the food they eat. Some of those exposures are especially dangerous: each day 610,400 children aged one to five consume neurotoxic insecticides the government considers unsafe, largely from apples and peaches.[109]

In 1996 Congress passed an important food-safety measure, the Food Quality Protection Act, which for the first time mandated protection of children from pesticides. The law has, at the very least, greatly increased expectations about protecting children from pesticides. But it hasn't come without a fight. Even three years after the law was passed, in 1999 congressional hearings, several representatives attacked "hasty" EPA actions to limit pesticide exposures. Bob Goodlatte, a Republican representative from Virginia, commented that EPA pesticide restrictions "have a dramatic effect on consumer confidence . . . you tell me what I should say when I hand my child an apple as a nutritious snack? With no imminent hazard present which you [EPA] fully acknowledge, a decision to announce such dramatic restrictions for two widely used pesticides seems unwarranted and an abhorrent abuse of power."[110]

But environmental groups say the EPA has been slow to develop any specific intake standards for children that account for multiple pesticide exposures. "Even the best application of the 1996 law will not protect the public from the combined effect of multiple pesticides," the Environmental Working Group wrote in 1999. "Although a handful of the most dangerous pesticides have been removed from the food supply in recent years, overall, the use of pesticides has remained steady or even increased. . . . If you eat in this country, you eat pesticides."[111]

EATING OUTSIDE THE BOX

Fatty foods. High cholesterol. Excessive salt and sugar. Shit-contaminated meat. Mercury and other metals in fish. Fruits and vegetables tainted by toxic residues. What is an eater of food to do? Nourishing oneself today entails navigating a minefield of immediate and long-term health hazards. Certainly there is plenty that individual consumers can do to circumvent the bad food trap, provided they have knowledge and money. Not all fruits and vegetables carry the same levels of pesticide residue, and some are safer than others (see the appendix for web sites with further information on this). Some fish contain less toxic metal than others. And of course there's organic produce and free-range organic meat and fowl, generally far less toxic and contaminated than the nonorganic alternatives. If you have the time, finances, and information, you can avoid most of the mainstream menu the American corporate food system so vigorously promotes.

But despite your best efforts, the deck is stacked against you. Despite the explosion in organic farming over the past two decades, by 1999 organics represented just 1.5 percent of all foods sold in the United States.[112] It is a burgeoning, and increasingly corporate, business, but still mostly unsubsidized by the government, and relegated to niche markets only affordable to middle- and upper-income classes. In most major cities there are at least a couple of stores offering organic produce, but across much of the country they are few and far between. Locating, and affording, free-range organic meat is even tougher.

Meanwhile, the government agencies charged with protecting consumer health are at best slow to the task, at worst deeply compromised by their close ties to the food industry (a subject explored in depth in Nestle's *Food Politics*). Through massive campaign contributions to key politicians—more than $54 million in 2002, with 72 percent going to Republicans—and revolving-door appointments to influential government posts, agribusiness corporations make sure that policy makers respect the industry's profits and cost-containment priorities.[113] In the past two decades, despite growing public concern about pesticides, contaminated meat, and food-borne illnesses, agribusiness has managed to maintain and sometimes increase its practices of spreading toxins on food, and has dramatically intensified the overcrowding and high-speed processing of animals. Eating meat has become a game of Russian roulette.

For individuals able and inclined to do so, the response to this mountain of junk food is to avoid as much of it as possible and seek out healthy unadulterated alternatives. For society, however, such an individualist response is wholly inadequate. It is certainly useful to broaden market demand for organics and free-range meat, and to cultivate the appreciation of health, taste, and environmental concerns reflected in the "slow foods" movement. Narrower campaigns to get McDonald's and other fast-food purveyors to serve cleaner, leaner meat, from "humanely" slaughtered animals, are also for the good. But these promising developments are, regrettably, small steps against steep odds. In the bigger picture, as I will explore in the final chapter of this book, what are urgently needed are aggressive policies addressing a system of food production and consumption that is profoundly unhealthy and unsustainable. Even through the lens of self-interest, consumers must begin to view what they eat as part of a larger economy and ecology of sustenance. Some consumers may be able to buy organic, but they're paying a stiff price, both at the register, for expensive unsubsidized food, and in their taxes, for the immense costs to public health and the environment of a food system gone deeply awry.

Part II

The Rise of the Corporate Cornucopia

INTRODUCTION

In these times of unprecedented corporate power (both economic and political), it is easy to succumb to the notion that we have left behind more halcyon days. It is enticing to imagine the small independent farmer of, say, the 1940s, making a decent living and living decently in a bucolic countryside, growing a diverse array of crops sold to small local markets. No big supermarkets or superhighways butting up against those fine green fields.

Certainly, the physical trappings of the American farm from the 1940s, or earlier, were far quieter and more picturesque than those of today's farms, which are often just an interstate exit away from Wal-Mart and McDonald's. And by degree, growers sixty years ago (or even twenty-five years ago) had far more power in the marketplace than today's harried farmer, who receives a lesser share of consumer money spent on food than ever before. Farmers then had more food companies bidding against one another for their crops, and supermarkets, then smaller and less concentrated, had less power to buy low and sell high. It was a better time for farmers, and, in many respects, for consumers as well.

But the postwar era, like times before and after it, was part of a historical continuum in which the corporate takeover of food has been a juggernaut. Even in the hardscrabble days after the Revolutionary War, when most farmers barely eked out a subsistence, moneyed interests and their political allies were laying the groundwork for agricultural consolidation. The century following the Declaration of Independence was marked by ferocious land buying by speculators, and later by well-connected railroad corporations. By the end of the nineteenth century, a near-omnipotent Beef Trust of just a few powerful companies wielded control over most of the nation's cattle supply.

American food and farming have never really been free of the impulses and imperatives of capitalism. As history makes clear, "free-market" agriculture—while arguably prolific and innovative—is marked by chaos and contradiction. The more farmers produce, the less money they make. Yet, the lower prices fall, the more individual farmers produce to recoup their losses through greater volume.

From a national perspective, farming has evolved (or devolved) to serve purposes that have little to do with nutrition and sustenance. Food—in some respects more precious than oil—is deployed both as a foreign-policy weapon and as an economic tool to help balance national trade deficits. Farm subsidies, at taxpayer expense, have helped big farms push aside small ones; they have also sustained a chronic situation of surplus production that at once both disciplines prices for farmers' crops and assures a national glut of food that can be exported at great profit to corporate traders.

The history of American agriculture is one of growing concentrated power over an essential resource, and of relentless industrialization. The consequences of these long-building trends are many, ranging from widespread ecological destruction and rural poverty to the aforementioned crises in food safety and the damaging international effects of America's overflowing supply of cheap food.

5

"GET BIG OR GET OUT"

"A business air sets the thresher to factory pace."
—George K. Holmes, "The Evolution of Farm Machinery,"
in *Readings in the Economic History of American
Agriculture* (1925)

"Most of our ills from the 1850s on could be traced to overproducing the market."
—Stanley Andrews, *The Farmer's Dilemma* (1961)

In the summer of 1972, while all of Richard Nixon's men were busy bugging offices and wreaking havoc with Democratic electoral hopes, his agriculture secretary, Earl Butz, was quietly tilling the path to his boss's reelection—and to the most radical upheaval in farm policy since the New Deal.[1] To deliver the farm vote, which had proved critical to Nixon's narrow victory in 1968, Butz went to Moscow.[2] Soviet crops were failing, and hungry workers and peasants were growing impatient. Food riots loomed as Leonid Brezhnev's government scrambled to keep its pledge of adding more meat to the Soviet diet.[3] Communist leaders in Russia and Eastern Europe were "under increasing pressure to provide their people with a standard of living commensurate with their military and industrial development," described Dan Morgan in his book *Merchants of Grain*. In Christmas 1970, Polish dock workers had burned Communist Party headquarters in Gdansk when officials tried to raise food prices.[4] Brezhnev needed grain, and Butz—for both immediate electoral and long-term policy reasons—needed an American food crisis.

Butz had already befriended farmers by doling out $4 billion worth of income supports, the highest such payments in history to that point, and paying farmers not to grow on 62 million acres. These were "big-government" sins that helped guarantee tight supplies and high prices for farmers.[5] The grain deal, coming amid drastic global food shortages, wouldn't win Nixon any international popularity contests. In the name of election-year politics, the U.S. government "was deliberately making the world grain shortage even worse by planting less."

Now, even as U.S. warplanes bombed Haiphong harbor in Vietnam to block Soviet food shipments to the Vietcong, Butz was laying the groundwork for a deal that would sell off America's dwindling grain surplus to Russia. Buyers on U.S. commodity markets "suddenly discovered that the only grain in storage in the world was unexpectedly gone."[6] The United States would soon encounter a grain shortage—precisely what Butz needed to increase grain prices and help deliver the farm vote as part of President Nixon's no-holds-barred reelection push. "The rain of financial benefices across the countryside in 1972 was politically motivated," writes historian John Shover in *First Majority, Last Minority*. "Butz took justifiable pride in his abilities as a Republican campaigner," and never intended to maintain record-level farm support payments.[7] Of course, electoral victory was just one of Butz's objectives; the deal also expanded private control over grain surpluses, and set off an era of prolific exports, increasingly controlled by grain corporations.

The U.S. government never actually sold a single ounce of grain to Russia. The Agriculture Department "could have sold the grain directly to the Soviets," writes Joel Solkoff in his 1985 book, *The Politics of Food*. "Instead, after negotiating with the Soviets, the government decided to sell all its grain in the marketplace. Private corporations bought it, and they in turn negotiated sales agreements with the Soviets."[8]

The deal was enabled by an unheralded regulatory maneuver in 1971 easing private exports. To grease the wheels, Nixon offered the Soviets $750 million in low-interest loans and cut-rate shipping costs.[9] With these inducements, the United States essentially privatized its precious food surplus, which propelled an export explosion—another key part of Butz's plan. The grain exports were also central to the Nixon administration's push to recover from shaky trade balances.[10] Exports, long an essential component propping up farm prices, tripled between 1972 and 1974.[11] Grain shipments went from 34 million tons in 1971, to 82 million tons by 1975.[12] The six major corporations doing the bulk of the trading controlled over 90 percent of the world's $11-billion-a-year grain-exports business in 1975.[13]

The magnitude of the highly secret transactions, revealed later in congressional testimony, was astounding. In a single deal with Continental Grain Co., Russian traders bought 4.5 million tons of yellow corn, 3.65 million tons of hard wheat, and 350,000 tons of soft wheat. The going export price for wheat at the time was $60 per ton, though Continental reportedly gave the Russians a price break: the firm "probably figured it could recover the discount by speculating on the government wheat subsidy."[14] All told, the deal was worth more than $1 billion.[15]

The deal worked short- and long-term magic. With the grain surplus erased almost overnight, domestic prices skyrocketed. By the November elections, "It was already clear that annual net farm income was going to be the highest in history." Buoyed by export-driven grain profits, farm income reached its historic zenith in 1973, a full 32.7 percent higher than in 1972.[16] Coinciding with worldwide droughts and food shortages, the Soviet purchase sent grain prices through the roof and set off "panic and hoarding on a planetary scale," explains Morgan. "The effect of the Soviet buying was comparable to the quadrupling of oil prices by the OPEC cartel a year later."[17]

The move also satisfied Republican cost-cutting imperatives: it eliminated grain-storage expenses and, by 1973, slashed government income-support payments to farmers by pushing crop prices up. The stage was set for Butz's sweeping overhaul of New Deal farm policy. Since the days of Franklin Delano Roosevelt, American agricultural policy had remained fairly consistent, pledging generally vigorous government spending to stabilize the farm economy and keep wholesale and retail food prices in check. Now Butz, in keeping with Nixonian ideology, aimed to cut farm-support spending and foist farmers onto the open market. Shover explains that "the objective of Republican agricultural policy was to move the government out of agriculture, obliterate government-held food stocks, and expand foreign markets for American commodities."

FEAST OF PROFITS—AND TROUBLE

Only after Nixon's reelection did the obvious ramifications of the farmers' boon and the shriveled surplus become evident: food prices soared. In January 1973, as Nixon was sworn in for a second term, the cost of food jumped by 20 percent over the previous month.[18] A report by the General Accounting Office would later find the grain deal had cost Americans about $1 billion in added food costs (according to Morgan the grain deal cost American consumers close to $2 billion). While gasoline prices ballooned from the OPEC oil embargo, the nation's food bill grew from $141 billion in 1971 to $226 billion by the time Georgia peanut farmer Jimmy Carter came to office in 1976.[19]

Consumers weren't the only victims of crushing prices. While big grain farmers and corporate grain traders reveled in their harvest of cash, meat and poultry growers were saddled with punishing grain-feed costs. Prices shot so high that "it became cheaper to slaughter cattle and poultry early and use them for feed, rather than wait until they were ready for market," wrote Stanley Aronowitz in his 1974 book, *Food, Shelter, and the American Dream*.[20] Many refused to sell their beef, poultry, and pork at the going price, and withheld their food from the market.[21] Once Nixon lifted price controls, in the spring of 1973, meat prices soared, satisfying farmers but outraging consumers, who soon joined in a mass boycott of beef.

Buffeted by countervailing pressures from farmers and consumers, Butz soon ordered 3 million acres of farmland back into production. But paradoxically, even as grain and meat supplies recovered, prices stayed stubbornly high. By autumn 1973, wheat hit $5 per bushel, triple its price fifteen months earlier; meat supplies remained strong, yet there were no signs of price cuts. The law of supply and demand wasn't controlling price levels.[22]

While juggling land use, prices, and supply, Butz was also engineering a sweeping policy overhaul—getting the government out of agriculture and, as he put it, compelling farmers to "get big or get out." The Nixon administration had already begun the process with the Agricultural Act of 1970, which for the first time put a ceiling on the amount individual farmers could be paid to prop up their incomes.[23] Then, in what many call the most important farm bill since the New Deal era, the 1973 Agricultural and Consumer Protection Act promised to shift "control of agriculture from the government to the marketplace." The government set exceedingly low minimum target prices, below which farmers would get support payments. "For the first time in decades farmers who produced wheat, corn, and other commodities depended entirely on market prices for their income."[24] Prices would have to plummet drastically before farmers would get government money. But a price plunge seemed unlikely: spurred by a weak dollar and intensifying global demand, U.S. farmers were reaping record incomes.

While thrusting farmers onto the capricious open market, the new law scrapped historic crop allotments and restrictions regulating how much farmers could grow. The floodgates were opened, and farmers, no longer guaranteed income protections, began what the USDA terms "wall-to-wall planting."[25] Most of the 62 million acres idled before the 1972 elections were soon plowed back into production. But nature and international politics intervened in 1974 to produce the worst American crop failures in nearly forty years.[26] Only 37 million acres of the surplus farmland, it turned out, was actually usable. Then major drought set in. Hammered by skyrocketing petroleum costs caused by the OPEC embargo, farmers cut back on petroleum-based fertilizers, and crops suffered. Even with reduced use, fertilizer costs alone shot up 1,000 percent between 1972 and 1974.[27]

American crop disasters in 1974 coincided with a gathering worldwide food crisis. A global emergency food reserve that could sustain the world's population for ninety-five days dwindled to a mere twenty-six-day supply by October 1974.[28] American reserves had been drained by the Nixon administration's intensive export push, and now U.S. food aid to poor nations, historically used under Public Law 480 (the federal "Food for Peace" program enacted in 1954) to dump surplus and stabilize prices, dried up. By late 1974, 700 million of the world's 4 billion people were near starvation.[29]

BOOM, BORROW, BUST

Despite the wild fluctuations in nature and the market, other more consistent trends were fattening the wallets of farmers at the top and rapidly thinning wallets at the bottom. The 1970s, writes Osha Gray Davidson in *Broken Heartland,* were "a heady time of rapidly rising farm income and skyrocketing land values," when "few questioned the notion that the good times would roll on forever."[30] The export explosion and support-slashing wrought by Nixon and Butz spawned a vigorous era of overplanting, farm buyouts and consolidations, and, perhaps most important, massive borrowing by farmers to finance the purchase of land and equipment necessary for the evergrowing superfarm. Banks were only too ready to oblige, encouraging farmers to "take out larger and larger loans to modernize and to expand operations."[31]

Enticed by optimistic projections of continued export growth, farmers burrowed deeper and deeper into debt in their fierce efforts to "get big." Farmland had turned to gold: the average acre in Iowa sold for $419 in 1970; by 1980 the going price was $2,066.[32]

For a time, U.S. exports continued to flow to a hungry world, and hearty prices validated to some extent the investment and debt rut, at least for wealthier growers. But in the early 1980s the bottom fell out. Export prices collapsed as the dollar strengthened. "In the split second between 1980 and 1983, the rising dollar overseas pushed American farm prices out of international competition," says historian John Opie.[33] Demand shrunk as global food production recovered, spurred by the controversial Green Revolution, which sent high-yield seeds along with pesticides and chemical fertilizers to Third World countries.[34] Traditional importers of U.S. grain, such as China, India, and Brazil, were reaping record harvests, and "flooded markets naturally led to lower grain prices worldwide."[35]

Farmers, already heavily indebted from the expansions of the 1970s, entered a devastating "circular process," writes Davidson: "In order to make up for diminishing profits, farmers were forced to grow more crops. The increased production forced grain prices even lower, which in turn led to farmers' putting more land into production, causing commodity prices to drop lower still."[36] Then, on October 6, 1979, came the back breaker: the Federal Reserve raised the cost of borrowing money, "a commodity that is as precious to farmers as rain."[37] Interest rates shot through the roof, while farmland values, influenced strongly by commodity prices, plunged by $146 billion between 1982 and 1985.[38] The U.S. economic recession was deepening, but for farmers it was more like depression. In Iowa the average net farm income went into deep-freeze, plummeting from $17,680 in 1981 to *minus* $1,891 by 1983.[39]

Though spawned most immediately by the export-at-all-costs policies of Dr. Butz, the 1980s "farm crisis," much like today's, was the natural outgrowth of age-old trends that saw a steady consolidation of farmland and wealth. The groundwork had been laid 200 years earlier.

1785: MAPPING THE FUTURE, CONQUERING THE LAND

For the white nonindentured settler emigrating from the religious and geographic confines of Europe, America in the 1780s must have seemed like a wide-open bounty literally ripe for the picking. Land wrested from Native Americans was copious and often rich with nutrients. The freshly independent nation, intent on widening its borders and filling its coffers, was cleansing the "frontier" of its native inhabitants and offering free land to anyone willing to farm it. But even then, nothing was really free. And America's political and financial leaders, once free of British colonialism, were eager to build up the young nation's economic clout—and to cash in on the wealth of the land.

Before crafting the Constitution, America's landholding leaders were busy taming the western wilderness, molding unruly land into quantifiable squares of civilization. When the Confederation Congress passed the Land Survey Ordinance of 1785, it structured the enduring contours of America's lands and regulated their settlement. A perfectly ordered grid would be imposed on the wild "new world," according to which it would be carved up into uniform squares that could be easily mapped and apportioned, regardless of whether their borders contained the resources necessary for farming. "The true geography of America," writes Opie, "disappeared under the checkerboard, which smoothed out the varied terrain into a single recognizable pattern. No other nation made a more positive affirmation of the rationality, order, and passion for control of the 18th-century enlightenment."[40]

Both a metaphor and concrete expression of early American conquest, the land survey mapped uncharted territory west of Pennsylvania in anticipation of its future settlement. With the swipe of a pen, the cocksure new Congress reined in a frontier it neither knew nor owned. "The abstract geometric survey lines were extended into unknown regions over the horizon. . . . [The survey] measured and described public lands, known or unknown or imagined, as the new nation continuously expanded westward over unseen forests, plains, mountains, deserts, and gardens to the Pacific shore."[41]

SPECULATORS VERSUS SQUATTERS

To bring in revenue fast, and keep land holdings large and consolidated, Congress crafted the land ordinance to grid and sell plots at least 640 acres (one square mile) for $1 per acre, far beyond the reach of the average grubby settler.[42] "Only rapid and large-scale sales of Western lands would keep the national government solvent," explains Opie.[43] The land survey was a policy of growth, but also of containment. The American land and its many riches was the new nation's primary path out of indebtedness and economic dependence on England—but land-hungry immigrants and settlers were already claiming the countryside, setting up "illegal" farms wherever they saw fit. Congress, with its eye on revenues, "took a high stand regarding these unauthorized settlements," according to historian Payson Jackson Treat, and moved quickly to stem this free-for-all tide with its newfound powers of lawmaking and military might. Two years after the survey's passage, in 1787, Congress dispatched troops to drive unlawful settlers from the lush land of the Ohio River Valley, making sure to destroy their cabins so they wouldn't return.[44]

In reality, the infant U.S. government couldn't possibly suppress the growing anarchic rush of pioneer farmer-squatters, although it did get some inadvertent help from Native Americans. Indigenous resistance to settler land grabs was even "more efficacious than the troops," writes Treat, and "kept back the pioneers until a stronger Federal government was able to administer the public lands."[45]

Meanwhile legislators and real estate speculators—and they often were the same people—were parceling out the frontier for federal and individual profits. On July 23, 1787, Congress sold 1 million acres of Ohio land, presumably free of pesky settlers, to the Ohio Company, which ultimately paid less than $100,000 in depreciated paper money.[46] A private investor named John Cleves Symmes bought up his own million-acre patch the same year.[47] While cash-strapped settlers scrambled to buy the minimum 640-acre plot at $1 an acre (raised to $2 an acre by Congress in 1796), the government offered up vast territories at bargain discounts, as low as 12 cents per acre, at sizes only affordable to the wealthy.investor-speculator.[48] Even as the land survey reined in the frontier under public auspices, it facilitated and formalized its rapid sell-off into private hands. It also facilitated the concentration of large tracts of land in the hands of the economic elite, even as it made smaller plots newly available to the white masses. African-American slaves were shut out of this land disposal spree, and Native Americans driven out and dispatched to bleak reservations and death.

Of course, farmers had their advocates, most notably Thomas Jefferson, who idealized the "yeoman farmer," whom he understood to be deeply invested in land and in food production, as the cornerstone of democracy. Jefferson and his many followers, influenced by John Locke's ideas about individual fulfillment and democracy, believed land ownership gave small farmers the economic independence and political stakes necessary to uphold a type of agrarian democracy. True freedom and independence, as well as genuine political participation, could only come through one's ownership and use of land. Jefferson

linked giving free land to small farmers, and taxing estates, with egalitar-
ian democratic development. Ultimately, however, Alexander Hamilton's
free-market agenda, which promoted land speculation and ownership
for the highest bidder, prevailed, despite the periodic interruptions of
homestead policies.[49]

Early American land battles prefigured today's political tension between federal and states' rights, and established the indelible primacy
of concentrated landholding over public space and farmland policy. As
the Constitutional Convention of 1787 neared, states and speculators
scuffled over land, which they clearly perceived as economic and political capital. Small states with small populations, like Connecticut and
Massachusetts, feared a loss of power in the new nation and lobbied for
a strong central government and federal control over new western ter-
ritories. Powerful larger states such as Virginia and North Carolina
promoted states' rights; speculators opposed a strong central government, which threatened to raise currency values and thus make land
more expensive, which would stifle their land-buying frenzy.

The million-acre Ohio land deal of July 1787 ultimately played a
pivotal role in shaping the future of American farmland, according to
Opie.[50] The Ohio Company was "infiltrated by Connecticut financiers"
who, suddenly rich with land, dropped their push for federal land control. The speculator lobby moved quickly "to make certain the new
government would continue the lucrative policy of trading land for
distressed or discounted government paper. . . . Under these pressures,
the Constitution would stay silent about land."[51]

Despite all their power, lawmakers and speculators couldn't keep settlers off the land. As word spread about fertile lands in Ohio, Iowa, and
Illinois, farmers who couldn't afford speculators' plots simply rushed the
land and "dared anyone to push them off"—it was America's first squat-
ter movement.[52] In Iowa in the 1830s, "tens of thousands of squatters
took the best sites, plowed the rich fields, built their homes and barns
and outbuildings, and prospered."[53] When government surveyors caught
up with them and arranged auctions on their land, farmers formed
squatters' claims clubs to scare off outside speculators and to ensure that

land they had worked was auctioned back to squatters at the minimum price.[54] In the 1790s squatting on empty public land "was a popular, and in frontier communities an accepted, means of acquiring a farm."[55]

LAND RUSH: RAILROADS VERSUS HOMESTEADERS

Still, with prices high and credit minimal and exorbitantly expensive, the federal government actually sold little land—just 50,000 acres in 1796. Pressure from settlers and western representatives, perhaps hoping to populate their districts, brought minor reforms with the Land Act of 1800, which extended credit and reduced the minimum purchase to 320 acres, at $2 per acre.[56] Even these improved terms were too steep for most settlers. But with the first major credit offerings, it was just enough to spur a massive land rush, called by Opie "history's fastest transformation of wilderness into farmland."[57] In 1801, some 397,000 acres were sold off; just three years later, in 1804, the government sold more than 1.3 million acres to private owners.[58] Meanwhile debt piled ominously high: only half of all the land purchased by 1819 had been paid for.[59]

This fire sale of public land had little to do with encouraging farming, even if farmers represented 90 percent of the twenty-five-year-old nation's population.[60] The chief goal—aside from favoring politically connected speculators—was revenue generation, and eastern congressional representatives resisted any efforts to sell land more cheaply. Land might have been made more accessible to small farmers, but, according to Treat, "Eastern men were unwilling to reduce the minimum further. It was believed that high land values in the West would stop the drain of population and prevent the rise of wages in the industrial states of the East."[61] In the 1850s, industrialists would stifle another threat to their captive low-wage labor, homestead legislation that promised western land to settlers and would thus tighten labor supply in the East. They had help from western farmers and speculators, who feared such a law would diminish their land values.[62]

By the time the much-heralded Homestead Act became law in 1862, land speculation had "passed out of the hands of small farmers and even rich individuals—and into the hands of large corporations and the railroads. It became big business."[63] The law, which has become associated with mythic notions of American agrarianism, disposed of just 80 million of the 500 million acres that were sold into private hands from 1860 to 1900.[64] Before the law, while industrialists fought off homestead bills, the vast majority of land was already going, free of charge, to huge railroad corporations, which had become, quite literally, the engine of America's exploding commerce. Snapping up massive, state-sized swaths of land, the railroads soon owned one fifth of Kansas and 15 percent of Nebraska; by 1857, the government had handed some 78 million acres to railroad firms, nearly equal to all the nation's homesteads.[65]

FOOD GOES NATIONAL—AND INTERNATIONAL

Railroads did more than buy up and open up the evaporating frontier. Coming fast on the heels of the canal developments of the 1820s, rail transport created an infrastructure that would thrust farmers out of subsistence and local-market agriculture, and onto emerging national and international markets. The rise of the rails, and concomitant leaps in farm-machine technology, lay the groundwork for the beginnings of American agribusiness.

The completion of the Erie Canal in 1825 opened the floodgates to domestic and international grain trading, suddenly providing western grain growers access to the expanding urban markets of the eastern seaboard and Europe. Steamships and canals soon pulsed with surplus grains that had been suppressing grower income, providing the first serious incentives for farmers to expand. When Chicago opened its shipping terminals in 1838, just seventy-eight bushels of wheat passed through the Windy City; by 1860 the terminal handled more than 12.4 million bushels a year.[66] But shipping was expensive, and cut deeply into farmers' earnings while also pinching consumers. The cost of transporting farm produce to the eastern seaboard was "greater than the value of the produce," concluded one expert. For farmers, that cost cut both ways: "The heavy cost of transportation was no less effective in increasing the expense for commodities consumed by the farmer than it was in reducing the return for his products."[67]

Yet exports had become a crucial component of U.S. economic growth, and a type of safety valve for dispensing with the burgeoning surpluses flowing from increasingly large, "efficient" farms. American food production ballooned between the 1830s and the Civil War, far outpacing domestic demand. And agricultural products, especially rice, cotton, and tobacco, were the country's chief exports, seen as vital to maintaining favorable trade balances.

The export boom was further boosted by policies and events overseas. In its push toward industrialization in the late 1840s, Britain phased out its Corn Laws, which had imposed stiff tariffs on imports. U.S. grains began pouring into the former mother country. Then, just as Britain's tariffs receded, Ireland "suffered a severe food famine and was obliged to import breadstuffs," joining the international bread line forming for U.S. goods. Total food exports shot up from $20.5 million in 1840 to $50.8 million in 1860.[68]

Canal and rail shipping and the ushering in of national markets transformed farming into a nonlocal operation; instead of serving the dietary demands of family and local community, farms began feeding distant markets. Competitive pressures increased, requiring farmers to specialize and produce in great bulk—a dynamic that has continued and intensified to the present day. The U.S. farm economy, built on a frenetic "free-market" model, was already moving toward large-scale monocrop production, a system in which farmers had to "get big" in order to survive. Regional divisions of labor evolved, leading to "economic differentiation and mutual dependence."[69] By the 1850s, most northeastern farmers had been knocked out of the wheat and corn business, owing chiefly to shipments of cheap grain from the Northwest through the Great Lakes and the Erie Canal. Meanwhile, "their proximity to market saved the Eastern farmers in the production of perishable products such as fluid milk, cheese and butter, poultry products and vegetables." By 1860, writes agricultural historian Willard W. Cochrane, "agriculture in the New England and Middle Atlantic states had become highly specialized."[70]

Big metal labor-saving machines, such as cultivators, threshers, and reapers, were hauling in bigger harvests in less time. The steam gang plow, with attached seeder and harrow, sliced open the soil and deposited seeds with record speed, slashing human labor per bushel of wheat from 32.8 minutes in 1830 to just 2.2 minutes by the end of the century.[71] The Civil War, dragging most farm labor from the gardens to the battlefields, kicked the farm-machine revolution into high gear: "Confronted with the alternative of losing their crops for want of labor the farmers became thoroughly interested in these new inventions."[72] Once farmers were armed with these tools of efficiency, there was no turning back. The Civil War, one observer reflected in 1920, marked the "transformation of farming from a primitive, pioneer, largely self-sufficing occupation into a modern business organized on a scientific, capitalistic, commercial basis."[73]

SURPLUS NATION

This new food Goliath was producing far more than Americans could eat—or afford. Booming harvests grew at twice the rate of the nation's population growth in the 1870s.[74] As writer William Trimble described in a 1921 essay: "Year after year came from widening acreages one might also say torrents of wheat, of pork, of cattle, of corn, swelling all the channels of trade and spreading over the whole civilized world."[75] This market dilemma of overproduction, a trap that continues to haunt American farmers today, required a foreign solution.

America's excesses were beginning to affect farmers abroad. Surpluses and reduced freight rates "transformed the local into the world market," stimulating even greater production, and flooding markets overseas, a flood that "compelled large numbers of the rural [European] population to abandon farming," and flock to urban industrial centers.[76] In the late 1870s, when European farmers suffered a succession of poor harvests, they weren't rescued by high prices. The United States, "plethoric with great crops," poured "an avalanche of grain upon Europe"—propping up American farm prices by flooding European markets with price-depressing surplus food.[77]

But if cheap American food suppressed European farmers, it also fed growing armies of low-wage factory workers. England, no doubt eyeing this food-wage connection, stymied European attempts to curtail American imports. "Superindustrial" Britain, one writer noted, was building "out of the great production of America a new weapon against the continental industries;" and cheap U.S. food enabled a "policy of dominating the manufacture of the world."[78] Canned beef from Texas also served a broader geopolitical purpose, as it "helped to fill the stomachs of soldiers of England who were extending the frontiers of the Empire in Africa and other regions."[79]

In the United States, too, bumper crops became the farmer's bane, and the industrialist's boon: they "greatly depressed agriculture in the Eastern states, though at the same time affording remarkably cheap food for the laboring classes," wrote Trimble.[80] And cheap food meant cheap labor.

Nonetheless, exports could only release so much of efficiency's bounty. According to Cochrane, rising domestic and foreign consumption of U.S. food "could not cope with the great surge in production," so farm prices and incomes "lagged and dragged."[81] The price of wheat plunged from $2.06 per bushel in 1866 to a mere 49 cents in 1894.[82] Meanwhile, payments for land and farm machinery kept coming due. Bigger markets, trumpeted as farmers' salvation, brought trouble, and ultimately farmer rebellion. Trimble noted, "The rise of organized discontent on a large scale among farmers in the United States synchronizes with the development of quantity production for a world market."[83]

FARMING THE FARMERS: MIDDLEMEN AND REBELLION

New markets created new layers of marketing middlemen, whom farmers quickly grew to despise. They were especially suspicious of unfair monopoly prices at the Chicago Board of Trade, set up in 1848, and at the cotton exchanges established in New York and Liverpool in the early 1870s.[84] Farmers in isolated areas were trapped in monopoly conditions, forced to buy machinery from a single retailer and sell their crops to a single buyer. Historians Patrick H. Mooney and Theo J. Majka describe the growers' bind: "Local merchants, who were also very often large landholders, provided production supplies . . . to farmers on credit in exchange for assurance that the crop would be sold to that merchant. This tended to eliminate competition for production, and because crops rarely sold for more than the cost of needed supplies, a dependency developed that approached peonage."[85]

Increasingly politicized, farmers complained that their produce was "obliged to pass through too many toll-taking hands before they reached the consumer."[86] Much-vaunted machinery, for all its efficient magic, was causing financial headaches. Capital-intensive monocrop agriculture "also led to overproduction and then to declining prices," according to Mooney and Majka. Prices on manufactured goods like farm equipment were kept high by protective import tariffs, while the government didn't see fit to protect farmers' produce in the same manner.[87]

A popular farmers' refrain arose in this age of monopolies and middlemen:

So it goes, the same old story, with the farmer as a goat.
He can only pay his taxes and the interest on his note.
Oh, it's fun to be a farmer and to till the dusty soil,
but the guys who farm farmers are the ones who get the spoil.[88]

Railroads, for which farmers had lobbied hard in order to access new markets, were now the enemy. In the far-flung grain regions of the West, powerful railroad monopolies often stuck farmers with discriminatory rates.[89] Like the middlemen, the railroads lopped hefty sums off farmers' already diminished prices, inspiring farmers' movements to lobby states for progressive railroad regulation. The most prominent among these was the Granger movement, founded in 1867 by Oliver Hudson Kelly, a clerk with the Department of Agriculture. James Dabney McCabe, a Granger, described how "the farmers find that to get the product of 1 acre of corn to market they must pay the railroad the product of three acres; the cost of transportation to the east eats up about 1/2 of the value of the wheat."[90] Illinois's 1870 state constitution explicitly commanded legislators to put caps on passenger and freight fees, and when the chief justice of the state supreme court ruled this unconstitutional, farmers organized voters to toss him out of office in the next election.[91] Grangers won again in 1876, when the U.S. Supreme Court upheld this taming of the railroad business by a state legislature.[92]

Grangers also launched their own marketing, processing, manufacturing, and purchasing cooperatives, and proposed eliminating local go-between merchants and shipping directly to merchants in large central markets.[93] Although these cooperatives were initially unsuccessful—farmers lacked necessary capital and business experience and couldn't compete with private firms—the idea took root. By the early 1900s, local cooperatives and a few large federated farmer associations like the California Fruit Growers Exchange were sprouting up across the country. Farmers organized 10,000 cooperatives between 1900 and 1920, sometimes improving their returns through efficient packing, shipping, and marketing.[94] The cooperative movement lost much of its steam after vigorous opposition and boycotts by a coalition of merchants and bankers.[95] But it created a lasting model, used to this day with varying success, by which farmers could band together to increase their economic clout in the marketplace.

Beyond competing in the market, Grangers and other farmers' associations, increasingly allied with labor, attacked the political system behind the market. In this respect, farmers' movements played a key role in the growing populist resistance to monopoly capitalism. The Indiana Grangers' platform railed against "banking and moneyed monopolies, by which, through ruinous rates of interest, the products of human labor are concentrated in the hands of non-producers."[96] Among these monopolies they highlighted "consolidated railroads," which taxed farmers' labors "for the benefit of the stockholders and stock-jobbers," as well as manufacturing monopolies "whereby all small operators are crushed out, and the price of labor and its products are determined with mathematical certainty in the interests of the capitalists."[97] In the electoral arena, farmers and workers rallied around the Anti-Monopoly Party (in Iowa known as the Farmers' and Laboring Men's Party) and the Independent Reform Party, among others, to place numerous populists in statewide and national office.

Exploitive debt peonage conditions in the South and West in the late 1880s inspired the People's Party, a national coalition of organizations representing the "tillers of the soil and the sons of toil."[98] Cotton growers, both white and black, were stuck in a crop lien system that kept them perpetually indebted to merchants. Historian M.B. Hammond described these farmers' plight in his 1897 book, *The Cotton Industry*. "Every mouthful of food that he purchases, every implement that he requires on the farm, his mules, cattle, the clothing for himself and family, the fertilizers for his land, must all be bought of the merchant who holds the crop lien."[99] Another People's Party cry of the 1890s has been echoed consistently across time: their protest against the widening gap between the price farmers received for their crops and the price at which they sold on market shelves.[100]

FROM GOLDEN AGE TO BANKRUPTCY

The rebellions quieted somewhat when farm prices recovered around the turn of the century, owing in part to a broader economic upswing. (According to Mooney and Majka, there were many other reasons for the decline of farmer resistance, particularly the defeat of cooperatives and progressives' shifting political emphasis.) "Even the usually discontented farmers were happy," chirped the *Louisville Courier-Journal*.[101] One reason for the turnabout was the immigration boom: population was outpacing production, enabling farm prices to go up. Food exports waned and were overtaken by manufactured exports as domestic consumption, and prices, rose.[102] By 1910 farmers had entered a haven of supply-demand equilibrium and price stability; it was known as the Golden Age of American Agriculture. It lasted just four years.

World War I was good to farmers—too good. It brought another export explosion, as food was sent abroad to feed the allies' soldiers and civilians. Farm prices kept rising, more than doubling their prewar levels by 1920, thanks in part to demand spurred by postwar relief efforts.

Enticed by this price binge, farmers "began bidding against each other for cropland."[103] Farmland costs, often inflated by realtors, began outpacing crop prices and rose by 70 percent between 1913 and 1920.[104] But when the war ended and relief programs ground to a halt, the farmers' party was over. Shriveling global demand and huge surpluses caused crop prices to be nearly halved in just one year.[105] Farmers could no longer pay the huge debts for land purchases that they had incurred during heady times; skimpy prices rendered them unable to pay their creditors. Thousands went bankrupt. The Roaring Twenties, that time of exploding American wealth, "were years of financial failure for many, many farmers and years of economic hardship for all farmers."[106]

MACHINES TAKE OVER

Farmers' economic well-being in the Golden Age and during World War I produced another, more insidious and long-term result: the expansion of large-scale industrial agriculture. Feeling that "a permanent era of higher prices had been reached," farmers began equipping themselves for larger production on their larger farms, just as they invested in expensive land. New, mass-produced gasoline tractors became essential tools of the trade, and their numbers increased from just 4,000 on farms in 1911 to 246,000 by 1920 and nearly 1 million by 1930. Farmers' use of manufactured nitrogen fertilizer doubled in this same period.[107] Whenever economic downturn hit, heavily capitalized farmers "found it very hard to contract his production to suit a contracted market."[108] The mechanization boom produced greater and greater surpluses, partially owing to increased efficiencies and also to "the release of lands which were formerly necessary to provide feed" for 26 million draft animals on farms.[109] And those surpluses made it harder and harder for farmers to run their surplus-producing machines: in 1919, a bushel of corn was worth five gallons of gasoline, but by 1921 it took two bushels just to buy a single gallon for their tractors.[110] As the Great Depression neared, debt-ridden farmers "were in a state of profound economic exhausation."[111]

6

AGRIBUSINESS TAKES OVER

"If a man lacks capital or the nerve to borrow for expansion, he is finished."
"In the country there is a surplus of food. In the city there is a surplus of labor."
—Edward Higbee, *Farms and Farmers in an Urban Age* (1963)

"The farm interest became almost identical with the general corporate interest since the control over agriculture had passed to the banks, large conglomerates such as Tenneco and ITT, and huge, vertically integrated food corporations which had extended their influence to all branches of the industry including growing, processing, distribution and marketing."
—Stanley Aronowitz, *Food, Shelter, and the American Dream* (1974)

DESTROYING THE COUNTRYSIDE IN ORDER TO SAVE IT

Drought, dust, and gaunt, grim-faced migrants huddled on old wooden porches. Farmland and families literally scattered to the wind. The penniless waiting in bread lines that snake around city blocks. These are the dominant and universally recognized images of the thirties. Such images obscure other, equally disturbing events of that bleak decade of Depression and Dust Bowl, enduring events that symbolize a "paradox of plenty" still with us today. On government orders, farmers coaxed reluctant mules to trample surplus crops into the ground. There was a mass slaughter of price-depressing surplus hogs while Okies teetered on the brink of starvation. Bread lines were "knee deep in wheat,"[1] a phrase coined by the historian Janet Poppendieck.

While crop disasters and the Dust Bowl drove tens of thousands of tenant farmers from the land, diminished supplies—which thus increased prices—offered temporary economic succor for better-off farmers. But there wasn't enough drought to go around, and surpluses continued to pile up. In the early 1930s, as domestic and worldwide Depression shriveled demand and exports, even drought couldn't prevent mounting surpluses, farmers' greatest enemy. Meanwhile, dispossessed farmers and the urban unemployed subsisted on wild greens and "water sandwiches," made of stale bread soaked in lard and water. The bread lines got longer, and deaths from malnutrition increased, plagued by what Poppendieck called "the poverty of abundance."[2] Arguably, the problem at its root was not abundance per se, but poverty and the perversity of a market economy that penalized this abundance by way of depressed prices and farm closures. Nonetheless President Herbert Hoover's primary concern was upholding the agricultural market: by October 1930 the Farm Board had bought up 65 million bushels of wheat (enough for 4 million loaves of bread) to protect prices.[3]

That autumn and winter, amid pleas for food relief, Congress battled over the wheat's fate, even as some pointed out that it already belonged to the public, since it had been bought with public monies. But as one influential senator explained, Congress shared Hoover's bottom line: "I do not want to do anything that would injure the efforts . . . of the Farm Board to stabilize the price of wheat. . . . If return of this wheat to domestic consumption and the channels of trade would have that effect, I would want to meet the situation in some other way."[4] Ultimately, proposals to distribute the wheat to the malnourished masses failed. In its first consideration of federal food assistance, Congress focused predominantly on "the impact of the proposed donation on the growers of wheat," writes Poppendieck. "No one argued that the wheat should be released regardless of its effect upon prices."[5] But Hoover's wheat hoarding would pale in comparison with the first market-relief measures of the Roosevelt years.

In June 1933, with cotton prices at a rock-bottom five cents per pound and a bumper crop on the way, the Roosevelt administration launched the first major agricultural initiative of the New Deal: paying farmers, many of them destitute sharecroppers, to destroy 10 million acres of budding cotton.[6] News reports told of an elderly black farmer asking his neighbor, a member of Congress, if he could use remaining cotton bolls to make himself a mattress. When told that it was against the law, the farmer reportedly replied, "Ain't you white folks a little crazieh 'n usual jus now?"[7]

Corn and hog growers, saddled with their lowest prices in decades, soon wanted their own dose of this "crazy" market medicine. To slow the price plunge, the National Corn-Hog Committee of Twenty-five, representing Corn Belt farm organizations and Roosevelt administration agriculture officials, decided to dispose of 6 million hogs. A poor corn harvest enabled the delay of corn crop demolitions, but hog prices were threatened by a bumper season. The surest way to prevent that was to slaughter young pigs and pregnant sows, thus removing 1 billion pounds of up-and-coming pork from the market.[8]

ROTTING SURPLUSES AND EMPTY STOMACHS

While food lines lengthened and families wrote in hungry requests for their first meat in years, nearly 80 percent of the hogs were liquefied and churned into inedible products such as soap and fertilizer. Pig carcasses were burned, buried, sometimes dumped in rivers and streams. The *Chicago Tribune* reported irately of the "indescribably revolting stench" of mountains of ground-up pigs piled in the hot sun, "redolent ghosts . . . which were martyred by the government so that the rest of the swine in the United States might become more valuable."[9] Roosevelt's new Agricultural Adjustment Administration was off to an auspiciously unpopular start, fueling doubts about the true aims of capitalism as it sought to protect markets. Eventually, scathing nationwide press attacks moved even the White House to lament the "economic paradox which has choked farms with an abundance of farm products while many of the unemployed have grown hungry."[10] An Iowa pastor noted, "Hunger and revolution are neighbors."[11]

But it wasn't a paradox, explains Poppendieck; the mean confluence of "rotting surpluses and empty stomachs" was the "normal, predictable working of the economy rendered extreme by the Depression."[12] That bitter era brought into sharp, wrenching relief the market's twisted calculus: apparently, the only way to save impoverished farmers—or the market, which was the real goal—was to starve impoverished consumers. Food had to be destroyed to save the market. Poppendieck writes, "Along with the enforced idleness of the unemployed, the contrast of hunger and abundance led to an unprecedented degree of skepticism about the desirability of capitalism."[13]

Although the June 1933 hog buy-up temporarily pumped cash into rural farming communities, it did little to prevent a broader free-fall, which forced one sixth of U.S. farmers to sell out between 1930 and 1935.[14] That September, recovering its political acumen, the Roosevelt administration announced it would buy $75 million worth of surplus foods to feed the unemployed; the Federal Surplus Relief Corporation was launched to give formal structure to this Robin Hood–style means of protecting the market. It also inaugurated a policy of "scarcity economics"—still in force today—which requires the reduction of food supplies to offset lapses in consumption and prices; one politician at the time called it "subsidized destruction."[15]

THE BIG GET BIGGER

World War II rescued farmers—and spawned modern agribusiness. A prolific wartime economy brought near-full employment and vast new markets for agricultural produce in U.S. wage earners, who saw their purchasing power increase; in the U.S. military; and in the population of allied nations. Fueled by rising U.S. wages and exports, farm prices and income skyrocketed and were propped up for more than a decade after the war by postwar price guarantees and food aid under the Marshall Plan. But if war heals economic wounds, its legacy creates new ones.

War-induced economic recovery spurred unprecedented consolidation in the countryside. As urban and suburban food consumption rose, farmers began, as the historian Edward Higbee put it, "knocking each other out in a scramble for the market."[16] Labor mobility prompted a farmer exodus to job-rich cities, thinning out 35 percent of America's farm population, which declined from 31 million in 1939 to 20 million by 1953.[17] The farms that remained got bigger as farmers plowed their hearty earnings into new farmlands and technologies of mechanization that had been sitting on the shelf since the impoverished thirties. A circular ideology of bigness evolved, explains historian Stanley Andrews, characterized by "the investment in bigger lands to utilize bigger machinery, and in still bigger machinery to farm bigger lands."[18] A "mechanical revolution" led to "the mechanization of almost every production process in farming," according to Willard Cochrane.[19] The number of tractors in use had slowed during the Depression decade, when just half a million new tractors had been put into the fields, but in the postwar decade tractor use kicked into high gear as farmers put nearly 2 million more machines to work on the fields.[20] Manual hay bailing was all but eliminated. By the 1950s nearly all cows were milked by machine. Commercial fertilizers and pesticides (many pesticide formulations had started out as nerve agents perfected by the Nazis) became increasingly integral to this new industrial agriculture. Meanwhile, the intensely competitive rush to large-scale mechanized farming was steadily weeding out small farmers: in 1958, one third fewer farmers produced 55 percent more crops than in 1938.[21] By 1959, 3.7 percent of farmers owned 49 percent of all U.S. farmland.[22]

Despite the influx of new machinery, growers still required human hands to harvest many crops, such as strawberries, lettuce, grapes, and tomatoes. As rural laborers increasingly pursued better-paying urban industrial jobs after the war, larger growers—represented by the American Farm Bureau Federation—sought the government's help to ensure a steady labor supply. They obtained this via the "Bracero" program, through which the U.S. government imported workers from Mexico who were paid rock-bottom wages to pick America's food. Begun in 1942 "as an emergency measure to deal with the wartime labor shortage," writes Miriam J. Wells in her book *Strawberry Fields,* the program "proved so profitable that growers secured its continuation for a total of twenty-three years." During that time the government imported nearly 5 million workers, who were summarily returned to Mexico after each harvest, according to Wells. The Bracero program came to symbolize the exploitation of farm workers, and, after much pressure, the government discontinued it in December 1964.[23]

TOO MUCH FOOD, TOO MANY FARMERS

For a time, expanded technologies and markets enabled a rare confluence of soaring production and rising prices. But the end of the Korean War in 1952 and the phasing out of postwar food relief brought another price plunge in the mid-fifties that temporarily slowed the big-farm boom. This time, however, farmers were protected somewhat by a government safety net of commodity price supports and income supports, augmented by production controls, commodity storage, and surplus disposal through foreign aid.[24] Income supports—farm subsidies—provided economic succor to a relatively prosperous minority, and had the further effect of normalizing the idea of surplus production. They accomplished this by promoting large-scale, heavily mechanized agriculture, and by assuring farmers (at least the big ones who received large payments) that their incomes would not be damaged by overproduction. Thus was born a precarious and little-discussed farm policy based on chronic excess capacity. American farming came to rely on huge government food purchases and storage to balance production and demand, which only intensified politicians' fear that ending these programs would devastate farm prices. As Cochrane, the agricultural historian, explains, "Government was so fearful of the price and income consequences of removing federal farm programs of price and income support that it continued those programs year after year. And with the continuation of those programs, the problem of excess productive capacity became a chronic problem."[25] By 1965 the bill was $4.5 billion annually. In one sense, taxpayers and consumers were paying for larger farmers' surplus-producing machinery, which consistently created more food than the market could bear. Meanwhile, the machine-produced market glut punished all farmers, not just the heavily subsidized few. Big farmers' overproduction, upheld by government price supports, drove small farmers deeper into poverty and, increasingly, off the land. Thus developed another paradox, described by Higbee: "Within that very segment of the economy which suffers from the overproduction of food there are farmers and farmhands who suffer from malnutrition because they cannot afford to eat properly."[26]

The new era of chronic surplus brought into focus the inherent conflict between efficient high-tech production and farmer income. Historically, industrial productivity has often led to higher wages for factory workers, whereas improved farm production has consistently depressed farmers' wages. A 1957 report by President Eisenhower's Council of Economic Advisers revealed that a 17 percent jump in output per man-hour on the farm was accompanied by a 23 percent drop in farmers' personal income. Meanwhile, a modest 11 percent productivity improvement off the farm brought nonfarm income up 12 percent.[27] During the fifties nonfarm productivity rose 21 percent and led to 58 percent higher wages, while farmers' amazing 65 percent output hike was rewarded by a 1 percent decline in wages.

As postwar farm production and policy generated chronic crop surpluses, it also created surplus labor, as "unneeded" farmers and farmhands flocked to low-income urban ghettos in search of work. The farm subsidies that helped big farms take over small ones also increased expenditures for urban welfare and unemployment. "City slums harbor hundreds of thousands of rural refugees, many on welfare rolls," reported Higbee in 1961. "To consider the problem of farm surpluses apart from the problem of human surpluses is to ignore the fact that the two are related in so far as it is more economical to raise food by the capital-intensive methods of the new agriculture rather than by the labor-intensive methods of the old style family farm."[28]

The postwar push for bigness ran headlong into the contradiction between productivity and profits. As wealthier farmers snapped up more land and machinery between 1947 and 1957, their production increased, but income remained flat and their costs for new land and machines mushroomed. By 1960 farmers were plunking down 82 percent of their sales to cover machinery and other costs, up sharply from the late 1940s, when expenses took 65 percent of sales. As output per man-hour during the 1950s rose by 50 percent, output per unit of farm machinery actually declined by 40 percent.[29]

THE VICTOR'S SPOILS: THE AGRICULTURE-INDUSTRIAL COMPLEX

Although surplus was the most obvious explanation for this production-price inversion (or perversion), other factors transformed the American food system in ways that have simultaneously boosted prices and eroded farmers' income. Rising incomes and purchasing power characterized a permanent war-time economy, which was marked by an increasingly frenetic car culture and suburban world obsessed with both physical and financial mobility. Convenience became king. Fast food was the order of the day, as were frozen and processed items pre-prepared for easy, quick consumption. In just four years, between 1965 and 1968, sales of frozen prepared dinners doubled.[30] Quite rapidly, the role and value of farmers' crops were reduced and cheapened by a phalanx of price-taking inter-mediaries who, aided by advertising, created and then served the grow-ing market for heavily processed convenience foods. By 1959, more workers were processing, transporting, and distributing food than were producing it on the farm.[31] Even as these expanding sectors created new jobs, they spelled plummeting prices and often unemployment for farm-ers. Government researchers in the late 1950s found that whereas costs for a market basket of food had gone up 9 percent since 1950, processing and marketing costs had increased by 28 percent; during this same pe-riod farmers' prices sank 12 percent.[32]

According to Andrews, so dramatic were these disparities that even the 1958 Economic Report of the President "concluded that so long as economic benefits of farm efficiency were absorbed in high marketing costs, increased costs of equipment and services, and high interest rates on the short-term and long-term credit bigger machines and increased mechanization were not going to do what they were supposed to do— increase net farm income."[33] President Eisenhower noted, "The chief beneficiaries of our price support policies have been the 2 million larger, highly mechanized farming units which produce about 85 per-cent of our agricultural output."[34] These remarks suggest a parallel

with Ike's prescient warning, when he left office, of the power of the
military-industrial complex.

PROCESSING PROFITS, DIVIDING THE FOOD DOLLAR

The rift between farmers and the broader food economy had widened
to the point where, says Andrews, depressed crop prices "more than
offset the disproportionate rise in costs of processing, packaging, and
distribution," which further deepened the divide between the income
interests of farmers and the purchasing interests of consumers.[35] Even
as farm subsidies became increasingly controversial, farmers' cheap
crops were subsidizing big profits for food processors and marketers, a
dynamic that has only intensified over time.

By the 1970s, marketing costs—shipping, processing, packaging, and
retailing—were gobbling up two thirds of every dollar consumers paid
out for food. Historian John Shover explains: "As an inviolable rule, the
more a food product is processed, the lower the return to the farmer."[36]
For instance, writes Shover, farmers in 1969 took in 67 cents per consumer dollar spent on eggs, while gaining just 50 cents per dollar for
milk, and 14 cents for two loaves of bread; wheat and cotton growers
lose so much to processors, they "could give away their entire crop free
without creating more than a minor effect on the price [to consumers]
of bread or shirts."[37] Meanwhile, processors and marketers benefit
from lower crop prices induced by oversupply, which diminishes the
value of raw farm crops used as inputs for processed products far more
than it does the price of store-bought food.[38]

Starting in the 1950s, food-company advertisers and large supermarkets nurtured the desire and market for higher-priced processed
food products, at the expense not only of farmers but also of consumers'
nutrition. Advertising, explains Shover, was "thrown disproportionately
behind highly processed, higher profit foods rather than those that are
less processed and which often have greater nutritional value."[39] Supermarkets, eager to move these profitable products off their shelves, began
featuring these intensely processed items along the most heavily traveled aisles, further prioritizing them over whole produce.[40]

THE FOOD OCTOPUS EMERGES

By the mid-1950s, most of the world's economies were, like the American economy, rapidly consumed by sprawling corporate conglomerates with webs of control cutting across numerous industries. The World War II boom had launched an intense flurry of mergers (about 750 a year) and corporate takeovers: between 1940 and 1947, more than 2,500 companies with total assets of more than $5 billion were gobbled up and erased from the business landscape.[41] Twenty years later—in an age of unbridled business affluence fueled in part by Cold War defense- and space-industry contracts, and upheld through U.S. "dollar diplomacy" and military might—corporations devoured one another with even greater acquisitive zeal, to the tune of 3,000 mergers in 1967.[42]

No longer satisfied with mere financial gain, corporations were "maximizing size rather than profit" in a frenetic quest for market control.[43] At the end of the 1960s, the top 500 industrial companies boasted sales amounting to nearly half the country's gross national product.[44] Massive firms "so dominated the economy that the welfare of the nation was now largely dependent on their success."[45] Antitrust law, with its narrow emphasis on monopoly, could do little to arrest the conglomerates' stampede, until the Johnson administration temporarily slowed the merger rush with a series of high-profile indictments in 1969.[46]

This corporate tornado wreaked economic havoc on farmers, whose ranks had been relentlessly thinning since the Depression. By 1973 just 2.5 million farms were left, and the biggest 2 percent accounted for one third of all sales.[47] Some corporations took over farmlands directly, adding them to their burgeoning portfolios. In 1970, the Houston-based giant Tenneco, among the nation's largest corporations in the oil and natural gas sectors, snared the California-based Kern County Land Company, one of the oldest and largest farm corporations in America. That same year Tenneco also acquired the country's largest distributor of fresh fruits and vegetables.[48] Corporations rarely put farmers out of business in any immediate sense, yet their consolidating control over the entire food industry speeded the demise of smaller independent farmers by reducing growers' selling options at the front of the market process and reducing their crops to cheap, raw inputs for processed retail food. The farmer was sandwiched between profit-taking sellers at one end and a diminishing number of powerful buyers on the other.

For the most part, corporations weren't interested in farming, given the risks of volatile weather and markets; they were more intent on controlling agribusiness through both vertical and horizontal integration—that is, commanding the food industry from farm to dinner table, and dominating near-monopoly markets. Tenneco, in addition to its farmlands, ran a "vast, integrated farm-to-market enterprise" that encompassed the giant Packaging Corp. of America, tractor and fertilizer manufacturers, a large data-processing plant, and a major shipping and dry dock company.[49] Another behemoth, General Foods, boasted a veritable supermarket of name-brand products—including Maxwell House, Sanka, Yuban, Postum, Grape-Nuts, Alpha-Bits, Bird's Eye frozen foods, baking powder, and Jell-O—as well as the Burger Chef restaurant chain and a seed company.[50] Even more impressive was the overarching oligopolistic control corporations had assumed over agriculture. By 1972, large vertically integrated firms controlled a remarkable 97 percent of all broiler chicken production, 95 percent of vegetable processing, 85 percent of all trade in U.S. citrus fruits, and 80 percent of seed crops.[51]

This quantitative corporate dominance over agriculture also had a qualitative effect on farmers. It wasn't simply that a narrowing group of powerful people owned more of the food supply. Aided by government subsidies encouraging large-scale agriculture, the postwar corporate takeover of the food business fundamentally and permanently transformed American farmers into input suppliers fulfilling the demands of food marketers and processors rather than consumers. Corporate input sellers and processors—those who sell farm equipment and seeds—only do business with large-scale farmers who can provide a huge, steady supply of crops. Ingolf Vogeler, in his intensive 1981 study of agribusiness, *The Myth of the Family Farm,* explains that to maintain maximum profits, agribusiness "has an incentive to create strong control over the farm production process to acquire an adequate and timely supply of uniform quality farm products for the food processing industries."[52]

These heavily industrialized "factories in the field," as historian Carey McWilliams aptly named them, hardly resembled the traditional family farm; they were big business with little social or economic connection to the surrounding community. Farming had become part of a well-oiled agribusiness assembly line, and big growers more than ever required huge arsenals of exorbitant capital equipment, and mountains of chemicals, to meet corporate buyers' demands. A tractor, which cost just $2,000 in 1960, by 1974 carried a price tag of $16,000, far out of reach for the 80 percent of farmers who sold less than $40,000 worth of food that year.[53] By 1970, farmers were spreading 70 pounds of chemical fertilizer per acre of soil—about twice the amount recommended by state agricultural officials.[54]

Decades before he helped lay the groundwork for the Soviet grain deals of the early 1970s, Dr. Earl Butz authored a paper titled "Agriculture in 1970," in which he predicted, somewhat cheerily, "unabated" growth of larger farms using more machinery and more chemicals. These bigger farmers "will use more capital, more science and technology, more managerial capacity, more purchased production inputs, more specialized marketing facilities" than ever before. Individual farmers "will be under pressure moving toward a corporate structure . . . with management representing only a portion if any of the ownership."[55]

By the time Butz was at the helm of the U.S. Department of Agriculture, this end game had taken hold. Armed with the latest gear, 2.1 percent of farmers posted 37 percent of all growers' sales, on just 14 percent of the nation's farmlands.[56] Equally dramatic was the widening income gap: the biggest farms were bringing in 600 times as much income as smaller operators. Even before the nightmarish 1980s, small-scale family farmers had been all but weeded out, not so much by drought or direct corporate bullying but by an entire system of corporate food-making which increasingly dictated every aspect of food and farming, from the planting of seeds on vast contract farms to the processing of crops in huge factories to the preparation and packaging of highly processed ready-to-eat meals in corporate kitchens and on corporate assembly lines.

7

ALMOST NOTHING LEFT: THE 1980s

"Death on the Iowa Prairie: 4 New Victims of Economy"
—New York Times headline (1985)

"When the news of the murders hit the Hills Tap bar, one patron
was incredulous that Dale Burr could have done such a thing:
'He was a hell of a nice guy,' the farmer said, stunned. 'He go nuts?'
'He went broke,' answered someone in the bar.'"
—from Osha Gray Davidson, *Broken Heartland:*
The Rise of America's Rural Ghetto (1990)

AFTER THE BOOM COMES THE BUST

Flush from the fast seventies, which set records for farm income and exports, farmers were perched on a paper-thin ledge overlooking a dark
future. Having borrowed and expanded during those alluring days of
growth, farmers were precariously overextended—poised for a crisis. Fat
on cheap credit, much of it borrowed against increasingly valuable land,
many growers had spent the mid to late seventies following the cheery
advice of the U.S. Department of Agriculture's export acolytes and of all-
too-generous banks—borrowing and getting big.

In 1980, Ronald Reagan swept into the White House on a landslide
aided by the farm vote. The Gipper, tag-teaming with Federal Reserve
Chairman Paul Volcker (appointed by President Jimmy Carter in 1979),
would soon repay them with a long cold bath of fiscal and monetary
austerity, which along with other factors dealt a punishing blow to
farmers and rural communities across America. As Reagan's agriculture

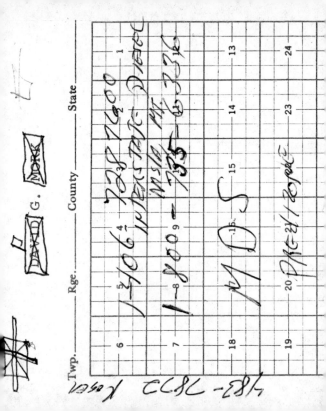

secretary, John Block, later put it, "American agriculture has been a pampered, spoiled child."[1] And those "spoiled" farmers, who had been coaxed as much by banks and export agencies as by their own thirst for growth, would be disciplined mightily by what became known as the "Volcker recession."

The double-barreled crush of inflation and economic stagnation, which gave rise to "stagflation," a term popularized by Reagan in the 1980 elections, arguably was as much a part of Carter's undoing as was the Iran hostage crisis. By election time, inflation, generally rising since the mid-1990s, had soared to double digits.[2] President Jimmy Carter's January 4, 1980, embargo of American grain exports to the Soviet Union, a get-tough election-year response to the Soviet invasion of Afghanistan, also cost him dearly. The resulting 17 million tons of lost grain sales dealt a strong blow to corn and wheat prices, so much so that, it was reported in the *Washington Post,* "Commodity tickers had become one of the barometers of potential political and economic trouble for the Carter administration this election year."[3]

In October 1979, as inflation spiraled, newly appointed Volcker jacked up interest rates, which limited money supply and drove up the cost of borrowing, an essential aspect of farming. By 1981, as Volcker's "monetarist squeeze" took hold, interest rates had skyrocketed to 16.4 percent, more than double the rate in 1979.[4]

Heavily indebted farmers soon found themselves over a barrel. By the early eighties, as "farmer income" became an oxymoron, the soaring interest rates drove farmers into severe debt.[5] Meanwhile, as commodity prices tumbled due to tightening international competition, so did farmland values (which are tied to commodity prices), further deepening farmers' debt and credit woes. According to Osha Gray Davidson, the value of total U.S. farmland plunged $146 billion between 1982 and 1985.[6] Any farmers who had borrowed to buy land in the seventies would face major losses if they sold land to pay off vicious interest rates—assuming they could find buyers. Even with the depressed prices, farmland was a tough sell. Land, once farmers' chief asset and their ultimate safety net against poverty, was worth little in the recessionary market.

By the end of the decade, American agriculture had undergone a brutal shakeout. Between 1982 and 1987 America lost 30,000 farms a year—153,217 farmers went out of business, victims of an increasingly competitive and consolidated agricultural economy. (In the eight years leading up to 1982, just over 73,000 farms went under.)[7] This dramatic winnowing put the long-term decline in farms, developing since the 1930s, into fast-forward. And this shakeout would ultimately help agribusiness concentrate its market power over those who managed to survive, enabling food corporations (retailers, processors, and traders) to further dictate farmers' crop prices and growing options.

The forces behind this economic cleansing were many. Externally, farmers were hammered by declining exports and vigorous international competition. On a domestic level, they were slammed by soaring interest rates, and by the broader effects of nationwide recession. Within agriculture itself, growers were hit with the ever-rising costs of capital-intensive industrial farming, such as expensive machinery and great volumes of pesticides; and as corporate economic clout expanded, farmers captured a rapidly dwindling share of the money consumers spent on food.

AN OLD CYCLE

In a sense, the eighties farm crisis reflected the classic boom-bust pattern of American agriculture and the economy at large: overproduction led to saturated markets and thus anemic prices; the more prices slid, the more farmers produced to try to recoup their losses. Historically, exports and food aid have served as economic safety valves by drawing down price-depressing surpluses. For over a decade, "U.S. farm policy and individual farmers' decisions to gear up production had been based on an assumption that the world would buy as much as Americans could grow," explained *Congressional Quarterly Almanac.*[8] Farm exports also played a key role in the larger U.S. economy, helping to balance trade accounts against the immense costs of imported oil.

But suddenly exports, the panacea of the seventies, which had induced farmer overexpansion and debt, hit a brick wall. "The underlying problem," *Congressional Quarterly* summarized, "was that world markets had gone sour while farm production peaked." The dollar was strong, and the strong dollar made U.S. exports more expensive.

A global recession, heightened international competition, and the comparative strength of the U.S. dollar against other currencies all conspired to reduce American exports. American farmers were not alone in their suffering: in 1982, France's farm income fell for the eighth consecutive year; in Germany and the UK, farmers' 1981 earnings were down 21 percent from where they were in 1974.[9] One account stated: "American farmers are producing as never before, and loading ever more excess grain on to a recession-flattened world market."[10] The decline in farm exports "reflected both the global recession and a rapid increase in competition for Third World markets, notably from members of the ten-nation European Community," Joseph Belden explained in his 1986 book, *Dirt Rich, Dirt Poor*. The European Community's Common Agricultural Policy helped bring Europe's share of world food exports from 8.3 percent in 1976 to 18.3 percent in 1981, while the U.S. share held steady at 18 percent. In 1983, amid this intensifying trade war, an American trade official warned that "the White House is ready to unload huge agricultural stockpiles on foreign markets in retaliation against West European export subsidies that push U.S. farm products out of those markets."[11]

After posting record exports of $43.5 billion in 1981, the United States suffered its first export decline in a decade, falling to $40.5 billion in 1982. Meanwhile, farmers produced record high yields for the second consecutive year, piling up the biggest surpluses in two decades.[12] The result: U.S. net farm incomes plunged by 30 percent in real terms between 1979 and 1981.[13] While the Rust Belt groped through deep recession, the talk on the Farm Belt was of a full-blown Depression.

HUNTING SEASON

The combination of astronomic interest rates, fattening surpluses, and diminished exports would prove deadly—sometimes literally.

On a crisp Thursday morning in October 1983, shots rang through the countryside just a few miles from the farm town of Ruthton in southwestern Minnesota. It was hunting season, but this time the prey was human, a rare homicide in this peaceful farm community. This was no random shooting: the targets were a banker and his chief loan officer, the assailants a struggling, debt-racked dairy farmer and his eighteen-year-old son, clad in military camouflage.[14] Worn down by business failures and foreclosure battles, the hunted farmer had become the hunter.

The police and ambulance found the bank president, Rudy Blythe, lying dead in a ditch near the house once owned by the farmer, James Lee Jenkins. The loan officer, Deems Thulin, a father of three, was also found dead nearby, hanging out of a car door. Days later Jenkins, fleeing a rural dragnet, shot himself. The *New York Times* said the shootings were likely "the most violent outburst yet in connection with the threatened or actual eviction of many of the nation's farmers."[15] But they were only the beginning, a grim signal of deepening distress and desperation across the heartland.

Some turned their desperation inward, hoping to salvage something for their loved ones. In Ohio, where net farm income in 1981 reached its lowest point in forty-nine years, a farmer named Larry Sheets "took out his gun and contemplated suicide," reasoning that if he killed himself, his family could collect on his life insurance. He told a reporter, "I owe about one million dollars. I figure I'm worth one million dead and I knew the wife and three kids could pay out. . . . It's just that tense." Sheets was by no means alone. "The highly leveraged farmers are carrying high insurance on themselves," said Eugene Patrick, the head of a local National Farmers' Union chapter. "You hate to think you'd have to kill yourself to save the family farm."[16]

Throughout the decade, the physical and psychological corpses wrought by economic misery piled up. One proud Iowa farmer tried to make his suicide attempt look accidental: he connected live wires over a manure pit, "hoping he would appear to have tumbled in and suffocated." Another farmer dug a grave for his banker. "We see more family abuse, more alcoholism, even more injuries to animals," said William Heffernan, a sociologist at the University of Missouri. "Veterinarians are treating farm dogs that have had their ribs kicked in."[17] In 1984 the Iowa legislature approved $200,000 for counseling for farmers.[18]

By 1982, as the nation's harshest recession in half a century ravaged much of the country with double-digit unemployment, the crisis on farms augured catastrophe. Hammered by hail storms and drought in 1980 and 1981, many farmers had lost their crops and piled up more and more debt. Meanwhile, Ronald Reagan's agriculture secretary, John Block, prayed for rain and exports to solve the problem of plunging farm income, telling Congress, "If [farm income] is improved, it will be from something other than legislation. . . . The weather, an export pickup someplace."[19]

Farm income estimates were so bleak in 1982 that the USDA stopped publishing the data for a time. While claiming to the news media that the income projections were simply not useful, Secretary Block acknowledged to a Senate subcommittee, "The truth is, the department doesn't want to give validity to the horror stories. The forecasts give credence to what farmers around the country are saying and feeling."[20]

BAD NUMBERS, EVERYWHERE

But nervous officials couldn't hide the nightmare that was rapidly unfolding. Even in 1981, when farmers produced record exports, the deeper signals were all grim. Net farm income was running roughly one third what it had been in 1973, in constant dollars, and was lower than at any point since the great Depression.[21] Farmers' income from nonfarm sources, such as a job in town, particularly critical to struggling small growers, was rising—a clear sign that farming was becoming less and less viable. Moonlighting became a vital part of agrarian life: farmers' earnings away from the fields totaled $36 billion in 1980, nearly double their net farm income of $19.9 billion.[22]

As the recession deepened, farmers' increasing reliance on outside income pressed them up against the boarded-up doors of the broader economy, further hastening their departure from agriculture. And with spreading unemployment, farmers' alternatives were bleak. "The most excruciating human aspect is that farmers being forced off their land will have a difficult time getting an off-farm job," remarked

Harold Breimyer, a well-known University of Missouri agricultural economist.[23]

The insanity of surplus economics saw cash-strapped American farmers praying not for rain but for food shortages abroad to pry open new markets. As the *Financial Times* described in April 1982, "unless there is a major crop disaster elsewhere in the world to fuel demand, the billions of bushels of grain that Americans reap this summer will only add to the bulging stocks held over from last year and make matters worse." The president of the Kansas Association of Wheat Growers told reporters, "Out here we all go to bed dreaming that we'll have a 40 bushel an acre crop and the rest of the world will have a drought."[24]

Meanwhile, costs for fuel, machinery, and interest payments were marching steadily upward. In the decade leading up to the farm crisis of the 1980s, agricultural production costs had tripled while crop prices slowly eroded.[25] Then, in the first two years of the eighties, production costs surpassed crop values, the first time since the 1930s that costs exceeded prices two years in a row.[26] Sandwiched in the vise between spiraling income and skyrocketing inflation, farmers saw the purchasing power of their net income in 1980 plummet to 40 percent below the annual average for the 1970s.[27] There was only one thing left to do: keep borrowing. By January 1982, farmers' debt exceeded their income by an astounding ratio of 10 to 1. In 1973, the ratio was 3 to 1.[28]

Not only were farmers mired deep in debt—by itself not necessarily a signal of serious trouble—but they also were increasingly unable to climb out of the financial muck. It was the severity of debt, and farmers' inability to repay their loans in order to access fresh credit, that really spelled disaster.

As 1981 drew to a close, farm debt piled up to a record high of nearly $195 billion, twice what it had been in 1975.[29] Debt now represented about one fifth of farmers' total assets: land, buildings, and machinery. The worsening debt-to-assets ratio, a key indicator of farmers' economic health, had reached a ten-year high.[30] Mounting debts made up a greater and greater portion of farmers' overall wealth. As debts outpaced assets, farmers' credit picture grew dimmer.

"VOLUNTARY LIQUIDATIONS"

Across the heartland, bills were coming due and piling up unpaid. The Farmers Home Administration (FmHA), a unit of the Department of Agriculture created in the 1930s as the lender of last resort, reported that more than half of its loans were overdue; delinquencies ran as high as 80 percent in some states.[31] Of 361 banks surveyed by the American Bankers Association, 85 percent said they had delinquent farm accounts.[32] Farm sales, in which all assets were liquidated to pay off creditors, were being held in record numbers. "In the *Des Moines Register* last Sunday there were thirty-one farm sales," an Iowa bank official, Richard Hixson, remarked in March 1982. "Normally when we get into this time of year the farm sales are over." He added, "The older people coming into the bank, the ones who went through the last Depression, they say it's just like it was before, only on a much, much larger scale."[33] In Stuarts Draft, Virginia, a family was forced to auction off its farm and equipment. Valued at $1.5 million, the entire estate was sold for $275,000—18 cents on the dollar.[34]

In just four months, between October 1981 and January 1982, the FmHA had 871 "voluntary liquidations," that is, farmers "voluntarily" selling out to settle their debts; another 421 farms foreclosed. In all of 1980, there had been just 127 voluntary liquidations and 133 foreclosures.[35] The 325,000-member National Farmers Union held farm crisis hearings across the country; it found that in many areas 20 to 35 percent of farmers were going out of business.[36]

The foreclosure epidemic had a self-fulfilling effect: the more farmers shut down, the worse things looked for farming, which further eroded land values and discouraged lenders. G. Edward Schuh, an agricultural economist, explained, "You get one group forced to sell out, which puts land values further down and that weakens the equity position of another group and their banks start getting nervous and the first thing you know, they're foreclosing and this just pushes itself right on across the land."[37]

In a one-year period between 1982 and 1983, some 30,000 farmers quit the business. According to USDA statistics, in 1983 there were

474,000 fewer farmers than in 1973, showing that even during the go-go seventies agriculture was consolidating its ranks. And the mass economic evacuation opened up more land for the survivors. The average farm size grew from 383 acres in 1973 to 437 acres in 1983; farms with annual sales of $100,000 or more, 13.2 percent of the total, took up 47.2 percent of all farmland.[38]

RAGE

By October 1983 the FmHA was awash in repossessed farmland, and was acquiring newly closed farms more quickly than it could sell them off. Its stock of acquired farmland had doubled since the beginning of the year. Pressure mounted for a moratorium or slowdown on foreclosures, and a moratorium bill passed the House of Representatives but was stalled in the Republican-controlled Senate. Outrage was building, both across the countryside and in state legislatures and Congress. Congressman Ed Jones of Tennessee wrote to his House colleagues, "The Farmers Home Administration has amassed so many farm properties due to foreclosures, bankruptcies and liquidations that the agency is now having to advertise in the media to solicit the services of auctioneers to assist in disposing of its inventory."[39]

But as the Minnesota shooting case vividly revealed, many "liquidated" farmers were far beyond the letter-writing stage. In a report to Congress the Iowa Farmers Union ominously warned, "The failure of government to respond to the problems has created a tinderbox that can ignite at any moment."[40]

Farm auctions became sites of fiery protest. One sheriff commented after enforcing a highly protested foreclosure in Kansas, "I would have to rate it as a success because the land was sold, just like the order from the court said, no one got hurt, and nothing was damaged."[41] But sometimes the sheriff's auction posses couldn't claim success. In November 1982 the FmHA canceled an equipment sale on a bankrupt Illinois farm after protest from nearly 100 angry farmers. One month later, farmers marched into the River Falls, Wisconsin, Production Credit Association office and secured a loan extension for a struggling colleague.[42]

When bankers and police moved to auction off a Springfield, Colorado, farm owned by Jerry Wright, one of the founders of the American Agriculture Movement, they were met by 300 farmers from several states chanting "No sale! No sale!" Sheriff's deputies sprayed tear gas to break up the protest and keep the auction going. Wright told reporters, "we're going to sacrifice the middle-class people of this country to satisfy a bank."[43]

Farmers also revived the penny auction, a Depression-era resistance tactic. In the 1930s, one account described, "Farmers would jam a foreclosure auction and buy back a bankrupt farmer's goods for pennies, threatening into silence any outsiders who wanted to bid."[44] According to James Gambone, a filmmaker who chronicled the thirties auctions, "After 10 or 12 penny auctions in a county during the Depression, the insurance companies stopped foreclosing. They learned to go talk to the committee that organized the penny auctions, where they would try to negotiate repayment for the farmer."[45] Local sheriffs, often friends with farmers, were sometimes reluctant enforcers. One foreclosed farmer described how "the sheriff came out. . . . You could tell he didn't want to be doing this. He shouldn't have to. The loan officers should have to face us and the kids."[46]

The auctions echoed farmers' earliest protests, the squatters' claims clubs of the 1790s, organized to fend off speculators. But now the primary targets were the banks and lending agencies that held farmers' fates in their hands.

Enemy number one was the FmHA, the last-resort lending agency, which seemed to have a voracious appetite for farm shutdowns. As more and more farmers fell behind on their payments, the FmHA ratcheted up the pressure. County-level employees of the agency were "put on notice that their jobs may depend on how well they collect on delinquent operating loans to farmers," the *Washington Post* reported. The agency's top administrator, Charles W. Shuman, promised to deny new loan money to any states with delinquency rates "higher than deemed appropriate."[47]

There was congressional and state-level action to secure a moratorium on foreclosures, and in Minnesota activists won a statewide mortgage moratorium after intensive lobbying and a brief occupation of the governor's office. Farmers also took their case against the FmHA to the courts.[48] In November 1983 a federal judge in North Dakota ruled that the FmHA was so aggressive it wasn't following its own rules. The agency sometimes promoted liquidations without presenting alternatives, and routinely rejected appeals.[49] One study in Iowa found that the agency rejected 95 percent of farmers' appeals,[50] and one Iowa farmer said, "The appeals are nothing but a farce, a save-face deal where they just protect the decisions made by their people in the field. There's no way you can win." The North Dakota judge's injunction, effective nationwide, prohibited the FmHA from foreclosing on farmers without notifying them about their right to seek loan deferrals and appeals.[51]

Farmers also coaxed legislators across the Midwest to push for the agricultural equivalent of a minimum wage: minimum grain prices. As crop prices fell below the costs of production, the idea of a minimum price that more closely reflected those costs took hold. Perhaps more important, the push for economic justice became "an emotional catalyst linking the interests of a variety of protest groups, including independent farmers, environmentalists, nuclear freeze proponents, civil libertarians and especially labor union members."[52]

Old farm-labor alliances, spawned during the Progressive era about a century earlier, were reignited. When one Minnesota legislator opposed a mortgage moratorium, the state's farm-labor coalition gathered signatures from his district and delivered them to him on the statehouse floor. Seated upstairs in the public gallery were 100 farmers alongside members of the United Automobile Workers and United Steelworkers, who "sat motionless, quietly staring down at the member. He later chose to support the bill."[53]

TRICKLING UP

The emerging coalition was more than a sentimental gesture. It reflected both heightened recession-era solidarity and the widening economic fallout from the evisceration of family farms.

As farmers were disappeared by capricious economics and aggressive creditors, the communities around them began to fade away. The economic value of a farm not only to its owners but to a community cannot be underestimated. In rural communities, farmers are an economic lifeblood, pumping dollars into everything from cafes and restaurants to fertilizer and feed stores and veterinarians, not to mention equipment vendors and mechanics. Governor Bob Kerrey of Nebraska, citing research showing that many small farm towns were on the verge of disappearing, declared, "We're not only liquidating producers, we're liquidating towns as well."[54]

Press reports abounded of rural business failures, and of a ghostly Main Street, America, that was all but boarded up. Government studies found that for every dozen farms that shut down, one town business went under.[55] Even banks, so often the most obvious villains, fell prey to the recession's crush. In 1984, seventy-nine banks shut their doors, the most annual bank closings since the Depression. Farm banks, those that made at least 25 percent of their loans to farmers, were most vulnerable: their losses from unpaid loans increased fivefold from 1980 to 1984.[56] It was, truly, mourning in America.

There were urban repercussions as well. As rural farm-implement dealers shut down or scaled back, production naturally fell off, slicing into manufacturing jobs. "In cities where farm equipment is manufactured, people are put out of work and they can't make payments on home mortgages or car loans," explained Thomas Huston, Iowa's superintendent of banking.[57] The number of farm machinery engines produced in the United States and Europe declined from 948,000 in 1978 to 767,000 by 1981, a falloff of more than 25 percent.[58] John Deere, long the most profitable U.S. farm-machine manufacturer, took a whopping 97 percent loss in earnings between 1981 and 1982.[59] Salary freezes and layoffs proliferated at Deere and other major farm-machinery producers such as International Harvester and Massey Ferguson.[60]

1985: SHAKEOUT

The worst was yet to come.

The year of Reagan's landslide reelection in 1984 (a.k.a. "Morning in America") also brought bumper crops, and more disastrous prices and credit woes for farmers. Despite the GOP's reluctance to ease credit or expand farmer aid, most farmers stuck with the Republican ticket. Many others in the farm sector put their hopes in the Republican insistence on trimming the deficit in order to rein in inflation and interest rates. But to critics it was clear that Reagan's massive defense buildup and "Star Wars" project were the real deficit culprits.

The Farm Credit System, a nationwide network of borrower-owned financial institutions and the nation's biggest agricultural lender, suffered an unprecedented $522 million loss in the third quarter of 1985, after gaining $363 million the previous year.[61] It was the system's first loss in twenty years.[62] Pleas for a bailout were rejected by the Reagan administration.

As credit evaporated and farms went under by the tens of thousands, the ironic specter of farmers standing on food lines became everyday news. "In Iowa, a state that produces one tenth of America's food, farmers lined up last Thanksgiving for free turkey dinners. The world's most efficient food producers cannot earn enough to feed their own families."[63]

In January desperate farmers filled the Iowa statehouse, lobbying for an economic emergency declaration to halt foreclosures. "Throughout the statehouse, talk of the farm economy dominated every conversation over coffee, and the rotunda was filled with farmers in seed-company caps carrying white crosses, the symbol of rural pain."[64] Despite much hand-wringing over the spreading crisis, it wasn't until October, after months of protest and vigils outside his office, that Republican Governor Terry Branstad enacted the emergency measure, which allowed farmers to seek one-year foreclosure moratoriums from the courts.[65] The Iowa Bankers Association opposed the move, claiming it would only cause banks to deny future loans to struggling farmers.

In Washington, at a farther remove from the Iowa cornfields, Republicans were more reluctant to loosen purse strings for farmers. Reagan's notoriously spendthrift budget director, David Stockman, proposed gutting $16 billion from farm subsidies, as the administration boosted military spending. At a Senate hearing, Stockman commented, "For the life of me, I can't figure out why the taxpayers have the responsibility to go in and refinance bad debt willingly incurred by consenting adults."[66] Angry farm-state Democrats stalled the nomination of Edwin Meese to attorney general, insisting Republicans first back emergency credit legislation to advance immediate cash to farmers to get them through the next growing season.[67] As then–House Speaker Thomas "Tip" O'Neill of Massachusetts put it, "If we can spend hundreds of billions putting missiles on the ground, we can spend half a billion to put seed in the ground."[68]

An aide to Congressman Jack Kemp, a major Republican booster of Reagan's supply-side economic policy, argued that "the farmers' plight was less the fault of over borrowing than of wide swings in the money supply. 'The problem is Paul Volcker, not the farmers.' "[69] Yet in March Reagan vetoed emergency farm credit relief, accusing Democrats of raiding the treasury to score political points.[70] It didn't play well, even among Republicans. Reagan "lost a lot of support out here," said Iowa's Governor Branstad. "That veto was received with great disappointment and outrage."[71] Most farm-state Republicans up for reelection distanced themselves from the pecuniary stinginess of Reagan and his budget director.

Beyond any partisan or regional bickering, however, there was a deeper policy consensus, at least among those in power, that held far greater meaning. There was going to have to be a shakeout, a thinning of the ranks in agriculture. *Business Week* wrote openly of the Reagan administration's "countenancing a farm shakeout on the grounds that it will make U.S. agriculture more efficient."[72] In his 1989 book, *Losing Ground,* Hugh Ulrich, a commodity trading adviser, explained: "The United States was planning to shrink its farm economy to fit its shrinking share of the world market. The policy establishment had vaguely acknowledged the folly of raising loan and target rates in a competitive world."[73]

But it wasn't really a matter of "inefficient" small farms—a myth that studies have repeatedly debunked (for more on this, see Chapter 8). In fact, to some extent it was the skyrocketing cost of agribusiness's ever-growing bigness that pressed many to the wall. As Ulrich writes, the farm economy's "years of addiction to debt, and to expensive chemical farming, and land speculation, and the latest equipment needed on the bigger farms [had] irrevocably raised many farmers' cost of production above the world price."[74]

ENDGAME

In the midst of it all, Earl Butz, the former agriculture secretary, descended on the bleak scene and declared it media hype. "You get the impression that agriculture is about to go down the tubes," he told an Iowa lumberman's convention. Half of U.S. farmers didn't have debt, he said, "but they don't make the headlines." As for those in trouble, Butz had this to say: "Some won't make it and some shouldn't make it. That's the American system, the system of risk and reward. . . . The right to succeed carries with it the right to fail."[75]

Harsh words, and not altogether true considering the inequitable subsidy system that disproportionately benefited the largest, wealthiest farmers (discussed in more detail in Chapter 12). Yet Butz, in characteristic form, laid bare a cold hard truth: the economic weeding and pruning of the 1980s was not entirely unwanted by policy makers and agribusiness, for it continued the system's long-term consolidation.

Senator Gary Hart of Colorado put it succinctly in 1985: "We will have an agriculture industry. But it is a question of who will own it. What we have here is an unannounced policy of revolutionizing agriculture. It would wipe out many of the 2.4 million family farmers and turn their land over to large corporations."[76]

8

HOSTILE TAKEOVER:
THE NEW FARM CRISIS

"Never before has there been so many dollars in food and never before has there been such a small percent of those food dollars going to the producer of that food."
—Mike Callicrate, testifying before Kansas Senate
Judiciary Committee, March 1, 2000

POVERTY PASTORAL: ENDANGERED SPECIES

Like ripples on a lake, the green hills of northern Missouri rise and fold across the horizon and on into Iowa in a series of ridges and wooded dales. For generations this rolling terrain has been home to small livestock ranchers. Now the horizon is marred by rows of factory buildings.

A metropolis of hogs—rearing 2.5 million animals for slaughter each year—resides in gleaming metal barns that dominate the landscape. It's one of the nation's largest concentrations of pigs, all property of Premium Standard Farms (PSF), among the ten biggest pork producers in the United States. Housing more than a quarter of Missouri's hogs, the factory farm generates putrefying manure, smog, and economic ruin for area farmers.[1]

Like some modern-day Leviathan, corporate hogs are taking over the countryside, forcing many local farmers out of business and off their land. "They have produced so many that the independent family farmer cannot compete," says Lynn McKinley, of Unionville, Missouri, whose 500-acre farm has been in the family since 1853. "The market for feeder pigs [pigs in feeding stage, being prepared for market] dried up because everyone who lived next to PSF either went out of business or started working for them."[2]

When Premium Standard launched its hog operations in northern Missouri in 1993—after obtaining a special exemption from the state's ban on factory farms—it quickly transformed the community. The pastureland, once expansive and fairly unblemished, was soon pockmarked with huge aluminum hog warehouses. The company snapped up 37,000 acres of land to house its massive flocks, and leased other lands to soak up its hundreds of millions of gallons of manure. The clean country air was suddenly thick with nauseating wafts of pig shit, a fetid odor far stronger than normal farm smell. (For more on the environmental and public health effects of these farms, see Chapter 10.)

The company transformed the local economy, too, turning some independent farmers into animal-factory employees. "It's a horrible thing to see the family farm being lost and these lower-wage jobs being created, and people moving into those jobs because they don't have a choice," says Gary Godfrey, whose family has farmed in northern Missouri for generations.[3]

After PSF and other hog corporations, drawn by hearty livestock prices at the beginning of the decade, began flooding the U.S. pork market in the early 1990s, prices in 1998 plunged to their lowest since the Great Depression, driving droves of small farmers out of business.[4] Since PSF built three factory-farm complexes in the early nineties, Missouri has lost half of its hog producers, mostly owners of small family farms. In nearby Nebraska and Iowa, independent hog farms are disappearing by the thousands. Nationally, more than 80,000 pig farms disappeared between 1992 and 1997, even as hog production rose dramatically.[5]

Today's farm fatalities are piling up largely as a result of what the Department of Agriculture calls a "historically high" concentration in agriculture. With vertically integrated corporations controlling food production "from seedlings to supermarkets," as agribusiness expert A.V. Krebs puts it, 86,650 farmers and ranchers have been plowed under since 1997. While many agribusiness firms posted massive profits in the late 1990s, more than 17,000 farmers went out of business each year, destroying local economies and turning many rural communities into ghost towns.[6]

Farmers and farmland are rapidly disappearing from the rural landscape, and most will never be replaced. For small, independent operators, the math of producing and selling food simply doesn't add up anymore. The ingredients—or "inputs"—necessary to launch a viable farm are increasingly exorbitant and high-tech. Laptop-equipped custom combines rigged with global positioning satellite technology cost hundreds of thousands of dollars (deluxe commercial tractor: $223,299; deluxe corn combine: $279, 847)—and all the big competitors have them.

As one midwestern writer cogently explained, the replacement of small farms by corporate agriculture has had far-reaching socioeconomic implications. "As the 1990 census made indisputable, farms increased in size while the number of farm families diminished. Residents of the countryside aged while youths left for distant opportunities. This demographic decline further weakened rural villages and towns. Increasingly stripped of business, social functions, amenities and communities themselves, the countryside finds itself less able to keep pace with metropolitan goods, services, wages and opportunities."[7]

"THE COMING HOLOCAUST IN THE COUNTRYSIDE"

The plummeting price of hogs in the late nineties was more than a mere market fluctuation, and carried deep significance for farmers. Pigs have long been a cornerstone of diversified farming, used as an income stabilizer to "round out" small farmers' earnings in lean years. Historically hogs have been considered the great "mortgage lifter," requiring little startup capital and producing quick returns.[8] If corn or wheat prices lagged, farmers could always sell off hogs to the local butcher or meat packer. But now farmers had lost their grip on a key tool of economic survival. Pigs, despite their tradition as a relatively efficient income source, nonetheless chew up a lot of food and money. In an unstable market now dominated by corporations and large-scale producers, pigs have become an economic liability rather than an asset to a small farmer's survival.

As PSF and its corporate colleagues conquer market after market, they eliminate long-standing farmer survival strategies like diversified agriculture. "There are many producers throughout the Midwest who have depended on diversifying their crop and livestock operations, which included hogs, to round out their production to make it more profitable," explains John Crabtree, of the Nebraska-based Center for Rural Affairs, a nonprofit farm advocacy group. The corporations have "taken one big important piece of that and made it less competitive and a less profitable market for small producers. Farming in the Midwest has always been reliant on the family-farming unit of production. Diversification has been the key to survival. But as we have driven more and more of the small producers out of particular sectors like hogs, they become less and less diversified and less and less able to survive those economic downturns."[9]

The demise of hog farms in the "Show Me" state is not an isolated sectoral crisis but part of a far broader trend of corporate takeovers steamrolling across rural America. This nationwide rural overhaul, intensifying in the late nineties, pushed and priced many survivors of the eighties crisis out of business altogether.

What's driving today's farm crisis is plummeting prices, not for food but for crops. Since 1980, the portion of the food dollar that goes to farmers has shrunk from 37 to about 19 cents, according to the USDA (in 1952, the farmer's share was 47 cents).[10] In 2000 farmers took in just $123 billion out of some $661 billion consumers spent on food, while the rest of the "marketing bill" went to processing, packaging, distribution, labor, and retailing. Meanwhile, the costs of farming have far outstripped crop values. In 1990, farmers earned slightly more than they spent on supplies and equipment, but now they are paying far more for seeds, pesticides, and machinery than they are receiving for their crops.[11]

In the late 1990s farmers were pummeled by a hailstorm of distressing trends. Pork and wheat prices plunged, pork to Depression-era lows, and farmers were saddled with massive losses and soaring debt, which hit its highest levels since 1985. Wheat farmers were losing $2 on every bushel. Milk and corn surpluses sent prices diving, as corn fell from about $5 a bushel in the highflying mid-nineties to well below $2.[12] Bad farm debt shot up 20 percent in just one quarter of 1998, and credit was drying up fast.[13] "Prices are so low that in some states around 20 percent of the farmers won't get financing next year to farm," warned Mark Ritchie, president of the Minneapolis-based Institute for Agriculture and Trade Policy in a 1999 interview. "The price they are receiving is below the cost of production, and so nothing can be done. . . . Farmers use terms like 'the coming Holocaust in the countryside.' "[14]

The *St. Paul Pioneer Press* in Minnesota reported grimly from the front lines of the crisis, "Implement dealers are going out of business. Hundreds of farm auctions are taking place. Farmers are becoming shift workers on snowmobile assembly lines. The mood is becoming bleaker with each week, each heavy rain, each low price report."[15]

This economic hurricane spread rapidly across the agricultural horizon. In an interview at the time John Crabtree called the late-nineties epidemic "a farm crisis of 1980s proportions." But in some respects it was worse: now, virtually all farmers were affected, not just particular sectors. "It is pretty much across the board, as opposed to the problems we saw in the early 1980s, when it was selected commodities," said Shawn Stevenson, a farmer in Fresno, California.[16] Chip Morgan, the executive vice president of the Mississippi Delta Council (a rural development group), observed in 1999, "There has been no other period in the history of agricultural record-keeping when all of the major commodities were experiencing depressed prices at the same time like is being seen now. It isn't just southern agriculture or Midwest agriculture. It isn't just livestock or crops. All of agriculture is in an extremely depressed state."[17]

Just a decade after the massive winnowing of the eighties, many of the survivors were taking a hit, deepening the recognition across rural America that even relatively successful farmers were in trouble. "What's frustrating is we're doing our job better than ever before, yet we are losing ground," said a California farmer, Robert Mitchell.[18] As the average farmer's age rose to fifty-eight (the portion of farmers under thirty-five declined from 26 percent in the early 1980s to just 15 percent by 1998) and adult offspring fled to the cities in droves, the future became bleaker still.[19]

The crisis of the late nineties was particularly worrying because now, unlike in the fierce battles for survival of the eighties, many farmers were thoroughly worn down by untenable economics and were resigned to failure. "In the 1980s, farmers asked for help to find a way to stay on the farm," said Jon Evert, a onetime grower and coordinator of Rural Life Outreach of Northwest Minnesota, a family-farm support group. "Now farmers come to us and tell us we gotta help them find a way to get out. It feels like you're at a funeral. . . . There's a kind of sadness that's pervasive."[20]

Bolstering that sentiment, a 1999 analysis by the Federal Reserve Bank noted a "marked pickup in voluntary exits from production agriculture" in 1998. The article observed that a "pronounced hike in farm auctions accompanying the deep slump in farm prices led to many comparisons with the mid-1980s farm crisis. Yet the differences were many, not the least of which was the fact that most farm auctions in 1998 were *voluntary,* and not the result of foreclosure."[21]

Getting out of farming was no simple matter. Beyond the intense psychic and social shattering wrought by a farm closure lay a potentially debilitating lifetime of debt. Jon Evert observed that "a lot of people can't see any future in farming anymore, and they're trying to get out. But they're having a really difficult time getting out because it's not easy. When you sell your land and your machinery, you get stuck with taxes—capital gains and income taxes—that mean you leave the farm with $50,000 or $100,000 in debts and go to a factory job that pays $8 an hour. You can't get out from under a $50,000 debt with a job like that. It's a catch-22 situation, and people are trapped. They've lost all hope."[22] (Of course taxes, while potentially burdensome, pale in comparison to the mountains of debt and interest that bury many farmers.)

Stories cropped up of reverse millionaires: farmers saddled with as much as $1 million in debts.[23] And it wasn't just bank loans anymore—many farmers, according to Evert, were "borrowing on their credit cards to try to get enough money to plant. . . . They are borrowing on their equity because they can't get operating loans because they can't show any payback. They're losing money, year after year."

Farm income had become so tenuous, according to Krebs, that more than 80 percent of U.S. farmers would be below the poverty line if they relied entirely on farm earnings. Indeed, the Department of Agriculture found that nearly 90 percent of total farm household income in 1999 was generated from something other than farming. More than half of America's farmers held jobs away from the farm to make ends meet, 80 percent of them working full-time.[24] (This moonlighting trend, especially pronounced since the 1980s, applies mainly to smaller growers, deepening the economic divide between big agriculture and small family farmers.) In 1999 farm income shriveled to roughly 30 percent below the average of the previous five years, and USDA economists said that about one out of every four farmers couldn't even cover his expenses.[25]

THE FREE(FALL) MARKET

What was going on? In some respects farmers were replaying the boom/bust pattern of the seventies and eighties all over again. Record-high commodity prices in 1995 spurred overconfidence in continued market expansion. Then, in 1996, the Freedom to Farm Act legislated the holy grail of "free markets," when it supposedly ended subsidies as we knew them and threw farmers to the treacherous four winds of the international marketplace. The new law promised an end to Depression-era price supports (identified by House Speaker Newt Gingrich as "East German socialist" programs), and "intended to wean farmers from subsidies by 2002," the *New York Times* summarized. "The idea was that farmers would flourish in an unfettered market."[26] Many farmers, however, dubbed the law the "Freedom to Fail Act."[27]

With subsidies and their attendant crop restrictions apparently on the wane (yet, as we'll see in Chapter 12, farm payments hardly ended, tripling between 1996 and 1999), farmers began feverish expansion, banking on another export boom.[28] "Led to believe they would be called on to feed the newly enriched urban consumers of Asia, [farmers] threw virtually every farmable acre into production."[29] In 1996 U.S. farmers exported a record $60 billion worth of products.[30] Just a year later, the Asian economic crisis hit home with a vengeance, and exports fell off dramatically, plunging to below $50 billion.[31]

The Asian recession exposed the soft underbelly of an American agricultural machine critically dependent on exports. David Waide, president of the Mississippi Farm Bureau, explained the situation: "One of the major obstacles I see is the economic decline of several foreign countries that were major purchasers of our commodities. They're not buying in the volume that they have bought in the past. That is hurting our ability to export. And we need to export because the U.S. only consumes roughly two-thirds of what agriculture produces in the U.S. We have to depend on foreign markets to sell the other third."[32]

THE CORPORATE CORNUCOPIA

Beyond these international economic trends lay a more fundamental, long-developing crisis for farmers and consumers: the intensifying consolidation of monopoly-level corporate control throughout the food system. Steadily brewing since the 1950s, when U.S. and multinational corporations increasingly solidified their grip over national economies and polities, corporate America's takeover of food acquired both quantitatively and qualitatively new significance in the 1990s. Mark Drabenstott, an economist with the Federal Reserve Bank, wrote in 1999, "Consolidation is certainly not new in agriculture—it has been under way for most of the 20th century. What *is* new is the type and speed of the consolidation."[33]

Hammered by waves of agribusiness mergers, new levels of vertical and horizontal corporate integration, and, perhaps most crucially, intense consolidation at the retail end, among supermarkets, farmers in the late 1990s were cornered into a position of profound powerlessness. There had always been battles to get a fair price for their crops from railroad and beef barons and the like, but now corporate control reached across the entire continuum of farmers' economic life, and a single company could dictate nearly every term, from the price of "inputs" such as seeds and pesticides to the value of crops and livestock to the prices of products on supermarket shelves. As a popular corporate slogan puts it, "From farm gate to dinner plate."

Thanks to corporate concentration and new seed patents, farmers must now buy self-terminating seeds every year from a narrowing clique of sellers. In what is best described as an "hourglass" economic arrangement, many of these same firms, such as Cargill and ConAgra, are waiting at the other end of the growing season to collect farmers' harvests at bargain-basement prices.[34] Farmers have never had much power at the negotiating table; now they have next to none. Intensifying corporate concentration means farmers must buy inputs high and sell crops low to a tightening field of giant global firms that hold all the bargaining power at all points of the food network.

GROWING WIDGETS: FARMERS AS "LAND-OWNING SERFS"

To leaf through the glossy pages of ConAgra's annual report is to take a tour up and down a tightly knit food web and across nearly every continent. The firm, which sports roughly $20 billion in annual sales (and at least 100 major brand-named product lines), boasts to its shareholders, "Diversification across the food chain provides limitless opportunities for growth."[35]

Such vast holdings thwart independent farmers. Cargill and Archer Daniels Midland have come to monopolize grain elevators throughout the Midwest, and ConAgra wields near total control over regional poultry production. ConAgra and other fully integrated meat-processing corporations such as Perdue accomplish this through "contract farming."

In effect, contract farming is turning more and more small producers into tenant farmers. "If you sign a contract," says Peter Rosset of Food First, a nonprofit research think tank, "every detail of the production process is spelled out. You must construct the animal housing according to their plans, wire the buildings according to their plans, feed the animals their feed, and use exactly the antibiotics they recommend. . . . And they have visits by contract supervisors to make sure that the farmer goes along with it."[36]

For instance, Perdue's poultry-producer agreement requires contract farmers to provide and maintain all housing, equipment, roads, utilities, and labor, and to use company-supplied feed, medications, and vaccinations. The farmer, labeled an "independent contractor," must own the land, buildings, and equipment—but Perdue may enter and inspect the premises at any time. And if Perdue decides the farmer is not following the corporation's "established procedures" for raising the flock, it can make the producer pay for necessary adjustments.[37]

A compelling eight-month investigation of contract chicken growers' struggles in thirteen states undertaken in 1999 by the *Baltimore Sun* documented case after case of southern poultry farmers who were crushed by powerhouse corporations such as Perdue, Tyson, and ConAgra, which wield tremendous economic and political power. "While the companies have been flourishing on Wall Street and extending their political reach to the White House," the paper wrote, the nation's 30,000 contract growers "have been increasingly beleaguered: the public denounces them as polluters whose chicken manure fouls waterways, while the poultry companies squeeze them ever tighter for profits. Formerly able to share in the bounty of an industry on the rise, they have become the land-owning serfs in an agricultural feudal system."[38]

Lured by sophisticated company sales pitches promising independence and a middle-class income, farmers and nonfarmers alike have migrated to the Deep South to grow chickens for ConAgra, Perdue, and others. They quickly find themselves deep in debt, their fates hitched entirely to the company. In 1992, Ed and Georgia Probst, responding to enticements from ConAgra, sold their home in Pennsylvania and moved the family to Alabama, where they invested about $250,000 to start up an operation running four used chicken houses. Every year, as Ed Probst and his family brought improvements to the farm, ConAgra squeezed them for more—"eventually demanding that he install $200,000 worth of new equipment and sign away his right to sue if things went wrong," according to the *Sun*. (It is common industry practice to require growers to give up their right to sue as a condition of securing a contract.) When Probst got fed up and put his farm up for sale in 1996, he "got his last, harshest lesson. . . . The company refused to offer a chicken-growing contract to any prospective buyer, and within three months the Probsts lost everything to foreclosure."

In return for a $250,000 startup investment, a contract chicken farmer takes in an annual net income of just $8,160, the *Sun* found. Of course there are no benefits, as the farmers are "independent contractors." The farmer "is saddled with round-the-clock responsibility, daily collecting dead birds by hand during strolls through dust and ankle-deep manure. A farmer battles heat waves, power outages and outbreaks of avian disease, and his every move is controlled by the vagaries of a contract that can be canceled virtually any time, cutting income to zero."[39]

Although the corporations supply the baby animals (which remain company property) and the feed and medicine, the farmer shoulders the risk if animals die off and the corporation determines that the farmer mismanaged its property. Factory farming increases this risk by exposing tens of thousands of animals to bacterial diseases such as *E. coli,* the cause of increasingly common outbreaks. "It's almost impossible to produce animals in that kind of concentration without promoting the spread of disease," Rosset says. "But if the animals die off, it's the farmer who goes out of business."[40]

Especially onerous are the economic pressures imposed on farmers when they sign these agreements. "We don't really have independent producers in poultry," says John Crabtree. "There *isn't* a chicken market—everybody is vertically integrated." Under such grossly unequal terms, Crabtree says, "It's not the contracting of production that is so troublesome; it's the fact that producers today have to contract with an industry that is so concentrated and consolidated that there is no way they can sit at a table and have any comparable economic power to be able to negotiate an agreement that is fair."[41]

LIFE IN THE CORPORATE COUNTRYSIDE

The town square in Unionville, Missouri (population: 2,041), is desolate. Most of its storefronts are boarded up or empty. Old brick buildings are crumbling into vacant lots. Signs of earlier prosperity are peeling away, and buildings bear "for sale" notices. Residents say the town once thrived as independent farmers' business propelled local commerce, such as fertilizer and feed stores.

But the foreclosures of the eighties and the consolidations of the nineties have reconfigured the economies of Unionville and countless other farm-country towns from diversified local interdependence into near-total dependence on corporations like PSF, which do not buy local goods and services. The corporation takes care of everything in-house. "As farms have grown bigger and bigger and more and more concentrated, the corporate farms don't buy their feed or their inputs, like veterinary services, locally," explains Crabtree. "This has had a devastating impact on rural communities that depend on that economic activity."[42]

There is far more at stake than individual farmers' livelihoods. The corporate countryside means a whole new way of life, one defined by short-term profit imperatives and hierarchical divisions between the company and the community. "There are farmers out here trying to make a living," says Rolf Christen, a cattle farmer in nearby Green City who has helped lead opposition and lawsuits against PSF's factory-farm pollution (for more on this, see Chapter 10). "We help each other, support each other, and here this corporation comes in and doesn't give any consideration to anybody around it. They come in, they take over and pollute the neighborhood, and when people complain they just say, 'This is the business of the new millennium.' . . . This corporate life just doesn't fit in here."[43]

Another of PSF's reluctant neighbors is cattle and grain farmer Gary Godfrey, whose great-great-grandparents first received title to their land from the U.S. government in 1857. His family still owns a 1,500-acre diversified farm in the county just south of Unionville. Godfrey has studiously researched life before and after PSF's arrival. His findings, extracted from public records, suggest a decidedly downward arc in some of the area's economic and social affairs since the Texas-based pork company opened its factory gates in northern Missouri. "We were making dramatic improvements when [PSF] came in and reversed that positive trend," says Godfrey, who, in addition to being a farmer, has served on the Northwest Missouri Private Industry Council and other economic development bodies.[44]

In the early 1990s, thanks largely to stratospheric livestock prices, the area was recovering economically from the 1980s farm crisis. In 1992 unemployment in Putnam and Sullivan counties stood at a mere 3.5 percent, less than half the national rate. Assessed property-tax values were on the rise, according to Godfrey's research based on county records. That August, the 800-person village of Green City held a ribbon-cutting ceremony for thirteen new and expanded businesses. Local school districts were ordering fiber-optic circuits to hitch their high schools up to the information interstate. And, Godfrey found, area bank assets were growing astronomically. All this during a recession.[45]

Predicting a continued livestock boom, PSF and its Wall Street investors (later led by Putnam Investments and Morgan Stanley) wanted a piece of the action. Nationwide, the hog business was going corporate, and PSF had poised itself to be a key player in the shift to high-tech industrialized hog production.

But the company was plagued by missteps. In 1989, PSF was essentially kicked out of Iowa: the state Department of Natural Resources rejected the firm's bid to build a huge wastewater lagoon for a planned hog facility already under construction just a half-mile away from a state park. Iowa officials were not convinced that PSF would deliver an economic boon sufficient to outweigh its steep economic, social, and environmental costs.[46]

So the company set its sights on three counties in northern Missouri, undeterred by a 1975 state law banning corporate hog farms. In 1993, in the waning hours of Missouri's legislative session, PSF caught a break. In an eleven-line amendment that was "piggybacked onto an economic development bill," according to the *St. Louis Post-Dispatch,* the legislature exempted those three counties from the corporate-farming law. The process enabling PSF to launch its huge corporate farms in Missouri didn't appear to be in keeping with the ethos of the "Show Me" state. "People living in the area got no advance notice or public hearings on the exemption," the paper reported. The last-minute amendment, allegedly passed around midnight, "was adopted before opposition could be mounted," remarked Estil Fretwell, a lobbyist for the Missouri Farm Bureau Federation.[47]

Despite the rancor, Premium Standard Farms was in business. In keeping with corporate tradition, they promised heady returns to both shareholders and northern Missouri communities. The firm hooked up with state legislators, economic developers, and the University of Missouri commercial agriculture program in a broad promotional blitz. The university extension department churned out a glowing 1994 report, based on continued hearty hog prices, predicting that PSF would produce nearly $655 million in annual economic output (including $195 million in revenues, and $459 million from spinoff economic multipliers) for the state.[48]

Godfrey and other locals were skeptical. "It seemed to me that with several hundred million dollars in junk-bond financing and with rates above 12 percent, that much of this money would be going to Wall Street investors," Godfrey wrote in an analysis he presented at hearings before a state legislative task force in 1998. "What really bothered me was that there were no estimates for the negative impact of removing all the farmers that sold out to them from our local economy."[49] A number of farmers in the area, already struggling, sold or leased their land to the company. The firm bought up thousands of acres of land, some of it for the pig factories, much of it to function as a vast receiving area for the factories' tons of manure.

In the late 1990s, a few years after PSF's auspicious arrival, hog prices nationwide nosedived, due to a variety of factors, including a corporate-induced oversupply and the Asian economic crisis of 1997–98, which dampened exports. As prices for slaughter-ready hogs plummeted to a century-low rate of 8 cents per pound, many producers in Missouri and elsewhere went out of business. Although PSF likely only contributed a small amount to the oversupply and price plunge, the company's dominant presence in Missouri shut smaller hog farmers out of the market. Premium Standard, the only major pork processor in the state, had its own supply of hogs for its slaughterhouses, creating a closed economic system to which small producers had no access. "There's not even a place to sell hogs in the state of Missouri right now since Premium Standard and these large operations have come in," explains Unionville cattle farmer Terry Spence. "A farmer raising hogs would have to go all the way to Iowa to even sell them."[50]

While PSF's impact on many small to midsized hog farmers has been unmistakably negative, the company touts the other side of the economic ledger: 1,100 new jobs and increased economic activity. Indeed for some area residents, PSF has been a lift, providing steady—if malodorous—employment. But starting pay for "power washers" who clean out factory barns is just $14,000. And that is to say nothing of the company's other job creation, employing poorly paid immigrant laborers in its processing facility.

It should be pointed out that the firm has showered local communities with generous "corporate citizen" gifts and has generated new economic activity even while eliminating many local farms. In Princeton, PSF's "showcase" town, the corporation built an air-conditioned apartment complex, complete with pool, and donated concrete for fresh sidewalks in the town square.[51]

Beyond these mixed economic effects, Godfrey has detected other "disturbing social trends" since Premium Standard's 1993 arrival. In 1996, the state Department of Social Services reported that Sullivan County had the state's highest rate of increase in reported cases of child abuse and neglect, a spike of 158 percent. Nearby Mercer County, also inhabited by PSF megafarms, was second on the list, at 69 percent. The statewide average showed a decline of 1.8 percent. In another study of child well-being, Sullivan and Mercer counties fell from number 27 and 58, respectively, of Missouri's 115 counties to 104 and 107—near the very bottom. Although the area unemployment rate remained below national averages, the number of households receiving food stamps shot up dramatically.[52]

A broad array of other costs, some of which I will explore later, must be counted against any economic benefits, such as increased spending activity and tax revenues, generated by the company's much-promoted $35 million payroll. Consider, for instance, all the staff time and resources of state environmental regulators responding to the dozens of PSF manure lagoon spills that have polluted local streams. Or the new pressures wrought on local budgets (including increased costs for law enforcement, schools, and public health) by the company's use of low-paid immigrant and migrant workers to chop up all those hogs in

PSF's sparkling new processing plant, a short drive away from the factory farms.

Critics say PSF has also created significant new costs borne by the public, including increased road maintenance incurred from the company's fleet of tractor-trailer trucks, and skyrocketing rents and less affordable housing to go around. Throw in a bevy of corporate tax breaks and discounted bulk utility rates, says Spence, and the public bill gets even higher. While PSF receives cut-rate utilities, "our bills just keep rising and rising. In actuality we are really paying for them being here. They promote their jobs and economic output, but the external costs like [higher] utility rates, the tax exemptions they're getting, you know somebody's picking that tab up, and it's the residents living here, not the corporation."[53]

Perhaps not all of the above problems can be laid neatly at PSF's well-guarded factory gates. But they provide demonstrable evidence of the firm's often quite harmful economic and social impact on its neighborhood, to say nothing of its destructive ecological effects (for more on this, see Chapter 10). The case illustration is important because PSF was at the forefront of an aggressive corporate rush to get control of the U.S. hog industry in the early to mid-1990s. And this, along with intensifying consolidations in beef and poultry, has transformed the nation's meat production and hastened the demise of small and medium-sized farmers.

A CORPORATE FEEDING FRENZY

Hard times on the farm come amid heady days for the largest agribusiness corporations, which throughout the 1990s engaged in a financial feeding frenzy of mergers and acquisitions. In one massive 1999 buyout, Cargill, then the nation's largest privately held company, snatched up the grain storage, transportation, export, and trading operations in North America, Europe, Latin America, and Asia of Continental Grain Company, one of the top five private U.S. grain traders. The purchase, estimated to be worth between $500,000 and $1 billion, gave Cargill control over one third of all U.S. grain exports, including 40 percent of all U.S. corn, one third of soybean, and 20 percent of wheat exports.[54]

Under a barrage of lobbying the generally listless Department of Justice antitrust division examined the merger, and ultimately gave its stamp of approval, but with a few caveats. The new, much expanded Cargill didn't hold any monopoly sway over global markets, Department of Justice lawyers ruled, but it threatened to create a monopoly in crucially important local and regional grain elevator markets, the economic gateway for grain farmers. As one analysis explained, "The combined firm might be able to set lower prices to grain producers without facing new entry [from competitors]."[55] To secure Department of Justice approval, Cargill and Continental agreed to sell off their elevators in markets where the merger would have created a monopoly.

But for agribusiness critics, the agreement amounted to so much fine print: at the end of the day, Cargill got nearly everything it wanted, and the private club of agribusiness had become yet more exclusive. The merger fanned the flames of resentment already spreading across the Farm Belt and became symbolic of farmers' growing economic woes in the face of rapidly consolidating corporate power. Seizing the moment, Minnesota's Senator Paul Wellstone proposed an eighteen-month moratorium on agribusiness mergers. Despite backing from powerful Midwest senators such as Democrat Byron Dorgan of North Dakota and Republican Charles Grassley of Iowa, the bill was soundly defeated.[56] Once the "farm crisis" faded from the headlines, the merger moratorium idea died on the vine.

"GRAIN TRADERS TRADE GRAIN"

The sheer scale of these food empires is breathtaking. Cargill, a commodities kingmaker with annual sales of nearly $60 billion, owns dozens of subsidiaries encompassing the manufacture, financing, wholesale, and transportation of dozens of food crops, livestock, and commodity futures. Its scope takes in nearly every aspect of food production, including seeds, fertilizer, feed grain, cattle feed lots, and contract hog production.[57]

Cargill heralded the Continental merger as a boon for farmers. "Together these grain operations will expand farmers' reach into new markets," said Cargill CEO Ernest S. Micek in a press release at the time. "Continental's worldwide grain handling and export facilities will help us move farmers' crops to our processing plants and to our customers more reliably and efficiently."[58]

Exports may expand markets, but Cargill's sunny prognosis is not shared by farmers and agribusiness critics, who say that consolidation chokes off any increased cash flow. "The bonanza [from exports] isn't shared with farmers; it's pretty much sucked up by the intermediaries like Cargill," says Food First's Peter Rosset. Krebs puts it succinctly: "Farmers don't trade grain, grain traders trade grain."

These megamergers hit farmers' pockets directly. Before the Cargill buyout, Floyd Schultz, an Illinois corn grower, could sell his crops to Cargill *or* Continental Grain. Now, he told the *New York Times,* he must drive an extra thirty miles to bargain with the nearest competitor, Archer Daniels Midland (ADM). The trip costs him an extra 10 cents a bushel. Mike Yost, a Minnesota corn and soybean grower, predicts that the Cargill deal will cost him about $2,700 a year in diminished crop value. "We see constant consolidation of both our input suppliers—for seed, fertilizer, pesticides—and the people who purchase our production," Yost told the *Times.* "Obviously, the trend's not healthy for the American farmer."[59]

Cargill's mammoth acquisition was just the tip of the merger-mania iceberg. While selling off its century-old grain business, Continental used Cargill's cash to further consolidate its livestock holdings; in 1998 Continental gobbled up PSF, the hog-raising and processing giant. That June, Monsanto bought up Cargill's international seed operations for $1.4 billion—cash that undoubtedly helped Cargill snag Continental Grain.

OUT OF CONTROL

As holdings and money change hands, these firms expand and deepen their control over market sectors and distribution channels, making consolidation more and more seamless. Just a few corporations, led by Cargill and ADM (which famously styles itself "supermarket to the world") control about 75 percent of the world's grain production.[60] Says Krebs, "Nearly every product on the market today that has corn in it [such as lysine, citric acid, and sweeteners] comes from ADM."

Aided by merger-friendly federal policies, payouts to corporations ("corporate welfare"), and grossly unequal subsidies, agribusiness firms are buying out their competitors and pricing out farmers. Although small farms (those with under $250,000 in annual sales) make up 94 percent of the nation's farms, they take in just 41 percent of all farm revenue. The 1998 USDA Commission on Small Farms found that "ownership and control over agricultural assets is increasingly concentrated," and, as a result, "farmers have little to no control over setting the price for their products."[61]

Nowhere is this trend more dramatic than in meatpacking, where four corporations now handle over 80 percent of all cattle and 54 percent of hogs slaughtered, and just three companies control 70 to 75 percent of the lambs slaughtered. Lest we take such levels of economic concentration for granted, consider this: in 1980, the top four companies handled just 36 percent of beef packing, and as late as 1985, the top four controlled 32 percent of the pork slaughter. In the chicken business, control by the elite four expanded from 35 percent in 1986 to 49 percent by 1998.[62] A 1996 USDA report on consolidation found a "depression of producer prices at all levels," and concluded that cattle ranchers' "losses seem out of control and hard to justify in light of the record profits being recorded at the higher levels of the beef industry." Indeed, in 1999, while most farmers slogged through the price crisis, Iowa Beef Processors reported record net earnings of $321 million, up from $205 million the previous year.[63]

This "out-of-control" corporate market share leads directly to lower prices for independent farmers—and, some studies show, to higher prices on supermarket shelves (more on that later). For years Great Plains cattle farmers and some rather powerful legislators, such as Senators Tom Daschle (D–South Dakota), Charles Grassley (R-Iowa), and Tim Johnson (D–South Dakota), have challenged corporate meatpackers' practice of building up their own "captive supplies" of surplus livestock as a means of imposing low cattle prices on independent farmers. Despite numerous high-level congressional efforts, and passage of a key Senate bill, the corporate cattle industry has so far succeeded in keeping a ban on packer ownership of livestock off the books.[64]

Nolan Jungclaus, a Minnesota grain and livestock farmer who has begun making the shift from "conventional" to organic agriculture, has witnessed firsthand the "concentration of economic power and wealth spearheaded by packers who own and feed their livestock," as he described it when testifying before a Senate committee in 2002. The repercussions, he says, are vast: "This shift in the economic balance from the rural sector to the corporate headquarters of the very large and monopolized packing industry is sucking the lifeblood out of our rural communities."[65]

Numerous farmer testimonies, backed up by press reports and studies, paint a picture of totalizing corporate power over the business of animal agriculture. Consolidated ownership and near-monopoly market share enable Cargill, ConAgra, Excel, Premium Standard Farms, and other powerhouse packers to dictate the going price, both on the daily spot market (where corporations' captive supplies help discipline farmers' selling price) and through one-sided "forward contracts," which trap livestock farmers into low prices.

In just five years, the nation's top six meatpackers extended significantly their web of control over the pork market; their ownership of sows (breeder pigs) grew from 442,000 in 1996 to more than 1.2 million in 2001. During that same period, hog farmers' share of the pork retail dollar plunged by nearly one third, from 42.5 cents in 1996 to just 30 cents in 2001. Jungclaus says, "That is money taken out of my pockets, money that is not circulating in my community, and it is hurting us severely."[66]

The widening "farm-to-retail price spread," or the difference between farmers' and retail prices, has skinned many independent farmers to the bone. Speaking to the Senate Agriculture Committee in July 2002, Herman Schumacher, of the Ranchers-Cattlemen Action Legal Fund described the widening disparity between what cattle farmers get paid for their livestock and what corporate beef packers and supermarkets charge for processed product: "Much has been said about the market share beef has lost to competing meats such as poultry, pork, and imported beef and cattle. However, the most damaging lost market share cattle producers suffer today is the lost share of the consumers' beef dollar from the packers and retailers. No industry segment can continue to survive the losses U.S. cattle producers have sustained."

Schumacher, himself a South Dakota cow and calf farmer and feedlot operator, testified that USDA data through April 1999 show that the farm-to-retail price spread had grown from $.40 to more than $1.40 per pound since 1970, "a loss to cattle producers of over $500 per head." Schumacher summed up the situation in simpler terms: "There is no greater evidence that something is wrong than to witness the record retail prices that you as consumers are spending and the tremendous losses producers are experiencing."[67]

In December 2002 Mike Callicrate, a Kansas cattle farmer, turned up the heat, suing one of the top four producers, Farmland National Beef. In his suit, Callicrate alleged that the corporation refused to buy his cattle after his feedlot sales manager penned a trade-industry article attacking Farmland and other corporate meatpackers for using their dominating market power to push farmers into signing unfair contracts. "They went from buying most of our cattle to buying nothing," Callicrate said. "It meant bankruptcy pretty damn quick." The USDA soon opened a complaint against Farmland for the alleged blacklisting.[68] But in 2001 the USDA agreed to call off its dogs, after Farmland agreed to cover the cost of the investigation—$95,000.[69] "It sounds like a sellout to me," Callicrate told the Associated Press. "Now we know that justice does have a price and it is very, very low. . . . We don't have a government to protect us. We have no government able to stand up to these big companies."[70]

As a result, Callicrate said in testimony before the agriculture committee of the Nebraska legislature, "We are now left with a packing monopoly that is stealing from both producers and consumers as well as threatening not only our food supply but a safe food supply."[71]

Farmland National is one fourth of an oligopolistic quartet, a few companies that effectively govern an industry. Another top player, IBP (now a subsidiary within the growing Tyson Foods empire), is in the proverbial fryer for alleged market manipulation, fending off complaints by farmers and the USDA.[72] As Callicrate testified: "It has been proven that IBP uses captive supplies, those inventories of cattle available to IBP outside of the competitive market, to lower prices paid to producers. . . . The cash market determines the value of these captive cattle. What is the cash market if price leader IBP doesn't need any cattle [because it has already assured its own supply]? . . . The market is totally disconnected from supply and demand and is simply what the packer wants it to be."[73]

FOOD CHAIN CLUSTERS

Such oligopolistic control is hardly unique to the meat industry. Corporate gangs of four with awesome economic clout now preside over many essential food sectors; four companies control at least 40 percent of all major commodities in the Midwest, a rate of concentration many economists consider anticompetitive.[74]

According to extensive research by University of Missouri sociologist Dr. William Heffernan, through 1999: the market share of the top four in flour milling (ADM, ConAgra, Cargill, and Cereal Food Processors, Inc.) was 62 percent; in dry corn milling the rate was 57 percent (again including ADM, ConAgra, and Cargill, along with Bunge); in wet corn milling the top four controlled 74 percent; and in soybean crushing the top four controlled 80 percent.

In nearly every category, the big three—ADM, Cargill, and ConAgra—were among the top four or five firms.[75] ConAgra is among the top four in processing beef, pork, turkeys, sheep, and seafood; Cargill is in the elite quartets producing animal feed, operating grain terminal facilities, processing beef and pork, raising turkeys, and in the top three exporters of corn and soybeans. And ADM, living up to its moniker as supermarket to the world, takes top billing in many major commodities, including flour milling, wet corn milling, soybean crushing, and ethanol production.[76]

Another area of increasing corporate control—exacerbated by a wave of mergers and acquisitions in the late 1990s—is the little-discussed seed industry. Here at the very beginning of food production, a small clique of companies control the lion's share of the business, which registers annual sales of $6 billion in the United States, and $30 billion worldwide. In the all-important corn seed sector, the largest four firms control 67 percent of market share; Dupont/Pioneer Hi-Bred alone has nearly 40 percent of the market. On a global scale, the top ten "life industry" corporations garner nearly one third of the commercial seed trade.[77]

This consolidated market power becomes increasingly worrying as firms such as Monsanto, Novartis, Dupont, and others begin to "manage proprietary crop genes [genetically modified plants] and chemicals [pesticides] as a pair," explains ETC, the international Action Group on Erosion, Technology and Concentration. Armed with market power and growing portfolios of seed patents, these firms control food's most basic ingredient, and dictate the terms on which farmers grow that food. Monsanto, for instance, vigorously pursues legal actions against farmers who try to save proprietary seeds from their harvest, according to ETC. "The penalties, warns Monsanto, may include criminal charges, on-farm field inspections, and damages that could exceed $1 million dollars. In some areas, the company has hired Pinkerton investigators to root out farmers who are saving the company's seed."

It has not always been like this. As recently as 1969, the top four controlled 30 percent of the wheat-milling business (already a pretty healthy share), but by 1995 they controlled 77 percent. Similarly, in the malt beverage industry the top four controlled 40 percent in 1969, but by 1992, this had ballooned to an astounding 90 percent share.[78] The Mafia can only dream of such market control.

It is not hyperbole to describe these corporations as empires unto themselves. Cargill operates in some seventy countries across the globe. As Heffernan points out, even if Cargill paid a full $1 billion in its 1999 purchase of Continental Grain, the price estimated by the *Wall Street Journal,* that's only half of their 1998 income: "Cargill could buy operations the size of Continental's global grain division with one year's earnings. That is economic power. . . . Cargill's corporate goal is to double in size every five to seven years, which it says it has achieved for the past 40 years."[79]

But that's not the end of it. Heffernan and his research squad have been mining agribusiness data for more than a decade, and their findings reveal a significantly new level of corporate power spanning the food system. With ongoing mergers, joint ventures, and other strategic alliances, food-industry giants have begun forming what Dr. Heffernan terms "food chain clusters," seamless megafirms and strategic alliances that "control the food system from gene to supermarket shelf."

In one 1998 venture, Cargill pooled its remarkable seed and commodity operations with the cutting-edge biotech and genetic engineering expertise of Monsanto, which was then on the cusp of controlling the "Terminator gene," a self-destructing mechanism that would prevent all crop farmers from using seeds from their harvest for planting their next crop (restrictions that, according to Heffernan, corn farmers have worked under for the past fifty years). Together, the two firms formed a cluster spanning "a complete food chain," says Heffernan: complete control of food products from seed to dinner table.

And here, Heffernan explains, consumers literally pay the price: "Within this emerging system, there will be no markets, and thus no 'price discovery,' [in other words, no understanding of how prices are derived] from the gene, fertilizer processing, and chemical production to the supermarket shelf. The only time the public will ever know the 'price' of animal protein is when it arrives in the meat case. . . . In a food chain cluster, the food product is passed along from stage to stage [of production], but ownership never changes and neither does the location of the decision making."[80]

WHAT WOULD ADAM SMITH THINK?

Just what constitutes anticompetitive market concentration is hotly debated in the obscure but important, and intensely political, universe of agricultural economics. Throughout many of America's mainstream university agriculture departments there is a scholarly celebration of the economic efficiencies supposedly wrought by increasing corporate-controlled agriculture. These departments are often joined at the economic hip with agribusiness, particularly with "life-sciences" companies such as Monsanto and Novartis. Economies of scale, huge centrally controlled production and distribution systems run by single companies, fewer and larger farms—these are the standard ingredients in today's corporate "supply chain." Centralized corporate control over this supply chain is ubiquitous throughout the economy (notably in sectors such as media and pharmaceuticals), so that industrial and now agricultural production is rationalized from the top down to fit the supply needs of the biggest wholesale and retail companies, be they meatpackers, food processors, supermarkets, or, most famously, fast-food chains like McDonald's.

An economic case has been made that up to a point, corporate consolidation does lead to some economic efficiencies and possibly some price benefits to consumers. A 1999 Federal Reserve Bank analysis claims that the share of Americans' consumer dollars spent on food has dropped from 21 cents in 1950 to 11 cents by 1999. The study concluded, "Consumers have been a major beneficiary of consolidation."[81] (Such hopeful accounts may be exaggerated: other analyses show that this shift may be due more to growth in Americans' disposable income than to decreased food prices.) Fewer and bigger farms and agribusiness companies, according to the mainstream economic argument, just makes good economic sense: consolidation's winners gain economies of scale leading to big cost savings passed along to the consumer. Smaller farms simply can't produce enough of any one crop to keep prices down, the argument goes. But studies have shown that small-to-medium-sized farms can produce just as efficiently as big ones, or even more efficiently.

"Small farms are far from being as unproductive or inefficient as so many would have us believe," argues Peter Rosset of Food First in a 1999 policy brief titled "The Multiple Functions and Benefits of Small Farm Agriculture." Citing an array of studies, Rosset says small farms are "more productive, more efficient, and contribute more to economic development than large farms." Although a large single-crop farm undeniably yields greater volume, such an operation wastes valuable "niche space" between crop rows, which goes unused. Small farms growing a diverse mixture of crops yield more total food per acre and sustain future productivity by replenishing the soil, Rosset maintains. Especially convincing is data from the U.S. Department of Agriculture on farm size and output. According to the 1992 agricultural census, farms just 27 acres in size averaged $1,050 in gross output per acre, while operations of 6,700 acres averaged just $63. Although much of that surprising disparity is due to the fact that "smaller farms tend to specialize in high-value crops like vegetables and flowers," says Rosset, "it also reflects relatively more labor and inputs" applied on large-scale farms. These arguments, if not conclusive, at least raise serious questions about the assumption that bigger is better, and more efficient.

Yet even agriculture scholars who agree that corporate control has created some economic benefits say today's near-monopoly consolidation goes too far, to the detriment of both consumers and farmers (farmers, of course, pay twice since they are also consumers). In a 2002 paper cleverly titled "Where's the Beef?" Professor C. Robert Taylor of Auburn University's College of Agriculture shows that while corporate meatpackers boast of cost cutting and efficiency gains, the gap between the prices received by farmers for their cattle and the wholesale price of beef has widened. Though farmers are making less, meatpacking companies are not passing those savings along to retailers or consumers.

"In the last few years, in particular, the efficiency gains from consolidation and concentration in meatpacking are arguably quite modest," writes Taylor, "yet the economic power imbalance worsens and participation in production agriculture increasingly comes by invitation only, which is a loss in economic freedom."[82]

And for those supposedly tough-minded followers of Adam Smith's free-spirited capitalism with its "invisible hand," Taylor had a cautionary note: "Even Adam Smith, patron saint of CEOs, pointed out that there is an inherent instability in a market economy; namely that through natural growth of firms or through mergers and acquisitions that the market system could evolve to monopoly. He added that monopoly would lead to poor management and to higher prices for consumers."

THE HIDDEN COSTS

This economistic scuffle over efficiency sidesteps the two most important issues facing food production and consumption today: soaring costs exacted by food-industry intermediaries and the massive hidden expenses caused by agribusiness's destructive effects on society.

Data show that the primary problem with food prices lies in all the "middlemen" costs of processing, packaging, and retailing, not in inefficient farms. Without all those intermediary costs—middlemen's profits—food could be far cheaper, and healthier, for consumers, and far more profitable for farmers. Equally expensive—to individual consumers, small farmers, and the economy—are the many hidden costs that lurk behind our grocery bill. When we all pay those costs (through taxes, public medical expenses, environmental cleanups, etc.), we need to ask: is cheap, efficiently produced food really so cheap?

It would appear that vast corporate food warehouses filled with mass-produced goods offer more food to more people, at lower prices, than, say, a group of small farmers and neighborhood stores. Certainly, that's what corporate supermarkets and lower-priced chains like Foods-Co advertise. But huge agribusiness conglomerates furnish their relatively cheap food at a high cost: pushing smaller farmers off the land and onto unemployment lines; polluting the environment and rendering much land and water unusable; recruiting, exploiting, and discarding low-paid immigrant workers; ultimately, selling food that is almost always mildly toxic (due to pesticides), relatively nutrient-poor, tasteless, and frequently contaminated—and which, for all its cheapness, remains overpriced, thanks to the middlemen who process, package, and market the bulk of what we eat today.

Broad socioeconomic trends, such as the rise of two-worker households and the demise of the home-cooked meal, have changed the way food is consumed and produced, largely to the detriment of farmers. As fast-food and frozen meals become increasingly popular, farmers' crops represent an ever-smaller fraction of the final, increasingly processed product. The more agribusiness processes and packages our food, the less money farmers make. There is a direct relationship between the proliferation of corporate-processed convenience food on the one hand and the demise of independent farmers. We cannot have one without the other.

Agribusiness critic A.V. Krebs describes how General Mills added just a few cents' worth of nutrients to Wheaties and increased the price by 50 cents. "The farmer doesn't see any of that profit. When you look at how much of what the farmer actually produces is in the final product, it is minuscule," says Krebs.[83]

The 1998 USDA Commission on Small Farms came to a similar conclusion, noting the widening gap between prices for farm crops and table food and, correspondingly, farm income and food prices. "As farmers focused on producing undifferentiated raw commodities, food system profit and opportunities were shifted to the companies that process, package, and market food," the commission explained. "Consequently, from 1910 to 1990 the share of the agricultural economy received by farmers dropped from 21 to 5 percent."[84] This dwindling economic share reflects farmers' shrinking role in a corporate-run food system. Not only are farmers rapidly disappearing; the few who remain are increasingly relegated to the role of ingredient suppliers on the agribusiness assembly line. In today's broken food chain, says Krebs, "most farmers are becoming producers of raw materials for a giant food manufacturing system. They are really not in any sense producing food anymore."[85]

Despite this bleak state of affairs, there are alternatives that afford at least a glimmer of hope for a future involving small independent farmers (for more on these alternatives, see Chapter 13). Farmers' markets and organics are booming, providing smaller growers a potential economic foothold. Community supported agriculture programs, in which consumers invest in and purchase directly from farmers, are also on the rise. Some small and midsize producers have been able to survive by processing and marketing the crops they grow, thus adding their own value and increasing their income. Those small farmers who remain on the tenuous margins of American agriculture represent more than just a fast-fading pastime. They represent a model for how things could be—but only if the public and policy makers insist on it.

Part III

Recipes for Disaster

INTRODUCTION

"The San Joaquin Valley—the most prolific farm belt in America—
may be the most dangerous place in the United States to breathe."
—*The Fresno Bee,* December 2002

In California's ever-fruitful Central Valley, Big Agriculture churns out some of the most bountiful harvests on earth. Watered by vast irrigation superhighways, this dry land produces a delectable explosion of strawberries, artichokes, almonds, walnuts, peaches, nectarines, and mountains of other fruits and vegetables, along with oceans of milk and wine. Home to sprawling, dusty vineyards, orchards, and vegetable fields and increasingly massive dairy farms, the valley boasts another product one might associate with heavy industry: some of the dirtiest air in America.

Farming "creates more lung-searing air pollution than the Valley's eight highest-polluting large businesses combined,"[1] according to a December 2002 investigative series by the *Fresno Bee.* "The San Joaquin Valley—the most prolific farm belt in America—may be the most dangerous place in the United States to breathe."[2]

Scouring air pollution data, the report found that by 2005 the valley's 2.6 million cows will surpass cars as the region's top emitter of reactive organic gases, a major smog ingredient. For emissions of nitrogen oxides, the other main smog pollutant, farm machinery—including diesel-guzzling tractors, plows, combines, and irrigation pumps—will rank second, behind diesel tractor-trailers. Livestock waste and pesticides will soon account for over 25 percent of the Golden State's smog-producing organic gases, some 117 tons a day during the hot summer months.[3] Many large farms in the valley, the *Bee* reported, "easily exceed 25 tons of pollutants a year," putting them in the same league with Big Oil.

Dust kicked up from heavy farm machinery plowing over huge tracts of eroded monocrop soil regularly clouds the valley air. Farms produce an astounding 54 percent of the region's particulate matter and are "far and away the biggest contributor of particle pollution in the Valley," according to the *Bee*. In recent years, "not even Los Angeles, the nation's smog king for the last half-century, has more violations" of daily or long-term air safety standards.

These are not just technical violations or odorous nuisances. Fresno County has the state's worst childhood asthma rate, the *Bee* found, and "treatment of respiratory illness has become an industry. The air, laced with some of the nation's highest concentrations of chemical particulates and dust, is a serious health hazard. . . . Medical experts, who have connected these particles to higher death rates, fear these specks are more dangerous than ozone or smog."[4]

In May 2001, the American Lung Association released a report showing that three of the four most ozone-polluted cities in the nation are located in the San Joaquin Valley: breathing is more dangerous in Bakersfield, Fresno, and the Visalia-Tulare-Porterville area than in any other place in the nation except Los Angeles.[5]

The *Bee* report concluded, "Tons of pollutants come from large, modern agriculture, and farmers have long resisted some of the air pollution controls common for other Valley industries." Farms have been "largely excluded from state air laws since the 1940s," and only recently have legislators begun prying agriculture's long-cherished exemption from air pollution rules, a move prodded by environmentalists and strenuously resisted by the California Farm Bureau.[6]

Agriculture reps insist the industry has cooperated with and often shepherded environmental reform, often at great expense to farmers. They've invested in thousands of new, cleaner diesel machines and water pumps, oiled hundreds of dirt roads to control dust, and reduced their pesticide use by 20 percent over the last six years. "We want to reduce pollution," proclaimed Roger Isom, vice president of the California Cotton Ginners and Growers Association. "I've got a daughter with asthma. I breathe the same air."[7] Yet the California Farm Bureau opposed stricter environmental rules, and farmers did not voluntarily reduce pesticide use. Agriculture industry lobbyists have swayed state and federal officials to exempt farm machinery from new dust-control measures.[8]

Some growers seek to protect their surrounding ecologies, either for future generations or their own pocketbook. One California farmer explained, "For fifteen years, I've watered my roads. Sure, it keeps down the dust, but I do it to keep the mites off of the crops. We do things that make sense economically and environmentally."[9] But when business and incomes are down, as they are increasingly in today's corporate-dominated agriculture, cash-tight farmers hang on to old machines and hold off on oiling or watering roads.

Good intentions and reforms have not been able to head off a gathering environmental crisis in American agriculture, one that stretches far beyond individual practices and reaches into nearly every corner of society today. Farming, historically associated with ecological stewardship, has become an environmentally devastating affair. Through the nexus of corporate takeover, abiding government policies, and the use of destructive chemicals and machinery, industrial agriculture has evolved to a point that is entirely unsustainable. It has gone far beyond being merely undesirable, unpleasant, or unhealthy. It is now a threat to our future food supply, and to the environment itself—rural, suburban, and urban.

Consider:

- Pesticide toxins by the millions of tons continue to saturate the environment each year, creating severe air pollution, killing millions of birds and fish, and poisoning drinking water.
- Corporate factory farms, where thousands of animals are packed into close confinement in huge barns, produce tons of

waste annually, polluting rivers and lakes and killing millions of fish.

- Huge algae blooms, caused in good part by pesticides and other agricultural runoff from the Mississippi River, are choking the life out of the Gulf of Mexico's northern coasts.
- Fish farms in Canada and the United States, where hundreds of thousands of fish are raised in pens, pollute oceans and bays with nutrient waste.
- Decades of intensive monocrop industrial agriculture have destroyed much of the farm soil across the Midwest. This topsoil, essential to our future food supply, is eroding at an alarming pace. In the breadbasket state of Iowa, the past century of intensive farming has used up half the available topsoil, which is "being lost about 30 times faster" than it can be replaced, according to research by Cornell University's Dr. David Pimentel and Italian nutrition expert Dr. Mario Giampietro. Soil erosion and other factors such as salinization and waterlogging destroy more than two million acres of prime U.S. cropland every year.[10]
- On the semiarid Great Plains, this same large-scale farming is rapidly sucking dry the enormous Ogallala aquifer on which the whole region relies for agricultural water; experts say the aquifer could be tapped out within thirty to forty years.[11]
- Irrigation to feed huge, water-intensive farms in the California desert has dried up Owens Lake, causing massive dust storms visible from outer space.

Not all these developments are new. Pesticides have been around since the 1930s and were creating a "silent spring" by the 1950s. Large-scale irrigation has existed since Uncle Sam lured wide-eyed European immigrants in the 1880s to settle and farm the dry West. Any one of these problems, in isolation, would be serious but rectifiable. Taken together, they form an awesome total impact comparable to the effects of strip mining or oil drilling. Never before have we experienced the confluence of all these environmental attacks, which are exacerbated by monopolistic corporate power and huge reductions in the level and effectiveness of government enforcement. In the last thirty years overwhelming evidence has made clear that mass-scale industrial agriculture, though it produces an apparent horn of plenty, is simply no longer sustainable, if it ever was.

9

KILLING FIELDS: THE SPRAYING
OF AMERICA

"For the first time in the history of the world, every human being is now subjected to contact with dangerous chemicals, from the moment of conception until death. In the less than two decades of their use, the synthetic pesticides have been so thoroughly distributed throughout the animate and inanimate world that they occur virtually everywhere."[1]

—Rachel Carson, *Silent Spring* (1962)

"Common sense tells us that rather than pouring nearly 3 billion pounds of pesticides on our food—and then trying to wash them off, commission scientific studies about them, [and] worry about how risky they might be—we ought to be figuring out how to use fewer pesticides in the first place."[2]

Carol Browner, EPA administrator under
President Bill Clinton

When Rachel Carson published *Silent Spring* in 1962, the American pesticide business was in full postwar bloom. These "elixirs of death" were suddenly ubiquitous, their use growing from 124 million pounds in 1947 to 637 million by 1960, a fivefold increase.[3] Roughly 60 percent, about 375 million pounds, of these synthetic potions were applied to farmlands. Toxic residues from pesticides were indeed everywhere: in most of the major rivers and groundwater; "lodged in the bodies of fish, birds, reptiles, and domestic and wild animals"; "stored in the bodies of the vast majority of human beings"; found even in that most sacred nectar, mother's milk.[4] DDT, a now-infamous poison originally thought to be harmless after it was sprayed on soldiers and prisoners to kill lice, with no immediately obvious harm, was "so universally used that in most minds the product takes on the harmless aspect of the familiar."

The proliferation of poison in the postwar era was no coincidence. For one thing, it was emblematic of the American push for global economic preeminence, marked by new heights of corporate power, mass production and "efficiencies" at any cost. Food, and especially bounteous surpluses, was increasingly a weapon in the nation's quieter wars for geopolitical leverage and market expansions. This was illustrated most vividly by the 1954 Food for Peace program, which dumped American surpluses onto poor nations, simultaneously boosting farm prices, opening new markets, and making good friends in the war against Communism. But there was a more concrete symbiosis between war and the food industry: the new synthetic pesticides spreading across the land were in fact "a child of the Second World War," born of toxic agents originally concocted for chemical warfare. The discovery, Carson explained, "did not come by chance: insects were widely used to test chemicals as agents of death for man."[5]

Carson, a biologist with a lifelong interest in wildlife, documented the lethal human and ecological toll exacted by insecticides that were known carcinogens, others that "permeate all the tissues of a plant or animal and make them toxic," and some that could cause fatal paralysis in minute doses.[6] In one case a man spilled a 25 percent solution of chlordane (a close relative of DDT) on his skin, and "developed symptoms of poisoning within forty minutes and died before medical help could be obtained."[7] More insidiously, pesticides like DDT were absorbed into the human body and stored in organs such as the adrenal glands, the testes, and the thyroid gland. "Relatively large amounts are deposited in the liver, kidneys, and the fat of the large, protective mesenteries that enfold the intestines."[8]

Beginning in the mid-1950s, as towns and beautification-conscious (and mosquito-fearing) suburbs lavished more pesticides on parks and tree-lined streets, scientists recorded a mounting toll of dead birds.

One analysis in Wisconsin reported a robin mortality rate of more than 86 percent in sprayed areas. Laboratories in Michigan and elsewhere were overloaded with robin carcasses; one woman called a lab to report a dozen dead robins lying in her lawn. It was, truly, a silent spring, eerily devoid of the orchestra of birdsong that had always heralded winter's thaw.[9]

The heavy rain of pesticides on farms created silent streams, as well. The contamination of groundwater by pesticide-soaked soils and irrigation canals became a hidden threat to entire water systems. As Carson explained, "It is not possible to add pesticides to water anywhere without threatening the purity of water everywhere." In one case, "A sample of drinking water from an orchard area in Pennsylvania, when tested on fish in a laboratory, contained enough insecticide to kill all of the test fish in only four hours." In another instance, "Water from a stream draining sprayed cotton fields remained lethal to fishes even after it had passed through a purifying plant." In Alabama, runoff from sprayed fields killed all the fish in fifteen tributaries to the Tennessee River.[10]

But hasn't DDT long since been outlawed? Aren't those dead robins and haunting images of crop-dusting planes dumping clouds of toxins on farmworkers a nightmare from which we've long since awakened? After all, the environmental movements of the 1970s ushered in new pesticide-control laws and regulations, heightened health consciousness, and a booming organics business.

True, some of the most vicious so-called "dirty dozen" pesticides, such as DDT and chlordane, were banished (only to resurface soon thereafter in developing countries such as Mexico). Yet, with little fanfare, American industrial farming uses close to *one billion pounds* of pesticides to produce a truly toxic harvest. The food industry, particularly the biotechnology sector, benefits from a decided hush when it comes to today's silent spring. Unless you read government reports or devour the reams of studies on the environmental and human-health effects of pesticides, you might think pesticides were just an unfortunate industrial episode of the past.

Now, in the brave new high-tech world of engineered crops that, like the Monsanto potato, emit their own pesticides from the inside out, we needn't worry ourselves with outmoded notions of poisoned farmworkers, pesticide drift, and children munching on toxic apples. The U.S. Department of Agriculture and corporate biotech officials have claimed publicly that genetically modified crops are helping to cleanse the environment by reducing pesticides. Addressing the UN Food and Agriculture Organization's thirty-first annual conference in November 2001, U.S. Secretary of Agriculture Ann Veneman said the "technologies of the new century," namely biotechnology and information technology, promise to "make agriculture more environmentally sustainable."[11] The facts show otherwise.

Despite public assurances that agriculture is now kinder and gentler, the reality is that the biotech and chemical industries march hand in hand as two sides of one corporate coin. The industry's most prominent genetically modified organism (GMO), Monsanto's "Roundup Ready" soybean, was designed to withstand intensive spraying, and thus expanded sales, of the firm's highly popular, and highly toxic, herbicide Roundup. Since the 1996 introduction of Roundup Ready, the use of glyphosate, a key Roundup ingredient that studies have linked to non–Hodgkin's lymphoma, has risen. "Industry claims that the use of genetic engineering in agriculture is environmentally sound and will reduce the use of agrochemicals. But this is clearly not the case," says Sarojeni V. Rengam, executive director of the Pesticide Action Network's Asia and Pacific branch. "They will only perpetuate and possibly increase the use of herbicides, especially glyphosate, as can be seen from the U.S. example."[12]

In 2003 a report touting various economic and ecological benefits of herbicides, titled, "The Value of Herbicides in U.S. Crop Production," was funded by the GMO-friendly CropLife America and was supported by the Biotechnology Industry Organization (BIO), the GMO industry's main group. Among the facts celebrated in the report: roughly 85 percent of all croplands in America are sprayed with herbicides, generating a substantial business that will remain stable as long as agribusiness fights off new bans on chemicals and maintains the myth that biotechnology is eliminating toxins in the fields.[13] And agribusiness's chemical dependence helps petrochemical companies stay solvent.

Since the publication of *Silent Spring*, the amount of pesticides applied on our food has more than doubled, and there even were large annual increases throughout the eco-conscious 1970s. In 1997, according to industry figures, U.S. growers applied more than 985 million pounds of pesticides and herbicides to their crops.[14] One indicator of the pesticide industry's financial dependence on American agriculture is the fact that the United States accounts for more than one third of the $33.5 billion global pesticide market, the vast majority used in farming.[15] That's an $11 billion business interest for the petrochemical and biotech industries to protect.

They've protected it well, perpetually—though not always successfully—fighting and delaying new regulations to limit toxins in the fields. After a modest decline in the 1980s, the amount of pesticides used each year has increased by more than 100 million pounds since 1991. Farm pesticide use shot up by 75 million pounds in 1994 alone. Simultaneously there's been a dramatic increase in pesticide costs borne by farmers, whose spending on herbicides has more than doubled since 1980. Meanwhile the use of pesticides has declined in all other sectors. In 1964, 59 percent of all U.S. pesticides were used in agriculture; by 1997 the figure was 80 percent.[16] Each year in California alone, over 100 million pounds of highly toxic active ingredients from pesticides are released into the environment.[17]

Why has pesticide use increased even in this time of growing ecological awareness? In *Living Downstream,* biologist and cancer survivor Sandra Steingraber describes the political economy that has driven agriculture into a self-feeding cycle of poison. First, the arrival of synthetic pesticides following World War II reduced labor on the farm. Simultaneously, profits per acre began to shrivel. "Both these changes pressed farmers into managing more acres to earn a living for their families," says Steingraber. Bigger farms, and federal subsidies promoting monocrop agriculture "further increased the need for chemicals to control pests. And the use of these chemicals themselves set the stage for additional ecological changes that only more chemicals could offset."[18]

The planting of the same crop, and only one crop, year after year enables insect populations to adapt and recover, intensifying the upward chemical spiral. Steingraber describes the process: "Eradicating insects with pesticides incites more severe pest outbreaks"; through natural selection, the few insects able to repel insecticides "become the progenitors of the next generation as their more chemically sensitive compatriots are killed off"; thus pesticides ultimately encourage genetic resistance. During the postwar pesticide revolution between 1950 and 1990, the number of insect species resistant to pesticides mushroomed from fewer than 20 to more than 500.[19] In roughly the same period, the amount of crops lost due to insect damage doubled.[20]

STILL TOXIC AFTER ALL THESE YEARS

One of the more potent cases against pesticides is the extensive evidence that DDT, chlordane, and other banned toxins still contaminate our water, long after their use was discontinued. These and other pesticides "are still detected in many streams today, more than 20 years after their use in agriculture was prohibited," one study found.[21] Through the late 1980s, scientists were still finding widespread concentrations of DDT in fish in the Great Lakes in areas fed by runoff from lands intensively sprayed with the chemical in the 1960s. According to the U.S. Fish and Wildlife Service, DDT residues are still found in freshwater fish in 97 percent of sites reviewed. In other studies, scientists have found exceptionally high levels of DDT in soil sediment and aquatic life, with "potential adverse effects on fish-eating wildlife" and "possible adverse human health effects." A 2000 report by the U.S. Geological Survey stated that in at least half of all sites examined, EPA safety levels for chlordane, DDT, dieldrin, and heptachlor epoxide, all banned long ago, were exceeded.

EVERYWHERE

If it were simply a matter of waiting for these ghosts of the 1960s to fade away, we might one day be in the clear. Rivers, lakes, fish, and birds might, over time, cleanse themselves of these virulent toxins, which are known to disrupt neurological and reproductive systems and contribute to cancer. But agriculture's chemicals runneth over, continuing to flood our water and air with contamination. What is particularly startling is the degree to which pesticides have spread, like a cancer, throughout the entire environment. One might lament the plight of poisoned farmworkers, or the effects of pesticides on farming communities, and consign it to the realm of regrettable but distant problems over which they have no control. Outside of California, fewer and fewer Americans live anywhere near farms anymore. Perhaps some, unaware of well-proven sustainable alternatives, will even think these seemingly remote casualties are a fair price to pay for a plentiful, relatively cheap food supply. While no one would openly counsel reckless disregard for the health of farmworkers and their families—who pay a very dear price for our pesticide-based food system—it is all too easy to ignore and to forget. It's not in my backyard.

Unfortunately, the evidence shows clearly that pesticides are, very likely, in your backyard: in your child's schoolyard, in the stream by the park, in the river or lake in which you swim, in the water you drink. According to a 1998 analysis by the California Public Interest Research Group, nearly 4 million Californians live within half a mile of heavy applications of pesticides, a third of which are "designated by state or federal regulatory agencies as carcinogens, reproductive toxins or acute nerve poisons."[22] These chemicals contribute mightily to a toxic environment in which cancer and other lethal chronic diseases multiply, partly through the buildup in human and other organisms—the gradual increase of the toxic load.

Spring, if not silent, is no doubt quieter for the continued onslaught of pesticides on birds, which threatens ecologies and trims the ranks of endangered species. Every year agricultural pesticides alone kill an estimated 67 million birds. An array of disturbing side effects is in store for those "lucky" enough to survive a sublethal dose, including weight loss, "increased susceptibility to predation, decreased disease resistance, lack of interest in mating and defending territory, and abandonment of nestlings," stated a 1999 report by Californians for Pesticide Reform and the Pesticide Action Network.[23]

A key indicator of today's pesticide pollution epidemic lies underground, in the hidden waters that ultimately percolate up into rivers, lakes, and wells. Groundwater, the source of 50 percent of America's drinking water, is intimately interconnected with surface water: "As water seeps through the soil, it carries with it substances applied to the land, such as fertilizers and pesticides."[24] As Carson wrote in 1962, "Pollution of the groundwater is pollution of water everywhere."[25]

Since the late 1970s, studies have found more than 139 different pesticide residues in groundwater in the United States, most frequently in corn- and soybean-growing regions. One study of a Nebraska aquifer found numerous pesticides at "lifetime health advisory" levels. Atrazine, America's most-used farm pesticide, which is sprayed on cornfields, was found in 100 percent of the samples. Some pesticides were found at levels considered unsafe for aquatic life or drinking water.[26] In Iowa, a Corn Belt state where agricultural productivity "goes hand in hand with the extensive use of herbicides to control weeds," toxic chemicals are found in roughly half of the groundwater, according to the U.S. Geological Survey.[27] Another survey analysis found levels of nitrates, often present as a result of fertilizers used in agriculture, exceeded EPA drinking-water standards in 15 percent of samples collected from groundwater beneath both agricultural and urban land.[28]

Closer to home, literally, were the findings of a 1992 national pesticide survey by the EPA which discovered that 10 percent of community wells "contained detectable levels of one or more pesticides."[29] Wellwater samples gathered by the California Department of Pesticide Regulation show residues for sixteen active ingredients and breakdown products from agricultural pesticides.[30]

Groundwater pesticide concentrations, disturbing as they are, pale in comparison with the chemicals' ubiquity in surface rivers and streams. Here, the data are truly frightening.

In California, state regulators detected pesticides in 95 percent of some 100 locations in the Central Valley. More than half of these sites exceeded safe levels for aquatic life and human consumption.[31] In Kentucky, where farmers annually apply roughly 4.5 million pounds of the top five herbicides, these chemicals cropped up routinely in the state's rivers. A two-year study by the Bluegrass State's Department of Environmental Protection discovered atrazine and metolachlor, both used heavily on corn, in fully 100 percent of the twenty-six river sites they examined; another chemical, simazine, was found at 91 percent of the sites. An additional 32,000 pounds of atrazine, metolachlor, and cyanazine had migrated from croplands to surface river waters.[32]

The spread of these toxins is a serious matter that affects both environmental and public health and should concern every American, rural, suburban, or urban. Atrazine, found widely in drinking water across the Midwest and detectable on many foods, is a "possible human carcinogen," says the EPA, and studies suggest it causes ovarian cancer. It "interferes with the hormone system of mammals," and has caused tumors of the mammary glands, uterus, and ovaries of female rats.[33]

Nationwide reports are equally troubling, revealing a bath of chemicals that, though often at low levels individually, combine in a toxic soup harmful to fish and the broader freshwater ecosystem. In a ten-year study in which it examined thousands of streams across the country, the United States Geological Survey traced the proliferation of numerous agricultural pesticides: atrazine was present in 90 percent of the streams; two others, deethylatrazine and metolachlor, were in 82 percent of all samples; others were detected in at least 40 percent of the samples.[34] Still more disquieting was a 1999 USGS finding that there was an average of twenty pesticides, mostly agricultural, at each river or stream tested. Chemical concentrations of some compounds "frequently were higher than the quality standards and criteria established for these compounds in drinking water," and one or more standards for protecting aquatic life were exceeded in thirty-nine of fifty-eight sites.[35]

The overall picture is clear: Over the past thirty years, nearly half of all pesticides targeted for research by numerous studies have been found in stream sediment and in some 64 percent of edible fish, mollusks, and other freshwater aquatic life.[36]

Even when fish are not directly poisoned, they commonly ingest toxins from the plants they eat, which are often marinated in pesticide residues.[37] Scientists are increasingly observing important changes in the hormones and reproductive systems in fish and other aquatic creatures exposed to pesticides. One study of sex hormones in carp revealed that the ratio of estrogen to testosterone, in both males and females, was "significantly lower at sites with the highest pesticide concentrations."[38] Pesticides may also be a factor behind rising numbers of frog deformities, such as extra or missing limbs. In a 2002 study published in the *Proceedings of the National Academy of Sciences,* the biologist Joseph Kiesecker compared frogs in Pennsylvania ponds that had pesticide runoff with those in ponds that did not. The rate of misshapen frogs was nearly four times higher in the ponds with pesticides.[39]

Environmentalists and scientists are not the only ones raising the alarm. Fishing enthusiasts are now up in arms about the poisoning of their prey. Randy Fry, of the Recreational Fishing Alliance of Northern California, has written that pesticide pollution "seriously impacts the estuary's food-web and thereby limits the productivity of Central Valley populations of salmon, steelhead, striped bass, and sturgeon while increasing the pollutants carried by these fish. . . . These fish bioaccumulate toxic chemicals, reducing reproductive success, which affects the size and health of their populations." Fry has noted declines in fisheries throughout the Valley.[40]

SOMETHING IN THE AIR

Perhaps the greatest, yet most elusive, measure of pesticides' long reach is their ubiquitous presence in the air we breathe. "Nearly every pesticide that has been investigated has been detected in air, rain, snow, or fog across the nation at different times of year," states the USGS.[41] Given just a lazy breeze, toxins can migrate for miles: "Pesticides released in one location may be a source of human exposure or environmental contamination several hundred feet or several hundred miles away."[42]

A seemingly innocuous spraying or fumigation of a rural farmfield can drift through air currents for hours, even days, ending up as residue in nearby towns, tainting organic crops downwind (and thus endangering their "organic" status), and further polluting waterways. Diazinon, a highly volatile agent sprayed widely on nuts and stone fruit (i.e., peaches), actually increases its drift concentrations as time passes, the greatest concentrations showing up in drifts two to three days after spraying.[43] Although levels generally diminish, pesticide drift can last for weeks, sometimes months, after it's been applied on the farm, "as volatile chemicals evaporate and contaminate the air."[44]

The epicenter for the pesticide drift problem, particularly its human effects, is California, where decades of suburban sprawl have wedged burgeoning population centers up against large industrial farms. The notion of blending agriculture with suburbs would seem a fine rural-urban complement, but for the rampant use and drift of pesticides, which are exceedingly toxic, even at low levels, for children. "Pesticides in air are often invisible and odorless, but like second-hand cigarette smoke, inhaling even small amounts over time can lead to serious health problems, especially for children," says Susan Kegley, staff scientist for the San Francisco–based Pesticide Action Network.

More than 90 percent of pesticides used in California (including nonagricultural pesticides) are likely to drift, and roughly a third of those are highly toxic to humans, according to a 2003 study by Californians for Pesticide Reform, a coalition of environmental groups.[45] Using state air quality records, the study concluded that Californians "are routinely exposed to concentrations of pesticides in air that exceed levels of health concern, often by large margins." Samples of two pesticides, chlorpyrifos and metam-sodium, taken near sprayed fields, produced residues that were some 184 and 111 times the acute exposure standards set by government for a one-year-old child.[46]

DOWN THE MISSISSIPPI, TO THE GULF OF MEXICO

Hypoxia sounds like a teenage skin problem. It is really the cause of a "dead zone" in the Gulf of Mexico, stretching across several thousand square miles along the Louisiana-Texas coast.[47] Here, a massive algae bloom feasts on a steady diet of nitrogen and other nutrients that flow down the Mississippi River and into the Gulf. In summer, when the river's flow peaks, the algae spread like an oil spill and choke the Gulf's northern coasts, cutting off oxygen that supports sea life. In 1999 the zone expanded to nearly 12,500 square miles, an area greater than the size of New Jersey.[48] The oxygen-depleted water near the floor of the Gulf here contains less than two parts per million of dissolved oxygen, not enough to sustain fish and bottom-dwelling life.[49]

One of the chief culprits behind this dead zone is American agriculture and its countless tributaries of fertilizer, pesticides, and animal feces. The Mississippi River Basin, which drains an area representing about 41 percent of the contiguous United States, is home to the majority of the nation's agricultural chemicals. About 7 million metric tons of nitrogen in commercial fertilizers are applied in the Mississippi Basin each year. These substances are the precursors of nitrates, which function as nutrients for algae blooms. Algae use up available oxygen and prevent the water from becoming reoxygenated. Since the late 1950s, when pesticides and synthetic fertilizers began to dominate the agricultural scene, the annual load of nitrates poured from the Mississippi River into the Gulf has tripled.[50] According to the USGS, "The largest change in annual nitrogen input has been in fertilizer, which has increased more than six fold since the 1950s." Another key nitrate source that is on the rise is the millions of tons of factory-farm animal waste (for more on this, see the next chapter).

Mainstream industrial agriculture is deeply wedded to chemical fertilizers, which boost yields when our economic system says it counts—right now. Unfortunately, they are highly destructive to the environment and the sustainability of farming over the long term. In 1999, when Congress, the EPA, and environmental groups pressed for cuts in farm pollution to clean up the Gulf of Mexico, some agricultural trade groups raised the specter of farm closures and diminished food production. The Associated Press summed up the agribusiness argument: "Crop yields in the Midwest could shrink if federal regulators try to reduce use of fertilizers to cut pollution in the Mississippi River and in the Gulf of Mexico." Asking farmers to reduce fertilizers would be "basically asking them to go out of business," said Cliff Snyder, a spokesperson for the Potash and

Phosphate Institute. "It would have a significant economic impact if producers were required to reduce nutrient input . . . at a time when the farm economy is dismal." Despite the economic trap, some forward-looking farmers share environmentalists' concerns and are looking at ways to either use less synthetic fertilizer (which in itself is quite costly) or at least drain their fields away from rivers, perhaps into wetlands that could hold the nitrogen until it evaporates.[51]

Chemical fertilizers laden with nitrogen, ammonia, phosphorus, and trace toxic metals like cadmium are a serious environmental problem, one whose dangers may be overshadowed in the public mind by pesticides. Yet chemical fertilizers pose a huge indirect threat. Synthetic chemical fertilizers drip toxic nutrients into the water supply; these injections of excessive nutrients into the ground and water ultimately rob soil of its fertility, rendering it useless for agriculture.[52] A 1984 World Bank report concluded there is "evidence that sustained use of chemical fertilizers can decrease soil fertility."[53] American agriculture's growing reliance on this perilous crutch "has allowed farmers to abandon practices—such as crop rotation and the incorporation of plant and animal wastes into the soil—which had previously maintained soil fertility," states the report. Synthetic fertilizers also decrease moisture and important minerals and organic matter, leading to further erosion and soil loss.[54]

Another danger from chemical fertilizers is toxic metals. Studies conducted in Sweden in the early 1990s show that increased cadmium contamination of food results largely from chemical fertilizer.[55] Cadmium and other heavy metals are poisonous. So why have U.S. fertilizer manufacturers begun loading up their products with incinerator waste containing highly toxic heavy metals including lead, cadmium, and beryllium, as documented by *Seattle Times* journalist Duff Wilson?[56]

THE PETROCHEMICAL ADDICTION

It doesn't have to be this way. Agriculture can be prolific and efficient without pesticides. In fact, the miraculous march of American agriculture toward unparalleled productivity long before the postwar pesticide revolution is a compelling testimonial to the effectiveness of organic farming. Before agribusiness and its petrochemical addiction, farmers used crop rotation and diversified agriculture to replenish soils and keep pests on the run. Crop diversity supplied sustenance for farm families and livestock, and was a natural insurance policy against pest outbreaks or weather disasters. "Growing many different types of crops over the years in the same field," writes Miguel A. Altieri, an agroecology expert, "also suppressed insects, weeds, and diseases by effectively breaking the life cycles of these pests."[57]

Although many conventional growers have bravely jumped the toxic ship and transitioned into organics—a lengthy, costly process for which there is virtually no government support—the current food economy and agribusiness profits rely on farmers' continued deployment of chemical warfare in the fields. The near-perennial American surplus fueled by petrochemicals keeps farm crops cheap, not so much for consumers as for the intermediary complex of food processors, fast-food chains, and supermarkets.

It's important to note that surplus preceded pesticides. Back in the *Silent Spring* days, the United States was already stockpiling surplus, with concomitant increasing subsidy payments to farmers and growing pressures on exports and food aid. As Rachel Carson remarked then, "We are told that the enormous and expanding use of pesticides is necessary to maintain farm production." Yet, noting that American taxpayers then were paying more than $1 billion a year for surplus food storage alone, she asked pointedly, "Is our real problem not one of over-production?"[58] Excess supply is indeed a problem for farmers, who, disciplined by the market, must "get big or get out." For the petrochemical industry and its close partner, the biotech business, however, today's system of overproduction, and of toxic industrial agriculture stripped of its natural sustainability, is not a problem at all but a precondition for profit. Except that they (and their children) must also inhabit a poisoned world.

10

THE AGE OF EFFLUENTS

"Agriculture has become the biggest polluter of U.S. waterways."
—*Los Angeles Times,* December 17, 2002

THE NEW ANIMAL FARM

Out on rural Route 4 near the crumbling farm town of Unionville, Missouri, Jeri and Lynn McKinley have an up-close view of an animal farm the likes of which George Orwell surely never imagined. They live next to 80,000 pigs. Crammed in Manhattan-like density, the pigs produce a suffocating methane-gas stench that "wakes you up in the middle of the night," Lynn says. Rivers of pig waste flow onto their land, polluting the water that sustains the McKinleys' cattle.[1]

Other residents in this northern Missouri community tell of waking up nauseous on many a summer's night, blanketed by hog fumes that send them running to the bathroom to retch. Throughout the warm months, when methane concentrations settle into a thick fog, homes within miles of these animal factories reek of pig shit: curtains, carpets, and clothes are marinated in the heavy smell, which hog and cattle farmers say is far more putrid than the hog manure from traditional farming, to which they are accustomed. This is a far heavier perfume, the product of thousands of pigs stuffed in a building, their lives spent doing nothing more than standing in one place, eating, urinating, and defecating.

Rolf Christen, a cattle and grain farmer who transplanted his family from Switzerland to the north Missouri hill country in 1983, finally got sick of the nausea and realized he had to either move away or fight the offender, the agribusiness giant Premium Standard Farms

(PSF). "I can't describe how terrible the odor from the lagoon, spray-fields and barns often is," Christen was quoted as saying in a 2001 report by the Clean Water Network and the Natural Resources Defense Council. "We can't keep our windows open, and sometimes you can even smell the odor through the shut windows. . . . A year or so ago, I went on vacation to a beautiful national park; when I entered my house upon my return and smelled the terrible odor, I broke down and cried."[2]

Along with other fume-weary farmers and residents in the area, the energetic fifty-year-old Christen formed Citizens Legal Environmental Action Network, or CLEAN. In July 1997, with the hog stench no doubt in full bloom, CLEAN took PSF to court. But this was more than an odor nuisance lawsuit. They charged the hog firm with major violations of the federal Clean Water Act and Clean Air Act, alleging massive unauthorized dumping of excess hog feces onto local fields and streams.[3] PSF, which agreed to settle the case in 2001, had already been charged with dozens of violations of state water and air laws, including numerous highly damaging spills of manure waste into streams and rivers.

Premium Standard Farm's pollution troubles are not isolated incidents. Agriculture, in particular today's enormous animal factory farms, "has become the biggest polluter of U.S. waterways." Those are not the excited claims of an agribusiness critic but rather a matter-of-fact statement tucked into the middle of a December 2002 *Los Angeles Times* article.[4] Even Christine Todd Whitman, then the Environmental Protection Agency administrator, bluntly acknowledged, "Animal waste generated by concentrated feeding operations poses a real threat to the health of American waters."[5] Whitman was safely behind the curve: potent evidence of an animal waste epidemic, emanating from mostly corporate-run concentrated animal feeding operations, or CAFOs, had been literally piling up for more than a decade.

The most concrete proof was all the dead fish—tens of millions of them killed by factory farm waste spilled into rivers and streams.

Why such carnage? Animal manure is a natural fertilizer, rich in nitrogen and phosphorus, that has been used to fortify farmland soils for centuries. But factory farms produce way too much of a good thing. In hog factories, according to a May 2000 report by the Consumers Union, pigs "are raised in closed barns, often from birth. They stand on slotted floors which allow their waste to drop below into a shallow tank which is flushed out with water." The "effluent," as the industry calls it, is then pumped into manure-filled lagoons often the size of several football fields. This type of toxic reservoir is also used by many large-scale cattle and dairy operations.[6]

When sprayed on farmlands, as is often the case, or dumped or leaked onto the ground, concentrated levels of nitrogen and phosphorus enter water supplies and create algae blooms that choke off oxygen and kill aquatic life. Hog manure is also loaded with ammonia, which when leaked or sprayed concentrates in soil and turns into nitrate when exposed to oxygen. Nitrate, toxic to humans in low doses, is very soluble and travels quickly through groundwater, thus threatening drinking water.[7]

Animal factories also generate serious air pollution. In North Carolina alone, according to an analysis by the Environmental Defense Fund, hogs send over 167 million pounds of ammonia nitrogen into the atmosphere every year—more than 458,000 pounds per day. "Blown downwind, this ammonia nitrogen subsequently rains down on sensitive rivers, estuaries, and coastal waters. . . . Studies in the North Carolina region where hog factories are clustered show that the level of ammonia in rain has doubled in the past decade."[8]

An in-depth report published in August 2000 by a coalition of environmental groups, titled "Spills and Kills," stated, "The root of the pollution problem caused by large confined livestock facilities is easy to understand: too many animals—and too much manure—concentrated on too little land." Exacerbating this problem is the "use of woefully inadequate 'technologies' for manure management. Lax regulatory enforcement also contributes to a pollution problem that is an environmental and public health crisis in this country."[9]

In Missouri, where PSF's hog pollution inspired citizen lawsuits, state environmental regulators repeatedly found themselves counting dead fish floating belly-up in rivers and streams near the company's swine warehouses that dot the hilltops. A single spill from one PSF lagoon in 1995 killed as many as 173,000 fish. In another case, a faulty sewage line led to the release of some 35,000 gallons of pig waste into a north-central Missouri creek.[10]

Despite the pleadings of company officials, the state Department of Natural Resources found that PSF failed to follow waste disposal rules, applied their waste on area farm fields at rates that "frequently exceeded primitive levels," and constructed lagoons that "didn't match the Company's plans filed with the state."[11] Missouri's attorney general, Jay Nixon, who sued PSF, called it a "Jurassic Pig operation."[12] But PSF wasn't alone: a state environmental review found that all but one of Missouri's large animal feedlots had been slapped with violations.[13]

Missouri's torrent of manure is but a modest trickle when compared with North Carolina, the nation's fastest-growing hog state. Without much regulation, North Carolina's hog population ballooned between 1987 and 1997 from 2.5 million to over 10 million, even as the number of farms decreased by 75 percent.[14] Now its swine population ranks second only to that of Iowa. The epicenter of this growth was a five-county area surrounding the world's largest hog slaughterhouse, opened in Bladen County, North Carolina, by Smithfield Foods in 1991. This one massive facility turns more than 24,000 pigs into pork each day.[15]

As the business consolidated, the environmental crisis grew. In eastern North Carolina's Neuse River Basin alone, hog and dairy farms were producing 2.5 billion gallons of waste annually by 1995. The region also boasted 493,000 tons of chicken shit, 3.3 million pounds of dead chickens and turkeys, and 200 million pounds of nitrogen- and phosphorus-laden manure coursing through Neuse River Basin waterways, according to an investigation by the Raleigh *News and Observer*.[16] Agriculture accounted for 61 percent of nitrogen pollution in the basin, far exceeding treated sewage, urban runoff, and air pollution. According to Dr. Melva Okun of the University of North Carolina's School of Public Health, "Excessive nitrogen levels in the Neuse River have led to thick mats of algae floating on the surface and submerged aquatic plants that are choking the river resulting in massive fish kills. At times the plant growth is so thick that it prevents boat access to docks and marinas."[17]

Hog manure exploded onto the nation's front pages in the summer of 1995, when an excrement-filled hog lagoon in North Carolina burst its seams, sending a tidal wave of 25 million gallons of nitrate-loaded manure gushing into the New River. As environmental inspectors tallied the carnage, it became clear this was the biggest, most deadly pig-waste spill yet recorded; its volume was twice the size of the Exxon Valdez oil spill.[18] The damage was both environmental and economic: the spill killed nearly 10 million fish, and shut down 364,000 acres of coastal wetlands to shellfishing.[19] Dead fish and poisoned rivers are bad not only for the state's $1 billion fishing business but also for tourism, North Carolina's second-leading revenue source.[20] Tom Madison, a Republican and veteran of the Marines who founded an environmental group called the New River Foundation, commented, "You just can't get tourists to come down to North Carolina to watch dead fish float by."[21]

In 1999, thanks to the ravages of Hurricane Floyd, North Carolina's booming hog industry was back in the news. While killing forty-eight people and racking up more than $1 billion in property destruction, the hurricane "left a vast amount of damage that might have been averted: incalculable and continuing hazards in groundwater, wells and rivers from animal waste, mostly from giant hog farms," the *New York Times* reported. "In the hurricane, feces and urine soaked the terrain and flowed into rivers from overburdened waste pits the industry calls lagoons." In a grim testimonial to the state's burgeoning corporate animal business, more than 2 million dead turkeys, chickens and hogs piled up in Floyd's aftermath, illustrated in the press by images of giant bulldozers plowing mounds of pig carcasses into something resembling mass graves.[22]

This catastrophe was more than just an accident of nature. As the *New York Times* assessed, "Loose regulations that helped eastern North Carolina become the nation's biggest producer of turkeys and the second-biggest of hogs have come back to haunt the state's public health and its environment."[23] According to a Sierra Club report titled "Corporate Hogs at the Public Trough," state lawmakers, fattened by hog-industry campaign contributions, doled out generous tax breaks and subsidies to large factory-farm outfits owned by politically connected businessmen.

Most prominent among these is a hog magnate named Wendell Murphy, the owner of Murphy Family Farms and previously a powerful state legislator who chaired the North Carolina Senate's agriculture committee. One of his legislative accomplishments, known as Murphy's Law, exempted factory farms from local zoning laws that might hinder the size of confinement houses and lagoons, especially along delicate floodplains. Journalist David Case wrote, "For a mere million or so dollars [in campaign donations], the hog barons were able to treat the eastern part of the state as one big sewer."[24] In 1997 the state prohibited building any new hog lagoons within a floodplain; but many of these "porcine ecological time bombs," as Case described them, remain in these precarious estuary-like hot spots.[25]

A NATIONAL EPIDEMIC

Lest the biggest factory farm spills appear as isolated disasters involving a few bad players, take a look at the situation nationwide. Fish kills caused by factory farm discharges have become epidemic: in ten states, more than 1,000 documented manure spills wiped out an astounding total of 13 million fish between 1995 and 1998.[26] But even that figure pales when compared with estimates by the EPA that *Pfiesteria piscicida*, an organism in manure, has killed more than 2 billion fish in rivers, estuaries and coastal areas in the Chesapeake Bay region of North Carolina, Maryland, and Virginia.[27]

The total volume of factory-farm waste is simply staggering. There is enough manure waste produced on these factory farms each year to fill 52 million large eighteen-wheeler semi trucks. This convoy of excrement would stretch bumper-to-bumper all the way across the United States— 148 times.[28]

In 1997, the United States Senate Agriculture Committee investigated the waste crisis and came to the following conclusion: including cattle, hogs, chickens, and turkeys, the nation's animal industries produce an astounding total of 1.3 billion tons of manure waste each year. That's five tons for every U.S. citizen—130 times the amount of human waste produced per year in America.[29]

The Senate Agriculture Committee's tally:

- The Central Valley's 1,600 dairies generate more waste than a city of 21 million people.
- Some 600 million chickens raised on the ecologically fragile Delmarva Peninsula (in eastern Delaware, Maryland, and Virginia) produce over 3.2 billion pounds of raw waste a year, which contains as much nitrogen as the waste from a city of 500,000.
- A 50,000-acre swine operation in southwest Utah "designed to produce 2.5 million hogs annually" will generate "a potential waste output greater than the entire city of Los Angeles." (The facility currently churns out 1 million hogs a year.)

The Senate report concluded, "As animals become increasingly concentrated in certain regions of the country and on larger operations, there is not always enough cropland to use all of the manure as fertilizer. These increasing concentrations of manure mean that the risk of water pollution from waste spills, runoff from fields and leakage from storage facilities is also increasing."[30]

Those "risks" have become a ubiquitous reality across much of America. Researchers at the EPA have found that agricultural runoff, "including nutrients from animal waste, is the largest contributor to pollution" in 60 percent of rivers and streams that are environmentally "impaired."[31] In twenty-two states that track agricultural pollution, animal wastes have polluted some 35,000 miles of river water.[32] In 88 percent of America's 2,056 watersheds, according to research by the U.S. Geological Survey, animal-farm waste puts more nitrogen in streams than do point sources such as municipal systems and industrial plants.[33]

Testifying before Congress in 1998, two high-level EPA officials, Michael Cook and Elaine Stanley, named agriculture (both animal and crop production) as the top culprit behind water pollution nationwide. "While many diverse sources contribute to water pollution, states report that agriculture is the most widespread source of pollution in the nation's surveyed rivers," the EPA officials said, adding that agricultural pollutants "degrade aquatic life or interfere with public use" of 173,629 miles of American rivers. Agriculture, they stated, "contributes to 70 percent of all water quality problems in rivers and streams."[34]

According to the writer Michael Pollan, studies have found "elevated levels of synthetic growth hormones in feedlot wastes; these persistent chemicals eventually wind up in the waterways downstream of feedlots, where scientists have found fish exhibiting abnormal sex characteristics."[35]

Perhaps most symbolic of the animal-waste plague is the destruction wrought on the South Branch of the Potomac, known as "the nation's river." A 1998 investigative report by the *Charlestown Gazette* in West Virginia stated that poultry houses in the South Branch valley, jammed with up to 30,000 birds in a single barn, "sit just yards away from streams, with little buffer to keep runoff out of the water." Many growers in the area "simply dump their litter in uncovered piles, where rain can easily wash it into nearby creeks." Government scientists have measured unsafe levels of fecal coliform bacteria in streams flowing near poultry and cattle facilities. The South Branch—"clogged with excrement from corporate poultry farms and cattle feedlots"—was listed among the ten most endangered rivers in the United States in a 1997 report by the nonprofit group American Rivers.[36]

The hazards of the Potomac's headwaters go beyond fish kills. According to a 1996 USDA report, "a high potential exists for contraction of waterborne illnesses in the Potomac headwaters because of the widespread presence of bacteria throughout the watershed and heavy dependence on the streams for drinking water and for contact recreation." Drinking-water treatment-plant operators, meanwhile, "have noted changes in water odor and taste, primarily from nutrients in the water," the *Gazette* reported.[37]

Elsewhere, anecdotal evidence suggests factory farms may pose a real hazard to drinking water and human health. In one case documented by the Centers for Disease Control, three women living near a hog confinement farm in northeastern Indiana suffered a total of six miscarriages after drinking well water contaminated with nitrates. In 1993, after these women suffered a string of spontaneous abortions, health officials in La Grange County Indiana identified nitrate contamination from a nearby hog facility as a possible factor. These spontaneous abortions "occurred coincident with the period of nitrate exposure," the CDC stated. Although this small cluster of miscarriages may have been mere coincidence, the CDC noted, "some studies have suggested a relation between nitrate consumption and spontaneous abortions."[38]

THERE GOES THE NEIGHBORHOOD

Living next door to thousands of hogs may indeed be bad for your health. In one of the few systematic surveys to examine the public health impacts of large-scale hog operations, Steve Wing, an epidemiologist with the University of North Carolina, found that daily whiffs of hog-factory waste appear to cause sinus problems, excessive coughing, headaches, nausea, and diarrhea.[39]

Wing and his research team interviewed three communities—one near a hog-raising factory, another near a cattle facility, and a control group far away from any animal yards—about a wide range of health symptoms. People living within two miles of the hog operation suffered far more headaches, nasal and throat irritations, heartburn, vomiting, diarrhea, burning eyes, and skin rashes than the other two groups.[40]

A similar 1997 study on the health effects of a hog operation in Iowa also documented high rates of upper-respiratory and mucous-membrane problems among residents living near giant pig factory farms. "The constellation of symptoms they reported are almost identical to the kinds of symptoms that we find among workers inside the facilities," says Kendall Thu, assistant professor of anthropology at Northern Illinois University, who helped conduct the study. Epidemiologists have also documented serious health problems, such as chronic bronchitis and occupational asthma, among workers in hog confinement facilities; more than 25 percent report suffering at least one chronic respiratory ailment.[41]

According to Gary Grant, director of Concerned Citizens of Tillery, a grassroots community group in eastern North Carolina, most hog factories in the Tar Heel State "are locating in rural communities that we call the avenues of least resistance—primarily African American, aged, and poor communities." Research prepared by his group uses census data to show that North Carolina's top hog-producing counties have high African American populations and poverty rates. Thirteen of the top fifteen counties are at least 25 percent African American, and about 30 percent of their residents are at or below the poverty line.[42]

Immediately after Wing released his findings, representatives of North Carolina's booming $1.8 billion pork industry pressured him and his assistant, Susanne Wolf, to identify the community where he had done his research. The North Carolina Pork Council hired a powerhouse law firm to secure the researchers' records, including documents that could be used to identify study participants who had been guaranteed confidentiality.

"We released our study at ten a.m. and by five p.m. we had a letter from the industry's attorney," Wing said in an interview. In the letter, an industry attorney, Charles Case, raised the possibility of a defamation lawsuit. Ultimately this threat brought the hog industry some bad press and the suit was dropped. Case insisted the industry merely wanted "to see if the results are reproducible" and did not seek "any information that discloses . . . the identity of the people they interviewed."[43]

Wing said the hog industry's aggressive reaction was "unprecedented." He was informed he could be arrested if he failed to turn over correspondence, community maps, and other data that would reveal the community he studied. He asserted that the documents demanded by the industry were "not restricted to things that would be considered necessary in academia to replicate the study." Wing turned over most of the documents, but resisted the industry's "harassing" demands for detailed community maps and demographic data that would reveal what town he studied.

Apart from his interest in protecting academic freedom, Wing expressed concern about the hog industry's threatening tactics. "I have spent many years building trust and relationships with people in eastern North Carolina," he explained. "I'm obligated to protect them from having their identity revealed to an organization that has a history of intimidating people. If they want to know personal information about these communities, forget it."

Such fears may be warranted. In June 1998, attorneys for a North Carolina hog farmer threatened to sue Elsie Herring, a black woman in her nineties who had complained repeatedly to state water-quality officials about the farmer's alleged overspraying of hog manure near her home in the town of Wallace. In a letter to Herring, the farmer's attorney promised to sue her for compensatory and punitive damages and impose a restraining order if she continued filing "false and groundless" complaints. "If you violate any such restraining order," the lawyer warned, "we will ask the court to put you in prison for contempt."[44]

REGULATION AND REFORM

All the stench and lagoon spills and nausea have inspired energetic citizen movements across the country to ban factory farms.

The groundbreaking citizen lawsuit against Premium Standard Farms in Missouri, while not entirely successful, has at least forced the corporation to commit to improvements. In November 2001 PSF and its partner Continental Grain Co.—which combined to form the second-largest producer of hogs in the United States—signed a consent decree with CLEAN, the farmer-led group, to settle the case. The firms agreed to pay a $350,000 civil penalty and spend another $25 million to develop "Next Generation Technology" to control its serious pollution problem. (A similar consent decree signed with the Missouri Attorney General's office in 1999, however, had not produced much improvement by 2001. Since that agreement, PSF had been charged with fifty-three violations of state water and air protection laws, according to the Missouri Department of Natural Resources.)[45]

In addition to CLEAN's lawsuit, a rash of court actions and state legislation have met with increasing success. North Carolina, Oklahoma, Minnesota, and other states—as well as counties in Iowa and

North Dakota—have passed moratoriums prohibiting new factory hog operations with lagoons.

There have been other victories as well. In May 1998 Tyson Foods agreed to shell out $6 million, including $4 million in civil penalties, to pay for runoff pollution from their giant chicken farms on the Delmarva Peninsula. Tyson was among the firms held responsible for links between agricultural waste and microbes that caused the deaths of millions of fish in bays along the Atlantic coast. The previous summer, agricultural runoff containing *Pfiesteria piscicida* was the culprit behind the die-off of millions of fish in three rivers that flow into the Chesapeake Bay. The area's seafood business lost $43 million worth of sales.[46] But as with many other such enforcement actions, these headline-grabbing fines, though they perhaps discouraged future misdeeds, came too late.

In February 2003, after years of intensifying pressure, the EPA set out rules designed to "support a vibrant agriculture economy," while ensuring that factory farms "manage their manure properly and protect water quality."[47] For the first time, factory farms would be regulated for their air and water quality impacts, and would be required to get permits for their wastewater lagoons. But again there's a catch: most states lack environmental enforcement staff to police these agricultural factories. In California, for instance, despite boasting one of the top environmental régimes in the nation, regulators can only afford to inspect large-scale dairies once a year, and officials acknowledge that many dairies go unmonitored for years.[48]

Too often, even successful regulation comes after the misdeed, which suggests that though the system sometimes "works" (on its limited terms), it is profoundly inadequate and misguided. Economic development and corporate welfare policies lay the groundwork for ecological disasters like animal-waste floods, while chronically underfunded environmental agencies at their best race around picking up the pieces—or, in this case, feces. A handful of state bans on factory farms is a promising start, as are federal moves to limit the permissible amount of animal waste. But factory farms, much like prisons, have become a rural economic stimulus program, one that many depressed counties and even some Native American reservations cannot resist, despite all the considerable drawbacks. While some communities have bravely just said no, others still compete to offer the most lucrative welfare incentives to lure meatpacking plants and factory farms. What's needed is a federal ban on the largest-scale animal factories, and transfer of billions of dollars in corporate welfare and subsidies into new incentives promoting smaller, more sustainable animal farms.

In the meantime perhaps the Kansas farmer-troublemaker Mike Callicrate has the cleverest idea to reform factory farming. On his web site he writes: "Maybe no home should be allowed closer to the waste containment lagoon of the big corporate hog factory than that of the corporate CEO. In fact, let's take it a step further. Perhaps every farmer should be required to actually live on the land he owns and profits from, intimate with its blessings, needs and limitations, so that he might daily be reminded that he is to care for it, and invest his heart and soul in it, not just mine it."[49]

11

SLICED AND DICED: THE LABOR YOU EAT

*"Like the many immigrant workers who came to the U.S. earlier in
the century [and who] made this nation great, today's immigrant
employees are hard workers and excellent employees. Because these
workers often have few skills and little or no training, jobs in the meat
and poultry industry are an ideal place to make a start. These jobs
provide the good pay and benefits that immigrant workers seek when
they leave their homelands."*

—American Meat Institute[1]

THE KILLING LINE

From the sprawling parking lot at the end of a road named Harms Way—
named, presumably, for Premium Standard Foods' cofounder, Dennis
Harms—the pig slaughtering plant in Milan, Missouri, has an immac-
ulate, information-age look. At the closely guarded entrance checkpoint, workers punch in by slipping their hands into a fingerprint
identification machine. Next to PSF's front door, a sign reads "On the
Job Safety Begins Here."

Mexican men in cowboy hats stream through the checkpoint as if
they're crossing another border. In the parking lot a school bus idles in
the biting January cold, slowly filling with workers awaiting their
nightly ride home to disheveled company housing. Few of the men
speak much English, but many, their arms bandaged and in slings,
speak the universal language of pain.

Behind the factory's polished front, assembly lines churn 7,100 pigs
into packaged product each day. It's not America's biggest meat-packing
plant, but it is brutally efficient. José, a rib cutter, works with three others

slicing rib plates into 14,200 pieces a day—that's 3,550 cuts made per person. "It's very tough," he says. "We usually take about three seconds for each rib, sometimes ten seconds if there's a lot of fat."[2]

The workers here, mostly impoverished immigrants from Mexico and elsewhere, don't last much longer than the pigs. "Every week there are new workers, and every week others leave," says José. "In two weeks, I have seen about two hundred people leave." They leave, he says, because the company keeps speeding up the assembly line. To protect its narrow profit margins, the firm pushes the line to the human breaking point—and often beyond it.

"When we first got here, we were killing five thousand pigs in ten hours," says Maria, a fifty-four-year-old recruit from El Paso who worked at PSF for more than one year packing and lifting thirty-pound boxes of pig feet. "Now the belt is at full blast with less people working on the line. We were doing pretty well when it was ten hours. Now they are trying to kill us by killing 7,100 in eight hours."[3]

There's little time for bathroom breaks. "When they were giving us the orientations, they told us to use the bathroom before work because they would not give us permission to go during work," says José. "We have four people working, and if one went to the bathroom, we would only have three to do the same amount of work. We would be making the others work even harder."[4]

Emma, a packing-line worker from El Paso, says she was denied bathroom trips even when she had morning sickness. Her supervisor told her to vomit in the garbage can next to the assembly line, she claims.[5]

There is also little time for medical care. Sergio Rivera felt stabs of pain in his first few days at PSF. "My hand hurt, I went to the nurse, and she put me back on the line in ten minutes," he says. Shane Bankus, a chiropractor in Milan, about a mile away from the PSF plant, says such treatment (or lack of it) is the norm. The injured meat-factory workers he sees "have got to get back to work, no matter how badly it hurts, which reaggravates it," says Bankus. Adding to the injuries, most of the migrant workers "don't get any health insurance, because they want to send money home."[6]

Rivera, thirty-four, winces as he tries to close his fist. He says he cuts thousands of chunks of fat each day without receiving any training or supervision. "Your wrists, elbows, arms—everything hurts," he says. "I'm still young, and I don't want my arms to be messed up." Like Rivera, José feels pulses of pain when he closes his fist. But when asked if he visits the company doctor, José says, "No, because the company told us if we went to the company doctor we would have to pay. None of the migrants have health insurance. It costs too much money."

Without a touch of irony, the company spokesman, Charlie Arnot, claims, "We have what is recognized as one of the safest facilities in the pork industry today."[7] True or not, the remark illuminates a broader reality. This is no renegade factory. This nation's production of meat (as well as chicken, fish, and vegetables) relies on our acceptance or ignorance of a deadly norm: the abuse and discarding of workers that is as relentless as the killing line itself.

From the phenomenally perilous meatpacking "jungle" of the Midwest to equally treacherous poultry and fish processing factories in the South to punishing farmwork in fields and orchards across the United States, our entire system of relatively cheap food is structured on cheap, endlessly replaceable labor. Conditions one might think had been banished by the twentieth century are still the norm in the food business. They are largely the result of flagging union power, lack of public pressure, and the industry's dependence on and recruitment of a constant supply of economically desperate immigrant workers. At minimum, tens of thousands of food industry workers are injured on the job each year, many of them permanently crippled by carpal tunnel syndrome and other repetitive-motion ailments. So this "cheap food" comes at a high cost, both to the injured workers and to the general public, which must pick up the tab when uninsured and low-paid food company employees end up in the emergency room.

FIELDS OF PAIN

Most of us are distantly familiar with the painstaking toil of farmworkers. Documentary footage of crop-dusting planes dumping toxic clouds on farmworkers as they work the fields seems an artifact of history.

Every twenty or thirty years, someone reminds us of barbarism and misery in the fields. In 1939 there was Carey McWilliams's classic, *Factories in the Field;* in 1960 there was Edward R. Murrow's *Harvest of Shame;* then, in the 1970s, Cesar Chavez and the United Farm Workers publicized exploitation of farmworkers through grape and lettuce boycotts and protests in front of supermarkets. These momentary spotlights, particularly Chavez's epic activism and marches, broadened consciousness and spurred important reforms, such as protections for migrant farmworkers and new rules to limit crop dusting. Yet in the mostly nonunion fields and orchards, a largely immigrant and Latino labor force of 1 million to 2 million still endures poverty wages, physically punishing work, widespread pesticide-related illnesses, and Third World living conditions.[8]

The U.S. Department of Agriculture acknowledges that farmworkers "perform some of the most exhausting, back-breaking labor in the United States," and are among the lowest-paid of workers. Some "live in houses that are little better than shacks. For migrant workers, the picture is particularly grim. They are sometimes forced to sleep in their vehicles, in tents, or completely outdoors. Even when shelter is available, it is often dangerous and unsanitary."[9] A survey by the U.S. Department of Labor published in 2000 found that 61 percent of farmworkers "had incomes below the poverty level." Equally alarming, farmworkers' wages are declining when adjusted for inflation: between 1989 and 1998, their real wage declined by more than 10 percent, and they now earn less than half the average wage for nonfarm production workers.[10]

Still, after all the exposés, farmworkers and their children, who often toil at their parents' side, pick our fruits and vegetables under the frequent threat of hazardous pesticide poisoning. "Working directly with and surrounded by a toxic soup of chemicals, farm workers and their families are on the front lines of pesticide exposure," states a report by the Pesticide Action Network of North America (PANNA).[11] Nearly 500 farmworkers suffer acute pesticide poisonings each year in California alone, most often caused by aerial pesticide drift. Symptoms vary by chemical but include nausea, vomiting, dizziness, "excessive sweating," trembling, and "momentary blackout."[12]

In one case, twenty migrant farmworkers in a Colorado lettuce field reported feeling sick "moments after a crop-duster buzzed nearby, spraying a field of sweet corn with pesticides." The workers, including one pregnant woman, reportedly "gasped for breath, had pounding headaches, irritated eyes and swollen, numb tongues. Some vomited as a cloud of white chemicals settled on fields around them."[13]

In farming areas, pesticides linger long after crop-dusting planes have departed and frequently end up in workers', and farmers', homes. According to a 1998 report published by the Natural Resources Defense Council, "There is an increasingly compelling body of scientific evidence indicating that farm children face particularly significant health risks" from pesticides. One study in Iowa found the herbicide atrazine (applied to virtually all corn) "inside all the houses" of farm families, compared with just 4 percent of nonfarm homes. Another study reported, "Metabolites of organophosphate pesticides used only in agriculture were detectable in the urine of two out of every three children of agricultural workers."[14]

Numerous studies have connected these exposures to cancer. A 2001 study of cancers among 146,000 Hispanic farmworkers in California reported by Californians for Pesticide Reform "showed that, compared with the general Hispanic population, they were more likely to develop certain types of leukemia by 59%, stomach cancer by 70%, cervical cancer by 63%, and uterine cancer by 68%."[15] Other studies have revealed that both farmers and farmworkers suffer higher rates of multiple myeloma and cancers of the stomach, prostate, and testes than the general population.[16]

Despite the occasional success story of the immigrant farmworker who makes good, and "settles out" of field labor into more comfortable pursuits, the predominant reality is one of intensely vulnerable migrant laborers from Mexico and Central America who are frequently undocumented. A full 77 percent of America's farmworkers were born in Mexico, and "the arrival of large numbers of immigrants from Mexico, the Caribbean, Central America, and Southeast Asia . . . have [sic] provided farm owners and operators and labor contractors with an inexpensive, steady supply of workers."[17] The 1994 passage in California of Proposition 187, aimed at cutting off health and social services (including public education) to undocumented immigrants and their children, has exacerbated farmworkers' plight. Since Prop 187, according to a government analysis of farm worker safety, "regressive work practices have resurfaced; as undocumented workers find it harder to get work and are more desperate, those who hire them have an easier time exploiting them."[18]

THE JUNGLE, AGAIN

Meanwhile, back in the rural jungle, a new generation of immigrant meat packers toils in a grim, bloody world far away from sanitized supermarket aisles, not much unlike the world depicted in Upton Sinclair's bleak novel *The Jungle* a century ago. It is a world fraught with peril. The portion of meat packers suffering injuries and illnesses has declined markedly in recent years, yet still stands at 15 percent, making it one of the most hazardous jobs in America. Often these workers are uninsured and undocumented; they are therefore less likely to report their injuries (for lack of knowledge about their rights, and for fear of deportation) or to receive decent medical care, if any at all.[19]

The United States produced a record 82.6 billion pounds of red meat and poultry in 2001, according to the U.S. Department of Agriculture.[20] The meatpacking industry maintains its prolific output and brutal labor conditions through the time-honored tradition of importing workers. Factories are cleaner and safer today, but "it's still a deadly and dangerous industry," says Robyn Robbins, assistant director of health and safety for the United Food and Commercial Workers union.[21] Turnover is higher than ever, more than 100 percent in some plants, owing to grueling conditions and the precarious employment of undocumented workers.

In this high-volume, low-profit-margin industry, faster lines are the primary path to profits, explains Mark Grey, associate professor of anthropology at the University of Northern Iowa who has studied meatpacking communities for more than a decade.[22] "That's how they make money—jamming lots and lots of animals through the plant—

and that's where your cumulative trauma problems come in." Nearly 12 percent of meat packers succumb to cumulative trauma injuries, such as carpal tunnel syndrome and tendonitis, according to the Bureau of Labor Statistics.[23] This is thirty times the average rate for all industries.

In a macabre, medieval scene, workers hack frantically at fast-moving carcasses while standing in pools of blood, fat, and chunks of abscess meat. Their knives, dulled from stabbing meat every three seconds or so, sometimes slice into the wrong piece of flesh, their own, or that of their coworker standing just a couple of feet away. Back injuries are common from slipping on the greasy floors. But the biggest risk comes from the mundane, steady, ceaseless cutting—of heads, necks, knuckles, legs, organs, stomachs, cutting a mind-numbing parade of animal parts flying down the line at dizzying speeds: thousands of cuts per day, about three seconds per piece of meat.

A BLUR OF CHICKENS

The dead chicken may be the fastest animal in North America, even speedier than the slaughtered pig or cow, as it moves from workers called "catchers" to "hangers" to those laboring in "evisc" (short for evisceration). The processing of roughly 8 billion chickens each year to meet the growing demand for cheap, versatile meals and slimmer hips rests on low wages and treacherous speed.

The typical poultry factory can turn 144,000 birds into packages of "RTC" ("ready-to-cook") chicken in a single eight-hour shift.[24] In addition to exploiting hyperstressed workers, the modern abattoir accomplishes this amazing feat with advanced technology such as the model 7660 killing machine, the model 7682-180 eviscerator, and the model 401-180 neck breaker.

The vaguely pornographic imagery and language used to advertise these execution devices (viewable at www.chickenequipment.com and similar web sites) features an unsettling blend of medieval brutality and modern efficiency. "To get the finished product you want, you must get the proper kill," begins an ad for the killing machine. "Feather problems, cadavers, red wing tips, poorly bled out parts and birds can all relate to your killer. Years of experience in the blood tunnel have produced this killer." Meanwhile, the neck breaker model 401-180 "produces the highest percentages with minimum bird damage. Works well on Cornish, small, and large broilers, and even heavy hens," a company advertisement boasts. "Downgrades and wing damage are not a problem with this machine. You can also expect to reduce bag breakage and improve off center KFC cuts due to long necks with this neck breaker." The eviscerator promises "low contamination, low gall breakage, combined with high lung removal rates."[25]

But this stainless-steel labor-saving technology doesn't eliminate all the dirty work, and there is plenty of physical punishment left over for harried workers, who must try to keep up with the blurry pace set by the machines.

Amid clouds of ammonia and fecal matter carrying *Salmonella* and other harmful bacteria, immigrant chicken catchers wade into 100-degree holding pens bustling with frantic, desperate birds. Dodging sharp beaks and claws, they grasp the birds by their feet and hurl them into cages destined for the processing plant. They catch about 8,000 per day. Many catchers fall prey to cuts, eye infections, and respiratory ailments, not to mention being urinated on by the terrified chickens. At the factory, "hangers" attach the chickens' feet into metal shackles so that a razor-sharp wire just down the line can lop off the dangling heads efficiently. At 50 birds per minute and 20,000 per day, it's not surprising that rotator cuff and other repetitive-motion injuries are widespread among hangers.[26]

After being scalded in huge vats to enable rapid plucking, the birds blast down the line to the evisceration section. Most plants now gut chickens by machine, but some workers perform "evisc" by hand, twisting and pulling the innards from thirty-five or more chickens a minute. In some plants, workers make up to 100 evisceration cuts a minute. Further down the line, workers in "debone" stand shoulder-to-shoulder, slicing and chopping their way through joints, tendons, and tough gristle to produce the most popular chicken part on the market, boneless chicken breasts. The process here "slows" to twenty or thirty hard twisting motions a minute. Scissors and knives quickly dull, and workers routinely lacerate themselves or their neighbors when blades slip off the slimy carcasses. Disabling carpal tunnel syndrome and other repetitive-stress disorders are common.[27]

As annual chicken consumption has soared from forty pounds per person in 1970 to seventy-five pounds today, the government has allowed industry to crank up assembly-line speeds. In a meticulously researched 1995 essay for the *Case Western Reserve Law Review,* Marc Linder, an Iowa-based attorney, details the poultry industry's effective campaign to pressure the USDA to authorize faster lines. The mere fact that the USDA is responsible for setting line speeds should be disconcerting, as the agency's mission is to increase food production, not to protect workers' safety. In 1979, late in the Carter administration, the official government-approved chicken factory speed limit stood at an already blinding seventy birds per minute. In 1984 President Reagan's business-friendly USDA "fulfilled its promise" to the powerful chicken industry by launching the so-called New Line Speed inspection system, which pushed the pace beyond seventy.

By the mid-1990s, that "new line speed" was an astounding ninety-one chickens a minute. An item in the *Federal Register,* quoted by Linder, reveals just how overtly the industry's productivity push had become a priority of government: "The driving force behind FSIS's [the USDA's Food Safety Inspection Service] program changes from the 1970s on was the need to keep up with industry's expansion and its productivity gains, including the incorporation of automation in the slaughter process that increased the rate at which carcasses could move through the slaughter facility. Automation has had a particularly great impact on poultry operations, where inspectors have had to face faster and faster line speeds, which today can be as high as 91 birds per minute."[28]

During this intense speedup, says Linder, the incidence of repetitive stress ailments skyrocketed. "Between 1980 and 1993, repetitive trauma disorders, as a proportion of all newly reported occupational illnesses, rose from 18% to 60%. The poultry processing industry recorded the second-highest incidence of repetitive trauma disorders in 1990—696 per 10,000 full-time workers. The highest incidence was recorded in the related meat packing industry." Government meat inspectors were not immune: "The USDA's admission that it sets the workload of its own employees 'at the limit' suggests that the USDA never orients its line-speed decisions towards workers' needs for longer lives, less plagued by physical pain and disability."[29]

There were parallel speedups in meatpacking. One plant in Sioux Falls, South Dakota, ramped up its hog-killing line from 640 per hour in the late 1960s to 1,065 in 1986—with no increase in workers.[30] As a result of this intensifying production, and of fading union power, over the past twenty-five years poultry-processing and meat-packing towns across the Midwest, and impoverished villages in Mexico and Central America, are littered with broken limbs. Historian Roger Horowitz cites industry data showing that occupational illness rates in meatpacking increased by a startling 264 percent between 1980 and 1988.[31]

ALL USED UP

Forty-year-old Connie Mayer, a lifelong resident of Unionville, Missouri, displays a long purple streak running down her arm to her mangled left hand—the result, she says, of cutting pig ears for PSF. It took just six weeks of holding and cutting apart pig temples before she suffered severe nerve damage. Each new head would slam into her hand before she could finish cutting the previous head.[32]

Mayer and her doctor insisted she needed surgery, she says, but her supervisors said she had to keep working. Soon PSF "fired the doctor who wanted to do my surgery," says Mayer. Then, when Mayer pursued workers' compensation to finance surgery on her arm, PSF supervisors harassed and attacked her, she alleges in a separate lawsuit, filed in 1997. First, the firm knowingly assigned her to jobs that "violated the medical restrictions that had been placed upon her by her treating physician," the suit says. Then, according to the complaint, Mayer's supervisors assigned her to "one of the most detested jobs" in the plants, sorting pig livers, spleens, and lungs. In April 1995, while Mayer sifted organs, "supervisory personnel deliberately caused to be dumped on [Mayer's] person pig kidneys, pig urine, pig blood, and other pig carcass fluids."

"When you stop making them money, they want you gone," she says. Company executives would not comment on her lawsuit.

The case of Connie Mayer may sound extraordinary, but actually it's not so unusual. There are plenty more cases much like hers, especially from the growing ranks of highly vulnerable immigrant workers who, induced by the industry, flock to the Midwest to pursue their own little slice of the American dream.

To support his wife and eleven children, Abel Merino left his ranch in the southern Mexican state of Michoacán in 1997 to work at PSF's Missouri slaughterhouse. Merino's attorney, Francisco Dominguez of Texas Rural Legal Aid, says that Merino was brought to Premium by a labor recruiter in El Paso—a fly-by-night operation called Ag-Labor Services, Inc., which charges the company $200 for each worker he delivers.[33]

On April 14, 1997, during his twelve-hour nightly shift cleaning the assembly line, Merino, forty-eight, tried to remove a chunk of meat that was stuck in a machine. But the line was still moving (supervisors told him the line could never stop, he says), and the motor pulled him in, crushing his arm and breaking a bone that ripped through the skin. He was caught in the machine for more than five minutes before he freed himself. He was taken to the emergency room and underwent surgery the next day. Surgeons took flesh from his leg to graft onto his arm.

Then, Merino charges in a lawsuit filed with five other migrant workers, the company pressured him to return to work despite his crippling injury. About a month after the accident, Merino testified in depositions, PSF "wanted me to go back. . . . But I told them that I couldn't because my hand was still bleeding and my leg was still bleeding and I would get dizzy. They told me that if I didn't go back to work, then there wouldn't be any money. . . . And I didn't have anything to eat."

Dominguez says PSF "harassed [Merino] to go back to work. They said, 'If you don't work, we don't pay you. And if we don't pay you, you are going to have to move out of the company housing.'"

Olivia Rascón, another plaintiff in the case, says that after six months of cutting meat with a round electric wizard knife, "my hands were completely closed" and in constant pain. But, she says, "the company said I had to keep working. . . . The doctor [employed by the company] said I was fine," and gave her wooden splints to pry open her fingers. For the next four months, she worked in the factory laundry room, but the pain persisted. "They told me I shouldn't complain or I might lose my job," she claims. Then, in March 1998, PSF fired her.

The company spokesman, Charlie Arnot, assures, somewhat guardedly, that harassing injured workers "certainly is not the policy, nor do I believe it is the practice of that facility. We have a dedicated safety and wellness staff . . . that work very diligently to make sure people receive the therapy they need in order to return to work when they are ready."[34]

FROM AMERICAN DREAM TO AMERICAN NIGHTMARE

How did things get so bad? Meatpacking was once a solid, if gritty, step toward the American middle-class dream. Before the union upheaval of the mid-1980s, symbolized most potently by labor's crushing defeat in a strike against the Hormel meatpacking company in Minnesota, unionized workers reported earning upwards of $30,000 a year.[35] Now the mostly nonunion industry relies on destitute migrants for whom $6 to $9 an hour seems like a godsend. Meat packers' real wages have declined by $5.74 per hour since 1981 (in 1998 dollars), according to Bureau of Labor Statistics data.[36] Employee turnover often runs more than 100 percent per year. Yet the people keep coming, and the conditions and turnover persist, largely the result of weakened unions and a virtually limitless reserve supply of immigrant laborers.[37]

The story of meatpacking workers' demise is the story of American economic restructuring and the 1980s shift to a nonunion economy increasingly dependent on immigrants to fill its bottom rungs. Responding to the economic crisis of the 1970s, in which corporate profits dwindled amid heightened global competition, U.S. companies redoubled their efforts to control labor and its costs.[38] The historian Peter Rachleff describes how, "as economic growth slowed, profitability declined, and international competition intensified, corporate challenges to unions increased."[39]

After sharing in the American affluence of the 1950s and 1960s, workers and unions were disciplined by an epidemic of plant closures and relocations, the severe recession of the early eighties, and the Reagan administration's full-fledged assault on organized labor. Meatpacking workers were exceptionally hard hit as dominant new firms like Iowa Beef Processors (IBP, now owned by Tyson Foods), starting in the early seventies, pulled the industry away from its heavily unionized urban base.

IBP was in the vanguard of the meatpacking industry as it steadily eviscerated union power and membership, and eliminated hard-fought wage gains, by transforming the labor process and workforce. One innovation that was key to IBP's rise and meatpacking workers' fall was boxed beef: mass-produced standardized prepackaged beef cuts ready for consumers. Previously, beef had been dressed in wholesaler and supermarket warehouses, but now packing companies took over this phase of production. This eliminated high-skilled workers and trimmed labor costs for wholesalers and retailers. A 1987 survey found that boxed beef's chief appeal to retailers was its reduced labor requirements.[40] New assembly-line technology "eliminated key skilled jobs in the initial slaughtering process and significantly reduced the need for labor in the processing of meat,"[41] according to Roger Horowitz.

In a geographic transformation begun in the 1950s and completed by the 1970s, packing firms relocated to the rural High Plains, moving slaughterhouses closer to feedlots and escaping the unions and higher wages of Chicago, Kansas City, and other midwestern cities.[42] The industry's migration was often strategic: IBP and others set up their sprawling new digs primarily in "right-to-work" states such as Iowa, Kansas, Nebraska, and Texas, which had outlawed union-only shops.[43] "Although relocating plants from city to countryside cut shipping and utility expenditures," explains Horowitz, "the most significant contribution to company profits came from reduced labor costs." In these new isolated plants, low-wage workforces had few options; huge distances between packing plants "further fragmented [the] packinghouse labor force and hindered the exercise of union power or the unionization of unorganized plants."[44]

As IBP, Excel, and ConAgra transformed the business and consolidated their control, the once-mighty and vigorous United Packinghouse

Workers of America, which had become a symbol of racially integrated unionism and had built up strong national labor agreements, began to crumble. The new Big Three, which by 1990 produced more than 75 percent of America's boxed beef, "shattered industrial unionism by eliminating the firms in which [unions] had been strong, the workers who were its base, and the labor organization that was its instrument."[45]

The industry's geographic shift served a parallel purpose, explains Horowitz, "eliminating the settled communities that had supported unionism since the 1930s and introducing new groups of workers, migrants from rural areas in America and immigrants from Asia and Latin America."[46] By the late 1980s these refugees, many of them "products of failed American foreign policy maneuvers and plundered economies," were flocking to rural Midwestern packing towns to do increasingly dangerous, low-paid work that most white Americans simply will not do.[47]

AN ENDLESS RESERVE ARMY

After just five days of cutting pig fat in northern Missouri, Sergio Rivera was ready to go home. So, too, was his sixty-year-old father, who had joined him on the Greyhound bus from El Paso in a desperate sojourn for work. They were broke in Missouri—financially and physically—and as eager to leave as they had ever been to cut up pigs for Premium Standard Foods in Green City, Missouri.

In 1999, with a $150 loan and assurances of decent paying jobs and clean housing from PSF, Rivera and his father ventured here with twenty-four other work-hungry souls from the Texas-Mexico border area. By the end of the first week, just thirteen remained. "People come here from all over—Mexico, Central America, El Paso—they stay for one or two weeks and then leave," says the elder Rivera. "The line moves too fast," he says, clutching a heavily bandaged arm that he says he injured during his weeklong stint cutting pig legs.[48]

Injured and indebted to the company, the Riveras decided to head back south to El Paso or Dallas—anywhere but the tiny, far-flung town of Green City, which Sergio bitterly calls Lonely City.

Many, like Sergio's housemate Luis, were fleeing desperate poverty when they came north and were hoping to pay off debts. "I was three months behind on my rent, and I needed a job," says Luis, a former factory worker who got his job as a neck cutter for PSF at the El Paso unemployment office. "The job is hard, but I'm making a living and paying my rent. My family matters more than my health right now."

Over a dinner of chicken mole with jalapeño peppers, Luis explains why he and so many others travel so far to do America's most dangerous work: "We are up here because of NAFTA. There are no good-paying jobs in El Paso. They've all gone across the border where they can pay you five dollars a day."

Luis and Sergio are part of a mass migration from Central America, Mexico, and border states to the packing towns of the U.S. interior. It is all part of a vast immigrant labor conveyor belt, driven by aggressive recruitment by the meatpacking and poultry industries and fly-by-night employment agencies, that continually ships fresh workers north and used-up workers south.

Even meatpacking executives acknowledge the parallel to a previous century. Says one: "I don't think it's a good deal different from when you saw a lot of immigrant labor coming to the East Coast in the 1920s." Today, instead of labor-stuffed steamships from Europe, it's Greyhound buses and pickup trucks toting migrants from South Texas, Mexico, and Central America, says anthropologist Mark Grey.

The industry isn't shy about the fact that it "relies heavily on workers from other countries who have recently come to the U.S. to make a new life," as the American Meat Institute puts it.[49] In some areas nearly half the meatpacking and poultry work force are noncitizens, according to industry surveys. The AMI puts a sunny spin on the trend: "Because these workers often have few skills and little or no training, jobs in the meat and poultry industry are an ideal place to make a start. These jobs provide the good pay and benefits that immigrant workers seek when they leave their homelands."[50]

According to Grey, by the 1990s it had become common industry practice to import workers through border-state labor recruiters who, for a fee, deliver busloads of Mexicans to plants throughout the Midwest. Many are undocumented, and prey to all manner of workplace abuse and widespread racist scapegoating. In 1998 the General Accounting Office found that 25 percent of meatpacking workers in Nebraska and Iowa were undocumented immigrants.[51]

The situation is similar in poultry: a 1998 survey by the U.S. Department of Labor showed that 30 percent of chicken processors conduct long-distance recruitment. "Only eight percent of these provided disclosure at the time of recruitment," investigators found, and "some contractors provide unsafe transportation and housing." Prophetically, the survey predicted that the companies could run into "potential problems" with violations of migrant labor law.[52]

Bill Roenigk, the vice president of the National Chicken Council, confirms that about 50 percent of the industry's 245,000 workers are immigrants.[53] Some companies, like IBP, run furtive yet busy recruiting operations in small Mexican towns that draw workers north by the thousands. Reporting from the town of Fresnillo, in central Mexico, the *Wall Street Journal* wrote: "Tucked away in an alcove in the back of a small pharmacy here is one of the busier recruiting outlets for IBP, Inc., the largest meatpacking company in the U.S." In less than one year some 1,500 Mexicans ventured north to IBP plants, "according to the bus company that IBP pays to transport them."[54]

Numerous union officials and a former Tyson worker, Jason Wolfe, say the company advertises for Mexican workers to come to its Midwestern plants and even transports them to Missouri and elsewhere. "Sometimes [Tyson's recruiters] get a freezer truck and load them up and take them up here," says Wolfe, who talked with Mexican workers at the plant.[55]

Ed Nicholson, a Tyson spokesman, denies that the firm recruits or imports Mexican workers: "We have not transported anyone across the border." Instead, Tyson offers bonuses for employees who bring in new workers, he says. "Some of the literature got passed along to people down there [in Mexico], and it gave the impression that we were advertising down there. The word gets out that jobs are available and people show up from Mexico, Texas, or Guatemala."[56]

But in December 2001, after a two-and-a-half-year investigation, the U.S. Department of Justice indicted Tyson Foods, charging that the company and six of its employees in particular conspired "to smuggle illegal immigrants into the United States to work at its poultry plants." The thirty-six-count lawsuit charged that fifteen plants in nine states were involved and that Tyson "cultivated a corporate culture in which the hiring of illegal alien workers was condoned in order to meet production goals and cut costs to maximize profits." Company officials allegedly "requested delivery of illegal aliens to work at Tyson plants in the United States and aided and abetted them in obtaining false documents," press accounts said. Tyson steadfastly denied any company-wide conspiracy, but terminated four managers named in the indictment. One former Tyson employee, forty-three-year-old Amador Anchondo-Rascon, himself an immigrant from Mexico, pled guilty, "admitting he smuggled illegal immigrants into the country to work for the poultry giant and provided them with fraudulent identification," according to the Associated Press. In March 2003, however, a federal jury acquitted Tyson Foods of conspiring to transport undocumented workers to its U.S. factories.[57]

THE RETURN OF THE COMPANY TOWN

At 4:30 each morning in small towns across the Midwest, migrant workers stumble through the cold dark onto company buses bound for the killing line. Thirteen hours later the bus picks them up at the factory and drops them off at their temporary homes, tiny motel rooms and dilapidated houses rented from the company—which sometimes even makes a profit. By 8:30 p.m. workers are sleeping off tendonitis and other aches and pains on wooden pallets, stained mattresses, or shag-rug floors.

Company towns, that infamous relic of the nineteenth century, are "back and booming," as a *Washington Post* headline announced in 1998. As the industry recruits immigrants with meager financial resources to staff its factories, many firms are crowding these workers into company housing and deducting rent from their paychecks. In some cases, "employer-assisted housing" is a clean and comfortable (if small) step up from the notorious dilapidated shacks that farmworkers commonly call home. In one especially luxurious—and quite rare—example described by the *Post*, some migrant workers for ConAgra-owned Butterball Turkey Co. rent a "dormitory-style apartment equipped with cable television, a full kitchen, housekeeping services, washer, dryer and picnic area." Most migrant meat and poultry workers do not have it so good. Even the best of these cozy arrangements tether already vulnerable meat-packing workers to the company, and, as the *Post* reported, "Losing a job can lead to eviction."[58] Often, workers are crammed into grim apartments that are no more desirable than their jobs on the killing line.

In Milan, Missouri, a Latino migrant worker from El Paso slumps down basement steps into the one-bedroom apartment he shares with two other PSF workers. The fake wood panel walls are cracked and torn. A tiny shower stall stands at the head of one bed, next to a hot plate and a small icebox. Rusty water drips from the ceiling into a pot on another bed.

Workers share sparsely furnished, overcrowded rooms. Many do not even have beds to sleep on. Ed Gilber, a local resident, recalls that PSF "brought [workers] up here and unloaded them and they didn't have nothing"—no beds, blankets, or furniture. "If they are going to bring them up here, they ought to be made to take care of them."[59]

PSF's Arnot says the company isn't responsible for substandard or overcrowded housing. "We intentionally put no more than two people to a bedroom," he says, "but once people are in the houses, they make their own living arrangements. . . . We provide a lot of furnishings for those folks when they first come up. Sometimes those things stay in the house, sometimes they don't." He insists, "None of the housing that we have operates at a profit." But in at least one case, the company overcharges for the shelter it rents to workers. One area landlord, Harry Frost, states that he rents a four-bedroom house to the company for about $400 a month—but PSF charges the six workers who live in the house $160 each, for a total of $960, meaning a $560 profit for the company.[60]

Rent is just one of countless deductions taken from each week's paycheck. A PSF memorandum distributed to recruits in Los Angeles in 1998 shows that an employee making $380 a week may take home as little as $175. The company tab includes $50 per week during the first few weeks to repay loans for Greyhound tickets and travel money; $40 per week for company housing; $10 per week for rides to work in the company bus; and $30 to $40 each week for meals in the company cafeteria. The workers pay for their meals by placing their hands in a fingerprint identification register.[61]

That's up to $140 taken out of each week's pay—before taxes. "There were many people who started at $7.25 an hour who for the first four weeks did not take home more than $100 a week because of all the paybacks that were being taken out," says the Reverend Velda Bell of the United Methodist Church in nearby Trenton. Reverend Bell has helped some workers settle in.

Worker pay stubs reveal yet more costs. José, who was recruited by PSF in the Los Angeles unemployment office, shows me his deduction-trimmed paycheck. Included are a $29 charge for "supplies"—a knife sharpener, essential to his work—and about $30 a pair for nonslip rubber boots, vital for navigating meat-factory floors slick with blood and fat. Surveys by the United Food and Commercial Workers show that many meatpacking employees are docked hundreds of dollars a year for everything from steel-mesh gloves to eye goggles, earplugs, and hair nets. The union found that poultry and meatpacking companies often overcharge their workers for protective gear. For instance, latex gloves typically cost workers $1.45 a pair, while companies pay just twelve cents to suppliers. Protective arm sleeves can cost workers up to five times what companies pay.[62]

José has found one way to save money. "I don't eat very much [at the company cafeteria] because it's very expensive and I wouldn't have any money left," he says. Workers are not allowed to bring their own food for lunch, says Maria, a former PSF worker. "I have seen people try to take their own food, and if they get caught they get fired or suspended."

DODGING BULLETS: "REDNECKS" AND INS AGENTS

On a cold winter night, the scratched windows of the Milan laundromat are fogged up, and you can hear men inside talking quietly in Spanish. They're not doing laundry. This is their hangout, where they share pizza, beer, and stories about working and living in an alien land.

Regulo Luhan, who worked in the company's cold room for three months before succumbing to a leg circulation ailment, says there is "antipathy toward Mexicans and blacks" in the town. To demonstrate this, he points out graffiti on the laundry bathroom walls: "Remember the Alamo"; "Hispanics Causing Panic"; "Niggers and Mexicans Need to Leave My Country, Our Girls, Our Women Alone or Die." At the ConAgra chicken plant in Milan, where Luhan now works, "Some workers put up Nazi signs saying they are the pure race, and put up a sign about the Ku Klux Klan."

Arnold, an El Pasoan who examined hog carcasses for PSF, says that when he and a friend were attacked by several white men wielding knives, a police officer on the scene "sat and watched, didn't do nothing. He turned a blind eye. He told us this is redneck country."[63]

The influx of immigrant Latinos to serve the industry's labor demands has roiled passions in many previously homogeneously white packing and poultry towns across the Midwest and South. While some communities have adjusted admirably to the newcomers, welcoming immigrant families into their neighborhoods and schools, others have lashed out. In Rogers, Arkansas, home to a Tyson Foods chicken-processing factory and its many immigrant workers, City Councilor Steve Womack, a former National Guard lieutenant colonel, rode anti-immigrant nativism to victory in the town's 1998 mayoral election. His top campaign plank: a "zero tolerance" policy for "illegal" immigrants, as a means of fighting crime. Incumbent mayor John Sampier, who advocated a more welcoming integration approach, lost handily despite ample backing from Tyson Foods and the poultry industry.[64]

Cops and thugs, though fearsome, pale in comparison to immigrants' top nemesis: the Immigration and Naturalization Service. Threats of INS sweeps and deportation loom over the precarious lives of undocumented workers, enforcing a generally silent, pliable labor force.

In fact, the INS often functions as an industry-friendly regulator of labor supply. Although the politics of immigration require sharp rhetoric about cracking down on "illegals" everywhere, the economics of industry require a constant supply of workers. The food industry has a long history of both advocating and opposing INS crackdowns, depending on its

seasonal labor needs and labor relations. As these competing imperatives came to a head across the Midwest in the 1990s, the meat industry
entered a "partnership" with the INS called the Employment Verification Pilot, a program ensuring that meatpacking and poultry companies' payrolls would remain both "legal" and fully staffed. Whether or
not they were complicit in hiring undocumented workers, companies
would get advance notice of INS sweeps, giving them ample time to recruit replacements—who typically might also be undocumented.

It was a win-win: the INS could have its victorious sweeps, and
companies could keep the killing line going, and wash their hands
of legal problems. The American Meat Institute placidly describes
the deal:

> Because the meat and poultry industry has cultivated a spirit of
> cooperation with the INS, disruptions to the workforce are being
> reduced. When the INS has reason to believe that companies have
> hired workers who presented documents that appeared legitimate
> but were false, the agency increasingly has contacted the compa-
> nies in advance to alert them that INS officials want to visit the
> plant, investigate the workers and possibly detain them. In alerting
> company officials ahead of time, plants can have replacement
> workers available and avoid production stoppages, which are so
> costly in an industry that relies on efficient production.[65]

DON'T GET TOO COMFORTABLE

Some residents and church groups have welcomed the workers and
tried to help them out socially and economically. Churches have organized furniture and clothing donations and pro bono legal and accounting advice for the workers, and persuaded some area grocery
stores to carry Mexican products and teach their employees basic Spanish. Many rural school districts throughout the Midwest have added
English as a second language to their curriculum.

But while these efforts may help ease the workers' alienation, hazardous working conditions and geographic isolation ensure that most

of these workers view Packingtown, USA, as a gritty pit stop on the way, they hope, to something better.

Company spokesman Arnot insists that PSF wants to "reduce turnover and to have a much more stable work force." He says the company plans to finance starter-home developments and encourage workers to settle and become "long-term residents in the community."

But Mark Grey and other critics, including officials of the United Food and Commercial Workers International Union (UFCW), contend that meatpacking firms actually prefer short-term, destabilized workers so they can cut injury costs and beat back union organizing efforts. A migrant and immigrant workforce, says Grey, also enables companies to "pass along a lot of costs," such as unemployment and disability payments, to the workers' home country. Jerry Helmick, an official of the Kansas City local of the UFCW, says that PSF successfully derailed a 1997 attempt to organize the plant with a massive campaign to recruit migrant workers. Just as the union secured majority support in the plant, PSF brought in its first wave of recruited workers; their precarious position made them reluctant to join the fight.[66]

"Instead of dealing with the wages, working conditions, and injury rates, [meatpacking firms] are just trying to find new ways to cycle through new workers," says Grey. "Ultimately, their concern is not about a stable workforce but maintaining a transient workforce." And migrant they are. José the rib cutter, like the Riveras, planned to leave in search of better work.

THE MIGRANT LABOR TREADMILL

In 1995, when Michelle Galvan heard the announcement on the radio of job openings at a Case Farms poultry plant in Winesburg, Ohio, she rushed to meet with recruiters in her hometown—McAllen, in southwestern Texas. The deal sounded good: she would pack boneless chicken breasts for $5.50 an hour, and the company would provide free furnished housing, with no more than two or three roommates, and transportation. Galvan, along with other hopeful unemployed residents of McAllen, soon set out for Winesburg, Ohio, namesake of Sherwood

Anderson's famous 1919 novel of Midwest Americana—and now home to a Case Farms chicken-processing factory.[67]

After traveling 2,000 frigid miles in a flatbed pickup truck in January 1996, Galvan was put in an unfurnished one-bedroom apartment along with seventeen roommates. She was cold and trapped, with no car or blankets. The Case Farms recruiter, she says, had promised to take care of everything: "I really believed they were going to have apartments, I was really excited. It was my first time out of Texas." Then, she alleges, the company took rent and transportation fees out of her paycheck.

After three days in the cramped apartment, people in town began to notice the newcomers and gave them a rough welcome—hurling rocks through the windows and writing, "Go back Mexicans, you don't belong here" on the outside walls. Inside the factory, "they were rushing you all the time, like animals. Sometimes they would tell you not to look at the line too much because you will get dizzy and fall because the line is going so fast," says Galvan. When the car she and others rode to work broke down, she was fired. "I felt like it was a trap, they were trying to get you up there with the least things that you can rely on, so you get stuck."[68]

But Galvan and twenty-three coworkers lured to the plant sued Case Farms for making false promises and providing "squalid" and overcrowded living quarters. They were part of a groundbreaking 1999 lawsuit (*Castillo v. Case Farms*) that sought, for the first time, to apply migrant farmworker protections to the growing numbers of workers recruited from Texas, California, and other states to work in poultry-processing factories in the Midwest and South. In a precedent-setting decision that held wide ramifications for the poultry industry, U.S. District Court Judge William Wayne Justice said the farmworker protection laws also cover migratory poultry laborers, whose job tenure has become so brief it is considered seasonal. Under these laws, meat-packing and poultry processing firms using migrant workers would be held liable for, among other things, providing substandard housing and making false promises when recruiting workers.[69]

Judge Justice reasoned that Case Farms' rapid worker turnover in effect rendered the workers temporary and seasonal: the recruits from Texas stayed on the job for just six weeks on average. Although Case

Farms' annual employee turnover is confidential, a company human resources official testified that 5 percent of the plant's employees leave each week, according to court documents.

Increasingly, the meat industry's vulnerable recruits are coming from the equally brutal and low-wage world of farm labor. Some farm-workers see meat-factory work as a step up from the fields—until they discover that chopping up animals might actually be worse than pick-ing vegetables.

Migrant labor experts say the meatpacking and poultry industries are following the long-distance labor recruitment model established in agriculture. "For years people in the agricultural labor business said let's try to make the agricultural labor market more like the nonfarm labor market, and I think the reality is nonfarm labor markets are taking on lots of characteristics of farm labor markets," explains Philip Martin, professor of agricultural economics at the University of California in Davis. "There used to be a very clear distinction between processing workers and fieldworkers and that clearly has changed in the last de-cade."[70] While many workers still view meat processing as a step up from farm labor, these two bottom rungs of the food-production ladder are increasingly parallel in their offerings of harsh migrant work.

Reverend Jim Lewis, of the Maryland-based Delmarva Poultry Jus-tice Alliance, says the Texas case could have an "enormous impact" on the many itinerant poultry workers in his region. "We started out see-ing around three or four hundred people come through [the factories] each month. Now we are seeing one thousand," he says. "They move from plant to plant, and if there is an INS raid or pressure on them for some reason they will move somewhere else."[71]

Laurence Norton, an attorney who represented the Texas workers, says the case could compel other poultry companies either to scale back their enticing promises of free housing and transportation or invest the money necessary to fulfill their guarantees. Regardless, he says, "They would have to make very clear disclosures about the terms of agreement at the time of employment in the language workers understand."[72]

In court, attorneys for Case Farms argued that the company isn't re-sponsible for worker housing, or for promises allegedly made in Texas by the company's recruiter, a defunct temporary employment agency called America's Tempcorp.

"We have no migrant workers at all," insists Richard Lobb, spokesman for the Washington, D.C.–based National Chicken Council. "When people are given a job in a poultry plant it is expected that it is a permanent full-time position as opposed to one that is naturally going to terminate in six weeks. They are not migrant, they are not seasonal."[73]

But the migrant labor law's reach is broad, and congressional records suggest it was designed to protect workers who migrate long distances for agriculture-related work, including poultry processing. Meat packers and chicken companies "are using the same recruitment, the same housing and transportation arrangements" as farm operators, argues Selena Solis, an attorney with Texas Rural Legal Aid who represents workers. "It's just recently that the meat-processing industry has caught on to the fact that this is a way to get workers, [who are] so desperate, so dependent on finding work" that they are easily lured by false promises. "They tell them, 'Don't take any furnishings, don't bring anything but your clothes, you don't need a car.' They get there and they are virtually dependent on the employer."[74]

For one Case Farms plaintiff, Israel Trevino, a veteran of poultry slaughterhouses and farm labor, processing chickens is just one stop on a long migrant labor road. He says he expected to sort chicken parts at Case Farms' plant in Winesburg, Ohio, for four months. But after arriving in midwinter to a cramped apartment infested with rats and cockroaches, he worked for just three weeks to save enough money to return to his home in Eagle Pass, Texas.

PLUCKING WORKERS: A CAPTIVE LABOR SUPPLY

As punitive welfare reforms swept the nation in 1995, Missouri officials discovered an especially efficient way to reduce the welfare rolls: send people receiving benefits to work as "pullers" on the killing lines of Tyson Chicken, ConAgra, or PSF. Gutting chickens would serve a macabre marriage of business demand for cheap labor and government's commitment to "caseload reduction." It was a job offer recipients couldn't refuse: those deemed uncooperative or reluctant were sum-marily "sanctioned"—their benefits were cut off.[75]

Tyson and other meat-processing corporations had tapped into a new cheap labor force created by welfare reform. Through this "Direct Job Placement" program (DJP) launched in 1995—"born out of Tyson's need for additional workers," according to a county welfare director—Missouri's welfare agencies began referring recipients directly to low-wage-paying private companies in need of labor. The pilot has since gone statewide to involve twenty-one counties and 2,500 employers, in-cluding several Tyson plants, ConAgra chicken-processing factories, PSF hog-slaughtering farms, and numerous temp agencies and nursing homes. In rural areas with tight labor markets, large companies have virtually monopoly control over job placement and the DJP turns county welfare offices into company hiring halls.[76]

State documents describe the DJP as a "cooperative effort between local employers and the Division of Family Services. . . . Employers ex-periencing labor market shortages fill vacancies with recipients." It's a classic "public-private partnership": the companies get new reserves of cheap labor, and harried welfare case managers can erase people from their welfare rolls to meet intense caseload-reduction pressures ema-nating from state and federal officials. "It's the same as slavery, you have no choice," says Helmick of the United Food and Commercial Workers. "The government has sent them there. If you can stand up and walk, Tyson's going to offer you a job and you either take it or you're out of the system altogether."[77]

As it turned out, more people lost their benefits due to "noncompli-ance" (refusing work or missing an interview) than accepted jobs at Tyson, according to local welfare officials. Of the 195 welfare recipients sent to Tyson in 1998 for mandatory interviews, just 22 accepted entry-level assembly-line jobs, which paid $6.70 an hour. Thirty-nine people were sanctioned. The penalty: no food stamps for sixty days. The other 134 simply disappeared from the rolls.[78]

Recipients who cooperated were in for a rude, often brief, return to the workplace. "The first job they get is the 'puller' job—pulling the in-ternal organs out," says Tim Barchak, Missouri political director for the

Service Employees International Union. "A lot of these workers will lose their fingernails in two to three weeks from the bacteria in the chicken fat."[79]

MEETING TYSON'S "CONSTANT NEED FOR EMPLOYEES"

When Tyson opened shop near Sedalia, Missouri, in 1995, it had a tough time finding workers. Unemployment was only about 3 percent. The company, lured there by Sedalia's powerful state senator, James L. Mathewson, spent six months advertising in area newspapers and job centers, to no avail. Brenda Proctor, a consumer economist with the University of Missouri cooperative extension service, says that Mathewson, then the state senate's president pro tem, "had been very instrumental in bringing the Tyson Chicken plant to Sedalia. When Tyson got into the area it couldn't find enough folks to fill these jobs, because the work is messy, and there's lots of carpal tunnel. . . . Tyson had trouble with the labor supply and was getting upset."[80]

Then the company hit on an idea. In addition to cycling through migrant workers, the plant could shore up its labor needs with an equally desperate group: welfare recipients under the gun to get off the dole. Tyson began "doing some informal visiting with Senator Mathewson about their need for more workers," says Pettis County Division of Family Services (DFS) Director Linda Messenger. Then, according to Proctor, "Mathewson sponsored a bill after this erupted, and got DFS to try a pilot where if somebody applied for benefits they were sent directly to Tyson. If they declined, they were refused benefits for sixty days."

Deb Hendricks, information officer for the Missouri DFS, explains: "Our case managers work directly with Tyson to place them in those jobs. Most of these are assembly-line, entry-level positions." She adds matter-of-factly, "They have pretty much a constant need for employees because there's a high turnover there. So our offices keep in touch with their employment needs."[81]

Messenger calls it "a perfect mesh." Prior to the Tyson program, she notes, "We had [welfare] clients who were job-ready, but for one reason or another had not responded to Tyson's job advertisements on their own. They have a reputation," she allows. "It's hard work, sometimes cold and dirty. It's not a glamorous job, and some people were turned off by that." Messenger's staff visited the Tyson plant, "so they were able to get [recipients] to the point of agreeing to an interview. We would set them up with an appointment, and if they failed to keep the interview, we sanctioned them and that meant they lost their food stamps. Actually, some of them did choose to lose their benefits instead of going to Tyson's."

Critics and former Tyson employees say that's precisely the problem with sending welfare recipients to pull chicken guts. "One of the real tragedies of an employer like Tyson being involved in this [welfare-to-work] program is that these are not jobs that give people a career," says the Services Employees International Union's Tim Barchak. "Jobs in poultry processing plants are temporary because people burn out quickly. Nobody who they take in and burn out in six months is taking with them any skill they can apply to the rest of the American workforce."

Crystal Wolfe, a nineteen-year-old former Tyson employee with her second child on the way, puts it more bluntly: "If you're just coming off welfare and you haven't worked in a while, that place will make you never want to work again."[82]

FIGHTING BACK

Despite the food industry's immense power over workers' lives—spanning political, economic, and social realms—there is growing resistance to the brutality of the killing line. Worker lawsuits, some victorious, are steadily piling up a record of abuse and resistance. The cases of Michelle Galvan, Abel Merino, Connie Mayer, and others show that the industry's walking wounded are rising up, part of a growing file of complaints against meat and poultry factories across the United States. But resistance to corporate intimidation, harassment, and other obstacles by individuals is just one aspect of a growing rebellion. Three unions—the United Food and Commercial Workers (UFCW), the Teamsters, and the Laborers' International Union of North America—are involved in organizing meatpacking and poultry-processing workers. By turns they cooperate and compete with one another. Less than one-third of chicken factory workers and roughly 20 percent of the nation's meatpacking workers are in unions.[83] Despite many victories in recent years, however, unions are fighting an uphill battle against an intensely consolidated industry in a context in which they have little negotiating power. And they are still recovering from the devastation of the 1980s, when, thanks largely to President Reagan's anti-union labor courts and increasing consolidation within the industry, meatpacking unionization and wages plummeted by 50 percent.[84] During that decade of lost labor power, between 1980 and 1987, the portion of unionized meat packers plunged from 46 percent to 21 percent.[85] Labor journalist David Bacon, writing in *The American Prospect* in 2002, stated that the UFCW has lost bargaining clout, and "its power to set wage standards has badly eroded."[86]

After decades of real-value wage losses and steep declines in union membership, the unions are exploring new community-based organizing strategies and posting some gains for workers. In 1998 the UFCW won a struggle for the most basic of rights—the bathroom break. According to the union, poultry and meatpacking workers are "arbitrarily denied the use of bathroom facilities," and "often are forced to relieve themselves at their workstations." They filed numerous worker complaints with the Occupational Safety and Health Administration. Finally, after many individual case rulings, OSHA ordered the industry to give all workers access to company bathrooms.[87]

Perhaps most promising is the growing collaboration between unions and community groups, which are organizing not only around wages and health care or working conditions but also around the needs of the broader communities of this largely immigrant workforce. In Nebraska a "union-community" campaign carried out jointly by the UFCW and Omaha Together, One Community led to a major victory—winning union membership in May 2002 for nearly 1,000 ConAgra meatpacking workers. Several months later, 500 of those workers ratified a two-year contract providing "affordable, quality health insurance," small employer contributions to a retirement plan, more vacation pay, "two pairs of safety work boots per employee per year," and up to thirty days unpaid leave for long-distance travel so immigrant workers can visit their families without losing their jobs.[88]

These victories, while important and uplifting, must also be placed in a broader context. For most meatpacking and poultry workers, wages remain miserably low. Hard-fought victories for bathroom breaks and a couple of pairs of safety boots are cause for both celebration and a sober reality check: food-processing workers and unions are battling relentlessly for things that ought to be taken for granted. While some immigrant workers have stood up courageously for better conditions, many remain isolated and intimidated by a whole collection of barriers, from social and cultural dislocation to lack of education and English-language skills to sheer economic desperation.

And at the end of the day, the killing line still runs faster than ever, with no signs that it will slow down anytime soon. Public outrage has swayed McDonald's to ensure that the cattle that end up in its hamburgers are slaughtered humanely, yet no comparable effort has been undertaken for humane treatment of the workers who make those burgers. Students and other concerned citizens boycott shoe and clothing companies whose products come from sweatshops—but what about the sweatshops that produce our food?

Despite astronomic injury rates that have generally increased along with the speed of the lines, government agencies have made no visible effort to reduce factory speed limits. For profit-minded corporations with fairly low profit margins, there is little immediate economic gain in slowing the carcass disassembly process. Unless, of course, companies should decide that it is worth it to reduce injuries and workers' compensation insurance costs, and retain a stable workforce. But the meatpacking and poultry industries have shown no evidence of such forward thinking.

The food industry, including the farm-labor sector, profits not only from cheap, highly exploited labor but also from the remarkably modest expectations of immigrant workers, who are accustomed to the lowest of wages, the toughest of work, the sparest of living conditions. What many immigrant workers demand—when they demand anything at all—is quite basic by American standards. As José, the rib cutter for PSF, put it, "If they paid a little more money and ran the line a little slower, the people wouldn't leave. I wouldn't leave."

12

SUBSIDIZING MADNESS, EXPORTING MISERY

"Civilization is what happens in cities, and the city is dependent on there being a surplus from the food producer and on some existing organization which can take it away from him. With this food surplus, the political organization feeds kings... armies, architects and builders, and the city comes into being. Political science in its earliest form is the knowledge of how to take the food surplus away from the food producer without giving him very much in return."
—Charles Walters, Jr., *Angry Testament* (1969)

In mainstream economic thought, the transformation from agrarian to industrial production is considered key to a nation's economic maturity. As productivity evolves into manufacturing and technical professions, it is said, the fewer people involved in agriculture the better. The transition from farms to factories is supposed to usher in both individual and national prosperity, higher wages, and technological and economic advance, as people are freed from the hard clutches of the land to pursue more profitable ventures for domestic sale and trade. Economists Robert Heilbroner and Lester Thurow, for instance, describe "a steady streaming of labor and capital out of agriculture, first into industry and later into the service sector" in the United States.[1] Such transitions are far from seamless. In the 1950s and 1960s, this "steady streaming"—fueled by a rapid buildup of mechanized agriculture—led to a huge rural exodus, mass farm closures, and increased urban poverty, as foreclosed farmers headed to cities looking for work.[2]

By these standards, the United States is an economic and agricultural miracle. In 2003, the U.S. farm population fell to an all-time low of about 1.8 million while producing as much as—in some crops more than—ever before. Between the war on farmers and the war on drugs, the United States has attained a dubious plateau: it now boasts more prisoners than farmers. In the steady march of industrial agriculture, productivity and total output rise ever upward, and American bounty overflows, even as farmers disappear from the landscape. Is this merely the natural—if brutal—triumph of technological efficiency? Or, is there something more than the vaunted "invisible hand" at work?

America's horn of plenty is coaxed not only by fertile soils and hardworking farmers (and laborers), but also by national policies that promote large-scale mono-crop farming and surplus production. Agricultural subsidies, running roughly 15 to 20 billion dollars a year, at once encourage big prolific farms and strive to keep much of that bounty out of the American market to balance food prices. So the glut pours onto world markets, enriching corporate export firms while often destabilizing food prices—and farmers—abroad. The vast majority of farmers in the United States, meanwhile, reap little from this harvest of subsidy payments and export profits.

Particularly since the 1950s, when the postwar technological revolution and economic boom swept U.S. agriculture into an age of perpetual overabundance, subsidies and exports have simultaneously relieved *and* sustained America's agricultural excess. James Wessel, in his excellent 1983 book *Trading the Future,* describes a "history of government programs since the New Deal designed to rescue American agriculture from the disasters of its own bounty by supporting farm prices through subsidies or controlling overproduction through 'set-asides.' "[3]

Although subsidies that pay farmers not to grow do help restrain surplus somewhat, the subsidy system as a whole maintains a "production treadmill" of oversupply. It does this by providing farmers an outlet for their excess—thus perpetuating a farm economy of surplus. Given the vagaries of the marketplace and the aid of government as the "buyer of last resort," farmers continue producing as much as they can (unless they are paid not to produce at all), leading to a virtually perpetual surplus. Subsidies also feed large-scale agriculture by promoting conditions favorable to big farmers.

This is the treacherous, destructive dance that is the nation's food economy and farm policy. But the term "farm policy" is misleadingly narrow: U.S. agricultural subsidies and exports have resounding domestic and international effects, not only on farmers but also on consumers, rural communities, the environment, and economic inequality. While neither trade nor farm subsidies are inherently harmful, both have evolved to predominantly meet the needs of large-scale farms and agribusiness conglomerates, at the expense of most everyone else. They accomplish this by nurturing an economy of expansionism, in which farmers are subsidized (with your tax dollars) to get big—or get out. And as the big get bigger, the copious fruits of their oversupply must be exported, or dumped at rock-bottom prices, often undermining small-scale agriculture and entire rural economies abroad.

SUBSIDIZING SURPLUS

The most basic purpose of the farm subsidy system, since its inception in the 1930s, has been to manage the marketplace by effecting an awkward balance among the conflicting forces of national food production, consumer prices, and farm income. In the throes of the Great Depression, which followed a decade of severe agricultural recession, President Roosevelt unveiled the core principles of contemporary U.S. farm policy with the Agricultural Adjustment Act of 1933. It laid out policy fundamentals still with us today: through a variety of mechanisms—including loans, subsidy payments pegged to target prices, surplus market controls, and acreage set-asides—the government would attempt to stabilize farmer income and keep food prices relatively affordable.[4]

Contrary to the popular conception, one of the key agricultural crises of the Depression era was surplus (see Chapter 6); even with Dust Bowl droughts, the machine of American agriculture piled up too much food for the depressed market, and prices kept tumbling. The historian Janet Poppendieck captured this paradox of plenty with the poignant phrase "bread lines knee-deep in wheat."[5] Under first President Hoover and then Roosevelt, huge hog and wheat reserves were destroyed amid hunger and starvation to prop up prices. This was the ignominious beginning of the subsidy system: the government paid farmers for their surplus, and squirreled away reserves (and even minimized food giveaways, fearing they would further depress prices), in order to rescue the market.

"Farm supports led American farmers to overproduce," writes Philip McMichael, professor of rural and development sociology at Cornell University. Following World War II, the United States "disposed of these agricultural surpluses overseas via the Public Law 480 program of food aid. It was within the context of this food régime disbursing food at concessional, and later, commercial, prices, that the huge grain traders, such as Cargill and Continental, prospered." Over time the corporations "gained a captive market through the subsidized exports of the food aid program."[6] Cloaked in the friendly garb of humanitarian assistance (which did bring some immediate benefits for the hungry), U.S. food aid programs helped carve out new markets for these corporations while undercutting farmers in poor recipient countries—again, at taxpayer expense.

Historically there have been three main forms of subsidy: price supports (paying farmers the difference between a Department of Agriculture target price and the actual market price), production controls (paying farmers to remove land from production as a hedge against surplus), and marketing orders (whereby "producers and the government agreed to restrict supplies of a particular commodity, improving prices by keeping surplus off the market.")[7] Another major element is surplus storage and disposal, largely through foreign food aid, which since the 1960s has played a politically suspect and economically destructive role in developing nations around the world.

THE PRICE OF CHEAP FOOD

Subsidizing inexpensive food seems a noble cause. But is that really the farm program's goal or accomplishment? Certainly, subsidies have helped keep food prices in the United States relatively low, at least when compared with prices in many countries in Europe (studies show Europeans as a whole spend anywhere from 25 to 50 percent more of their family income on food than do Americans).[8] The issue of price might appear simple: Who could object to making food more affordable? Yet, if prices fall too low, farmers can't survive. Indeed, lower prices for raw commodities (in tandem with rising costs for equipment, seeds, labor and other "inputs") have broken many a farmer's back in recent years.

Once again we are confronted with the contradiction between farm prices and food prices—what economists call, rather drearily, the "farm-retail price spread." Even as most farmers make less money off their crops, food prices in supermarkets and restaurants keep going up (occasionally held in check by recession). While the value of farmers' crops remained roughly the same between 1987 and 1997, retail prices rose sharply, and the farm-retail gap also shot up.[9] Consumer spending on food rocketed from $449 billion in 1990 to $661 billion in 2000, an increase of almost 50 percent. In that same time farmers' gross sales inched up by just 16 percent, from $106 billion to $123 billion. The rest of consumers' dollars went to the ballooning "food-marketing" bill, including labor, packaging, transportation, fuel, advertising, and corporate profits. Marketing and processing now eats up 81 percent of consumer costs for food, while farming represents just 19 percent. According to a 2001 USDA analysis, "Consumers' preference for quick, easy-to-prepare convenience foods, including more away-from-home eating, translated into an increased demand for food marketing services."[10]

But what does all this have to do with subsidies? By keeping the price of farm crops in check, subsidies stabilize costs for the food industry's marketing and processing intermediaries. In this way the farm program helps provide cheap food "inputs" for corporations and retail businesses—food processors, packagers, transporters, supermarkets, and restaurants. This is the hidden yet vitally important impact of farm subsidies as they are currently constructed. Farmers pay a stiff price for this market depression, especially the majority of growers, who receive minimal subsidies, yet must sell their crops at the artificially low wholesale market price. In this regard, today's system of farm payments skews an already tilted market in favor of agribusiness and away from a level playing field for growers.

Subsidies also guarantee a price *floor*, preventing depressed markets from pushing U.S. farm prices too *low*. Transnational agribusiness firms, such as grain traders and chemical producers, therefore often oppose subsidies as a meddlesome market invention. As Philip McMichael explains, these corporate intermediaries "generally favor using the WTO [World Trade Organization] to phase out farm programs, eliminating supply management and driving down prices by exposing producers to world-wide differential labor costs." By reducing price supports, "the corporations maximize their ability to structure comparative advantages in the world market."[11]

On the domestic scene, agribusiness and its many allies in Congress have successfully pushed policies—such as the 1996 so-called "Freedom to Farm Act"—that effectively cheapen farm products, particularly grains and some livestock. Such policies supply cheap foods to corporate processors and retailers that, as we have seen, do not pass these savings along to consumers. According to a report by the Agricultural Policy Analysis Center at the University of Tennessee, U.S. policies since the late 1980s have engineered "a free fall in domestic farm prices while simultaneously promoting rapid liberal trade measures to open new markets for U.S. products. U.S. farmers, the intended beneficiaries of these policies, have languished, despite official rhetoric to the contrary. Meanwhile, major agribusinesses have thrived."[12]

The report explains how this cheap-food policy has intensified the economic concentration of the food industry: "The precipitous decline in prices of primary commodities, especially grains, is providing agribusiness and corporate livestock producers access to agricultural commodities at below the cost of production, consolidating their control over the entire production and marketing chain."[13]

"A CHRONIC STATE OF SURPLUS"

Agriculture historian Willard Cochrane chronicles the strange confluence of price supports and a surplus food economy. As domestic and global markets recovered following World War II, farmers began expanding and investing in industrial technologies at a vigorous pace. The war "lifted the financial constraints from farmers, and they adopted the new technologies and they substituted capital for human labor with a reckless abandon," Cochrane writes. Farm output shot up by 25 percent in the 1940s and rose again by 20 percent during the 1950s. Demand still outpaced production through 1951, but "the inevitable occurred in 1952. Foreign demand contracted with the end of the Korean hostilities and the phasing out of post–World War II relief and rehabilitation activities, and farm prices began to fall."[14]

But instead of plummeting as they had in the 1920s, farm prices were now propped up by a phalanx of government commodity supports. The subsidy system protected prices and thereby sustained burgeoning farm expansion and surplus food production. Some economists estimated farm prices would have fallen by about 40 percent without the safety net. (The 1950s was a pivotal epoch in the rise of consolidated, large-scale agriculture and the demise of small family farming.) Cochrane explains, "At the level at which farm prices were supported during the 1950s and 1960s the farm sector was producing, or had the capacity to produce, more total product each year than the commercial market, both domestic and foreign, would take at those prices. The farm economy was in a chronic state of surplus."[15]

What began as emergency aid and economic stimulus during the New Deal became a persistent political culture and economics of subsidized surplus. "Government was so fearful of the price and income consequences of removing federal farm programs of price and income support that it continued those programs year after year. And with the continuation of those programs, the problem of excess productive capacity became a chronic problem."[16]

It is important to distinguish between individual farmers and the broader market. While bolstering farmers' income is always good politics (subsidy increases and emergency payments are standard fare in election years), and might be a safeguard against rebellion in times of depression, the larger purpose of subsidies has always been to protect agricultural markets. If subsidies were intended to promote farmers, they would be distributed evenly to all producers—or in fact, unevenly, with the majority of payments going to stabilize incomes for smaller, struggling farmers, to anchor rural economies and expand food security in communities across the country. But the historical record clearly shows that subsidies have done nothing to fend off the economic tidal wave of farm consolidation. Rather, they have helped to speed the rise of large-scale, environmentally damaging monocrop agriculture, at the expense of small-scale sustainable farming.

SUBSIDIZING INEQUALITY

In 1996, amid the hoopla over "ending welfare as we know it," Congress sought a similar free-market, budget-cutting coup regarding farm subsidies. Since the 1985 farm bill (in some respects since President Nixon's war on subsidies in the early 1970s), the president and Congress have been steering farm policy away from government guarantees and toward the supposed open range of deregulated markets. The idea has been to cut government farm spending and, allegedly, to let the free market sort out who survives and who doesn't. Under the 1996 Federal Agricultural Improvement and Reform Act, better known as "Freedom to Farm," subsidies would be phased out, with the apparent purpose of letting farmers grow without government restrictions. Prices were high at the time, and politicians, in typical shortsightedness, said the time was right to cut the chord. As a Department of Agriculture summary described, rather optimistically, "farmers would trade a strict set of supply-control programs for a new era of market-driven cropping decisions, tempered with seven years of transition payments to help move the government out of farming."[17] (Critics called the 1996 act "Freedom to Fail," as it purported to end both acreage restrictions and subsidies and to push farmers onto the sink-or-swim open market.)

Despite the rhetoric of ending subsidies, payments have risen astronomically since then. From $7.4 billion in 1997, subsidies soared to a record $22.7 billion in 1999.[18] Congress doled out whatever was necessary to balance against foundering prices magnified by the late-1990s Asian economic crisis, which greatly diminished exports. When the export valve closes, shrunk by recession and competition abroad, price supports and emergency payments become a farmer's bread and butter. During the price plunges of the late 1990s, government payments tripled, yet net farm income kept declining, by 16.5 percent between 1996 and 2001. By that year, total subsidy payments amounted to 47 percent of farmer income, up from 20 percent in the 1990s.[19] But for large, better-off farmers (and plenty of well-heeled nonfarmers), it's much more than bread and butter. And their slice of the pie has grown substantially bigger since the Freedom to Farm Act.

Critics of the 1996 law ranged from Midwest family farm groups to President Clinton's Agriculture Secretary Dan Glickman. "The Freedom to Farm Act embraced and in fact worsened Congress's tendency to say the bigger and richer you are, the more money you get," said Chuck Hassebrook, of the Nebraska-based Center for Rural Affairs, a nonprofit advocacy group. In an April 2000 interview with the *New York Times,* Glickman (then nearing the end of his tenure) concurred: "[T]here's no question that a big chunk of payments go to larger producers. The more pounds you produce, the more money you get. Congress has always resisted changing that."[20]

During this subsidy renaissance, payments (which are pegged to production volumes) to the top 10 percent of farmers became increasingly concentrated, mirroring the ongoing consolidation of agribusiness. "Smaller farms have consistently received smaller payments than have larger ones, and this gap has widened," concluded a 2001 report by the Congressional General Accounting Office.[21] According to an analysis by the Environmental Working Group, using government data, the portion of subsidies taken in by this top tier rose from 55 percent of all payments in 1995 to 65 percent by 2002. In 2001, wealthier farmers' share ran as high as 73 percent, while the bottom 80 percent of recipients got just 12 percent of all farm payments. Among some major commodities, subsidy inequality was even more stilted. Top-tier wheat farmers harvested 73 percent of all wheat subsidies, while 78 percent of cotton payments went to that commodity's top 10 percent.[22]

American taxpayers spent $12.2 billion on farm subsidies in 2002, two thirds of which went to the top 10 percent of farmers and businesses. That amounts to $8 billion paid to just over 170,000 of the 1.7 million recipients of farm aid, an average of over $46,000 each. The bottom 80 percent of recipients, meanwhile, took home a meager $1,680 each on average. At the pinnacle of farm subsidy privilege, the top 1 percent of all the nation's beneficiaries got payments averaging

$175,651, according to the Environmental Working Group.[23] Among the biggest winners in U.S. farm policy were a couple of rice cooperatives in Stuttgart, Arkansas. Riceland Foods Inc. pulled down $110 million in taxpayer subsidies, and Producers Rice Mill Inc. netted $83 million. Riceland has been the happy recipient of more than $426 million in subsidies since 1995.[24]

Dozens of other farmers also fared pretty well in the subsidy game, members of a "millionaires club" of beneficiaries who snared anywhere from $3.2 million to $23.8 million in government farm payments between 1996 and 2000. Numbers like that clearly put the lie to any notion that the farm subsidy system is there to help the average farmer survive. "There ought to be a limit on how much those operations get," says Kenneth Cook, president of the Environmental Working Group.[25]

Famously, the subsidy program has featured some rather unlikely beneficiaries, wealthy people and institutions with no apparent connection to agriculture. In 2003, for instance, John Hancock Mutual Insurance snared nearly $2 million in peanut subsidies by selling off to the government special price-support licenses. Pilgrims Pride Corp., a Texas-based chicken producer, received $15 million, despite the fact that there is no official subsidy for poultry. The basketball star Scottie Pippen and the TV news guru Sam Donaldson also raked in farm program money. Others on this all-star team of "farmers" who have gotten checks, most for not farming land they owned, are Ted Turner, David Rockefeller (once chairman of the Chase Manhattan Bank), and the former Enron CEO Kenneth Lay.[26]

A host of Fortune 500 corporations have gorged themselves at the farm-subsidy trough. In the period from 1996 through 2000, Chevron collected more than $260,000 in farm payments, according to data compiled by the Environmental Working Group. International Paper did even better, hauling down over $375,000. Providing a stark contrast to politicians' election-season posturing about saving the family farm, the list of big business beneficiaries of farm subsidies includes DuPont ($188,000), Caterpillar ($171,000), Archer Daniels Midland ($36,000), and Georgia-Pacific ($37,000). During this time period the average payment to farmers among the bottom 80 percent of subsidy recipients was just $5,830.[27]

Beyond the scandal of corporate farm welfare to the rich and famous, there's a deeper structural bias in the subsidy system that en-
riches agribusiness and wealthy farmers at the expense of small
independent growers. Because farm payments are "generally based on
volume of production," big growers rake in most of the cash—money
that enables them to buy up more land, purchase more equipment, and
push smaller competitors out of business. In 1999, the average small
farmer (with gross sales under $50,000) received a payment of about
$4,141, while large-scale farmers (with gross sales over $250,000) were
given subsidy checks averaging $64,737. Although smaller producers
represented 76 percent of all farmers, they took in just 14 percent of
subsidy payments, according to the General Accounting Office. Growers
with 1,000 acres or more represented just 8 percent of all farmers in
1999, yet received 52 percent of all subsidies.[28]

The image of millionaire farmers living off subsidy checks provides
anti-government conservatives with a useful poster child, a rural parallel to the urban myth of the "welfare queen." Indeed, the right has cleverly hijacked populist class-consciousness to rail against a government
farm program that is, well, ripe for the picking. The conservative Heritage Foundation, no friend of the working class, blasted farm subsidy
inequalities in a 2002 report, stating quite accurately that "the subsidy
programs tax working Americans to award millions to millionaires
and provide profitable corporate farms with money that has been used
to buy out family farms." But don't be fooled: the right-wing group
wasn't calling for economic redistribution, just less government. "The
issue of concern is not consolidation" of agriculture, the report argued,
but instead "whether multimillion-dollar agricultural corporations
should continue to receive welfare payments."[29]

While the right deploys the populist vernacular to attack this "corporate welfare," there is a deeper, more forward-looking critique to be
made. The easy populist argument lodged by some on the left assails
corporate greed and the blatant unfairness of enriching agribusiness
while neglecting small farmers. It's a compelling commentary, rich
with moral fiber and simple justice. Yet it must be recognized that the
current subsidy system is, despite its gaping flaws (such as farm

payments to famous athletes) quite rational on its own terms. If the goal is to maximize national production of cheap bulk commodities for corporate food manufacturers and traders—without much regard for rural economies or ecological sustainability—then America's farm subsidy program is working reasonably well. There are, to be sure, subsidies for resource conservation, and various small government programs offering scraps to family farmers. But these are typically budgetary leftovers. The essence of the subsidy problem lies in its core purpose—not simply enriching agribusiness, but more fundamentally cultivating a precarious national project of producing and managing surplus, and flooding foreign nations with exports to beef up U.S. revenues.

GUSHING GREEN

Less discussed yet equally important are the billions of dollars in water subsidies, paid by taxpayers to supply large-scale farming operations with cheap irrigation. Agriculture consumes roughly 80 percent of all water used in America each year, according to the EPA. Huge irrigation projects, the result of early twentieth-century efforts to settle and farm dry western lands, channel precious underground and surface waters to growers at cheap, heavily subsidized rates. According to *Common Cause Magazine,* in 1995, Americans paid $3 billion in irrigation subsidies. Critics say this only encourages waste. The EPA points out, "the loss of water from irrigation conveyance systems" can be "significant." Cornell University's David Pimentel, a widely published expert on ecological and resource issues, argues, "if farmers paid the full cost of water, they would manage irrigation water more efficiently. We should reward water conservation, not water use."

Of course, not all farmers are implicated equally. Under the original 1902 National Reclamation Act, only family farmers with up to 160 acres of land could receive federally subsidized water. But corporate farming interests have over time convinced the government to extend the subsidy to farms as large as 960 acres, according to the Natural Resources Defense Council. "These large farms divide ownership on paper, form trusts, and use other subterfuges to drink up significant amounts of taxpayer-subsidized, below-cost federal water."

One major beneficiary of irrigation subsidies is the lucrative french fries business, 80 percent of which comes from the Columbia River Basin Russet Burbank potato. An industry analyst told *Common Cause* that this particular breed "makes a perfect frozen french fry but needs to grow in a desert with lots of water." So cheap subsidized Columbia River water flows amply to this otherwise parched land, benefiting large-scale potato growers and corporate processors of frozen french fries, such as potato magnate J.R. Simplot.[30]

THE SUBSIDY-EXPORT CONNECTION

Far from guaranteeing food security and crop diversity, the subsidy program is narrowly targeted to sustain and promote a few select crops—which happen to form a significant portion of America's agricultural exports. Payments to wheat, corn, and cotton farmers represent roughly 75 percent of all farm subsidies; just two other crops (oil seeds represent 12 percent and rice, 7 percent) get major payments. Among food crops, oil seeds and grains attracted 54 percent of all government farm payments. As it happens, heavily subsidized grains, oil seeds, and cotton are far more aggressively exported than fruits, vegetables, and meat[31]—crops that were subsidized minimally if at all. In fact, crops representing 60 percent of the value of U.S. agriculture production in 1999 attracted only 3 percent of all subsidies.[32] Much of the big subsidy money ends up in America's breadbasket: in 1999 just six states—Iowa, Illinois, Texas, Kansas, Nebraska, and Minnesota—took in 48 percent of all farm subsidies in America.[33] These numbers make abundantly clear that subsidies are not designed to sustain family farming, nor to ensure a decent and diverse national food supply.

Political history has also played a role in these imbalances. Iowa State University's Bruce Babcock sums up the situation: "Subsidies are concentrated geographically, they are concentrated on relatively few crops, and they are concentrated on relatively few producers." Some of these inequities are, he says, "an artifact of the way that commodity programs were initially set up in the 1930s. Tobacco, barley, corn, wheat, cotton, oats, rice, and grain sorghum were by far the most important commodity crops that had firm political backing because production was geographically concentrated" in a few states.[34]

While farm payments enrich agribusiness and big growers and skew the playing field against small farmers in America, they wreak their greatest havoc overseas. By maintaining surplus production and a ready supply of cheap commodities, subsidies enable agribusiness corporations to obtain farmers' crops at below the cost of production and then export them at bargain-basement prices. It's good business for export firms like Cargill and ADM, but these cheap subsidized foods often flood markets in poor countries and undermine Third World farmers. Farm subsidies, coupled with aggressive U.S. trade policies, have helped American agriculture carve out a commanding 20 percent share of all agricultural exports worldwide, a dominance rivaled only by the European Union, which also heavily subsidizes many farming sectors.[35] The deep inequities in U.S. farm supports are mirrored by huge disparities between wealthy, highly subsidized exporters such as the United States, the European Union, and Japan and poorer nations that can't compete. In this country, protests regarding this subsidized elimination of small independent farmers have been few and quiet, but the international ramifications have inspired fiery mass resistance from Third World farmers and peasants who are so impoverished they've got nothing to lose.

THE "GLOBALIZATION OF DEATH"

The peasants are at the gates—literally.

The scene is Cancún, Mexico, in September 2003. On the two-year anniversary of the horrific 9/11 attacks, while flags and prayers mingled with President Bush's promises of continued unilateral militarism in Iraq, peasant farmers stalked the heavily guarded perimeters of a World Trade Organization get-together in the posh Mexican resort city. "Protesters, led by farmers from around the globe . . . threw rocks, bottles and flaming signs at police, who pushed them back with tear gas and night sticks," one press account described.[36] Walled off by security fences and an army of cops, thousands of farmers and activists demanded to be heard. They had no place at the WTO bargaining tables, where trade ministers and other officials from member nations met in conference rooms several miles from the security-zone fencing.

The 146-member WTO, which has since its 1995 inception been a U.S.-dominated juggernaut designed to deregulate "free trade," was meeting for a battle royal over the incendiary matter of agricultural subsidies and trade barriers. The United States, Canada, and the European Union countries, though often sharply divided on agricultural trade, stood together to press poor developing nations to lower their trade barriers, proposing, for instance, that Bolivia and Kenya slash tariffs by 80 percent. Meanwhile these countries from the well-heeled global North would make far smaller tariff cuts: just 28 percent for the EU, and 24 percent for the United States. The British *Guardian* newspaper called it "a calculated insult, designed to prevent any agreement on this issue from taking place."[37]

It was also a departure from wealthier nations' pledge at the 1994 Doha, Qatar, meeting on world trade "to phase out farm subsidies if poor countries opened markets to Western corporations." The WTO talks in Cancún were "supposed to lead to phasing out of all export subsidies," but that idea was suddenly off the table.[38] The wealthy North, living large off subsidized inequality, *The Guardian* opined, "must know that the combination of their broken promises and their outrageous terms could force the weaker governments to walk out of the trade talks in Cancún, just as they did in Seattle in 1999."[39] And that's precisely what happened.

The stakes for developing nations were high. Squeezed by deepening worldwide inequalities and intensifying poverty, many countries throughout Africa and Latin America are desperate for new markets and see protectionist tariffs as their only defense against incursions by Northern corporations. For many less-developed countries—typically former colonies still recovering from more than a century of resource plunder and exploitation by the colonial North—agriculture is an economic mainstay. They lack the financial capital, industrial technology, and infrastructure to compete with the United States, Canada, Europe, and the more developed Asian nations. One indicator of the wealth gap: as of 2003, the 500 richest people on the planet owned a combined $1.54 trillion, "more than the entire gross domestic product of Africa, or the combined annual incomes of the poorest half of humanity."[40]

"The situation in the countryside is terrible," said Rafael Alegria, a Honduran corn and bean farmer and head of Via Campesina, an influential international peasant group. "The policies of the WTO and free trade agreements are filling the countryside with dead people and misery."[41] Honduras is a bleak yet not atypical case study in how U.S. agribusiness subsidies, in combination with diminished Third World trade protections, lead to poverty and hunger abroad. In the 1980s, Honduran farmers produced a full 100 percent of the nation's domestic rice needs. But in 1991, Honduras, "under pressure from the IMF [International Monetary Fund], abolished the system of import controls and threw the rice market wide open," recounts *The Guardian*. Unable to compete with heavily subsidized American rice farmers' low prices, Honduran rice production collapsed, falling to just 1 percent of domestic needs. Poverty and unemployment increased, and economically desperate peasants crowded into cities. Only after Honduras began requiring processors to purchase home-grown rice before turning to imports did the nation's staple crop recover.[42]

The Northern countries' proposal in Cancún must have been especially galling in light of their highly subsidized dominance of global trade. American foodstuffs and agricultural products have long flooded international markets—the by-product of chronic surpluses and export subsidies that enable American exporters to undercut markets by selling at below the cost of production. The United States backed its cotton industry to the tune of $2.2 billion in 2001–2, comprising nearly half of all the cotton subsidies in the world. This has spelled economic disaster in numerous developing countries. Sudan's foreign debt has mushroomed by one third since 1998, largely because of cotton trade barriers, according to the country's WTO representative, Adil Alfaki.[43] A similar crisis is brewing in Benin: "if nothing is done urgently and solidly, this [American cotton subsidy] could lead to the total loss of revenue for our producers, an increase in poverty and the destruction of our economic system," said Benin's trade minister, Fatiou Akplogan.[44] A study by the UK-based nonprofit Oxfam calculated that Africa lost $301 million in 2001–2 because of American cotton subsidies.[45]

Likewise the World Bank estimates that reduced U.S. cotton subsidies would "translate into revenue gains of US $250 million a year for West and Central African farmers." In an effort to compete with the hefty American cotton subsidy, African nations are expending precious money on their own subsidies, according to the World Bank, "money that instead could be used to build schools, train doctors or immunize children."[46]

It's not merely a problem of a couple of crops in a couple of countries. Farm subsidies in the United States and the European Union total $150 billion annually—that's nearly half a billion dollars a day—and "shut poor countries out of the richest markets," the *Los Angeles Times* reported. Prior to the Cancún talks, the Bush administration promised American farmers an additional $190 billion over the next decade, while the EU delayed reforms to its subsidy-laden Common Agricultural Policy.[47]

Even less impoverished countries like Chile can hardly compete in so-called "free trade" agreements with subsidized American agribusiness. Chilean farmers were up in arms after their government signed a trade pact with the United States that eliminated numerous Chilean price controls on imports. "We just cannot compete with U.S. subsidies," said Nicolas Garcia, a Chilean wheat and oat farmer. Hundreds of thousands of farmers in southern Chile, who rely almost entirely on domestic sales, were immediately threatened by cheap subsidized American imports. According to the Minneapolis-based Institute for Agriculture and Trade Policy, in 2001, American agribusinesses sold wheat exports at 44 percent below its cost of production. The *Miami Herald* reported, "Below-cost U.S. grain exports are pushing down the world prices, thereby undercutting competition in developing countries that cannot compete in a subsidy war."[48]

The World Bank, always a staunch foe of protectionist state planning, jumped on the blatant disparities highlighted by Cancún to sound a populist alarm about subsidies run amuck: "It is hypocritical to preach the advantages of trade and markets and then erect obstacles [e.g., subsidies] in precisely those markets in which developing countries have a comparative advantage," said the bank's chief economist, Nicholas Stern. The bank called the U.S. and EU subsidies "egregious examples of rich countries opting to underwrite the status quo rather than using their wealth to support growth and facilitate development."[49] But the bank's real agenda is to lower protectionist tariffs everywhere, part of its wider mission of deregulated global markets and economic privatization. Stern noted in this same speech, "Many developing countries have protective barriers which are still very high."

Subsidies and protectionism have become bad words, largely because they run counter to the neoliberal objective of a pure worldwide "free market"—free, that is, of meddlesome labor and environmental regulations, state economic planning, or tariffs. The World Trade Organization has been at front and center of the push for total market access, even (or especially) when it means that lower labor and environmental standards in an exporting country undercut wages or ecological protections in importing nations. The institution's web site proclaims that, "by lowering trade barriers, the WTO's system also breaks down other barriers between peoples and nations." In promoting the benefits of unbridled free trade, the WTO argues stridently against protectionism. Economists debate the costs and benefits of protectionism, but the WTO's opposition to state-erected trade barriers is unmistakably political: tariffs, subsidies and other barriers make it harder for corporations to penetrate poor nations' fragile markets.[50]

Many critics see the WTO not merely as a promoter of free trade but as part of a broader assault on the sovereign right of countries to enforce rules protecting workers and the environment. The "neoliberal" model, prizing economic efficiency and corporate penetration of markets everywhere, "sidelines environmental rules, health safeguards and labor standards to provide transnational corporations (TNCs) with a cheap supply of labor and natural resources," explains Public Citizen. And while free-trade boosters promote open and unfettered markets, the watchdog group argues, "WTO rules have led to increased dumping of subsidized agricultural commodities resulting in steep drops in the prices paid to farmers around the world for their crops." In rich and poor countries alike, farmers "have only seen their incomes decline, with many losing farms and livelihoods under the WTO régime."

Under such policies, in which U.S. farm subsidies and cheap agricultural exports play a major role, farmers in poor "developing" nations are driven from the land. As Public Citizen describes, "In country after country, displaced farmers have had little choice but to join swelling urban workforces where the oversupply of labor suppresses wages and exacerbates the existing crisis of chronic under- and unemployment in the cities of the developing world."[51] Thus, we have come full circle back to the economic theory touting the transformation from agrarian to industrial society—except that, in many cases, the results can hardly be called progress.

The problem lies not in subsidies or protectionism per se, which can be vital policy tools for developing countries to protect their economic and cultural sovereignty, especially in the context of American and corporate power. Rather, critics point to the intense economic disparities and policy hypocrisies that enable global wealth and power to become increasingly concentrated in a small group of players in a small group of countries.

One such critic on the streets of Cancún was Lee Kyung-hae, a Korean farm leader, a former member of the South Korean parliament and farmer of the year whose successful farming operation was later plowed under by cheap imports. On September 10 Lee marched with his Korean compatriots and a few thousand farmers and activists from around the world, up to the edge of the WTO's heavily policed barricades. Amassed up against "a fence 10 feet high reinforced by a matrix of steel and concrete," the demonstrators, led by Lee and the Koreans, began attacking the wall that had silenced their voices at the trade conference. According to Writers Block, a group of reporters on the scene, "The fence begins to rock back and forth. . . . A few of the Koreans climb on top hanging banners and leading the chants of their comrades below."[52]

With a sign from his neck stating "WTO Kills Farmers," Lee urged the crowd to "go through" the WTO blockade. Then, the reporters recount, "Lee turns away from us, towards the police, the WTO and the corporate media functionaries who cower among them. His right hand is raised; he plunges a knife into his heart and falls backward from the fence into the waiting arms of his astonished comrades." There was scuffling with police, then a quiet parting for the ambulance. Some of Lee's contingent followed him to the hospital. Later, recovering from the initial shock and pandemonium, the Korean contingent launched an all-out assault on the barbwire barrier, "a fence that excludes not just the farmers present here but 3.5 million Korean farmers and countless others being strangled by the policies of the WTO," describes Writers Block. Inspired by Lee's sacrifice, they later tore down portions of the barricade.[53]

The media and WTO officials portrayed Lee's dramatic suicide as an individual tragedy, but his final act galvanized the movement on the streets and emboldened representatives of poor WTO member nations to resist the United States and European Union at the conference negotiating tables. Developing nations headed by Brazil, India, and China, known as the Group of 21—representing 60 percent of the world's farmers—refused to sign an agriculture agreement that failed to eliminate wealthier nations' subsidies. On September 14, amid "ministerial paralysis . . . the confabulations ended in a spectacular and crashing collapse. No agreements were reached," wrote Christian Parenti in *The Nation*.[54] To many of the "globofobicos" in the streets of Cancún, it was a remarkable victory of public resistance over narrow corporate-state policy interests. Some, like Tom Hayden, a longtime activist and California legislator, drew parallels with rising global opposition to American militarism: "Just as U.S. military unilateralism has failed at the UN, U.S. economic unilateralism is being resisted in the WTO."[55]

"DUMPING ON THE POOR": FOOD IMPERIALISM

The rage in Cancún was decades in the making. Agribusiness subsidies are only part of the story. The bigger picture, of which subsidies are one important piece, concerns the political-economic role of food—especially surplus food—in the international arena.[56]

Surplus food, in the form of exports and food aid, does not just flow benevolently from countries with too much to countries with too little. One nation's excess can be another nation's political and economic weakness. We are continually reminded of the potent and destructive role oil plays in international politics. In lieu of forward-thinking renewable energy policies, oil is viewed as essential to both the mechanics of daily life and national infrastructures and productivity, not to mention political clout. But what about food? No nation can survive without it. And few countries are blessed with the natural resources to sustain themselves without trade or assistance.

In capitalist economies, excess and overaccumulation are both a natural by-product and a potential threat to profits. Competition may produce qualitative improvements, for example, in convenience, and technology, but it almost unrelentingly produces a greater quantity of things. This is especially true in the case of U.S. agriculture, as historical evidence has shown; to survive in the marketplace, individual farmers produce as much as they can, even though they understand that oversupply hurts prices. In this regard the people of the world and the money at their disposal form one giant potential market for which all sectors and industries compete. As global competition intensifies, nations, industries, and corporations battle for economic leverage and market share. There is nothing inherently immoral or sinister about this battle; it is the amoral, inherent logic of capitalism. But the impacts of global food markets and trade wars have severe human consequences.

As we have seen in the American example, surplus has to go *somewhere* in order to protect the market from price depression. As a U.S. Department of Agriculture trade reform summary makes clear, "with 96 percent of the world's population living outside the United States, our farmers and ranchers rely on international trade to sell their surplus. Dollar for dollar, we export more wheat than coal, more fruits and vegetables than household appliances, more meat than motorcycles, more corn than cosmetics, and more bakery products than motorboats." If it is dumped abroad, either as food aid or as bargain-basement-price exports, excess food no longer threatens U.S. markets, but instead penetrates and destabilizes agriculture markets in other countries. There is rampant evidence suggesting highly destructive economic and social effects wrought by the spread of cheap surplus food, predominantly from the United States and Europe into developing countries whose agricultural sectors are both vital and precarious.

One problem with the current U.S. farm subsidy program, other than its fostering of intense domestic inequalities, is that it helps corporate export firms to sell crops at below their cost of production. These exports "create an unfair trading advantage because they depress international prices and narrow or even eliminate market opportunities for producers in other countries," explains a 2003 report by the Institute for Agriculture and Trade Policy. According to government data compiled by the institute, several major U.S. commodities were "dumped" on the international market at remarkably low prices between 1990 and 2001: wheat was sold at 40 percent below its production cost; corn, at about 25–30 percent; soybeans, at nearly 30 percent.[57] This means that the crops are dirt cheap and can easily penetrate foreign markets and push prices down.[58]

Cheap, below-cost imports "drive developing country farmers out of their local markets," the Institute report said. "If the farmers do not have access to a safety net, they have to abandon their land in search of other employment." This is no small matter: in poor, developing countries, anywhere between 50 and 80 percent of the people make their living from agriculture.[59] The great bounty that overflows from the United States and Europe creates economic mayhem in the developing world, exacerbating rural poverty, migration, and hunger.

Export dumping also manipulates markets abroad, and can punish consumers as well as farmers. According to a 2002 report by the Catholic Fund for Overseas Development, farmers told investigators that dumped food "is used by powerful traders to manipulate prices to their [the farmers'] disadvantage, for example by importing large quantities just before harvest time, in order to drive down prices to farmers. Once the traders have bought the harvest, imports are then reduced and prices rise again—farmers lose out, and consumers fail to gain."[60]

AIDING HUNGER: FOOD AS A WEAPON

Even more insidious than the continuous flood of American exports is the seemingly gracious flow of U.S. food aid to developing countries.

One country giving food to another sounds like a simple act of humanitarianism. Certainly food shipments to starving countries have often temporarily staved off hunger—at least for those lucky enough to get a taste. But since it was launched in the early 1950s, America's Food for Peace program, while promoting the idea of feel-good charity, has been first and foremost a convenient "secondary market" through which to channel U.S. surpluses. The primary goal has always been to stabilize the domestic market and to penetrate and expand foreign markets for U.S. food. "From its very inception in 1951, the food aid program has been an extension of foreign policy, farm interests, and corporate interests," according to *The Paradox of Plenty: Hunger in a Bountiful World,* published by Food First.[61]

The United States has been using food shipments for political leverage since at least 1812, when it sent emergency food to earthquake victims in Venezuela, with the ulterior purpose of fueling a revolt against Spain, writes Susan George in her classic, *How the Other Half Dies.*[62] But as is meticulously documented in *Aid as Obstacle,* published by Food First in 1980, the genesis of modern U.S. food aid was America's burgeoning food surplus after World War II, which was "costing taxpayers $1 million per day just for storage."[63] The politically potent farm lobby and grain-trading corporations "did not want the surpluses put on the domestic market," nor on the world market, where they would suppress prices. Through the Food for Peace program, agribusiness and Congress created a secondary market "allowing food-deficient countries to pay for American food imports in their own currencies instead of in dollars." These Third World countries were not part of the international market anyway, so their purchases (often facilitated by U.S. loans) relieved American surplus while protecting world prices and creating new commerce for American agribusiness.[64] A win-win-win scenario, at least for the U.S. corporations trading cheap subsidized American grains on the world market.

But the effects on Third World economies were anything but benign. In case after case, American food aid has led to deeper dependency on the U.S.—depleting Third World agriculture while carving out steady markets for U.S. exporters. A 1969 study published in the

Journal of Farm Economics "concluded that for every pound of [Public Law] 480 cereals imported, there was a net decline of almost one-half pound in Indian domestic production over the following two years, because of the reduced return to the farmer."[65]

South Korea has historically been among the top recipients of U.S. food aid, having "purchased more U.S. agricultural goods than any other underdeveloped country," according to *Aid as Obstacle*. "The U.S. grain imported into South Korea has allowed the government to maintain a 'cheap food' policy, undercutting many Korean farmers." As a result, between 1963 and 1976 Korea's rural population "fell from one-half to slightly more than one-third of the total population. . . . People lost their livelihoods and were forced to seek jobs in the cities."[66]

In another stark instance of destructive food aid, Colombia imported more than 1 million tons of U.S. wheat under public law 480 between 1955 and 1971—wheat that "could have been produced more cheaply locally." The American glut was priced so low it sabotaged domestic production and "resulted in 50 percent lower prices to Colombian farmers." During those years of American food aid, Colombia's domestic wheat production plunged by 69 percent, and imports skyrocketed 800 percent. By 1971 imports "accounted for 90 percent of domestic consumption."[67]

Even projects that claim to help developing nations help themselves often end up hurting farmers and helping agribusiness. In another case documented by Food First, the U.S. Agency for International Development (USAID) promoted export-oriented agriculture for poor Central American farmers. The idea was to shift growers away from producing staple foods for domestic markets and instead to encourage them to produce nontraditional crops for export. But it also imposed a system of American-style agriculture involving more pesticides and other costly "inputs"—meaning more business for U.S. petrochemical firms. Many of the new crops, such as melons and pineapples, reaped greater export profits, but not for the farmers—rather, for U.S. agribusiness firms such as Dole and Del Monte. Farmers went into debt to purchase the new seeds, fertilizers, and pesticides. Meanwhile, production of staple foods such as corn and beans plummeted. The export program, coupled with structural adjustment policies designed to eliminate subsidies for corn, beans, and rice, "destabilized traditional Central American farming while creating new markets for transnational agricultural inputs such as pesticides, fertilizers and hybrid seeds," according to *A Cautionary Tale: Failed U.S. Development Policy in Central America.* "While the nontraditional-export program's stated aim was to reduce poverty, it ended up further eroding the precarious economic foothold of small-scale farmers."[68]

SUBSIDIZING CHANGE

In its aggressive promotion of genetically modified foods, agribusiness claims that new, superefficient, vitamin-boosted crops are the answer to world hunger. The Green Revolution, whereby new strains of wheat and rice were introduced into developing countries in the 1950s and '60s, was billed much the same way, and at times produced wondrous quantity. Yet hunger persists. America's vast subsidies and exports, as well as those from Europe, make clear there is no shortage of food. But simply giving food to poor countries, while temporarily feeding the hungry, exacerbates food dependency. The problem isn't supply, it's poverty and access. And as we've seen, American subsidies, exports, and food aid have created some of that poverty, by marginalizing small farmers and disrupting local markets in poor countries. "In a world economy in which food is a commodity, poverty will lead to starvation no matter how productive agriculture becomes," argues Douglas H. Boucher in *The Paradox of Plenty.* "The basic problem for hungry people is not a scarcity of food, but a scarcity of income."[69] While agriculture produces enough food to supply every person on earth with 76 grams of protein and 2,800 calories per day—more than nutritionists consider necessary—some 842 million people are undernourished.[70]

Phenomenal money and energy are expended by the U.S. government—in other words, by taxpayers—to relieve the market of surplus. America's farm-support program emerged in the 1930s not only as a New Deal boost for farmers but also as a means of removing excess food from the market. Vast quantities were simply destroyed, even amidst rampant hunger, to keep farm prices from bottoming out. Then, in the 1950s, the government launched Food for Peace to unload postwar glut. In the 1980s, while deep recession plowed growers under and filled food banks with hungry farmers, grain overflowed from storage facilities into farm-town streets. All the while, American exports and food aid have decimated market after market abroad, intensifying poverty and migration and food dependency in developing countries. Something is seriously amiss here.

The problem is not subsidies and exports per se. Global trade, for better and worse, has been a fixture of human society since the 1500s. Economies and cultures can benefit from exchange. In an economically equitable and environmentally sustainable context, trade can enrich our lives. Subsidies, like technology, can be a tool for diminishing economic disparities instead of widening them. There is no reason that we can't have an entirely different subsidy system that promotes diversified, small-scale organic farming and that expands food security to make healthy and sustainable food economically viable. The only obstacle to such policies is the opposition of deeply entrenched financial and political interests.

There is no shortage of alternatives to the current agribusiness-based food system. There is also widening public outrage regarding the five negative impacts of corporate agribusiness's control over food, such as the proliferation of growth hormones, genetically modified crops, and food-borne illnesses. But woefully little political or economic capital is committed to serious sweeping change. It is important to assess America's farm subsidy program in the context of resource allocation: the money our society spends today, tens of billions of dollars a year, finances predominantly large-scale, ecologically unsustainable agriculture. Our tax dollars are spent in the name of stabilizing food prices and farm income, even as food costs continue to rise and farmer earnings decline. Meanwhile corporate intermediaries such as food processors, export firms, and supermarkets bask in profits at the expense of both farmers and consumers. Is this what we want?

13

THE GOOD NEWS: A MENU FOR CHANGE

"On college campuses, in religious organizations, among certain state and national legislators, in co-op movements, and among ecology and natural food groups there is a feeling that food is the right place to start to focus attention and energy for change."
—Frances Moore Lappé and Joseph Collins, *Food First:*
Beyond the Myth of Scarcity (1977)

"These forces are so big and so powerful, that it's very easy to feel despair.... When you look more closely at the subsidies, at the bribery, at the corruption, there was nothing inevitable about this system. And if there's nothing inevitable about it, the corollary is, things don't have to be the way they are."
—Eric Schlosser, author of *Fast Food Nation*, panel discussion
at University of California at Berkeley, 2003

THE CONSEQUENCES OF CONSUMPTION

The title of this book is meant in all earnestness: we are steadily farming and eating our way to oblivion. The way we make and eat food today is killing us and the planet. The effects may be direct, as when large numbers of individuals suffer from food-borne illnesses, obesity-related diseases, and, possibly, the chronic effects of pesticide residues. Food-industry workers are harmed by pesticide exposures and dangerous conditions in meatpacking and poultry plants. Indirectly, the depredations of Big Food are far and widely felt, as farmers are dispossessed and become unemployed; millions on millions of fish and birds are slain by factory-farm and pesticide pollution; unsustainable monocrop industrial farming drains aquifers and destroys irreplaceable topsoil; genetically modified crops endanger biodiversity; and millions of Third World farming peasants are impoverished and dislocated when their livelihoods are plowed under by the economic might and excesses of American agribusiness.

The total worldwide destructive impact of agribusiness and the corporate food industry should be considered as being on a par with that of other threats with planetary reach, such as global warming and nuclear weapons. The question of how the world feeds itself is as urgent and fundamental as any other question concerning human survival.

Before Thanksgiving Day in America, millions of turkeys stuffed with hormones and pesticides and manufactured on corporate factory farms hurtle down the immigrant-labor assembly line. Then it's on to diesel tractor-trailer trucks, to corporate supermarkets hundreds if not thousands of miles—and hundreds of gallons of diesel fuel—away, to be sold at inflated prices to those who can afford a turkey. This happens every day, but Thanksgiving—a moment when the perennial realities of feast and famine are graphically illuminated, when gluttony and hunger are thrown up in especially stark contrast—dramatizes the event. At Thanksgiving, America's heaping bounty stands on enviable display, alongside deprivation and individual acts of generosity.

Thanksgiving is also a time of unparalleled food shopping, a magnified expression of the daily choices we make. Every time we shop or dine, intentionally or not we participate in this intensely destructive food system. Unless, of course, we have the time, knowledge, and money to seek out something different. Our mundane everyday purchases at the supermarket, convenience outlet, fast food joint, health food store, or farmers' market are literally investments in either the dominant agribusiness system or an alternate one that prizes consumer health and economic and environmental sustainability. Many consumers ask themselves when they shop: What sort of future do I want to invest my money in? Can I afford to match my spending to my ideals? What are the consequences of my consumption?

More and more people are posing these questions. That said, far too much responsibility for change is heaped on the shoulders of individual consumers. Too many critics of corporate capitalism view consumer behavior as the final, decisive act of resistance, instead of as a modest yet useful point of departure. Clearly, consumer demand has helped drive the blossoming of organic foods. Strategic boycotts of crops such as grapes and lettuce, or of powerful firms like Monsanto or Tyson, can have real (though ultimately limited) economic and symbolic impact.[1] But the Long March of the wallet alone is not enough. Much more is needed than merely reforming business practices, though that is a step in the right direction. Industries and corporations find ways to survive, adjusting their niches and portfolios to protect their markets, maintain corporate power, and take advantage of new opportunities—for example, General Mills is now moving powerfully into the organics business. Eliminating the rotten apple presumes the rest of the harvest is just fine.

Everyone—consumers, producers, packagers, marketers, and retailers—is implicated and involved in a system far bigger than the mere economic sum of our purchases. Consequently, reversing our current agribusiness madness requires much more than toppling or rehabilitating "bad" corporations, more than switching our business from big companies to small ones, more than just creating new markets for the products we cherish. The solution must ensure equal access to wholesome, affordable food, ecological stewardship, and the survival of farmers. Whether or not we become activists, we, as citizens and consumers, must begin to view ourselves as part of a broader push for a serious overhaul of the food system as a whole.

A BUMPER CROP OF RESISTANCE

That big push is already happening. Resistance to this unhealthful, unsustainable food system—what the French farmer-activist José Bové calls "bad food"—is everywhere. The range and variety of responses to the global corporate food menu is compellingly vast, and reflects the nature of the target: the food industry's ubiquitous impacts, embedded in the fabric of our daily lives, have inspired a multitude of rebellions.

Protests against agribusiness's zealous promotion of genetically modified foods, food dumping, and pro-corporate subsidies have ignited across the globe, and their size and ferocity have increased over the past five years. Organic foods are selling like hotcakes. Farmers' markets and urban gardens are literally sprouting in cities across the United States. Under pressure from family farm groups and environmentalists, several states have banned toxic corporate hog farms. Just to list the resistance efforts evokes the scope and promise of the many movements attempting to abolish, replace, undercut, reform, or transform the harmful incarnations of agribusiness. (See the appendix, page 261, for contact information.)

Protests against the corporations' cheap-food-at-all-costs, "dead planet" agenda is taking place on a local, national, and international level. Here is a snapshot:

- *Organic and sustainable agriculture.* Perhaps the fastest-growing consumer and grower alternative to conventional, pesticide-centric farming. There's a booming niche market for organics, and a gathering movement to go "beyond organic," to ensure food is grown sustainably, on a small-scale locally available basis when possible. These efforts range from consumer-oriented health-conscious shopping alternatives such as niche marketing of locally-produced organics, to holistic "Natural Systems" agriculture (diversified farming in harmony with nature) championed by Wes Jackson, a widely published agroecology expert and founder of the Land Institute, a farm research project based in Kansas.
- *The anti-GM-foods fight.* Waged on multiple fronts, the worldwide struggle against genetically modified foods has mobilized millions against this latest cutting edge of corporate control over farmers and human sustenance. Anti-GM efforts have included large and loud protests, sabotage to destroy corporate GM crops, lawsuits and legislative battles challenging the GM takeover, well-documented scientific and environmental critiques of GM foods' safety and sustainability, and campaigns for open and honest food-labeling regulations.

- *The anticorporate, fair-trade movements.* The struggles for sustainable family farming, both in the United States and in Third World countries hammered by agribusiness dumping and corporate-friendly "free trade" agreements, have been a key element in broader campaigns for fair trade and against neoliberal policies promoting unbridled corporate access to markets. This has ranged from the Cancún protests against dumping and unequal subsidies to resistance to NAFTA and its infant cousins, the Free Trade Agreement of the Americas and the Central American Free Trade Agreement.

- *Direct farmer-to-consumer links.* Farmers' markets and Community Supported Agriculture (CSA) are not as overtly political as the anticorporate and fair-trade movements. Nevertheless, the momentum-gathering project of establishing direct contact between farmers and consumers is a vital piece of the resistance puzzle. Though many farmers' markets are still small, and not all sellers are organic, these markets are creating real connections between consumers and the growers of their food and are cutting out the supermarkets and other corporate middlemen that deprive farmers of income and inflate food prices.

- *Food safety and consumer health.* A panoply of highly effective food-safety movements aim to combat corporations' headlock on the regulatory system and to convince fast-food corporations to clean up their act. The efforts range from "soccer mom"–type groups fighting to clean up meat to Public Citizen and other organizations working to strengthen food-safety regulations. There are also campaigns against irradiation, growth hormones, antibiotics, and genetically modified foods.

- *Saving the family farm.* Independent family farms may be in critical condition, but they're not dead yet. Groups like the National Farmers Union, the National Family Farm Coalition, and others are struggling fiercely, through education, protests, and legislation, to give smaller producers an economic foothold. They're campaigning for, among many things, vigorous antitrust protections against agribusiness consolidation, creation of real com-

petitive markets by restricting agribusiness subsidies and corporate welfare, and the abolition of huge corporate factory farms.

- *Community Food Security.* Since the mid-1990s this national coalition bringing together hundreds of sustainable agriculture, antihunger, environmental, and nutrition groups has helped secure
federal money for dynamic food security projects linking farmers
to consumers and providing healthy, affordable, locally produced
food for communities across the United States. This small but
growing movement has created a compelling holistic model for a
different food system, one that integrates and addresses the concerns of farmers, consumers rich and poor, and the environment.

This abbreviated inventory leaves out other important and influential
resistance, such as organized labor's dogged opposition to deregulated
free trade and union efforts (against huge odds, and not always successful) to improve conditions for meat packers and farmworkers. Not to
mention work by the Humane Society, People for the Ethical Treatment
of Animals, and others forcing the meat industry to reform its brutal and
torturous slaughtering practices. Every group deserves praise for its
members' achievements. But it is important, as well, to undertake critical
assessment: What are the possibilities and limitations of today's landscape of opposition? Where and how do consumers fit in? And, perhaps
most critical—how can these movements work together most coherently
toward a clear goal that is bigger than any individual reform?

GOING ORGANIC ISN'T ENOUGH

The organic movement is exciting. The market for organics has grown
phenomenally, and is surging into the mainstream. Market researchers
estimate that sales of organic produce stood at $13.4 billion in 2003, up
from $5 billion just two years earlier. Nearly half of those sales came in
conventional grocery stores, as opposed to health-food outlets. Acreage
of certified organic pastures and croplands rose by 1 million between
1997 and 2001. A survey conducted by the Whole Foods grocery chain
found that 86 percent of shoppers said they "would buy more organic

food if the prices were lower," and 76 percent said they would increase their organic purchases if supermarkets offered more items.[2] Numerous school districts across the country have replaced junk food with organic treats in their vending machines.[3] The Minnesota-based Organic Consumers Association now claims 400,000 members; they estimate that there are some "30 million American organic consumers and farmers genuinely committed to purchasing and growing organic food."[4]

For reasons of environmental stewardship and sheer economic survival, many small and mid-sized farmers are shifting to the organic niche. It takes about three years to restore toxic and depleted conventional soils and gain certification, and there is minimal government support for the process. Organic meat and poultry is especially popular in higher-end markets and can bring farmers better revenue than conventional meat sold at depressed prices to giant corporate stockyards and processors. To be sure, it takes time and investment to make the switch to organic farming, but doing so can save a bundle by eliminating expenditures for pricey fertilizers and pesticides. (Some organic growers use certain pesticides, but ones that are far less toxic than those used in conventional farming.) The explosive organics market in the United States and elsewhere has also prompted burgeoning, loosely regulated organic production in China, where, reports Reuters, "government is understandably supportive of organic farming as a way of lowering input costs while tapping high-value markets."[5]

These impressive trends would seem to offer great hope for an organic revolution, in which the market would compel all farmers to grow organic, which would clean up the environment and improve human health. Toxic pesticides would be all but eradicated. Farming would be more sustainable, and more economically viable. But there's a catch: Corporations have caught on to the trend.

"Years ago it was looked upon as like a fringe movement, hippies eating their organic vegetables," says Kenny Swain of California Certified Organic Farmers, but now corporations like General Mills and Kraft are launching lucrative organic ventures.[6] "The more it becomes available and the more people hear about it, the more companies figure, 'Here's a new market that I can get into,'" observes Holly Givens, communications director for the Organic Trade Association. "Wal-Mart sent a representative to our trade show last year. There are some Wal-Marts that carry organic products. Now, that's great. They're offering additional accessibility, and that's great."[7] But is it really great that organics have become big business, what the *New York Times* termed "the organic-industrial complex"?[8]

Horizon, perched at the top of organic agribusiness, "is a $127 million public corporation that has become the Microsoft of organic milk, controlling 70 percent of the retail market," says Michael Pollan, writing in the *New York Times Magazine*. Cascadian Farm, one of the early organic outfits that arose in the early 1970s, is now "a General Mills showcase—a P.R. farm," and its back-to-the-land founder "is a General Mills vice president and a millionaire." Roger Blobaum, an organic advocate, told the *Times,* "Organic is becoming what we hoped it would be an alternative to."[9]

Despite the advent of corporate organics, to many, the organic business boom nonetheless signifies the arrival of a healthier, more ecologically sound way of life, a ray of hope that better, cleaner days are ahead. For all its stunning growth, however, organics remains a niche market, representing about 2 percent of foods consumed in the United States.[10] Yet even at this nascent stage, the same corporate centralization trends that have savaged so many conventional growers are already looming on the organic horizon, and there is no reason to expect this market to work any differently from the conventional agriculture market. Unless there are real public investments and stringent new antitrust protections, corporations and big growers will eventually knock out small organic producers. If the market flocks to frozen and processed organics, growers will again lose their share of the consumer dollar, unless they have the capital to do their own processing.

There are other serious limitations to the organics revolution, which are likely to become more evident and problematic as corporations move in. Large-scale monocrop organic farming is the most applicable model for corporations seeking volume and market share. Although this would be an improvement over conventional farming because it is less toxic, it still fails to sustain soils the way diversified agriculture does. The bigger organic producers are "applying the same model of industrial agriculture, just not using the allowable amounts of synthetic inputs," says Ryan Zinn of the Organic Consumers Association. "This is going to have a very comparable detrimental impact on the environment, by expanding the scale."

Organics also don't guarantee an end to back-breaking, exploitive conditions for farmworkers. Contrary to the bucolic scene connoted with organics—furthered no doubt by brand names like Nature's Valley—many "alternative" farms treat their workers quite conventionally. "The assumption of many who buy organics is that growers treat their workers with as much care as they do their tender shoots and berries," states a 2002 account in *U.S. News & World Report*. Although organic laborers "are spared the exposure to toxic pesticides that they would endure on regular farms, labor inspection reports show that they often toil in dangerous, unsanitary conditions for wages that sometimes don't approach the legal minimum."[11]

Ronnie Cummins, the national director of the Organic Consumers Association and a movement guru, notes: "If we don't watch out, organic food is going to be produced in an industrial manner, where you're going to have gigantic plantations in northern Mexico or wherever with standardized labor producing under USDA organic standards which ignore labor, and so it's not gonna taste that good if you know slaves had to produce it."[12]

Finally, there is the very serious problem of price. Currently, organics, lacking any government subsidy supports, are only really accessible to the middle and upper class, leaving working-class and poor people out of this privileged new way. Despite their growing presence in supermarket aisles, organic foods—which are often heavily processed and thus more expensive—remain largely pricey boutique items, often more than double the price of conventionally grown foods. A strong case can be made that organics provide more nutrition per dollar and that Americans have been spoiled to expect cheap food; nevertheless the organics movement must address the accessibility problem if it is to be about something more than good food for the better-off.

Many in the organics movement are aware of this challenge. "Up until now, the primary demographic of organic consumers is usually white middle-class mothers," says Zinn, who directs the Organic Consumers Association campaign on global trade and justice. "What we're seeing is that lower-class [people], people of color, especially people on Indian reservations do not have access to organic, fresh, safe food." Zinn and others are trying to "bring a class and race analysis within the organic movement."[13]

Cummins says the broader social-justice vision of the movement is still intact, and is part of the very definition of organic. "The organic ideal that we started building thirty years ago really was all-inclusive," he says. "It was health, it was justice, it was far beyond [just] me and my family and my health, and we've got to make sure that the organic integrity and traditional ideals get incorporated." Another prominent advocate, commentator Jim Hightower, a former Texas commissioner of agriculture, agrees: "It can't be organic if Wal-Mart produces it, if China produces the food in intolerable working conditions and then it's shipped to us and Wal-Mart brings it in here and does the retailing of it," he said in a 2003 interview. "The system itself has to be organic. It's about justice as much as it is about no chemicals."[14]

BEYOND ORGANIC—COMMUNITY FOOD SECURITY

Transportation is a central yet little-discussed part of the food system. According to research by David Pimentel of Cornell University, it takes roughly ten calories of fossil-fuel energy to produce, process, and transport a single calorie of food. Worldwatch Institute estimates that the average food item in the United States travels 1,500 to 2,500 miles from farm to table. As one writer explains, "While organic farming methods can save some energy in the production department, they don't have the same healthy effect on transportation; organic or not, oranges burn a lot of fuel on their way to Minneapolis."[15] Zinn notes, "We're really shooting ourselves in the foot if our only focus is on organic. While we are saving ourselves from ingesting all sorts of nasty synthetic chemicals, at the same time we are destroying the environment by [transporting] that clear across the country."

Even while organics' arrival in the mainstream—symbolized most potently by the 2002 adoption of (somewhat controversial) USDA organic standards—is celebrated, many groups, such as the Washington, D.C.–based Center for Food Safety, are pushing for a system that is "organic and beyond." They advocate a more sweeping mission to "maintain strong organic standards and to promote agriculture that is local, small-scale, and family operated, biologically diverse, humane, and socially just."[16]

It sounds wonderful, but what does it mean on the ground? Is it feel-good idealism for a privileged few or can it make a real difference? Actually, the goals and accomplishments of numerous "community food security" projects around the country reveal a movement that is striving to make locally produced food less expensive and more accessible to urban and rural working-class and poor people. The national Community Food Security Coalition, bringing together antihunger, environmental, and sustainable-farming advocates, defines community food security as "all persons obtaining at all times an affordable, nutritious and culturally appropriate diet through local, non-emergency food sources."[17] This means developing small farms near—and sometimes within—cities and towns, and prioritizing local food production over food banks, which, however benevolent, feature mostly processed, nonorganic food made by large corporations. To achieve this, small (and poorly funded) independent groups are establishing real economic relationships between farmers and city folk, and creating exemplary models for sustainable food systems built around community resources and needs.

For the urban and rural poor, "beyond organic" takes on a different, more basic meaning, for many don't have access to decent food of any sort, organic or conventional. Many inner-city poor are shut out of the supermarket: as studies document, either the produce store in their neighborhood charges much more than supermarkets in middle-class and suburban areas, or there is no food market at all. As detailed in Chapter 2, the only "food" readily available in many public housing communities is all-too-available McDonald's or Burger King, or a convenience store offering liquor, chips, and candy. Supermarket chains have become a meeting place for agribusiness conglomerates and middle- and upper-class consumers, leaving small farmers and rural and urban low-income groups hungry and out in the cold.[18]

In response to this crisis in food security, a veritable cornucopia of innovations is taking hold. In Los Angeles, San Francisco, Denver, and other cities, urban gardening projects using city lands are producing fresh nutritious food for public housing residents, and offering paid job training for budding gardeners and landscapers. Some of these endeavors emphasize entrepreneurship, employing poor residents (many of them teenagers from public housing) to produce and market niche products. In the heart of the poorest neighborhood in Austin, Texas, where more than 40 percent of the families live below the poverty line, residents and organizers have set up a community garden and farmers' market. It provides a hub for nutrition education and accessible food, as well as a direct market opportunity for local farmers, many of them organic.[19]

Urban subsistence and market farming generates both dietary and economic nourishment, and creates at least the potential for community-based economic development and a local food supply in poor, isolated neighborhoods. But while individual projects create very real hope, they are no panacea for the immense problems of structurally entrenched poverty, malnutrition, and hunger. Many entrepreneurial efforts, ironically, involve selling pricey jams and sauces to "yuppie" markets. Such is the perverse economic trap for the poor within capitalism: the entrepreneurial path out of poverty enlists the poor to sell niche products to the middle and upper class. This may help a few individuals, but it's an insufficient model for broad community sustainability.

In 1995, while the Republican-controlled Congress (with an ample assist from President Clinton) was vigorously attacking welfare and food stamp programs, an emergent grassroots movement gained passage of the Community Food Security Act, which provides funds for projects that address food, farm, and nutrition problems. It legislated the concept that the USDA could promote a whole different food system marrying the needs of small producers and low-income consumers. For the federal government, it was still mostly PR: Congress ladled out a meager $3.5 million in "seed grants" to thirteen community foodsecurity projects that would ultimately have to become self-sustaining. Programs from Indiana to Montana to Maine to South Central Los Angeles would develop an array of rural-urban food links: community kitchens and gardens would be training grounds for public housing residents to produce food and sell it to local stores and restaurants; area urban-rural food policy councils would be set up to help develop new farmers' markets; local sustainable agriculture networks would bring together farmers and neighborhood gardeners to produce food for people in need.[20] By 2003, the USDA was funding projects in twenty states to the tune of $4.6 million a year.[21]

There also are ongoing efforts around the country to convince local institutions such as schools and hospitals to purchase locally produced and, when possible, organic foods. The California Food and Justice Coalition is promoting a statewide "farm-to-cafeteria" program in which schools would purchase foods from area farmers, to improve kids' nutrition and boost farmers' incomes. "To the farmers, it really means access to a market that was previously closed to them, particularly the smaller family farmer in California, which makes up the vast majority," says Karrie Stevens Thomas, program director for Community Alliance with Family Farmers. "The food-service industry is typically only open to large-scale farmers."[22]

With some help from USDA, small farmers in Florida, North Carolina, and Kentucky are selling fresh produce to nearby school districts. According to a USDA report, these farm-to-school marketing projects "typically yield concrete benefits to everyone involved in the program: school children can incorporate a greater volume and variety of fresh fruits and vegetables into their diets, local school districts can obtain products packed to meet their exact specifications without having to pay for long-distance transportation and handling costs, and local growers gain an additional—and generally stable—source of farm-based income."[23]

One of the most promising trends in direct farm-to-consumer connections is the explosive growth of farmers' markets. By 2002 there were over 3,100 farmers' markets in the United States, according to the USDA, 79 percent more than in 1994. Nearly 20,000 farmers "reported selling their produce only at farmers markets," and 82 percent of the markets were self-sustaining, covering all their costs. Though on a limited scale, urban farmers' markets also improve food access for the poor: more than half the markets participate in the food stamps program, the federal Women, Infants and Children Farmers' Market Nutrition Program (WIC), and local or state nutrition programs.[24] One especially promising effort the USDA likes to promote is its WIC coupon program, in which up to 2 million mothers on welfare in forty-four states can get special coupons to shop in farmers' markets. Since launched in 1992, the program has provided millions of welfare mothers with fresh fruits and vegetables and boosted earnings for thousands of farmers. There's just one problem: the program gives each recipient just $10 to $20 a year in farmers' market coupons.[25] And even this tiny drop in a very big bucket is perennially under assault by antiwelfare budget cutters.

THE BIGGER PICTURE

This compelling array of alternatives provides at least a glimpse into how true food security could change our food system. Concrete examples are out there, and they're working. But there are serious limitations. First and foremost, the money devoted to these projects is a pittance, not much more than some of the largest subsidy payments made to individual big farmers. In addition, although farmers' markets and farm-to-school projects help small growers survive, they don't ensure that the food is organic or sustainably produced. Entrepreneurial projects help a few individuals and can symbolize progress in poor communities, but they don't challenge structural poverty and food corporations' astounding economic power. For those who can afford it, shopping organic is a fine individual investment in a healthier future. But we cannot simply eat our way to a better world: consumers and the various food-resistance movements must demand and pressure for sweeping policy changes concerning the many interrelated crises described throughout this book.

Food First's Peter Rosset is a trained agricultural ecologist and longtime food analyst (and activist). When asked about the way forward, he said: "We're not going to get [there] by just wishing or hoping that social change or popular culture will just come around. It requires policy change. The system we have right now is ... the product of specific policies and policy biases. Policies by which 50 percent of American farmers, the smaller ones, get zero or only symbolic amounts of subsidies and the largest and richest 25 percent get almost all of it. That is a policy that is written in a particular way that could just as easily be written in reverse. And would produce the reverse. There's nothing inevitable about it."[26]

The annual $20 billion bill for subsidies, if redirected to small, diversified agriculture, organics, and community food security projects, would go a long way toward making food more healthy, environmentally responsible, local, and economically sustaining. As the smallest of steps in that direction, says Michael Pollan, we could require that the USDA "turn back the clock a little bit and go back to the New Deal," when subsidies were far more equitable and were designed (in part) to keep farmers afloat.[27] So subsidies are certainly one piece of the puzzle.

Another piece is the overwhelming, near-total control of the food industry by a handful of corporations, most prominently ConAgra, Archer Daniels Midland, Tyson Foods, Monsanto, Cargill, Wal-Mart, Safeway, and Albertson's. Their grip on the entire food supply must be broken. In the lingo of an earlier age, the trusts must be busted.

The third piece of the puzzle, one with still broader implications, is the need for overt federal and local food policies that articulate and implement the goal that our food should, to the greatest extent possible, be locally, organically, and sustainably produced on small diversified farms that feed their surrounding economy. Federal rules should set far tighter standards for protecting food workers and farm ecologies; our tax dollars should be invested in community food security instead of corporate welfare; antitrust measures to prevent monopolies and at least diminish corporations' destructive market share must be strictly enforced.

On a local level, every community should have its own food policy as a central part of planning, of which food security is an intrinsic element. Cities and towns see it as their job to plan for housing, transportation, education of children, some social services, economic development, sewage and garbage collection, drinking water supply, and other essential services. But when it comes to food, the most basic and constant ingredient in our lives, we leave it up to the market and Band-Aid charity.

What kinds of measures could a local food policy incorporate? Many ideas are being tried, including convincing water agencies to donate water for community gardens and other urban agriculture ventures; offering tax incentives for sustainable agricultural land use; providing a site and other supports for a farmers' market; extending subsidies and other incentives to urban farms and small rural growers in the surrounding area; and providing purchasing incentives that entice restaurants, food markets, schools, and other food-service outlets to buy local organic produce.[28] Local food policy would also use zoning and other policy devices to ensure that food markets are accessible and evenly distributed.

Numerous states and some cities have food policy councils that are bringing long-ignored groups such as low-income residents and small farmers to the table. The Hartford Food System, in Hartford, Connecticut, begun in 1978, addresses root causes of hunger and poverty and works with farmers, policy makers, antihunger groups, schools, and other institutions to establish "an equitable and sustainable food system that addresses the underlying causes of hunger and poor nutrition."[29] The Arizona Food Policy Council, run by a group called Community Food Connections, emphasizes most of the core principles of community food security in statewide planning.[30] The Minnesota Food Association has three main programs. It encourages communities and residents to "buy local," and provides directories to farmers' markets and Community Supported Agriculture (CSA) programs; it has helped more than 1,000 conventional growers make the move to organics; and it is working to help food banks purchase products from struggling small farmers, a policy that focuses on both hunger and the farm crisis.[31] The list of individual programs and policy initiatives is hearteningly long.

Ultimately, however, we need to make a fundamental shift in our priorities. We must put healthy, accessible, sustainably produced food at the forefront of our society's political and economic agenda. What could be more important for sustaining both present and future generations than providing good food in a manner that sustains not only its consumers and its producers but also the planet itself? The answer will not come simply through boycotts of "bad" corporations, consumer revolts to reform McDonald's or Burger King, gentle antitrust reforms that essentially leave corporate power intact, or entrepreneurial niche marketing for the poor—though each of these steps plays an important role. There must be a larger commitment that encompasses all these hopeful parts, that takes into account the needs of the whole society—consumers, workers, farmers, the environment, and even animals—and not just the concerns of one group or another. Food is part of the web of life. How we produce and consume it is a measure of a people. We need to make a commitment as a society to change this diet for a dead planet—before it is too late.

APPENDIX: RESOURCES

Numerous forward-looking organizations are working to create sustainable solutions to the problems generated by agribusiness. Some organizations are overtly political and tackle broad systemic issues such as concentrated corporate power and neoliberal free-trade policies and highlight their connection to poverty and hunger. Others focus on just one concrete issue and avoid broader political questions. What follows is a starter's kit, by no means exhaustive, for learning more about the issues and locating ways to get involved. Many of these organizations' web sites provide extensive resources as well as links for further exploration. The listings are organized into eight categories:

Social Justice, Poverty, Trade
Consumer Protection and Public Health
Workers' Rights and Labor Organizations
Environment
Farming and Rural America
Community Food Security and Food Justice
Animal Rights and Humane Farming
Government Resources

SOCIAL JUSTICE, POVERTY, TRADE

Institute for Food and Development Policy (Food First)

http://www.foodfirst.org/index.html
398 60th Street, Oakland, CA 94618 USA
Phone: (510) 654-4400, Fax: (510) 654-4551
Email: foodfirst@foodfirst.org

Launched in 1975 by Frances Moore Lappé (author of *Diet for a Small Planet*) and Joseph Collins, this Oakland, California–based progressive nonprofit "people's think tank" has been a vital source of information, analysis, and initiatives pushing for sustainable food production, global economic justice, and overhauls of farm and trade policy. The institute produces books, reports, articles, and other media and works in coalition with other groups to advocate small-scale sustainable agriculture, combat corporate agribusiness, and fight global hunger and poverty.

Institute for Agriculture and Trade Policy

http://www.iatp.org
2105 First Avenue South, Minneapolis, MN 55404 USA
Phone: (612) 870-0453, Fax: (612) 870-4846
Email: iatp@iatp.org

The Institute for Agriculture and Trade Policy is an important advocate for fair trade and sustainable agriculture and the survival of small family farms. It works on a broad array of issues ranging from food security to exports and global trade to food safety. The institute's web site is a vital resource center for plugging into information, reports, and numerous campaigns.

ETC Group (Action Group on Erosion Technology and Concentration), formerly RAFI—The Rural Advancement Foundation International

http://www.etcgroup.org
478 River Avenue, Suite 200, Winnipeg, MB R3L 0C8 Canada
Phone: (204) 453-5259, Fax: (204) 284-7871

ETC Group's mission states that it "is dedicated to the conservation and sustainable advancement of cultural and ecological diversity and human rights. To this end, ETC Group supports socially responsible developments of technologies useful to the poor and marginalized, and it addresses international governance issues and corporate power." This critically important international group fights agricultural concentration, corporate takeover of seed patents, and rural poverty, and advocates sustainable farming. It pushes for "sustainable self-reliance within disadvantaged societies."

Via Campesina

http://www.viacampesina.org/welcome_english.php3
Secretaría Operativa
Operative Secretariat Tegucigalpa
Apdo. Postal 3628MDC, Honduras, C.A.
Phone: (504) 239-4679, Fax: (504) 235-9915
Email: viacam@gbm.hn

Via Campesina (literally, "the peasant's way"), an international organization with its head office in Tegucigalpa, Honduras, describes its mission as "coordinat[ing] peasant organizations of small and middle-scale producers, agricultural workers, rural women, and indigenous communities from Asia, Africa, America, and Europe. . . . Via Campesina is organized in eight regions as follows: Europe, Northeast and Southeast Asia, South Asia, North America, the Caribbean, Central America, and South America and Africa." Via Campesina has played an important role in fighting the World Trade Organization and neoliberal trade policies.

Public Citizen

http://www.citizen.org
1600 20th Street NW, Washington, DC 20009 USA
Phone: (202) 588-1000
Email: member@citizen.org

Public Citizen was founded by Ralph Nader in 1971 "to protect consumer interests in Congress, the executive branch, and the courts." Since that time it has been a critical locus of advocacy and research on a number of food-related fronts, including fair trade, water privatization, and food-safety issues such as meat irradiation and meat processing.

Worldwatch Institute

http://www.worldwatch.org
1776 Massachusetts Avenue NW, Washington, DC 20036-1904 USA
Phone: (202) 452-1999, Fax: (202) 296-7365
Email: worldwatch@worldwatch.org

Best known for its work on global ecology and sustainable development, Worldwatch Institute provides outstanding research and analysis on food-related issues such as the environmental and public health consequences of large-scale animal agriculture and supersized consumption. The Worldwatch web site is a useful resource for reading up on poverty and food inequality, as well as energy issues and environmental sustainability, and the institute also puts out an excellent monthly magazine, which can be found at most libraries.

CONSUMER PROTECTION AND PUBLIC HEALTH

Center for Food Safety

http://www.centerforfoodsafety.org
660 Pennsylvania Avenue SE, Suite 302, Washington, DC 20003 USA
Phone: (202) 547-9359, Fax: (202) 547-9429
Email: office@centerforfoodsafety.org

The Center for Food Safety, with home offices in Washington, DC, is a vital, aggressive advocate for consumers, farmers, and ecological sustainability. The group "works to protect human health and the environment by curbing the proliferation of harmful food-production technologies and by promoting organic and other forms of sustainable agriculture. CFS engages in legal, scientific and grassroots initiatives to guide national and international policymaking on critical food safety issues." To spearhead its "Organic and Beyond" campaign, in 2002 the center published an important anthology titled *Fatal Harvest: The Tragedy of Industrial Agriculture* (http://www.fatalharvest.org/index.htm).

Organic Consumers Association

http://www.organicconsumers.org
6101 Cliff Estate Road, Little Marais, MN 55614 USA
Phone: (218) 226-4164, Fax: (218) 353-7652
Email: ryan@organicconsumers.org

This 400,000-member group is a powerful advocate for sustainable organic agriculture and genuine organic standards. The web site of the Organic Consumers Association provides an outstanding information resource for those interested in (or already working on) issues such as organic foods, genetically modified crops, food irradiation, mad cow disease, and many other topics relating to food safety and agribusiness. It provides a useful database of mainstream and alternative press reports, research, campaign updates, and ways to get involved.

Consumers Union

http://www.consumersunion.org
Consumers Policy Institute
1666 Connecticut Avenue NW, Suite 130, Washington, DC 20009-1039
Phone: (202) 462-6262, Fax: (202) 265-9548

Highly respected for its research on a wide array of consumer issues, the independent Consumers Union, which publishes *Consumers Reports*, has undertaken studies in order to provide consumers with important information on food-safety matters such as genetically modified foods and mad cow disease.

Government Accountability Project

http://www.Whistleblower.org
1612 K Street NW, Suite 400, Washington, DC 20006 USA
Phone: (202) 408-0034

Since its founding in 1977, the Government Accountability Project's mission has been "to protect the public interest by promoting government and corporate accountability through advancing occupational free speech and ethical conduct, defending whistleblowers, and empowering citizen activists." The nation's leading whistleblower organization, it litigates whistleblower cases, publicizes whistleblower concerns, and develops policy and legal reforms of whistleblower laws. The group has done important work publicizing serious flaws in meatpacking and food-safety protections.

Safe Tables Our Priority

http://www.stop-usa.org
P.O. Box 4352, Burlington, VT 05406 USA
Media & Business: (802) 863-0555, Victims & Victims' Families:
(800) 350-S.T.O.P.
Email: mail@safetables.org

Founded by parents of fatal meat-poisoning victims in the early 1990s, Safe Tables Our Priority, or S.T.O.P., is a nonprofit organization that has helped put a human face on the deadly problems of tainted meat. The group's mission is specific: "to prevent unnecessary illness and loss of life from pathogenic foodborne illness." S.T.O.P. believes that "in the United States today, people should not be made seriously ill, permanently injured or killed by pathogens such as bacteria or viruses in our food. S.T.O.P. does not take a stand on other types of food safety issues such as pesticides."

Pesticide Education Center

http://www.pesticides.org/educmaterials.html
P.O. Box 225279, San Francisco, CA 94122-5279 USA
Phone: (415) 665-4722, Fax: (415) 665-2693
Email: pec@igc.org

The web site of the Pesticide Education Center, located in San Francisco, is a one-stop spot for information on all the health aspects of pesticide use by consumers themselves (in pet and lawn care and home maintenance) and by agriculture.

WORKERS' RIGHTS AND LABOR ORGANIZATIONS

United Food and Commercial Workers International Union

http://www.ufew.org
UFCW International Union
1775 K Street NW, Washington, DC 20006 USA
Phone: (202) 223-3111
Email: www.ufcw.org

Representing 1.4 million workers who toil in some of the most dangerous, low-paying jobs in the United States and Canada, the UFCW fights for better wages, affordable health insurance, workplace safety, and basic workers' rights in various sectors such as meatpacking, poultry and food processing, and large retail food outlets. Recent battles have included resisting Safeway's attempt to cut employees' health-care benefits and ensuring that meatpacking and poultry plant workers get their pay for break time, essential safety gear on the job, and the right to go to the bathroom.

Farm Worker Justice Fund, Inc.

http://www.fwjustice.org
1010 Vermont Avenue NW, Suite 915, Washington, DC 20005 USA
Phone: (202) 783-2628, Fax: (202) 783-2561
Email: fjf@nclr.org

A steadfast advocate for highly exploited migrant and seasonal farmworkers, the Farm Worker Justice Fund promotes legislation and public education and also litigates to "improve [farmworkers'] wages and working conditions, labor and immigration policy, health and safety, and access to justice." The group has strong ties to labor unions, farmworkers, and legal-aid advocates.

Farm Labor Organizing Committee

http://www.floc.com
1221 Broadway, Toledo, OH 43609 USA

Phone: (419) 243-3456, Fax: (419) 243-5655
Email: info@floc.com

Since 1968, the feisty Farm Labor Organizing Committee has advocated for migrant farmworkers and has won some key battles to improve rock-bottom wages, rebuild dilapidated migrant housing, and to reduce pesticide poisoning in the fields. They have fought large corporate growers and processors in the fields and plants where cucumbers are grown and processed into pickles, winning contracts and eliminating the industry's "independent contractor" system so that pickle companies now must contribute to unemployment, workers compensation, and Social Security funds.

United Farm Workers

http://www.ufw.org
P.O. Box 62, Keene, CA 93531 USA
Email: UFWofamer@aol.com

The historic labor and civil rights movement that launched the United Farm Workers was led by Cesar Chavez, who rallied consumers to migrant workers' cause by calling grape and lettuce boycotts in the late 1960s. The United Farm Workers has won major victories for California farm laborers, including migrant worker protection laws, basic workers' rights, contracts restricting pesticide exposures, the establishment of worker credit unions, clean-ups of conditions in labor camps, profit-sharing plans, and parental leave.

National Interfaith Committee for Worker Justice

http://www.nicwj.org
1020 W. Bryn Mawr Avenue, 4th Floor, Chicago, IL 60660 USA
Phone: (773) 728-8400, Fax: (773) 728-8409

The National Interfaith Committee for Worker Justice is a key ally for low-wage immigrant workers. It has aided unions in organizing, public education, and legislative campaigns, with particular emphasis on improving working conditions and basic safety in U.S. poultry plants. The committee is part of an emerging broad coalition of labor and religious communities.

ENVIRONMENT

Pesticide Action Network of North America

http://www.panna.org
49 Powell Street, Suite 500, San Francisco, CA 94102 USA
Phone: (415) 981-1771, Fax (415) 981-1991
Email: panna@panna.org

The Pesticide Action Network of North America provides critical research and background information on the proliferation and hazards of pesticides. Its popular "dirty dozen" campaign helped push U.S. policy makers to phase out a number of the more deadly pesticides, and the group continues to push for the elimination of the many hazardous toxins that wind up in our food. The network's web site provides information on pesticide use, and ways to get involved to reduce it.

National Campaign for Sustainable Agriculture

http://sustainableagriculture.net
P.O. Box 396, Pine Bush, NY 12566 USA
Phone (845) 361-5201, Fax: (845) 361-5204
Email: campaign@sustanableagriculture.net

The National Campaign for Sustainable Agriculture "is dedicated to educating the public on the importance of a sustainable food and agriculture system that is economically viable, environmentally sound, socially just, and humane." The group has been an energetic advocate for organic and small-scale farming, and has worked on these and other issues in concert with organizations around the country.

Sierra Club

http://www.sierraclub.org/factoryfarms
85 Second Street, 2nd Floor, San Francisco, CA 94105   USA

Phone: (415) 977-5500, Fax: (415) 977-5799
Email: information@sierraclub.org

The nation's most venerable national environmental group, the Sierra Club has been on the scene since its founding by John Muir in 1892. It has spearheaded education and action campaigns on factory-farm pollution, family farmers, antibiotics, and other issues. The group's web site includes resources for activists, fact sheets, articles, and reports.

Environmental Working Group

http://www.ewg.org
1436 U Street NW, Suite 100, Washington, DC 20009 USA

Perhaps best known for its farm-subsidy database—an intensively documented indictment of waste, abuse, and fundamental inequities in American farm-support programs—the Environmental Working Group has since 1993 produced meticulous, comprehensive, and widely pub-licized reports on pesticides in food, toxins in farmed fish, and many other environmental and consumer issues. These reports rely largely on original government data and extensive public records. The EWG's website is a valuable research resource.

Natural Resources Defense Council

http://www.nrdc.org
40 West 20th Street, New York, NY 10011 USA
Phone: (212) 727-2700, Fax: (212) 727-1773
Email: nrdcinfo@nrdc.org

One of the larger national U.S. environmental groups, the Natural Resources Defense Council is a valuable legislative advocate and regu-latory watchdog that produces well-researched reports on issues such as pollution by factory farms and pesticides.

GRACE (Global Resource Action Center for the Environment) Factory Farm Project

http://www.factoryfarm.org
215 Lexington Avenue, Suite 1001, New York, NY 10016 USA
Phone: (212) 726-9161, Fax: (212) 726-9160
Email: info@factoryfarm.org

This organization's goal is "to eliminate factory farming in favor of a sustainable food-production system that is healthful and humane, economically viable, and ecologically sound." The group's web site features an "Eat Well" guide, with which consumers can locate organic produce and free-range animal meat available in their area.

Ecological Farming Association

http://www.eco-farm.org
406 Main Street, Suite 313, Watsonville, CA 95076 USA
Phone: (831) 763-2111, Fax: (831) 763-2112
Email: info@eco-farm.org

The Ecological Farming Association is a nonprofit educational organization based in Watsonville, California, that promotes ecologically sound agriculture. It organizes special events "to bring people together from all over the world to share ideas and experiences in producing healthful food from a healthy earth." At their web site are links to a number of their projects and action alerts, including Worldwide Opportunities for Organic Farms (WWOOF), and Californians for GE-Free Agriculture.

Leopold Center for Sustainable Agriculture, Iowa State University

http://www.leopold.iastate.edu
209 Curtiss Hall, Iowa State University, Ames, Iowa 50011-1050 USA
Phone: (515) 294-3711, Fax: (515) 294-9696
Email: leocenter@iastate.edu

The Leopold Center for Sustainable Agriculture, operating under the umbrella of Iowa State University, "explores and cultivates alternatives that secure healthier people and landscapes in Iowa and the nation." It has research programs in marketing and food systems, ecology, and policy.

The Land Institute

http://www.landinstitute.org/vnews/display.v

Founded more than twenty years ago in Salina, Kansas, by widely published agroecology expert Wes Jackson, this experimental research farm aims to "develop an agricultural system with the ecological stability of the prairie and a grain yield comparable to that from annual crops," the institute's web site says. Their research on Natural Systems Agriculture, the concept of farming in harmony with the surrounding ecology, has appeared in numerous peer-reviewed journals.

FARMING AND RURAL AMERICA

National Farmers Union

http://www.nfu.org
11900 East Cornell Avenue, Aurora, CO 80014-3194 USA
Phone: (303) 337-5500, Toll Free: (800) 347-1961, Fax: (303) 368-1390

The National Farmers Union is a national farmers-advocacy group with a membership of nearly 250,000 family farmers throughout the United States. For more than a century, the union's primary goal has been "to sustain and strengthen family farm and ranch agriculture," through grassroots initiatives on the local, state, and national levels. The union's website states that it "believes that good opportunities in production agriculture are the foundation of strong farm and ranch families and that strong farm and ranch families are the basis for thriving rural communities. Vibrant rural communities, in turn, are vital to the health and economic wellbeing of the entire U.S. economy."

National Family Farm Coalition

http://www.nffc.net/com.htm
110 Maryland Avenue NE, Suite 307, Washington, DC 20002 USA
Phone: (202) 543-5675, Toll Free: (800) 639-3276, Fax: (202) 543-0978
Email: nffc@nffc.net

The National Family Farm Coalition unites family farmers and farm advocacy groups from across the country to join in numerous national campaigns on issues such as sustainable agriculture, genetically engineered crops, fair trade, Farm Aid, and building direct economic relationships between farmers and consumers through alternative markets and cooperatives.

Center for Rural Affairs

http://www.cfra.org
145 Main Street, PO Box 136, Lyons, NE 68038-0136 USA
Phone: (402) 687-2100, Fax: (402) 687-2200
Email: info@cfra.org

A Nebraska-based nonprofit, the Center for Rural Affairs is a strong advocate for family farming. It promotes legislation, programs, and education to stimulate new small-farm development and rural economic stability, and has worked with farmers and ranchers against agribusiness consolidation. Its web site contains useful reports and background information, and ways to get involved.

Western Organization of Resource Councils

http://www.worc.org/index.html
2401 Montana Avenue, #301, Billings, Montana 59101 USA
Phone: (406) 252-9672, Fax: (406) 252-1092
Email: billings@worc.org

The Western Organization of Resource Councils is a network of grassroots community groups that help support and coordinate a range of environmental and rural economic justice campaigns. The council's mission is to "advance the vision of a democratic, sustainable, and just society through community action"; it seeks to promote a balance between economic growth and "the health of people and stewardship of their land." The 8,700-member strong organization has fought economic concentration in meatpacking and grain trading and on factory farms, and has fought for farm lending reform.

CropChoice

http://www.cropchoice.com/about.html
P.O. Box 33811, Washington, DC 20033 USA
Phone: (202) 797-7554
Email: editor@cropchoice.com

CropChoice describes itself as "an alternative news and information source for American farmers and consumers about genetically modified crops, corporate agribusiness concentration, farm and trade policy, sustainable agriculture, wind farming and alternative energy, and rural economic and social issues."

American Farmland Trust

http://www.farmland.org
1200 18th Street NW, Washington, DC 20036 USA
Phone: (202) 331-7300, Fax: (202) 659-8339
Email: info@farmland.org

American Farmland Trust is a nonprofit founded in 1980 to protect farmland. The trust "works to stop the loss of productive farmland and to promote farming practices that lead to a healthy environment." Based in Washington, D.C., the group promotes sustainable agriculture, community and state-level land-use planning involving agriculture, and environmental conservation.

Organization for Competitive Markets

http://www.competitivemarkets.com/ocml.html
P.O. Box 6486, Lincoln, NE 68506 USA

Phone: (402) 792-0041, Fax: (786) 549-0277

Email: ocm@competitivemarkets.com

Advocating on behalf of family farmers and ranchers for fair market competition, the Organization for Competitive Markets provides information and promotes policies to create a more level playing field between small and larger farms. It fights corporate monopoly control over the food system, and pushes to boost farmers' share of the food dollar by advocating new marketing approaches and combating economic consolidation in food processing.

Corporate Agribusiness Research Project

http://www.electricarrow.com/CARP

P.O. Box 2201, Everett, WA 98203-0201

Phone: (425) 258-5345

Email: avkrebs@earthlink.net

The purpose of the Corporate Agribusiness Research Project is to "monitor corporate agribusiness from a public interest perspective through awareness, education, and action while at the same time advocating the importance of building alternative, democratically controlled food systems." Its web site, offering useful background information and published newspaper and other articles on the machinations of agribusiness, is edited by the longtime agribusiness critic and commentator A.V. Krebs.

COMMUNITY FOOD SECURITY AND FOOD JUSTICE

Community Food Security Coalition

http://www.foodsecurity.org

P.O. Box 209, Venice, CA 90294

Phone: (310) 822-5410, Fax: (310) 822-1440

The nonprofit Community Food Security Coalition describes itself as "dedicated to building strong, sustainable, local and regional food systems that ensure access to affordable, nutritious, and culturally appropriate food for all people at all times. We seek to develop self-reliance among all communities in obtaining their food and to create a system of growing, manufacturing, processing, making available, and selling food that is regionally based and grounded in the principles of justice, democracy, and sustainability." The coalition, which consists of 250 member organizations, has successfully pushed Congress to finance community food-security programs around the country. The group's excellent web site provides links to dozens of organizations working on sustainable agriculture, poverty and hunger, community development, and broader food-system issues.

The coalition maintains a section of its web site as an information center for urban agriculture and community gardening programs in the United States and Canada (http://www.foodsecurity.org/links.html# communitygardens).

Slow Food USA

http://www.slowfoodusa.org
434 Broadway, 6th Floor, New York, NY 10013 USA
Phone: (212) 965-5640, Fax: (212) 966-8652
Email: info@slowfoodusa.org

The rapidly growing international slow food movement, which originated in Italy, promotes environmental sustainability and healthful, mindful eating. Slow Food USA is "dedicated to stewardship of the land and ecologically sound food production; to the revival of the kitchen and the table as centers of pleasure, culture, and community; to the invigoration and proliferation of regional, seasonal culinary traditions; and to living a slower and more harmonious rhythm of life."

Just Food

http://www.justfood.org
P.O. Box 20444, Greeley Square St., New York, NY 10001-0008 USA
Phone: (212) 645-9880, Fax (212) 645-9881
Email: info@justfood.org

This New York City–based nonprofit vigorously promotes sustainable local food production and access to healthy food for low-income and other urban residents. Like similar projects around the country, Just Food emphasizes "new marketing and food-growing opportunities" that connect small family farms and urban community gardeners with city neighborhoods that often have little access to fresh food. Their Community Supported Agriculture project "helps to support family farms that are struggling to stay in business, while providing city people, particularly those in low-income neighborhoods, with access to high-quality, locally grown, affordable produce."

Hartford Food System

http://www.hartfood.org/index.html
Email: info@hartfordfood.org

One of the most venerable community food-security projects in the United States, Hartford, Connecticut's Hartford Food System, launched in 1978, has been a key player in the growth of this movement. While working concretely to meet the food security needs of low-income and elderly Connecticut residents, the group also advocates broader collaborative programs involving farmers, grassroots community groups, chefs, educators and government, and public policies to create "an equitable and sustainable food system that addresses the underlying causes of hunger and poor nutrition."

Community Alliance with Family Farmers

http://www.caff.org
P.O. Box 363, Davis, CA 95617 USA
Phone: (530) 756-8518, Fax: (530) 756-7857

Based in California's agribusiness-rich Central and San Joaquin valleys, the Community Alliance with Family Farmers helps family farmers and their surrounding rural communities by creating direct economic and social relationships between farmers and consumers, through farm-to-school education projects and other programs. In an area dominated by environmentally destructive big agriculture, the alliance also pushes for smaller-scale sustainable farming and ecological restoration, including biodiversity projects.

Urban and Environmental Policy Institute Center for Food and Justice

http://departments.oxy.edu/uepi/cfj
2106 Colorado Boulevard, Los Angeles, CA 90041 USA
Phone: (323) 341-5090, Fax: (323) 258-2917
E-mail: cfj@oxy.edu

Occidental College's Urban and Environmental Policy Institute Center for Food and Justice promotes "a sustainable and socially just food system," through "collaborative action strategies, community capacity-building, and research and education." The center's website offers valuable background information on community food security, supermarket redlining, farm-to-school projects, and healthy-school-food campaigns.

American Community Gardening Association

http://www.communitygarden.org/about/index.html

Founded in 1979, the American Community Gardening Association, a national nonprofit, promotes the expansion of community gardening, which it promotes as a means for greening neighborhoods, increasing social cohesion, and boosting the supply of fresh, healthy food.

ANIMAL RIGHTS AND HUMANE FARMING

Farm Sanctuary

http://www.farmsanctuary.org
P.O. Box 150, Watkins Glen, NY 14891 USA
Phone: (607) 583-2225, Fax: (607) 583-2041
Email: info@farmsanctuary.org

Farm Sanctuary provides education, numerous campaigns focusing on humane treatment of farm animals, and "operates farm animal sanctuaries and wages campaigns to stop the exploitation of animals raised for food." Its web site offers some basic information on the meat industry's treatment of poultry and livestock, and promotes vegetarian alternatives.

Humane Society of the United States

http://www.hsus.org/ace/352
2100 L. Street NW, Washington, DC 20037 USA
Phone: (202) 452-1100

The Humane Society of the United States, the nation's most venerable and well-known animal protection group, works on a range of fronts, fighting against brutal and excessive animal testing, marine overfishing that snares dolphins, and inhumane livestock raising and slaughtering practices, among other issues.

GOVERNMENT RESOURCES

U. S. Department of Agriculture

http://www.usda.gov
Email: agsec@usda.gov

The sprawling U.S. Department of Agriculture is involved with most aspects of the nation's farming and food production, including subsidy policies, crop research, marketing programs and data, rural assistance programs, food stamps, nutrition, soil conservation, and agricultural export policies. Its web site is a powerful research tool that makes available historical and current data from the national agricultural census. Particularly useful is the USDA Economic Research Service, available at http://www.ers.usda.gov.

Food and Drug Administration

http://www.fda.gov
5600 Fishers Lane, Rockville, MD 20857-0001, USA
Phone: (888) INFO-FDA (888-463-6332)

Part of the U.S. Department of Health and Human Services, the Food and Drug Administration is responsible for ensuring food safety, monitoring and reporting on aspects of food processing, livestock raising, pesticide use, and nutrition and labeling, and pharmaceuticals. The agency's website provides regulatory updates, statistics, and background on issues such as mad cow disease, mercury levels in fish, and pesticide residues on food, as well as a wealth of information on food safety and food-borne illness alerts. To access the FDA's food-safety site directly, go to http://www.foodsafety.gov.

Centers for Disease Control

http://www.cdc.gov
1600 Clifton Road, Atlanta, GA 30333 USA
Phone: (404) 639-3311, Public Inquiries: (404) 639-3534, (800) 311-3435

Another division of the U.S. Department of Health and Human Services, the Centers for Disease Control tracks and analyzes human illnesses and diseases. Its website is packed with background information and statistics on disease, including food-borne illnesses.

Environmental Protection Agency

http://www.epa.gov
Ariel Rios Building
1200 Pennsylvania Avenue NW, Washington, DC 20460, USA
Phone: (202) 272-0167

Indirectly, covering food issues is part of the Environmental Protection Agency's job, because the EPA regulates and monitors pesticide use and water supply and pollution. Its web site contains useful reports and background information on pesticide use and toxicity.

General Accounting Office

http://www.gao.gov
441 G Street NW, Washington, DC 20548 USA
Phone: (202) 512-4800 (Office of Public Affairs)
Email: webmaster@gao.gov

The investigative agency of Congress made famous during the Watergate era for its aggressive research into wrongdoing by President Nixon's reelection campaign, the General Accounting Office provides a critical service to Congress and the public by undertaking often vigorous investigations of the successes and failures and costs of government programs and regulations. At the agency's web site can be found a rich database of reports, many of them on food-related topics such as meat inspection, pesticides, mad cow disease, and others.

U.S. Congress

http://thomas.loc.gov

The United States Congress maintains a powerful web site that provides links to congressional committees dealing with food and agricultural policy. It also provides an easy way to contact your representatives about your concerns.

United Nations Food and Agriculture Organization

http://www.fao.org
Viale delle Terme di Caracalla, 00100 Rome, Italy
Telephone: (+39) 06 57051
Phone: (+39) 62 5852, (+39) 61 0181
Fax: (+39) 06 570 53152
Email: webmaster@fao.org

The UN's food and agriculture agency conducts research and analysis and carries out programs that deal with the global food supply, hunger, and malnutrition issues. Its website is an excellent educational and research resource, including reports and databases on world food production, subsidies, trade, disease outbreaks, water supply, and many other issues.

World Health Organization

http://www.who.int/en
Avenue Appia 20, 1211 Geneva 27 Switzerland

Phone: (+ 41 22) 791 21 11
Fax: (+ 41 22) 791 3111
Email: inf@who.int

Established by the United Nations in 1948, the WHO monitors and reports on global health issues, including disease outbreaks, famine, nutrition and malnutrition, and provides detailed information and background on food-related health crises such as mad cow disease and avian flu.

NOTES

PART I: CONSUMED

1. AGRICULTURAL APOCALYPSE

1. The Fertilizer Institute; U.S. Department of Agriculture (USDA).

2. Drs. David Pimentel and Mario Giampietro, "Food, Land, Population and the U.S. Economy," report published by Carrying Capacity Network, November 21, 1994, available at http://www.dieoff.com/page40.htm.

3. Calculations based on data from 2002 Census of Agriculture, USDA National Agricultural Statistics Service.

4. Based on data collected by USDA Economic Research Service; Centers for Disease Control.

5. See Andrew Kimbrell, ed., *Fatal Harvest: The Tragedy of Industrial Agriculture* (Washington, DC: Island Press, 2002).

6. See Eric Schlosser, *Fast Food Nation* (New York: Houghton Mifflin, 2001).

7. Wendell Berry, speech on panel discussion titled "Fast Food World: Perils and Promises of the Global Food Chain," University of California, Berkeley, November 24, 2003.

8. Mary Hendrickson, William D. Heffernan, Philip H. Howard, and Judith B. Heffernan, "Consolidation in Food Retailing and Dairy: Implications for Farmers and Consumers in a Global Food System," report to the National Farmers Union, University of Missouri, 2001.

9. James M. MacDonald, Michael E. Ollinger, Kenneth E. Nelson, and Charles R. Handy, "Consolidation in U.S. Meatpacking," Agricultural Economics Report No. 785, USDA, Economic Research Service, March 1999, available at http://www.ers.usda.gov/publications/aer785/aer785a.pdf.

10. Risks of Genetic Engineering, backgrounder by Union of Concerned Scientists, available at http://www.ucsusa.org/food_and_environment/biotechnology/page.cfm?pageID=346.

11. Food and Drug Administration, U.S. Department of Health and Human Services. A memo from October 18, 2000, states in part, "based on the information Monsanto has presented to FDA, we have no further questions concerning grain and forage from the Roundup Ready NK603 corn at this time."

12. See, for instance, Frances Moore Lappé, Joseph Collins, and Peter Rosset with Luis Esparza, *World Hunger: 12 Myths*, 2nd ed. (New York: Grove Press, 1998); Frances Moore Lappé, Joseph Collins, and David Kinley, *Aid as Obstacle: Twenty Questions About Our Foreign Aid and the Hungry* (San Francisco: Institute for Food and Development Policy, 1980); and Susan George, *How the Other Half Dies: The Real Reasons for World Hunger* (Montclair, NJ: Allanheld, Osmun, 1977).

13. UN Food and Agriculture Organization statistical database, available at http://apps.fao.org/faostat/form?collection=FS.CropsAndProducts&Domain=FS&serv let=1&hasbulk=0&version=ext&language=EN.

14. "FAO Reports a Setback in the War Against Hunger," UN Food and Agriculture Organization, November 25, 2003.

15. Michael Pollan, speech at "Fast Food World," November 24, 2003.

2. ONE BIG SUPERMARKET

1. Senate Committee on Small Business, witness B testimony, "The Effects of Slotting Fees on Small Businesses," hearing 106-359, September 14, 1999 (Washington, DC: U.S. Government Printing Office).

2. Kent Hoover, "Supermarket Slotting Leaves Small Firms Out," *Cincinnati Business Courier,* October 8, 1999.

3. Senate Committee on Small Business, Senator Christopher S. Bond, opening statement, "Slotting Fees: Are Family Farmers Battling to Stay on the Farm and in the Grocery Store?," September 14, 2000 (Washington, DC: U.S. Government Printing Office).

4. Ibid.

5. Senate Committee on Small Business, "Effects of Slotting Fees."

6. Mary Hendrickson, William D. Heffernan, Philip H. Howard, and Judith B. Heffernan, "Consolidation in Food Retailing and Dairy: Implications for Farmers and Consumers in a Global Food System," report (Washington, DC: National Farmers Union, 2001).

7. Senate Committee on Small Business, "Slotting Fees."

8. Ibid.

9. Arizona State University, National Food and Agriculture Policy Project, "Slotting Fees: Symptom of a More Fundamental Problem?," NFAPP paper no. 01-4, March 2001, available at http://nfapp.east.asu.edu/policy/2001/pb01-04.pdf.

10. Wyatt Andrews, "Missouri Rep Describes Payola at the Supermarket," *Midwest Today,* summer 2000.

11. Federal Trade Commission, Robert N. Pyle, "Statement Before the Federal Trade Commission Slotting Fees Hearing," November 8, 1995, available at http://ftc.gov/opp/global/slott.htm.

12. George Anthan, "Supermarket Chains Are Secretive About Fees," *Des Moines Register,* March 18, 2001.

13. Kent Hoover, "Grapes of Wrath: Slotting Fees Squeeze Fresh Produce Growers," *Houston Business Journal,* September 22, 2000.

14. "Slotting Fees, Consolidation in Food Industry Examined," *Food & Drink Weekly,* October 25, 1999.

15. Senate Committee on Small Business, "Effects of Slotting Fees."

16. Institute of Agriculture and Natural Resources, University of Nebraska, "Food Industry Consolidation Mostly Hikes Consumer Prices, NU Research Shows," news release, September 5, 2002, available at http://ianrnews.unl.edu/static/0209054.shtml.

17. Senate Committee on Small Business, "Slotting Fees."

18. See Western Growers Association, "Consumer Produce Price Index," online database available at http://www.wga.com/pub/consumer/ppi/index.aspx.

19. USDA Economic Research Service, "Understanding the Dynamics of Produce Markets: Consumption and Consolidation Grow," August 2000, available at http://www.ers.usda.gov/publications/aib758/.

20. USDA Economic Research Service, "Consolidation in Food Retailing: Prospects for Consumers and Grocery Suppliers," *Agricultural Outlook,* August 2000, available at http://www.ers.usda.gov/publications/agoutlook/aug2000. a0273g.pdf.

21. Hendrickson et al., "Consolidation in Food Retailing and Dairy."

22. Ibid.; Lorrie Grant, "Wal-Mart Moves Up," *USA Today,* September 24, 2002.

23. Patricia Callahan and Ann Zimmerman, "Wal-Mart, After Remaking Discount Retailing, Now Nation's Largest Grocery Chain," *Wall Street Journal,* May 31, 2003.

24. Kevin Kenyon, "Mergers Fueling Supermarket Competition," *Shopping Centers Today,* June 1, 1999.

25. Grant, "Wal-Mart Moves Up."

26. Callahan and Zimmerman, "Wal-Mart, After Remaking Discount Retailing."

27. Karen Olsson, "Up Against Wal-Mart," *Mother Jones,* March–April 2003.

28. Steven Greenhouse, "Wal-Mart Continues to Create Chaos in Retail Food Business After Driving Nearly Two Dozen National Supermarket Chains into Bankruptcy," *New York Times,* October 19, 2003.

29. Hendrickson et al., "Consolidation in Food Retailing and Dairy."

30. Linda Scott Kantor, "Community Food Security Programs Improve Food Access," *FoodReview* (USDA Economic Research Service), January–April 2001.

31. Prevention Institute, "Supermarket Access in Low-income Communities," Nutrition Policy Profiles paper, available at http://www.preventioninstitute.org/CHI_supermarkets.html.

32. "Study Cites Grocery Store Gap in Poor Areas," *Hartford Courant,* May 18, 1995.

33. Gregg Krupa, "Groceries Cost More for Poor," *Detroit News,* August 21, 2001.

34. Institute for Food and Development Policy (Food First), "Redlining Food: How to Ensure Community Food Security," report, available at http://www.foodfirst.org/progs/humanrts/redlining.html; "Supermarket Drain Leads to Empty Pantries," *Cincinnati Post,* November 16, 1992.

35. Amanda Shaffer, "The Persistence of L.A.'s Grocery Gap: The Need for a New Food Policy and Approach to Market Development," report (Los Angeles: Occidental College, Urban and Environmental Policy Institute, 2002).

36. Ed Bolen and Kenneth Hecht, "Neighborhood Groceries: New Access to Healthy Food in Low-income Communities," report (San Francisco: California Food Policy Advocates, 2003).

37. Krupa, "Groceries Cost More for Poor."

38. Kantor, "Community Food Security Programs Improve Food Access."

39. Ibid.

40. California Food Policy Advocates, "Improving Access to Food in Low-income Communities: An Investigation of Three Bay Area Neighborhoods," report (San Francisco: CFPA, January 1996).

41. Cited in Shaffer, "Persistence of L.A.'s Grocery Gap."

42. California Food Policy Advocates, "Neighborhood Groceries."

43. Shaffer, "The Persistence of L.A.'s Grocery Gap."

44. Cited in Elisa Ludwig, "Not So Super Markets," *Philadelphia Weekly,* June 20, 2001.

45. Maida P. Galvez, Thomas R. Friedan, and Philip J. Landrigan, "Obesity in the 21st Century," *Environmental Health Perspectives,* October 2003.

46. Eric Schlosser, *Fast Food Nation: The Dark Side of the All-American Meal* (New York: Houghton Mifflin, 2001).

47. Hendrickson et al., "Consolidation in Food Retailing and Dairy."

3. FOOD GONE MAD

1. Karl Taro Greenfeld, "On High Alert," *Time Asia,* January 24, 2004.

2. World Health Organization and UN Food and Agriculture Organization, "Unprecedented Spread of Avian Influenza Requires Broad Collaboration," press release, January 27, 2004.

3. "Vietnam 'Almost Bird Flu Free,'" *Australian News,* March 18, 2004; Tini Tran, "Vietnam Confirms 16th Bird Flu Death," Associated Press, available at http://customwire. ap.org/dynamic/stories/V/VIETNAM_BIRD_FLU?SITE=DCTMS&SECTION=HOME& TEMPLATE=DEFAULT; Gretchen Parker, "Avian Flu Discovery Leads to Big Chicken Killoff," Associated Press, March 8, 2004; World Health Organization, "Avian Influenza—Fact Sheet," January 15, 2004, available at http://www.who.int/csr/don/2004_01_15/en/.

4. World Health Organization, "Avian Influenza—Fact Sheet"; World Health Organization, "Confirmed Human Cases of Avian Influenza A(H5N1)," available at http://www. who.int/csr/disease/avian_influenza/country/cases_table_2004_03_17/en/.

5. U.S. Department of Agriculture, Animal and Plant Health Inspection Service, "Bovine Spongiform Encephalopathy Overview."

6. U.S. General Accounting Office, "Food Safety: Controls Can Be Strengthened to Reduce the Risk of Disease Linked to Unsafe Animal Feed," September 2000.

7. UK Creutzfeldt-Jakob Disease Surveillance Unit, figures available at http://www. cjd.ed.ac.uk/figures.htm.

8. Claudia Rowe, "More 'Bad Food News' Goes Down Easy for Consumers," *Seattle Post-Intelligencer,* January 9, 2004.

9. Ronald A. Hites, Jeffrey A. Foran, David O. Carpenter, M. Coreen Hamilton, Barbara A. Knuth, Steven J. Schwager, "Global Assessment of Organic Contaminants in Farmed Salmon," *Science,* January 9, 2004.

10. Jessica Portner, "Salmon Warning: Intake Should Be Limited to Once Every 2 Months, Researchers Say," *San Jose Mercury News,* January 9, 2004.

11. Jane Kay, "US Urges Limits on Eating Albacore," *San Francisco Chronicle,* March 20, 2004.

12. USDA pesticide residue data, compiled by Organic Materials Review Institute, available at http://www.omri.org/OG_chartsgraphs_final2.pdf.

13. Sheldon Rampton and John Stauber, *Mad Cow U.S.A.: Could the Nightmare Happen Here?* (Munroe, ME: Common Courage Press, 1997).

14. U.S. Food and Drug Administration, "Expanded 'Mad Cow' Safeguards Announced to Strengthen Existing Firewalls Against BSE Transmission," press release, January 26, 2004.

15. Paul Brown, Robert G. Will, Raymond Bradley, David M. Asher, and Linda Detwiler, "Bovine Spongiform Encephalopathy and Variant Creutzfeldt-Jakob Disease: Background, Evolution, and Current Concerns," *Emerging Infectious Diseases* (Centers for Disease Control) 7, no. 1 (January–February 2001).

16. Rampton and Stauber, *Mad Cow U.S.A.*

17. Brown et al., "Bovine Spongiform Encephalopathy and Variant Creutzfeldt-Jakob Disease."

18. Rampton and Stauber, *Mad Cow U.S.A.*

19. Shankar Vedantam, "First Case of Mad Cow in US," *Washington Post,* December 24, 2003.

20. Randy Fabi, "Two More U.S. Herds Quarantined over Mad Cow," Reuters, January 22, 2004; "USDA Mad Cow Investigation Expands to Oregon," Reuters, January 22, 2004.

21. USDA, "Veneman Announces Expanded BSE Surveillance Program," news release, March 15, 2004.

22. Physicians Committee for Responsible Medicine, "Mad Cow Disease: Facts, Resources, and Free Veggie Starter Kit," January 20, 2004, available at http://www.pcrm.org.

23. Doreen Muzzi, "Veneman, Senators Spar over BSE," *Delta Farm Press*, January 28, 2004.

24. Christopher Drew, Elizabeth Becker, and Sandra Blakeslee, "Industry Resisted Warnings over Beef," *New York Times*, December 28, 2003.

25. Vedantam, "First Case of Mad Cow in US."

26. Eric Schlosser, "The Cow Jumped over the USDA," *New York Times*, January 2, 2004.

27. Ibid.

28. Vince Beiser, "Big Beef's Dirty War," *LA Weekly*, January 16–22, 2004.

29. Jon Ortiz, "Stricter Beef Rules Urged," *Sacramento Bee*, January 16, 2004.

30. Sabin Russell, "Foreign Reaction: Import Bans Turn Tables on US Industry," *San Francisco Chronicle*, December 24, 2003.

31. Insurance Information Institute, "Hot Topics & Insurance Issues," available at http://www.iii.org/media/hottopics/.

32. Katie Fairbank, "Government, Beef Industry Are Trying to Reopen Trade," *Dallas Morning News*, January 10, 2004.

33. Joe Ruff, "Mad Cow Scare Hurts Meatpacking Belt," Associated Press, January 20, 2004.

34. "Mad Cow Costs Tyson Foods $US 61 Million," www.theage.com, January 27, 2004.

35. National Cattlemen's Beef Association, "Veneman to Cattlemen: Administration Proposes Boost in BSE Prevention," press release, January 30, 2004.

36. National Cattlemen's Beef Association, "Beef Industry Plan Keeps Consumers Confident in US Beef Safety," press release, January 28, 2004.

37. Beiser, "Big Beef's Dirty War."

38. Ibid.

39. U.S. Food and Drug Administration, Center for Veterinary Medicine, "Ruminant Feed (BSE) Enforcement Activities," surveillance report, July 6, 2001.

40. Todd Bishop, "Corraling Mad Cow a Challenge to FDA," *Seattle Post-Intelligencer*, December 25, 2003.

41. U.S. Food and Drug Administration, "U.S. Department of Justice Files Consent Decree of Permanent Injunction Against X-Cel Feeds Inc. Based on Violations of FDA's 1997 Animal Feed Rule," press release, July 11, 2003.

42. U.S. Food and Drug Administration, "FDA Announces Test Results from Texas Feedlot," press release, January 30, 2001.

43. Steve Mitchell, "UPI Exclusive: No Mad Cow Tests in Washington," United Press International, January 15, 2004.

44. U.S. General Accounting Office, "Mad Cow Disease: Improvements in the Animal Feed Ban and Other Regulatory Areas Would Strengthen US Prevention Efforts," report, January 2002.

45. U.S. General Accounting Office, "Food Safety: Controls Can Be Strengthened to Reduce the Risk of Disease Linked to Unsafe Animal Feed," press release, September 2000.

46. Ibid.

47. Beiser, "Big Beef's Dirty War."

48. Center for Responsive Politics, "Agribusiness: Top Contributors," database available at http://www.opensecrets.org/industries/contrib.asp?Ind=A&Cycle=2002.

49. Schlosser, "Cow Jumped over the USDA."

50. Beiser, "Big Beef's Dirty War."

51. Drew et al., "Industry Resisted Warnings over Beef."

52. Ibid.

53. Statement of George J. Pauley III, consumer safety inspector, Northeast Region, USDA, signed statement provided to Public Citizen, January 15, 2004.

54. Affidavit of Paul Carney, consumer safety inspector, USDA, signed and provided to Public Citizen, January 14, 2004.

55. Affidavit prepared by Trent J. Berhow, signed and provided to Public Citizen, January 14, 2004.

56. Drew et al., "Industry Resisted Warnings over Beef."

57. Rampton and Stauber, *Mad Cow U.S.A.*

58. Schlosser, "Cow Jumped over the USDA"; "Tests Confirm Japan's 10th Mad Cow Case," *Los Angeles Times,* February 23, 2004.

59. Jon Bonne, "US Plans Many More Mad Cow Tests," MSNBC.com, March 9, 2004.

60. Schlosser, "Cow Jumped over the USDA."

61. *Boston Globe,* "Testing All Beef," editorial, January 3, 2004.

62. Christopher Doering, "Poll: Farmers Oppose Testing All Cattle, Favorite ID's," Reuters, January 22, 2004.

63. Ibid.

4. DYING FROM CONSUMPTION

1. Marion Nestle, *Food Politics: How the Food Industry Influences Nutrition and Health* (Berkeley: University of California Press, 2003), 31.

2. Paul S. Mead, Laurence Slutsker, Vance Dietz, Linda F. McCaig, Joseph S. Bresee, Craig Shapiro, Patricia M. Griffin, and Robert V. Tauxe, "Food-Related Illness and Death in the United States," *Emerging Infectious Diseases,* September–October 1999, U.S. Centers for Disease Control, available at http://www.cdc.gov/ncidod/eid/vol5no5/ mead.htm.

3. Warren Leon and Caroline Smith DeWaal, *Is Our Food Safe?* (New York: Three Rivers Press, 2002), 9; Nestle, *Food Politics,* 22.

4. U.S. Centers for Disease Control, National Center for Health Statistics, "National Health and Nutrition Examination Survey," 2000; "Prevalence of Overweight among Children and Adolescents: United States, 1999–2000," available at http://www.cdc.gov/ nchs/products/pubs/pubd/hestats/overwght99.htm; Leon and DeWaal, *Is Our Food Safe?*

5. U.S. Centers for Disease Control, "Overweight and Obesity: Economic Consequences," available at http://www.cdc.gov/nccdphp/dnpa/obesity/economic_consequences. htm; U.S. Centers for Disease Control, "Actual Causes of Death in the United States, 2000," available at http://www.cdc.gov/nccdphp/factsheets/death_causes2000.htm; Kim Severson, "Perils of Portion Distortion," *San Francisco Chronicle,* March 7, 2004.

6. USDA Economic Research Service, "Beef Supply, Utilization, and Per Capita Consumption, 1971–2001."

7. Jeremy Rifkin, *Beyond Beef* (New York: Penguin Books, 1992), 175.

8. L.M. Butler, R. Sinha, R.C. Millikan, C.F. Martin, B. Newman, M.D. Gammon, A.S. Ammerman, and R.S. Sandler, "Heterocyclic Amines, Meat Intake, and Association with Colon Cancer in a Population-based Study," *American Journal of Epidemiology* 157, no. 5 (2003), available at http://dceg2.cancer.gov/pdfs/butler1572003.pdf; Domenico Palli, Antonio Russo, Laura Ottini, Giovanna Masala, Calogero Saieva,

Andrea Amorosi, Alessandro Cama, Cristina D'Amico, Mario Falchetti, Raffaele Palmirotta, Adriano Decarli, Renato Mariani Costantini, and Joseph F. Fraumeni Jr., "Red Meat, Family History, and Increased Risk of Gastric Cancer with Microsatellite Instability," *Cancer Research,* July 15, 2001, available at http://dceg2.cancer.gov/pdfs/palli612001.pdf.

9. Based on reports by USDA Economic Research Service. See: Jean C. Buzby, Tanya Roberts, C.T. Jordan Lin, and James M. MacDonald, "Six Foodborne Illnesses Cost U.S. an Estimated $2.9–$6.7 Billion Annually," Agricultural Economic Report No. 741, August 1996; Jean C. Buzby, Tanya Roberts, and Ban Mishu Allos, "Estimated Annual Costs of Campylobacter-Associated Guillain-Barré Syndrome," Agriculture Economic Report No. 756, July 1997, available at http://www.ers.usda.gov/publications/aer756/AER756.pdf; and "Reported Cases of Salmonellosis, 1967–1996." The Iowa State University Extension web site refers to research by the National Restaurant Association showing "that a foodborne illness outbreak can cost an establishment not only dollars, but loss of customers, reputation, increased insurance premiums, lawsuits and court fees," available at http://www.extension.iastate.edu/families/success/2002/clarkn0231.html.

10. "Modern Meat," produced and directed by Doug Hamilton, PBS, April 18, 2002.

11. Marian Burros, "Health Concerns Mounting over Bacteria in Chickens," *New York Times,* October 20, 1997.

12. Leon and DeWaal, *Is Our Food Safe?*

13. Ibid.; Environmental Protection Agency, Office of Policy Analysis, *Unfinished Business: A Comparative Assessment of Environmental Problems,* vol. 1, February 1987. (As cited in Leon and DeWaal, *Is Our Food Safe?,* notes, 228.)

14. The phrase "food pyramid scheme" is borrowed from Che Green, "Got rBGH?," *Independent Weekly,* August 7–13, 2002.

15. Nestle, *Food Politics,* 1.

16. Ibid.

17. Leon and DeWaal, *Is Our Food Safe?*

18. Nestle, *Food Politics,* 93.

19. John Robbins, *Diet for a New America* (Walpole, NH: Stillpoint, 1987).

20. Nestle, *Food Politics,* 34.

21. Ibid., 35.

22. Ibid., 36–37.

23. Ibid., 38–39.

24. Ibid., 41–42.

25. Rifkin, *Beyond Beef,* 175.

26. Council for Agricultural Science and Technology, "US Meat Consumption Changing," October 13, 1997, available at http://www.cast-science.org/cast/pub/anpr_nr.htm.

27. Frances Moore Lappé, *Diet for a Small Planet* (New York: Ballantine Books, 1971).

28. Ibid., 5–8, 47–50.

29. Ibid., 183.

30. Ibid., 173–74.

31. Rifkin, *Beyond Beef,* 174.

32. Mikkel Hindhede, "The Effect of Food Restriction During War on Mortality in Copenhagen," *Journal of the American Medical Association* 74, no. 6 (February 1920). Text from original article available at http://www.mindfully.org/Health/Hindhede-Food-Restriction.htm. Also cited in Robbins, *Diet for a New America,* 152.

33. Robbins, *Diet for a New America,* 151–53.

34. Witold Zatonski, Anthony J. McMichael, and John W. Powles, "Ecological Study of Reasons for Sharp Decline in Mortality from Ischaemic Heart Disease in Poland since 1991," *British Medical Journal,* April 4, 1998.

35. Rifkin, *Beyond Beef,* 170–74.

36. Walter Willet et al., "Relation of Meat, Fat, and Fiber Intake to the Risk of Colon Cancer . . . ," *New England Journal of Medicine,* December 13, 1990; Willet quoted in Gina Kolata, "Animal Fat Is Tied to Colon Cancer," *New York Times,* December 13, 1990.

37. Rifkin, *Beyond Beef,* 170–74.

38. Ibid., 174.

39. Hamilton, "Modern Meat."

40. USDA Economic Research Service, "Reported Cases of Salmonellosis, 1967–1996."

41. "Food-Related Illness and Death in the United States," *Emerging Infectious Diseases,* U.S. Centers for Disease Control.

42. USDA Economic Research Service, "Reported Cases of Salmonellosis."

43. Nicols Fox, *Spoiled* (New York: Basic Books, 1997), 52.

44. Ibid., 50–52.

45. Ibid., 55–56.

46. Hamilton, "Modern Meat."

47. "I Gave My Employer a Chicken That Had No Bone: Joint Firm-State Responsibility for Line-Speed-Related Occupational Injuries," *Case Western Reserve Law Review* 46, no. 1 (Fall 1995): 85–87; Allison Thaler, USDA, interview with the author, 1998; Christopher D. Cook, "Fowl Trouble," *Harper's Magazine,* August 1999.

48. Michael Pollan, "Power Steer," *New York Times,* March 31, 2001.

49. Marion Nestle, *Safe Food: Bacteria, Biotechnology, and Bioterrorism* (Berkeley: University of California Press, 2002), 37.

50. Buzby et al., "Six Foodborne Illnesses Cost U.S. an Estimated $2.9–$6.7 Billion Annually."

51. Fox, *Spoiled,* 51.

52. Buzby et al., "Estimated Annual Costs of Campylobacter-Associated Guillain-Barré Syndrome."

53. Fox, *Spoiled,* 8.

54. Ibid., 6–7.

55. Ibid.

56. Nestle, *Safe Food,* 67.

57. Ibid., 65–78.

58. Public Citizen and Government Accountability Project, "The Jungle 2000: Is America's Meat Fit to Eat?," report, September 2000.

59. Stan Grossfeld, "Animal Waste Emerging as U.S. Problem," *Boston Globe,* September 21, 1998.

60. Michael Janofsky, "U.S. Hopeful on Food Safety Efforts, but Critics Are Skeptical," *New York Times,* August 21, 1997.

61. Curt Anderson, "New System for Inspection of Meat Prompts Concern; Federal Monitors Say Too Much Faith Is Placed in Corporations," Associated Press, January 26, 1998.

62. Public Citizen, "The Jungle 2000."

63. Ibid.

64. "Discussing the Pros and Cons of the Mega-Reg," *Meat & Poultry,* September 1, 1996, cited in Public Citizen, "The Jungle 2000."

65. Public Citizen, "The Jungle 2000."

66. USDA Food Safety and Inspection Service, "Agriculture Fact Book," 2002, available at http://www.usda.gov/factbook/chapter9.pdf.

67. David Stout, "Tainted Patties Are Estimated in Millions," *New York Times,* August 16, 1997.

68. Jerry Gray, "U.S. Seeks New Power to Regulate Meat Safety," *New York Times,* October 9, 1997.

69. Ibid.

70. Sabin Russell, "USDA Lacks Power to Inform Public, Mandate Returns," *San Francisco Chronicle,* January 6, 2004.

71. Marian Burros, "Experts Concerned About Return of Deadly Bacteria in Cold Cuts," *New York Times,* March 14, 1999.

72. Ibid.

73. Hamilton, "Modern Meat."

74. Eric Schlosser, "Bad Meat: The Scandal of Our Food Safety System," *The Nation,* September 16, 2002.

75. Associated Press, "Meat Company Orders Big Recall in Listeria Scare," October 14, 2002.

76. Diane Carmen, "Just Cook the Crud Out of It," *Denver Post,* July 25, 2002.

77. Pollan, "Power Steer."

78. Union of Concerned Scientists, "Hogging It: Estimates of Antimicrobial Abuse in Livestock," 2001. Cited in press release available at http://www.organicconsumers.org/toxic/massiveantibiotics.cfm.

79. Nestle, *Safe Food,* p. 45.

80. Pollan, "Power Steer."

81. Ibid.

82. Ibid.

83. National Corn Growers Association, available at http://www.ncga.com/education/pdf/unit6lesson2.pdf and http://www.ncga.com/03world/main/consumption.htm.

84. Pollan, "Power Steer."

85. "Consumer Concerns about Hormones in Food," Institute for Comparative and Environmental Toxicology, Cornell University Program on Breast Cancer and Environmental Risk Factors in New York State, June 2000, available at http://envirocancer.cornell.edu/factsheet/diet/fs37.hormones.pdf. Also see Orville Schell, *Modern Meat* (New York: Vintage Books, 1984).

86. Robbins, *Diet for a New America,* 109.

87. Nestle, *Safe Food,* 46; "Consumer Concerns about Hormones in Food."

88. Pollan, "Power Steer."

89. Hamilton, "Modern Meat."

90. Nestle, *Safe Food,* 46.

91. Ibid., 46.

92. Burros, "Health Concerns Mounting over Bacteria in Chickens."

93. Ibid.

94. Nestle, *Safe Food,* 46.

95. Robbins, *Diet for a New America,* 344.

96. Sandra Steingraber, *Living Downstream* (New York: Vintage Books, 1997), 238.

97. Robbins, *Diet for a New America,* 345.

98. Steingraber, *Living Downstream,* 239.

99. "Pesticides in the News," *Rachel's Environment and Health News,* July 22, 1999.

100. Leon and DeWaal, *Is Our Food Safe?,* 30–31.

101. Ibid., 86.

102. Ibid., 87–88.

103. "Chlorpyrifos, part 2: Human Exposure," *Journal of Pesticide Reform,* Spring 1995.

104. Leon and DeWaal, 88.

105. Environmental Working Group, "They Are What They Eat: Kids' Food Consumption and Pesticides," report, February 25, 1999.

106. National Research Council, National Academy of Sciences, "Pesticides in the Diets of Infants and Children," 1993.

107. "FDA's Total Diet Study: Monitoring U.S. Food Supply Safety," *Food Safety Magazine,* FDA, June–July 2002.

108. Environmental Working Group, "Pesticides in Baby Food," July 26, 1995, available at http://www.ewg.org/reports/Baby_food/Baby_Home.html.

109. Richard Wiles, Kenneth A. Cook, Todd Hettenbach, and Christopher Campbell, Environmental Working Group, "How 'Bout Them Apples? Pesticides in Children's Food Ten Years After Alar," February 25, 1999, available at http://www.ewg.org/reports_content/apples/apples.pdf.

110. United States House of Representatives, Committee on Agriculture, "The Impact of the Food Quality Protection Act Implementation on Public Health," hearings, August 3, 1999, available at http://commdocs.house.gov/committees/ag/hag10629.000/hag10629_0.htm.

111. Environmental Working Group, "How 'Bout Them Apples?"

112. Ibid.

113. Center for Responsive Politics, "Agribusiness: Long-Term Contribution Trends," available at http://www.opensecrets.org/industries/indus.asp?Ind=A.

PART II: THE RISE OF THE CORPORATE CORNUCOPIA

5. "GET BIG OR GET OUT"

1. John Shover, *First Majority—Last Minority* (DeKalb: Northern Illinois University Press, 1976).

2. Joel Solkoff, *The Politics of Food* (San Francisco: Sierra Club Books, 1985), 43.

3. Ibid., 47.

4. Dan Morgan, *Merchants of Grain* (New York: Penguin Books, 1980), 38.

5. Solkoff, *Politics of Food,* 43; Shover, *First Majority—Last Minority,* 252.

6. Solkoff, *Politics of Food,* 43.

7. Shover, *First Majority—Last Minority.*

8. Solkoff, *Politics of Food,* 48.

9. Ibid.

10. Stanley Aronowitz, *Food, Shelter, and the American Dream* (New York: Seabury Press, 1974), 48.

11. Solkoff, *Politics of Food,* 45.

12. Morgan, *Merchants of Grain,* 39.

13. Solkoff, *Politics of Food,* 52.

14. Morgan, *Merchants of Grain,* 207.

15. Aronowitz, *Food, Shelter, and the American Dream,* 49.

16. Solkoff, *Politics of Food,* 44.

17. Morgan, *Merchants of Grain,* 39.

18. Solkoff, *Politics of Food,* 57.

19. Ibid., 45.

20. Aronowitz, *Food, Shelter, and the American Dream,* 49.

21. Ibid.

22. Ibid., 50.

23. Shover, *First Majority—Last Minority,* 251.

24. Solkoff, *Politics of Food,* 61.

25. Ibid.

26. Ibid., 69.

27. Ibid., 70.

28. Shover, *First Majority—Last Minority,* 259.

29. Ibid., 253.

30. Osha Gray Davidson, *Broken Heartland: The Rise of the Rural Ghetto* (New York: Anchor Books/Doubleday, 1990), 15.

31. Ibid.

32. Ibid.

33. John Opie, *The Law of the Land* (Lincoln: University of Nebraska Press, 1987), preface.

34. Ibid.

35. Davidson, *Broken Heartland,* 17.

36. Ibid.

37. Ibid.

38. Ibid.

39. Ibid.

40. Opie, *Law of the Land,* 19.

41. Ibid., 2.

42. Ibid.

43. Ibid., 10.

44. Louis Bernard Schmidt and Earle Dudley Ross, eds., *Readings in the Economic History of American Agriculture* (New York: Macmillan, 1925), 154.

45. Ibid.

46. Opie, *Law of the Land,* 17.

47. Ibid.

48. Ibid.; and Willard W. Cochrane, *The Development of American Agriculture* (Minneapolis: University of Minnesota Press, 1984), 45.

49. Davidson, *Broken Heartland,* 22–23.

50. Opie, *Law of the Land,* 16.

51. Ibid., 17.

52. Ibid., 33.

53. Ibid., 49.

54. Ibid., 50.

55. Cochrane, *Development of American Agriculture,* 45.

56. Schmidt and Ross, *Readings,* 156–57.

57. Opie, *Law of the Land,* 33.

58. Ibid., 38.

59. Cochrane, *Development of American Agriculture,* 46.

60. Opie, *Law of the Land.*

61. Schmidt and Ross, *Readings,* 157.

62. Cochrane, *Development of American Agriculture,* 59.

63. Ibid., 83.

64. Ibid.

65. Opie, *Law of the Land,* 73–75.

66. Schmidt and Ross, *Readings,* 231.

67. Ibid., 216–17.

68. Ibid., 233.

69. Ibid., 335.

70. Cochrane, *Development of American Agriculture,* 74.

71. Schmidt and Ross, *Readings,* 358.

72. Ibid., 333.

73. Ibid., 331.

74. Cochrane, *Development of American Agriculture,* 94.

75. Schmidt and Ross, *Readings,* 437.

76. Ibid., 336.

77. Cochrane, *Development of American Agriculture,* 438.

78. Schmidt and Ross, *Readings,* 439.

79. Ibid., 441.

80. Ibid., 438.

81. Cochrane, *Development of American Agriculture,* 94.

82. Ibid., 93.

83. Schmidt and Ross, *Readings,* 441.

84. Cochrane, *Development of American Agriculture,* 113.

85. Patrick H. Mooney and Theo J. Majka, *Farmers' and Farm Workers' Movements: Social Protest in American Agriculture* (New York: Twayne Publishers, 1995), 31.

86. Schmidt and Ross, *Readings,* 448.

87. Mooney and Majka, *Farmers' and Farm Workers' Movements,* 31.

88. Davidson, *Broken Heartland,* 21.

89. Ibid., 93.

90. Nathan Fine, *Labor and Farmer Parties in the United States, 1828–1928* (Berkeley: Center for Socialist History, 1984), 57.

91. Ibid., 58.

92. Cochrane, *Development of American Agriculture,* 95.

93. Schmidt and Ross, *Readings,* 448.

94. Cochrane, *Development of American Agriculture,* 114.

95. Ibid., 47.

96. Fine, *Labor and Farmer Parties in the United States,* 59.

97. Ibid.

98. Ibid., 75.

99. Ibid., 73.

100. Ibid., 74.

101. Cochrane, *Development of American Agriculture,* 100.

102. Schmidt and Ross, *Readings,* 438.

103. Cochrane, *Development of American Agriculture*, 100.

104. Ibid.; and Janet Poppendieck, *Bread Lines Knee Deep in Wheat: Food Assistance in the Great Depression* (New Brunswick, NJ: Rutgers University Press, 1986).

105. Cochrane, *Development of American Agriculture*, 100; Poppendieck, *Bread Lines Knee Deep in Wheat*, 4.

106. Cochrane, *Development of American Agriculture*, 101.

107. Ibid., 108–9.

108. Schmidt and Ross, *Readings*, 299.

109. Stanley Andrews, *The Farmer's Dilemma* (Washington, DC: Public Affairs Press, 1961), 11.

110. Poppendieck, *Bread Lines Knee Deep in Wheat*, 5.

111. Ibid., 14.

6. AGRIBUSINESS TAKES OVER

1. Janet Poppendieck, *Bread Lines Knee-Deep in Wheat: Food Assistance in the Great Depression* (New Brunswick, NJ: Rutgers University Press, 1986).

2. Ibid., 32.

3. Ibid., 37.

4. Ibid., 48.

5. Ibid., 52.

6. Ibid., 109.

7. Ibid.

8. Ibid., 109–11.

9. Ibid., 114.

10. Ibid., 121.

11. Ibid., 117.

12. Ibid.

13. Ibid.

14. Ibid., 18.

15. Ibid., 127.

16. Edward Higbee, *Farms and Farmers in an Urban Age* (New York: Twentieth Century Fund, 1963), 3.

17. Willard Cochrane, *The Development of American Agriculture* (St. Paul: University of Minnesota Press, 1984), 124.

18. Stanley Andrews, *The Farmer's Dilemma* (Washington, DC: Public Affairs, 1961), 50.

19. Cochrane, *Development of American Agriculture*, 202.

20. Ibid., 126.

21. Andrews, *Farmer's Dilemma*, 9.

22. Higbee, *Farms and Farmers in an Urban Age*, 3.

23. Miriam J. Wells, *Strawberry Fields: Politics, Class, and Work in California Agriculture* (Ithaca: Cornell University Press, 1996), 57–58.

24. Cochrane, *Development of American Agriculture*, 139.

25. Ibid., 140.

26. Higbee, *Farms and Farmers in an Urban Age*, 11.

27. Andrews, *Farmer's Dilemma*, 49.

28. Higbee, *Farms and Farmers in an Urban Age*, 5.

29. Andrews, *Farmer's Dilemma*, 50–51.

30. John Shover, *First Majority—Last Minority* (DeKalb: Northern Illinois University Press, 1976), 179.

31. Andrews, *Farmer's Dilemma,* 58.

32. Ibid., 49.

33. Ibid., 51.

34. Higbee, *Farms and Farmers in an Urban Age,* 17.

35. Andrews, *Farmer's Dilemma,* 58.

36. Shover, *First Majority—Last Minority*, 177.

37. Ibid.

38. Ibid., 178.

39. Ibid., 181.

40. Ibid., 191.

41. Ben B. Seligman, *The Potentates: Business and Businessmen in American History* (New York: Dial, 1971), 329.

42. Samual Bowles, David M. Gordon, and Thomas Weisskopf, *Beyond the Wasteland: A Democratic Alternative to Economic Decline* (Garden City, NY: Anchor, 1983), 69.

43. Seligman, *The Potentates,* 329.

44. Ibid.

45. Ibid., 325.

46. Robert Sobel, *The Age of Giant Corporations: A Microeconomic History of American Business, 1914–1970* (Westport, CT: Greenwood, 1972), 208.

47. Stanley Aronowitz, *Food, Shelter, and the American Dream* (New York: Seabury Press, 1974), 51.

48. Shover, *First Majority—Last Minority,* 183.

49. Ibid., 184.

50. Ibid., 179.

51. Ibid., 180.

52. Ingolf Vogeler, *The Myth of the Family Farm: Agribusiness Dominance of United States Agriculture* (Boulder: Westview Press, 1981), 106.

53. Shover, *First Majority—Last Minority*, 162; Vogeler, *Myth of the Family Farm,* 135.

54. Shover, *First Majority—Last Minority,* 153.

55. Andrews, *Farmer's Dilemma,* 61–62.

56. Vogeler, *Myth of the Family Farm,* 134.

7. ALMOST NOTHING LEFT: THE 1980S

1. Ward Sinclair, "There Is No Joy in This Fall's Harvest as Farmers Worry; Record Crop Also Means Lower Prices," *Washington Post*, September 19, 1982.

2. Bennett Harrison and Barry Bluestone, *The Great U-Turn: Corporate Restructuring and the Polarizing of America* (New York: Basic Books, 1988), 90–91.

3. Dan Morgan, "Administration Is Facing Grain Embargo Backlash," *Washington Post*, April 6, 1980.

4. Christian Parenti, *Lockdown America: Police and Prisons in the Age of Crisis* (New York: Verso, 1999), 38.

5. Osha Gray Davidson, *Broken Heartland: The Rise of America's Rural Ghetto* (New York: Anchor Books, 1990), 17.

6. Ibid., 7.

7. *Congressional Quarterly Almanac* (1982), 351.

8. Terry Povey, "Warning on World Farm Incomes," *Financial Times*, June 16, 1982.

9. "Farmers' Plight Now Similar to That of Depression Years," Dow Jones News Service, October 18, 1982.

10. Ibid.

11. *Congressional Quarterly Almanac* (1982), 351.

12. Povey, "Warning on World Farm Incomes."

13. Andrew H. Malcolm, "Murder of Banker in Minnesota Spurs Manhunt for Failed Farmer," *New York Times*, October 2, 1983.

14. Ibid.

15. Ward Sinclair, "The Heyday Has Ended for Ohio Farmers; Low Prices, High Interest Leave Most Hanging on for Dear Life," *Washington Post*, June 29, 1982.

16. John McCormick, "Uprooting a Way of Life," *Newsweek*, February 18, 1985.

17. "Strapped Farms Fear 'Quiet Death' Near," Associated Press, May 3, 1984.

18. Ward Sinclair, "Farmers Look Beyond Weather for Help," *Washington Post*, April 2, 1982.

19. *Congressional Quarterly Almanac* (1982), 351.

20. "Moonlight on the Farm," *New York Times*, October 11, 1981, section III, 22.

21. Ward Sinclair, "Farm-State Democrats Assail Reagan Policies, Urge Rescue Measures," *Washington Post*, March 19, 1982.

22. "Moonlight on the Farm."

23. Gregory Jaynes, "U.S. Farmers Said to Face Worst Year Since 1930s," *New York Times*, March 28, 1982.

24. David Lascelles, "A Bumper Crop of Troubles," *Financial Times*, April 16, 1982.

25. "Farms: The Cost Spiral," *New York Times*, January 18, 1981.

26. Jaynes, "U.S. Farmers Said to Face Worst Year Since 1930s."

27. "Moonlight on the Farm."

28. Seth S. King, "On the Farm, a Problem of Abundance," *New York Times*, January 10, 1982.

29. "Farm Debts Are High," Associated Press, December 20, 1981 (published in *New York Times*, December 21, 1981, D6).

30. Jaynes, "U.S. Farmers Said to Face Worst Year Since 1930s."

31. "Farm Debts Are High," Associated Press.

32. Sinclair, "Farmers Look Beyond Weather for Help."

33. "Rate of Delinquencies on Farm Loans Is Rising," Dow Jones News Service, May 26, 1982.

34. Jaynes, "U.S. Farmers Said to Face Worst Year Since 1930s."

35. "Sold! For 18 Cents on the Dollar," *U.S. News & World Report*, March 11, 1985, 26.

36. Ibid.

37. "Embattled Farmers," editorial, *Christian Science Monitor*, April 19, 1982.

38. Jonathan Harsch, "Budget Cuts Reap Protest on the Farm," *Christian Science Monitor*, March 16, 1982.

39. "Farm Total Falls in Most States," *U.S. News & World Report*, September 19, 1983, 13.

40. Larry Feinberg and Myron Struck, "Farm Foreclosures Rising," *Washington Post*, October 4, 1983.

41. United Press International, October 4, 1983.

42. "Pleas Aside, Farmland Auctioned," United Press International, October 4, 1983.

43. "Despair, Violence Down on the Farm," *U.S. News & World Report*, January 17, 1983, 13.

44. Dow Jones, October 18, 1982.

45. "Farmers' Plight Now Similar to That of Depression Years," Dow Jones News Service, October 18, 1982.

46. "Farmers Become Activists as Economy Forces Foreclosures," Dow Jones News Service, September 10, 1982.

47. *Washington Post,* February 4, 1982.

48. Ward Sinclair, "U.S. Increasing Pressure to Collect on Delinquent Farm Loans," *Washington Post*, February 4, 1982.

49. Andrew H. Malcolm, "Farm Protesters' Focus: Prices and Foreclosures," *New York Times*, June 23, 1983.

50. "Farmers: Ruling to Curb FmHA," United Press International, November 5, 1983.

51. United Press International, November 5, 1983.

52. "Farmers: Ruling to Curb FmHA."

53. Malcolm, "Farm Protesters' Focus: Prices and Foreclosures."

54. *Omaha World Herald,* May 19, 1984.

55. James Allen Flanery, "Finance Overhaul Urged; Officials at Ag Summit See Debt Escalation," *Omaha World-Herald*, May 19, 1984.

56. "Ag's Prosperity Suffers Reversal," *Successful Farming*, March 1985.

57. Patricia M. Scherschel, "Banks, Too, Hit Hard by Rural Woes," *U.S. News & World Report*, March 11, 1985, 29.

58. *Financial Times,* October 5, 1982.

59. Ian Rodger, "Agricultural Equipment Producers Are Hardest Hit," *Financial Times*, October 5, 1982.

60. Christopher Parkes, "Deere Profits Plunge by 97%," *Financial Times*, May 26, 1982.

61. Winston Williams, "Even Deere Feels the Pinch," *New York Times*, May 6, 1982.

62. "Farm Credit System Posts $522 Million Loss," Associated Press, October 24, 1985.

63. Peter T. Kilborn, "Farm Bank Plea Gets Cool Reply," *New York Times*, September 7, 1985.

64. Michael Bosc, "A Small Town's Last-Ditch Fight for Survival," *U.S. News & World Report*, March 11, 1985, 27.

65. Mike Glover, " 'People Are Scared': Growing Farm Crisis Jolts Nervous Iowa Lawmakers," Associated Press, January 20, 1985.

66. James R. Dickenson, "Iowa Governor Activates Debt-Moratorium Law; Farmers Can Seek a One-Year Reprieve from Foreclosure," *Washington Post*, October 2, 1985.

67. Peter Grier, "Block Announces Farm-Credit Aid Plan," *Christian Science Monitor*, March 7, 1985.

68. David M. Alvern, Howard Fineman, Margeret Garrard Warner, and John McCormick, "Bitter Fight Over Farms," *Newsweek*, March 4, 1985.

69. Seth S. King, "Farm Credit Bill Is Passed by House," *New York Times*, March 6, 1985.

70. Alvern et al., "Bitter Fight Over Farms."

71. David Hoffman, "Senate Panel Balks at Agriculture Cuts, Deficit Reduction; Emergency Farm Aid Vetoed by President," *Washington Post*, March 7, 1985.

72. William Robbins, "Saving in Farm Aid Veto Questioned," *New York Times*, March 11, 1985.

73. Michael A. Pollock, "How the Farm Credit Crisis Is Crushing America's Breadbasket," *Business Week*, February 18, 1985.

74. Ibid., 183.

75. "Earl Butz Says U.S. News Media Exaggerating Farming Troubles," Associated Press, January 15, 1984.

76. Nancy Dunne, "U.S. Farmers Fear a Weeding Out," *Financial Times*, February 8, 1985.

8. HOSTILE TAKEOVER: THE NEW FARM CRISIS

1. Information and quotations regarding Premium Standard Farms and Missouri, unless otherwise cited, are from Christopher D. Cook, "The New Farm Crisis: Scenes from the Corporate Countryside," *In These Times*, June 13, 1999, available at http://www.iatp.org/iatp/News/news.cfm?News_ID=324. Sources include: USDA, Agricultural Marketing Service, "Concentration in Agriculture: A Report of the USDA Advisory Committee on Agricultural Concentration," report, June 1996; USDA National Agricultural Statistics Service; USDA, National Commission on Small Farms, "A Time to Act," report, January 1998; Missouri Agricultural Statistics Service; Premium Standard Farms Company web site, interviews with spokesman Charlie Arnot by the author (1998, 1999), press releases and company documents; Federal Reserve Bank; Cargill press releases and company documents, available at www.cargill.com; ConAgra annual reports and financial documents.

2. Lynn McKinley, interview with the author, Green City, Missouri, December 1999.

3. Gary Godfrey, interview with the author, Green City, Missouri, December 1999.

4. Gary Godfrey, unpublished paper, 1999 (in possession of the author). Sources include Missouri Department of Labor and Industrial Relations, Missouri Department of Social Services, and Putnam County Clerk.

5. USDA, 1997 Census of Agriculture; Missouri Agricultural Statistics Service.

6. USDA, 2002 Census of Agriculture.

7. Nick Coleman, "Many Farmers Fail to See Future in Their Livelihood," *St. Paul Pioneer Press*, June 27, 1999.

8. David Morris, "Factory Farms Foul Water, Air, and Democracy," opinion, Minnesota Department of Natural Resources, Division of Fish and Wildlife, spring 1997.

9. John Crabtree, telephone interview with the author, 1998.

10. USDA, Economic Research Service, "Food Marketing and Price Spreads: USDA Marketing Bill," updated June 19, 2002, available at http://www.ers.usda.gov/Briefing/FoodPriceSpreads/bill/table1.htm.

11. USDA, "Indexes of Prices Received by Farmers, by Months and Annual Average, United States, 1975–1993."

12. Warren Cohen, "The Seeds of Discontent," *U.S. News & World Report*, May 24, 1999.

13. Christopher D. Cook, "Consolidated Cornucopia: How Corporate Food Is Ploughing Small Farmers into the Ground," *The Witness*, January–February 1999. Sources include USDA, Economic Research Service, USDA National Agricultural Statistics Service, USDA *Agricultural Outlook*, USDA Agricultural Income and Finance Summary (September 24, 1998), *American Banker-Bond Buyer* (1998), Federal Reserve Bank.

14. Mark Ritchie, telephone interview with the author, 1998.

15. Coleman, "Many Farmers Fail to See Future in Their Livelihood."

16. "Western Farmers Say They Are in an Economic Crisis," *Modesto Bee*, December 7, 2000.

17. Becky Gillette, "Farm Crisis Could Spread to Entire U.S. Economy," *Mississippi Business Journal*, March 8, 1999.

18. Richard T. Estrada, "Worst of Crisis Is Over, but Farmers Still Face Tough Times," *Modesto Bee,* May 5, 2001.

19. USDA, National Commission on Small Farms, "Glickman Announces National Commission on Small Farms," July 16, 1997, available at http://www.reeusda.gov/smallfarm/announcement.htm.

20. Coleman, "Many Farmers Fail to See Future in Their Livelihood."

21. Mark Drabenstott, "Consolidation in U.S. Agriculture: The New Rural Landscape and Public Policy," report, Kansas City Federal Reserve Bank, 1999.

22. Coleman, "Many Farmers Fail to See Future in Their Livelihood."

23. Ibid.

24. Ashok K. Mishra, Hisham S. El-Osta, Mitchell J. Morehart, James D. Johnson, and Jeffrey W. Hopkins, USDA, Economic Research Service, "Income, Wealth, and the Economic Well-being of Farm Households," July 2002, available at http://www.ers.usda.gov/publications/aer812/; A.V. Krebs, telephone interview with the author, 1998.

25. Cohen, "The Seeds of Discontent."

26. Tim Weiner, "Congress Agrees to $7.1 Billion in Farm Aid," *New York Times,* April 14, 2000.

27. William Greider, "The Last Farm Crisis," *The Nation,* November 20, 2000, available at http://www.thenation.com/doc.mhtml?i=20001120&s=greider.

28. Cohen, "The Seeds of Discontent."

29. Doug LeDuc, "Farm Crisis Quietly Take [*sic*] Toll on Heartland," *Ft. Wayne News-Sentinel,* August 18, 1998.

30. Cohen, "The Seeds of Discontent."

31. Ibid.

32. Gillette, "Farm Crisis Could Spread to Entire U.S. Economy."

33. Drabenstott, "Consolidation in U.S. Agriculture."

34. William Heffernan, "Consolidation in the Food and Agriculture System," report to the National Farmers Union, February 5, 1999.

35. "ConAgra Foods at a Glance," ConAgra Co. document, available at http://www.conagrafoods.com/documents/at_a_glance.pdf; ConAgra, Inc. Annual Report, 1997.

36. Peter Rosset, interview with the author, Oakland, California, 1998.

37. Poultry Producer Agreement, obtained from United Poultry Growers Association web site, accessed November 20, 1998. For more information, go to http://www.unitedpoultrygrowers.com/.

38. Dan Fesperman and Kate Shatzkin, "The Plucking of the American Chicken Farmer," *Baltimore Sun,* February 28, 1999.

39. Ibid.

40. Rosset, interview with the author, 1998.

41. John Crabtree, telephone interview with the author, 1998.

42. Ibid.

43. Rolf Christen, interview with the author, Green City, Missouri, December 1999.

44. Godfrey, telephone interview with the author, April 13, 2004.

45. Godfrey, unpublished paper.

46. Iowa Department of Natural Resources, correspondence with Premium Standard Farms, February 10, 1989. Veronica Fowler, "Ledges Hog Lot Accused of Building without Permit," *Des Moines Register,* January 4, 1989; Jay P. Wagner, "Rural Residents Rail at Impact of Hog Lots," *Des Moines Register,* April 2, 1995; Lynn Okamoto, "Sukups Radio Ads Attack Gross," *Des Moines Register,* May 9, 2002.

47. Terry Ganey, "Corporate Farm Got Special Help from Legislature," *St. Louis Post-Dispatch,* April 24, 1994.

48. Godfrey, unpublished paper.

49. Ibid.

50. Terry Spence, interview with the author, April 7, 2004; Gary Godfrey, interview with the author, April 13, 2004.

51. Dan Mihalopoulos, "Hog Plant Both Boon and Burden for Farmers," *Missouri Digital News,* May 9, 1995, available at www.mdn.org.

52. Missouri Department of Labor and Industrial Relations, labor force data, 1996; Missouri Department of Social Services.

53. Terry Spence, interview with the author, April 7, 2004.

54. *Grainnet,* December 1998; Heffernan, "Consolidation in the Food and Agriculture System."

55. James M. MacDonald, Economic Research Service, USDA; and Marvin L. Hayenga, Iowa State University, "Concentration, Mergers, and Antitrust Policy," in *The 2002 Farm Bill: Policy Options and Consequences,* Joe L. Outlaw and Edward G. Smith, editors, publication no. 2001-01 (Oakbrook, IL: The Farm Foundation, September 2001).

56. "Senate Nixes Food Merger Moratorium," Associated Press, November 17, 1999.

57. Cargill Company profile, Business Index ASAP, database, January 1998. Also see www.cargill.com.

58. "Cargill to Purchase Continental's Worldwide Grain Assets," news release, November 10, 1998, available at www.cargill.com.

59. Allen R. Myerson, "Cargill Set to Buy Main Unit of Continental Grain, Its Chief Rival," *New York Times,* November 11, 1998.

60. A number of press accounts say just two firms, Cargill and ADM, control 75 to 80 percent of the market. See, for instance, Vijay Prashad, "Farms as Factories," *Frontline,* available at http://www.frontlineonnet.com/fl2104/stories/20040227000506400.htm; or Zac Goldsmith, "When Common Sense Is a Crime," *New Statesman,* June 30, 2003.

61. USDA, National Commission on Small Farms, "A Time to Act," report, January 1998.

62. MacDonald, "Concentration, Mergers, and Antitrust Policy."

63. "IBP Reports Record Sales & Earnings," *Meat Industry Insights News Service,* available at http://www.spcnetwork.com/mii (accessed February 12, 2000).

64. Center for Rural Affairs, "Center for Rural Affairs Exposes Excel's Deceitful Campaign to Overturn Amendment to Ban Packer Ownership of Livestock," news release, January 28, 2002, available at www.cfra.org. See also "Ranchers Fight Meatpackers' Grip on Livestock," March 12, 2002, available at www.thepigsite.com.

65. Nolan Jungclaus, testimony before United States Senate Committee on Agriculture, Nutrition, and Forestry, July 16, 2002.

66. Ibid.

67. Herman Schumacher, testimony before the United States Senate Committee on Agriculture, Nutrition, and Forestry; hearing on the proposed ban on Packer ownership of livestock and the USDA's enforcement of the Packers and Stockyards Act, July 16, 2002.

68. Eric Palmer, "Feedlot Owner Files Lawsuit Against KC-Based Meat Packer," *Kansas City Star,* December 17, 2002; Eric Palmer, "Farming Being Transformed by Huge Mergers, Globalization," *Kansas City Star,* September 2, 1999.

69. Palmer, "Feedlot Owner Files Lawsuit."

70. "USDA Settles Complaint against Farmland," *Meat Industry Insights News Service*, June 6, 2001, available at www.spcnetwork.com.

71. Callicrate, testimony, February 2, 1999.

72. Testimony of Michael V. Dunn, Undersecretary of Agriculture for Marketing and Regulatory Programs, Hearing on Agricultural Consolidation, Committee on Agriculture, Nutrition, and Forestry, U.S. Senate, July 27, 1999, available at http://agriculture.senate.gov/Hearings/Hearings_1999/dun99727.htm.

73. Mike Callicrate, testimony before the Agriculture Committee of Nebraska's Legislature concerning competitive livestock markets, price discovery, and meat labeling, February 2, 1999.

74. Heffernan, "Consolidation in the Food and Agriculture System."

75. Ibid.

76. Mary Hendrickson and William Heffernan, "Concentration of Agricultural Markets," report, February 2002.

77. Jorge Fernandez-Cornejo, USDA, Economic Research Service, "The Seed Industry in U.S. Agriculture: An Exploration of Data and Information on Crop Seed Markets, Regulation, Industry Structure, and Research and Development," February 2004; American Seed Trade Association, "Seed Statistics," available at http://www.amseed.com/about_statistics.asp; Action Group on Erosion, Technology and Concentration, "Seed Industry Consolidation: Who Owns Whom?," July 30, 1998, available at http://www.etcgroup.org/article.asp?newsid=186.

78. Richard J. Sexton, "Industrialization and Consolidation in the US Food Sector: Implications for Competition and Welfare," *American Journal of Agricultural Economics* 82, no. 5 (December 2000): 1087–1104.

79. Heffernan, "Consolidation in the Food and Agriculture System."

80. Ibid.

81. Drabenstott, "Consolidation in U.S. Agriculture."

82. C. Robert Taylor, "Where's the Beef? Monopoly and Monopsony Power in the Beef Industry," *Agricultural and Resource Policy Forum*, College of Agriculture, Auburn University, March 2002.

83. Cook, "Consolidated Cornucopia."

84. USDA, "A Time to Act."

85. Cook, "Consolidated Cornucopia."

PART III: RECIPES FOR DISASTER

INTRODUCTION

1. Mark Grossi, Barbara Anderson, and Russell Clemings, "Last Gasp," special report, *Fresno Bee*, December 15, 2002, available at http://www.fresnobee.com/special/valley_air/story/5572630p-6538262c.html.

2. Ibid.

3. Ibid.

4. Ibid.

5. American Lung Association of California, "33 California Counties Flunk Annual American Lung Association Clean Air Test," news release announcing "State of the Air 2001" report, May 1, 2001, available at http://www.californialung.org/press/010501stateofair.html.

6. Grossi et al., "Last Gasp."

7. Ibid.

8. Ibid.

9. Ibid.

10. Drs. David Pimentel and Mario Giampietro, "Food, Land, Population and the U.S. Economy," report published by Carrying Capacity Network, November 21, 1994, available at http://www.dieoff.com/page40.htm.

11. Ibid.

9. KILLING FIELDS: THE SPRAYING OF AMERICA

1. Rachel Carson, *Silent Spring* (London: Readers Union, 1964), 13.

2. World Wildlife Federation, available at www.worldwildlife.org/toxics (accessed June 6, 2003).

3. Carson, *Silent Spring*, 14.

4. Ibid., 13.

5. Ibid.

6. Ibid., 25, 28.

7. Ibid., 21.

8. Ibid., 18.

9. Ibid., 89.

10. Ibid., 34–35.

11. Remarks by Secretary of Agriculture Ann M. Veneman, UN Food and Agriculture Organization 31st Conference, Plenary Session: State of Food and Agriculture, Rome, Italy, November 5, 2001.

12. Pesticide Action Network Asia and the Pacific, "New Study Links World's Biggest Pesticides to Cancer," June 21, 1999.

13. Leonard P. Gianessi and Sujatha Sankula, "The Value of Herbicides in U.S. Crop Production," report, National Center for Food and Agricultural Policy, April 2003.

14. Ibid.

15. U.S. Environmental Protection Agency, "Pesticides Industry Sales and Usage, 1998 and 1999 Market Estimates," 2000, available at www.epa.gov/oppbead1/pestsales.

16. Ibid.

17. Susan Kegley, Lars Neumeister, and Timothy Martin, "Disrupting the Balance: Ecological Impacts of Pesticides in California," report, Pesticide Action Network and Californians for Pesticide Reform, 1999.

18. Sandra Steingraber, *Living Downstream* (New York: Vintage Books, 1997), 151.

19. Ibid., 152.

20. Ibid., 154.

21. U.S. Geological Survey, Pesticide National Synthesis Project, "Pesticides in Stream Sediment and Aquatic Biota," fact sheet, 2000, available at http://ca.water.usgs.gov/pnsp/rep/fs09200/.

22. Zev Ross and Jonathan Kaplan, "Poisoning the Air: Airborne Pesticides in California," Californians for Pesticide Reform and CALPIRG Charitable Trust, 1998, available at www.environmentcalifornia.org/reports/poison98.pdf.

23. Kegley et al., "Disrupting the Balance."

24. U.S. Geological Survey, Circular 1225, "Sources of Nutrients and Pesticides," fact sheet, available at http://water.usgs.gov/pubs/circ/circ1225/html/sources.html.

25. Carson, *Silent Spring*, 36.

26. Roy F. Spalding, Mary E. Exner, Daniel D. Snow, David A. Cassada, Mark E. Burbach, and Stephen J. Monson, "Herbicides in Ground Water Beneath Nebraska's Management Systems and Evaluation Area," *Journal of Environmental Quality* 32 (January/February 2003): 92–99.

27. U.S. Geological Survey, Toxic Substances Hydrology Program, "Where Are the Pesticides?" fact sheet, 2003, available at http://toxics.usgs.gov/highlights/herbicides_deg_gw.html.

28. U.S. Geological Survey, Circular 1225, "National Findings and Their Implications for Water Policies and Strategies," fact sheet, available at http://water.usgs.gov/pubs/circ/circ1225/html/wq_agric.html.

29. Edwin D. Ongley, "Control of Water Pollution from Agriculture," FAO Irrigation and Drainage Paper 55, Food and Agriculture Organization of the United Nations, 1996.

30. John Troiano, Don Weaver, Joe Marade, Frank Spurlock, Mark Pepple, Craig Nordmark, and Donna Bartkowiak, "Summary of Well Water Sampling in California to Detect Pesticide Residues Resulting from Nonpoint-Source Applications," *Journal of Environmental Quality* 30 (2001): 448–59.

31. California Sportfishing Protection Alliance, "Angling Groups Protest Agricultural Pollution, Cite Impacts of Fishery Health and Human Consumption," *Fish Sniffer Online*, available at http://www.fishsniffer.com/guest/111602cspa.html, accessed November 16, 2002.

32. Kentucky Department of Environmental Protection, Division of Water, *Pesticides in Kentucky Rivers*, report, September 2000.

33. "Pesticides in the News," *Rachel's Environment and Health News*, July 22, 1999, available at http://www.rachel.org/bulletin/index.cfm?St=4.

34. Jeffrey D. Martin, Charles G. Crawford, and Steven J. Larson, *Pesticides in Streams at Agricultural Sites, 1991–2001* (National Water Quality Assessment Program).

35. Steven J. Larson, Robert J. Gilliom, and Paul D. Capel, "Pesticides in the Streams of the United States—Initial Results from the National Water Quality Assessment Program," U.S. Geological Survey Water Resources Investigations Report 98-4222, 1999.

36. U.S. Geological Survey, "Pesticides in Stream Sediment and Aquatic Biota."

37. Kegley et al., "Disrupting the Balance."

38. U.S. Geological Survey, "National Findings and Their Implications."

39. "Study: Pesticides, Parasites Deform Frogs," Associated Press, July 9, 2002.

40. California Sportfishing Protection Alliance, "Angling Groups Protest."

41. U.S. Geological Survey, Circular 1225, "Sources of Nutrients and Pesticides."

42. Ross and Kaplan, *Poisoning the Air*.

43. Ibid., 21.

44. Ibid., 22.

45. Pesticide Action Network, California River Legal Assistance Foundation, Pesticide Education Center, *Secondhand Pesticides: Airborne Pesticide Drift in California*, report, 2003; Brian Skoloff, "Study: California Pesticide Drifts Routinely Exceed Acceptable Levels," Associated Press, May 8, 2003.

46. Pesticide Action Network et al., *Secondhand Pesticides*.

47. "Task Force Looks at Options to Cut Farm Pollution in River, Gulf," Associated Press, November 20, 1999.

48. Donald A. Goolsby and William A. Battaglin, "Nitrogen in the Mississippi

Basin—Estimating Sources and Predicting Flux to the Gulf of Mexico," U.S. Geological Survey, fact sheet, December 2000.

49. U.S. Geological Survey, "Hypoxia in the Gulf of Mexico," fact sheet, 2003.

50. Goolsby and Battaglin, "Nitrogen in the Mississippi Basin."

51. "Task Force Looks at Options," Associated Press.

52. U.S. Geological Survey, Circular 1225, "Sources of Nutrients and Pesticides."

53. Peter Goering, Helena Norberg-Hodge, and John Page, *From the Ground Up: Rethinking Industrial Agriculture* (London: Zed Books, 1993), 11–12.

54. Ibid.

55. Ibid., 12.

56. For more, see Duff Wilson, *Fateful Harvest: The True Story of a Small Town, a Global Industry, and a Toxic Secret* (New York: HarperCollins Publishers, 2001).

57. Fred Magdoff, John Bellamy Foster, and Frederick H. Buttel, eds., *Hungry for Profit: The Agribusiness Threat to Farmers, Food, and the Environment* (New York: Monthly Review Press, 2000), 77.

58. Carson, *Silent Spring*, 8.

10. THE AGE OF EFFLUENTS

1. Lynn McKinley, interview with the author, Green City, Missouri, December 1999.

2. Michael Mansur, "Environmental Coalition Urges Ban on Waste Lagoons on Factory Farms," *Kansas City Star,* July 24, 2001.

3. *Citizens Legal Environmental Action Network, Inc., v. Premium Standard Farms, Inc., and the U.S. Environmental Protection Agency*, U.S. District Court for Western District of Missouri, St. Joseph division, July 2, 1997.

4. Elizabeth Shogren and Melinda Fulmer, "EPA Widens Rules for U.S. Farms," *Los Angeles Times,* December 17, 2002.

5. Ibid.

6. *Animal Factories: Pollution and Health Threats to Rural Texas,* report, Consumers Union Southwest Regional Office, May 2000.

7. *Hog Lagoons: Pitting Pork Waste Against Public Health and the Environment,* report, Environmental Defense Fund, North Carolina Office, June 1999.

8. Ibid.

9. *Spills and Kills,* report, Clean Water Network, Izaak Walton League, Natural Resources Defense Council, August 2000.

10. Scott Canon, "Hog-Farm Waste Spills into Creek," *Kansas City Star*, December 28, 1995.

11. "PSF Blamed for Improper Disposal of Animal Wastes at Missouri Sites," Associated Press, January 9, 1996; "State to Look at Hog Farm's Building Plans," *Associated Press,* January 3, 1996.

12. Stan Grossfeld, "Animal Waste Emerging as US Problem," *Boston Globe*, September 21, 1998.

13. Associated Press, "Most Large Missouri Feedlots Accused of Violating the Law," July 12, 1998.

14. "Hog Waste's Effects on the Economy," Environmental Defense Fund fact sheet, November 2002.

15. "America's Animal Factories: How States Fail to Prevent Pollution from Livestock Waste," Clean Water Network and Natural Resources Defense Council, December 1998.

16. See Stuart Leavenworth and Joby Warrick, "Sold Down the River," *Raleigh News & Observer*, four-part series, March 6–9, 1996.

17. Melva Okun, "What's That Smell in the Air? Hog Population Report," Environmental Resource Program (Chapel Hill: University of North Carolina, School of Public Health, 1997).

18. U.S. House Committee on Agriculture, Subcommittee on Livestock, Dairy and Poultry and Subcommittee on Forestry, Resource Conservation and Research, *Reducing Water Pollution from Animal Feeding Operations,* testimony by Michael Cook, director and officer of Wastewater Management, and Elaine Stanley, director and officer of compliance of the EPA, Washington, May 13, 1998.

19. "America's Animal Factories."

20. "Hog Waste's Effects on the Economy."

21. Quoted in David Case, "The Love Canal of the 90s? Floating Hog Carcasses Not Surprising in Floyd's Wake," *American Spectator,* October 6, 1999.

22. Peter T. Kilborn, "Storm Highlights Flaws in Farm Law in North Carolina," *New York Times*, October 17, 1999.

23. Ibid.

24. Case, "The Love Canal of the 90s?"

25. "America's Animal Factories"; and Case, "The Love Canal of the 90s?"

26. *Spills and Kills.*

27. Grace Factory Farm Project, *"Facts and Data: Waste Pollution and the Environment,"* available at http://www.factoryfarm.org/facts-wastepollutionandenvironment.html.

28. Calculations based on a fifty-foot tractor-trailer truck carrying twenty-five tons. See also David E. Rosenbaum, "Senator Looks to Home with Bill on Manure Use," *New York Times,* July 29, 2001.

29. *Animal Waste Pollution in America: An Emerging National Problem, Environmental Risks of Livestock and Poultry Production,* Minority Staff of U.S. Senate Committee on Agriculture, Nutrition, and Forestry, December 1997.

30. Rosenbaum, "Senator Looks to Home with Bill on Manure Use."

31. *Animal Waste Pollution in America.*

32. U.S. House Committee on Agriculture, Subcommittee on Livestock, Dairy, and Poultry and Subcommittee on Forestry, Resource Conservation, and Research, *Reducing Water Pollution from Animal Feeding Operations;* and Sierra Club, "Water Contamination from Factory Farms," Factory Farm Fact Sheets, cites EPA, USDA.

33. *Water Contamination from Factory Farms.*

34. U.S. House Committee on Agriculture, Subcommittee on Livestock, Dairy and Poultry and Subcommittee on Forestry, Resource Conservation and Research, *Reducing Water Pollution from Animal Feeding Operations.*

35. Michael Pollan, "Power Steer," *New York Times,* March 31, 2001.

36. Ken Ward Jr., "Threat to the Nation's River?," *The Charlestown Gazette*, October 12, 1998.

37. Ibid.

38. U.S. Centers for Disease Control, "Spontaneous Abortions Possibly Related to Ingestion of Nitrate-Contaminated Well Water—La Grange County, Indiana, 1991–1994," *Morbidity and Mortality Weekly Report* 45, no. 26 (July 5, 1996). See also *America's Animal Factories,* 29.

39. Information about the North Carolina Hog study, unless otherwise cited, is from Christopher D. Cook, "Pork Council Roots Out Researchers," *The Progressive,* September

1999. Quotes not otherwise cited are from interviews with the author, July 1999. Sources include: North Carolina Pork Council; North Carolina Agricultural Statistics Service; primary study: Steve Wing and Susanne Wolf, University of North Carolina, "Intensive Livestock Operations, Health and Quality of Life Among Eastern North Carolina Residents," report prepared for North Carolina Department of Health and Human Services, May 6, 1999; North Carolina Department of Health and Human Services; Elsie Herring case: correspondence from Burrows & Hall, attorneys-at-law, to Elsie Herring, June 24, 1998 (letter is in possession of the author).

40. Wing and Wolf, "Intensive Livestock Operations, Health and Quality of Life Among Eastern North Carolina Residents."

41. Kendall Thu, telephone interview with the author, July 1999.

42. Gary Grant, telephone interview with the author, July 1999. Grant's research cites data from the U.S. Census.

43. Steve Wing, telephone interview with the author, July 1999.

44. Correspondence from Burrows & Hall to Elsie Herring.

45. U.S. Department of Justice and U.S. Environmental Protection Agency, "Nation's Second Largest Hog Producer Reaches Settlement with US & Citizen's Group," news release, November 20, 2001; Missouri Department of Natural Resources, "Department to Take Strong Action against Premium Standard Farms," news release, August 21, 2001.

46. "Tyson Firm Will Pay $6 Million for Maryland Water Pollution," Reuters, May 9, 1998.

47. "Rules and Regulations," *Federal Register* 68, no. 29, February 12, 2003.

48. Anonymous official, California Environmental Protection Agency, telephone interview with the author, June 2003.

49. Available at http://www.nobull.net.

11. SLICED AND DICED: THE LABOR YOU EAT

1. American Meat Institute, "Background: Immigrant Workers in the Meat and Poultry Industry Workforce," promotional materials sent to the author, June 1999.

2. This and all other quotations not footnoted are from interviews with the author, originally published in the following stories: Christopher D. Cook, "Hog-Tied: Migrant Workers Find Themselves Trapped on the Pork Assembly Line," *The Progressive*, September 1999; Christopher D. Cook, "Revolt over Conditions in Poultry Plants," *Christian Science Monitor*, April 28, 1999; Christopher D. Cook, "Plucking Workers: Tyson Foods Looks to the Welfare Rolls for a Captive Labor Force," *The Progressive*, August 1998; Christopher D. Cook, "Fowl Trouble," *Harper's Magazine*, August 1999.

3. Maria, PSF slaughterhouse employee, interview with the author, Sullivan County, Missouri, 1999.

4. José, PSF slaughterhouse employee, interview with the author, Milan, Missouri, 1999. In a November 1997 interview, Greg Denier, spokesman for the United Food and Commercial Workers, told me, "Poultry workers will wet or soil themselves because they are not allowed to go to the bathroom."

5. Emma, PSF slaughterhouse employee, interview with the author, Trenton, Missouri, 1999.

6. Sergio Rivera, PSF slaughterhouse employee, interview with the author, Green City, Missouri, 1999; Dr. Shane Bankus, interview with the author, Milan, Missouri, 1999.

7. Charlie Arnot, interview with the author, Kirksville, Missouri, 1999.

8. Estimates of the total farmworker population vary. The USDA Economic Research Service estimated 840,000 farmworkers in 1999; a Centers for Disease Control document discussing farmworker health and safety in 1998 estimated 2.5 million people involved in farm labor; other estimates place the figure between 1 and 2 million.

9. "Building a Better Future for Farmworkers," USDA Rural Development, Rural Housing Service, August 2000, available at http://www.rurdev.usda.gov/rd/pubs/pa1669.pdf.

10. "Findings from the National Agricultural Workers Survey 1997–1998; a Demographic and Employment Profile of United States Farmworkers," research report no. 8, U.S. Department of Labor, March 2000.

11. "Protecting Farmworkers from Poisons in the Field," Pesticide Action Network of North America, spring 2002, available at http://www.panna.org/about/pu/pu_200203.02.dv.html.

12. Margaret Reeves, Anne Katten, and Martha Guzmán, "Fields of Poison 2002: California Farmworkers and Pesticides," report by Californians for Pesticide Reform, Pesticide Action Network North America, 2002.

13. Coleman Cornelius, "Report: Farmworkers Plagued by Pesticides, Legal Aid Group Alleges Laws Violated," *Denver Post,* August 19, 2002.

14. "Trouble on the Farm: Growing up with Pesticides in Agricultural Communities," report (Washington, DC: Natural Resources Defense Council, 1998).

15. Reeves et al., "Fields of Poison 2002."

16. Ibid.

17. "Surveillance of Hired Farm Worker Health and Occupational Safety," National Institute of Occupational Safety and Health, Centers for Disease Control, 1998.

18. Ibid.

19. U.S. Department of Labor, Bureau of Labor Statistics, "Highest Incidence Rates of Total Nonfatal Occupational Injury and Illness Cases, Private Industry, 2002," available at http://www.bls.gov/iif/oshsum.htm.

20. "Table 102—Total Red Meat and Poultry Supply, Utilization, and Per Capita Consumption, 1971–2001," U.S. Department of Agriculture, Economic Research Service, available at http://www.ers.usda.gov/data/sdp/view.asp?f=livestock/94006/.

21. Robyn Robbins, United Food and Commercial Workers spokesperson, telephone interview with the author, 1998.

22. Mark Grey, professor of anthropology, telephone interview with the author, 1998.

23. U.S. Department of Labor, Bureau of Labor Statistics, "Highest Incidence Rates and Number of Disorders Associated with Repeated Trauma, Private Industry, 2001."

24. National Institute for Occupational Safety and Health, Health Hazard Evaluation Report, surveillance study of workplace safety at Perdue Farms, Inc., February 1990. Supporting information provided by National Broiler Council. Portions of this section originally appeared in Cook, "Fowl Trouble."

25. All descriptions of machines are taken directly from http://www.chickenequipment.com.

26. These and other details about poultry factory conditions, when not otherwise noted, are from Cook, "Fowl Trouble." One example of line speed comes from Teddy Griffin, a former Tyson Foods employee who, according to court documents, "picked up boxes of chicken and laid them on a conveyor belt, handling up to 3,400 boxes in three hours." *Tyson Foods, Inc., Appellant, v. Teddy Griffin, Appellee,* No. CA 97-1184, Court of Appeals of Arkansas, Division I, April 8, 1998. 61 Ark.App. 222, 966 S.W.2D 914.

27. For instance, government investigators clocked evisceration at one poultry plant in Georgia at sixty-two birds per minute. National Institute for Occupational Safety and Health, Health Hazard Evaluation Report, surveillance study of workplace safety at Cargill Poultry Division, November 1989. Information on evisceration line speed also provided by: former Tyson Foods employee Jason Wolfe, telephone interview with the author, 1998; Liz Sessoms, Center for Women's Economic Alternatives, North Carolina, telephone interview with the author, 1998; and Richard Fairfax, Occupational Safety and Health Administration, telephone interview with the author, 1998.

28. Marc Linder, "I Gave My Employer a Chicken That Had No Bone: Joint Firm-State Responsibility for Line-Speed-Related Occupational Injuries," *Case Western Reserve Law Review* 46, no. 1 (fall 1995); see also Cook, "Fowl Trouble."

29. Ibid.

30. Roger Horowitz, *"Negro and White, Unite and Fight!": A Social History of Industrial Unionism in Meat Packing, 1930–90* (Urbana and Chicago: University of Illinois Press, 1997), 277.

31. Ibid., 278.

32. All comments from Premium Standard Foods employees, unless otherwise noted, are from interviews with the author, Sullivan County, Missouri, 1999. Cited in Cook, "Hog-Tied." For details on Connie Mayer allegations, see *Connie Mayer v. PSF Finance* [a corporate entity representing Premium Standard Foods], case no. CV596-43CC, Circuit Court of Mercer County, Missouri, filed November 20, 1997.

33. Francisco Dominguez, telephone interview with the author, June 1998. For details of allegations by Merino and other injured PSF workers, see *Abel Merino et al. v. Premium Standard Foods, Inc., and Armando Alvarez, DBA Ag-Labor Services, Inc.*, United States District Court, Western District of Texas, EP-98-CA-254, filed July 15, 1998.

34. Charlie Arnot, telephone interview with the author, 1998.

35. Horowitz, *"Negro and White, Unite and Fight!,"* 270.

36. Calculations, based on real inflation-adjusted wages in 1998 dollars, provided by Iain Gold, Field Services Department, United Food and Commercial Workers, based on data from U.S. Department of Labor, Bureau of Labor Statistics, National Employment, Hours, and Earnings, data series, 1999. Real wages fell from $16.08 per hour in 1981 to $10.34 in 1998.

37. Based on multiple interviews with meatpacking workers, Missouri, 1998 and 1999. Most workers interviewed lasted just a few months on the job, sometimes less. A couple of workers lasted about a year. Estimates of roughly 100 percent annual worker turnover also provided by Greg Denier, research staff of United Food and Commercial Workers: "They have to constantly feed the labor pool. You could find tons of native-born workers to do the job if you paid higher wages and cleaned up the plants" (telephone interview with the author, November 3, 1997). Independent research has produced similar findings. For instance, see Mark A. Grey, "Immigrants, Migration, and Worker Turnover at the Hog Pride Pork Packing Plant," *Human Organization* 58, no. 1 (1999).

38. Bennett Harrison and Barry Bluestone, *The Great U-Turn: Corporate Restructuring and the Polarizing of America* (New York: Basic Books, 1988), 7–9.

39. Peter Rachleff, *Hard-Pressed in the Heartland* (Boston: South End Press, 1993), 10.

40. Horowitz, *"Negro and White, Unite and Fight!,"* 250–51.

41. Ibid., 249.

42. Jimmy M. Skaggs, *Prime Cut: Livestock Raising and Meatpacking in the United States, 1607–1983* (College Station: Texas A&M University Press, 1986), 190.

43. Ibid., 193.

44. Horowitz, *"Negro and White, Unite and Fight!,"* 252.

45. Ibid., 247.

46. Ibid.

47. Louise Lamphere, Alex Stepick, and Guillermo Grenier, eds., *Newcomers in the Workplace: Immigrants and the Restructuring of the U.S. Economy* (Philadelphia: Temple University Press, 1994), 3.

48. Information and quotations from Premium Standard Foods workers are from Cook, "Hog-Tied." Comments by Sergio Rivera and Luis are from interviews with the author, Green City, Missouri, 1999.

49. American Meat Institute, "Background."

50. Ibid.

51. United States General Accounting Office, "Community Development: Changes in Nebraska's and Iowa's Counties with Large Meatpacking Plant Workforces," report, February 1998, available at http://frwebgate.access.gpo.gov/cgi-bin/useftp.cgi?IPaddress=162.140.64.21&filename=rc98062.pdf&directory=/diskb/wais/data/gao.

52. U.S. Department of Labor, Poultry Processing Compliance Survey Fact Sheet, February 10, 1998.

53. Bill Roenigk, National Chicken Council, telephone interview with the author, 1998.

54. Laurie Cohen, "With Help from INS, U.S. Meat Packer Taps Mexican Work Force," *Wall Street Journal*, October 15, 1998.

55. These and other quotes and information about Tyson, unless otherwise cited, are from Cook, "Plucking Workers"; Jason Wolfe, telephone interview with the author, 1998.

56. Ed Nicholson, telephone interview with the author, 1998.

57. "Tyson Foods Indicted," *Money,* CNN, December 19, 2001; "Ex-Tyson Foods Employee Admits to Immigrant Smuggling," Associated Press, January 7, 2002; and "Jury Acquits Tyson Foods in Immigrant Conspiracy Case," Associated Press, March 26, 2003.

58. Kirstin Downey Grimsley, "Company Towns Are Back and Booming," *Washington Post,* November 27, 1998.

59. Ed Gilber, interview with the author, Green City, Missouri, 1999. Descriptions of worker housing are from visits by the author, Milan and Green City, Missouri, 1999.

60. Charlie Arnot and Harry Frost, interviews with the author, Missouri, 1999.

61. Premium Standard Farms, "Empleo De Tiempo Completo en Premium Standard Farms" [Full-Time Employment with Premium Standard Farms], PSF memorandum, October 1998.

62. United Food and Commercial Workers, "Payment for Personal Protective Equipment," staff memorandum, October 9, 1997; correspondence from Peter J. Ford, Assistant General Counsel, United Food and Commercial Workers, to Tom Harris, Director, North Carolina Department of Labor Wage and Hour Division, September 17, 1993, and December 6, 1994.

63. Regulo Luhan and Arnold, interviews with the author, Milan, Missouri, 1999.

64. Dick Kirschten, "A Melting Pot Chills in Arkansas," *National Journal,* November 14, 1998.

65. American Meat Institute, "Background."

66. Luhan and Arnold, interviews with the author.

67. Portions of this section originally appeared in Christopher D. Cook, "Revolt over Conditions in Poultry Plants," *Christian Science Monitor,* April 28, 1999.

68. Michelle Galvan, Case Farms packing plant employee, telephone interview with the author, March 1999.

69. *Gerardo Castillo et al. v. Case Farms of Ohio, Inc. et al.*, United States District Court, Western District of Texas, No. DR 97-CA-89. Decision ordered by Judge William Wayne Justice, March 23, 1999.

70. Philip Martin, telephone interview with the author, March 1999.

71. Rev. Jim Lewis, telephone interview with the author, March 1999.

72. Laurence Norton, telephone interview with the author, March 1999.

73. Richard Lobb, National Chicken Council, telephone interview with the author, March 1999.

74. Selena Solis, telephone interview with the author, March 1999. See also *Castillo et al. v. Case Farms of Ohio, Inc. et al.*, Order, March 23, 1999.

75. All information for section on Tyson Foods and Direct Job Placement was originally cited in Christopher D. Cook, "Plucking Workers," *The Progressive*, August 1998.

76. Linda Messenger, Missouri Division of Family Services, Pettis County Welfare Director, telephone interview with the author, spring 1998; Missouri Department of Social Services, Division of Family Services, memorandum, June 24, 1997.

77. Missouri Department of Social Services, Division of Family Services, Direct Job Placement program description, 1997; Jerry Helmick, telephone interview with the author, July 21, 1997.

78. Messenger, telephone interview with the author, July 30, 1997.

79. Tim Barchak, state political director of Service Employees International Union in Missouri, telephone interview with the author, July 18, 1997.

80. Brenda Proctor, University of Missouri Cooperative Extension Service, telephone interview with the author, July 30, 1997. Another source, Tim Barchak (see above note), told me, "This is really his [Senator Matthewson's] baby. He's a powerful senator in Missouri. This program was his baby from the get-go, it passed through the Legislature because of his clout. He was pretty much a one-man show for this project."

81. Deborah Hendricks, public information officer, Missouri Division of Family Services, telephone interview with the author, July 23, 1997.

82. Crystal Wolfe, former Tyson worker, telephone interview with the author, July 1997.

83. James M. MacDonald, Michael E. Ollinger, Kenneth E. Nelson, and Charles R. Handy, USDA, Economic Research Service, "Consolidation in U.S. Meatpacking," March 1999, available at http://www.ers.usda.gov/publications/aer785/; David Moberg, "Poultry Giants Fight Organizers," *In These Times,* January 30, 2004.

84. "Hispanics in Iowa Meatpacking," *Rural Migration News,* October 1995, available at http://www.laborers.org/Rural_Meatpacker_10-95.htm.

85. MacDonald et al., "Consolidation in U.S. Meatpacking."

86. David Bacon, "The Kill-Floor Rebellion," *The American Prospect,* July 1, 2002.

87. "Union Charges at Poultry Plant Bring New Policy on Workplace Bathroom Rights," press release, United Food and Commercial Workers, April 15, 1998.

88. "UFCW Vote Pays off for ConAgra Workers," press release, United Food and Commercial Workers, October 24, 2002.

12. SUBSIDIZING MADNESS, EXPORTING MISERY

1. Robert L. Heilbroner and Lester C. Thurow, *Economics Explained* (New York: Simon & Schuster, 1987).

2. See, for instance, Edward Higbee, *Farms and Farmers in an Urban Age* (New York: Twentieth Century Fund, 1963).

3. James Wessel, *Trading the Future: Farm Exports and the Concentration of Economic Power in Our Food System* (San Francisco: Institute for Food and Development Policy, 1983).

4. Joseph N. Belden, *Dirt Rich, Dirt Poor: America's Food and Farm Crisis* (New York/London: Routledge & Kegan Paul, 1986).

5. Janet Poppendieck, *Bread Lines Knee-Deep in Wheat* (New Brunswick, NJ: Rutgers University Press, 1986).

6. Philip McMichael, "Global Food Politics," in *Hungry for Profit: The Agribusiness Threat to Farmers, Food, and the Environment,* ed. Fred Magdoff, John Bellamy Foster, and Frederick H. Buttel (New York: Monthly Review Press, 2000).

7. Belden, *Dirt Rich, Dirt Poor,* 43.

8. USDA, Economic Research Service, "U.S.-EU Food and Agriculture Comparisons," February 2004, available at http://www.ers.usda.gov/publications/WRS0404/WRS0404f .pdf; also see USDA, Economic Research Service, international food consumption patterns table, available at http://www.ers.usda.gov/Data/InternationalFoodDemand/ StandardReports/Foodbudgetshares.xls.

9. USDA, Economic Research Service, "Food Price Review 1950–1997," available at http://www.ers.usda.gov/publications/aer780/aer780.pdf.

10. Howard Elitzak, "Food Marketing Costs at a Glance," *FoodReview,* USDA Economic Research Service, September–December 2001.

11. McMichael, "Global Food Politics."

12. "Rethinking U.S. Agricultural Policy: Changing Course to Secure Farmer Livelihoods Worldwide," report, University of Tennessee, Agricultural Policy Analysis Center, September 2003.

13. Ibid.

14. Willard W. Cochrane, *The Development of American Agriculture* (Minneapolis: University of Minnesota Press, 1979), 139.

15. Ibid.

16. Ibid., 140.

17. U.S. Department of Agriculture, "Building a 2002 Farm Bill," *Science & Education Impact,* available at http://www.csrees.usda.gov/newsroom/impacts/01index/farmbill. html.

18. Environmental Working Group, Farm Subsidy Database, 2003, available at http://www.ewg.org/farm/; Tim Weiner, "Congress Agrees to $7.1 Billion in Farm Aid," *New York Times,* April 14, 2000.

19. "Rethinking U.S. Agricultural Policy."

20. Weiner, "Congress Agrees to $7.1 Billion in Farm Aid."

21. "Farm Programs: Information on Recipients of Federal Payments," Report to the Chairman, Committee on Agriculture, Nutrition, and Forestry, U.S. Senate, U.S. General Accounting Office, June 2001.

22. Environmental Working Group, Farm Subsidy Database, 2003.

23. Environmental Working Group, "Concentration of Payments for Farms in the United States," Farm Subsidy Database, 2002, available at http://www.ewg.org/farm/ concentrationtable.php?fips=00000&yr=2002.

24. John Henry, "Report Reveals Top Farm Subsidies," *Arkansas Business,* September 15, 2003.

25. Environmental Working Group, "The Millionaire's Club," Farm Subsidy Data-

base, 2002, available at http://www.ewg.org/farm/; Kenneth Cook quoted in Emily Gersema, "Report Reveals Top Farm Subsidies of 2002," Associated Press, September 9, 2003.

26. Ibid.

27. Environmental Working Group, "Concentration of Payments for Farms in the United States," Farm Subsidy Database, 2004, available at http://www.ewg.org/farm/concentrationtable.php?fips=00000.

28. "Farm Programs: Information on Recipients."

29. Brian M. Riedl, "Still at the Federal Trough: Farm Subsidies for the Rich and Famous Shattered Records in 2001," Heritage Foundation backgrounder, April 30, 2002.

30. Edward A. Chadd, "Manifest Subsidy," *Common Cause Magazine,* Fall 1995; U.S. Environmental Protection Agency, "How We Use Water in These United States," 2003; Natural Resources Defense Council, "Wasting Water on California Farms"; Roger Segelken, "End Irrigation Subsidies and Reward Conservation, CU Study Advises," *Cornell Chronicle,* January 30, 1997. For more on J.R. Simplot and the french fry business, see Eric Schlosser, *Fast Food Nation.*

31. USDA, Economic Research Service, "Export Share of U.S. Ag Production Is a Stable 21 Percent," *Agricultural Outlook,* November 2002.

32. Bruce A. Babcock, "The Concentration of U.S. Agricultural Subsidies," *Iowa Agricultural Review* (Center for Agricultural and Rural Development), Fall 2001.

33. Ibid.

34. Ibid.

35. USDA, Economic Research Service, "U.S. Agricultural Trade: Global Agricultural Trade."

36. Associated Press, "Poor Nations Air Subsidies Gripe," September 11, 2003.

37. George Monbiot, "The Worst of Times," *The Guardian,* September 2, 2003.

38. Ibid.

39. Ibid.

40. Ibid.

41. Chris Kraul, "WTO Meeting Finds Protests Inside and Out," *Los Angeles Times,* September 11, 2003.

42. Patricia Hewitt, "Making Trade Fairer," *The Guardian,* September 12, 2003.

43. Kraul, "WTO Meeting Finds Protests Inside and Out."

44. Associated Press, "Poor Nations Air Subsidies Gripe."

45. James Meek, "The Subsidies Gap," *The Guardian,* September 8, 2003.

46. Afrol News, "West's Cotton Subsidies Cost Africa Hundreds of Millions," July 15, 2002. Article cites data and analysis from World Bank and the International Cotton Advisory Committee.

47. Charlotte Denny and Larry Elliott, "Protecting the Land," *The Guardian,* September 8, 2003; World Bank, "Cutting Agricultural Subsidies," press release, November 20, 2002.

48. Jimmy Langman, "Chilean Farmers Protest Trade Pact," *Miami Herald,* June 11, 2003.

49. World Bank, "Cutting Agricultural Subsidies."

50. For more information, see World Trade Organization web site, at http://www.wto. org/english/thewto_e/whatis_e/ inbrief_e/inbr00_e.htm.

51. Public Citizen, "A Citizen's Guide to the World Trade Organization: Everything You Need to Know to Fight for Fair Trade"; also, Public Citizen, "The WTO on Agriculture: Food As a Commodity, Not a Right"; both available at www.citizen.org.

52. Writers Block, "Protest and Death in Cancun," *CounterPunch*, September 12, 2003.

53. Ibid.

54. Anuradha Mittal, "Daily Report from Cancun #5," Food First, September 12, 2003; Christian Parenti, "Postcard from Cancun," *The Nation*, September 15, 2003.

55. Tom Hayden, "Cancun Report: As Empire Builder, the U.S. Feels the Heat," AlterNet, September 9, 2003.

56. The phrase "dumping on the poor" is borrowed from Duncan Green and Matthew Griffith, "Dumping on the Poor: The Common Agricultural Policy, the WTO and International Development," report, Catholic Fund for Overseas Development, September 2002.

57. Mark Ritchie, Sophia Murphy, and Mary Beth Lake, "United States Dumping on World Agricultural Markets," report, Institute for Agriculture and Trade Policy, 2003.

58. Ibid.

59. Green and Griffith, "Dumping on the Poor."

60. Ibid.

61. Douglas H. Boucher, ed., *The Paradox of Plenty: Hunger in a Bountiful World* (Oakland, CA: Food First Books, 1999).

62. Susan George, *How the Other Half Dies: The Real Reasons for World Hunger* (Montclair, NJ: Allenheld, Osmun, 1977), 164.

63. Frances Moore Lappé, Joseph Collins, and David Kinley, *Aid as Obstacle: Twenty Questions About Our Foreign Aid and the Hungry* (San Francisco: Institute for Food and Development Policy, 1980), 94.

64. Lappé et al., *Aid as Obstacle,* 94.

65. Ibid.

66. Ibid., 95.

67. Ibid., 95–96.

68. Michael E. Conroy, Douglas L. Murray, and Peter M. Rosset, *A Cautionary Tale: Failed U.S. Development Policy in Central America* (Boulder: Lynne Rienner Publishers, 1996). Christopher Cook and Peter Rosset, "Exporting Misery," *In These Times,* May 26, 1997.

69. Boucher, ed., *Paradox of Plenty*, introduction, xii.

70. United Nations Food and Agriculture Organization, statistical database, 2004; United Nations Food and Agriculture Organization, "The State of Food Insecurity in the World," 2003, available at www.fao.org.

13. THE GOOD NEWS: A MENU FOR CHANGE

1. The idea of boycotting Tyson was lofted publicly by Vandana Shiva and Eric Schlosser at "Fast Food World: Perils and Promises of the Global Food Chain," a panel discussion at the University of California, Berkeley, November 24, 2003. Neither suggested this was the whole solution; rather it is one aspect of a broader movement.

2. Analisa Nazareno, "Organic Grows in Popularity," *San Antonio Express-News,* November 15, 2003.

3. Ellen Byron, "Will Kids Buy Organic Food in School Vending Machines?" *Wall Street Journal,* October 15, 2003.

4. AScribe Newswire, "Organic Consumers Association Criticizes New Federal Labeling, Says 'USDA Organic' Is 'Grade B' Organic," October 1, 2002.

5. Nao Nakanishi, "Chinese Farmers Cash in on Need for Organic Food," Reuters, October 25, 2003.

6. Kenny Swain, interview by the author, San Francisco, California, November 8, 2003.

7. Nazareno, "Organic Grows in Popularity."

8. Michael Pollan, "The Organic-Industrial Complex," *New York Times Magazine,* May 13, 2001.

9. Ibid.

10. Nazareno, "Organic Grows in Popularity."

11. Kit R. Roane, "Ripe for Abuse—Farmworkers Say Organic Growers Don't Always Treat Them as Well as They Do Your Food," *U.S. News & World Report,* April 22, 2002.

12. Ronnie Cummins, interview by the author, San Francisco, California, November 8, 2003.

13. Ryan Zinn, interview by the author, San Francisco, California, November 8, 2003.

14. Jim Hightower, interviews with the author, San Francisco, California, November 8, 2003.

15. Michelle Nijhuis, "Beyond the Pale Green: Activists and Small-Scale Farmers Are Going 'Beyond Organic' to Push Local Foods," *Grist Magazine,* November 12, 2003.

16. Andrew Kimbrell, ed., *Fatal Harvest: The Tragedy of Industrial Agriculture* (Washington, DC: Foundation for Deep Ecology/Island Press, 2002).

17. The Community Food Security and Empowerment Act, a proposal for the 1995 Farm Bill, submitted by the Community Food Security Coalition, January 1995. This proposal laid the groundwork for the Community Food Security Act, passed by Congress in 1996. For more information, contact the coalition at http://www.foodsecurity.org/index.html.

18. Christopher D. Cook and John Rodgers, "Community Food Security: A Growing Movement," Food First Backgrounder, Spring 1996; for additional studies, see "Improving Access to Food in Low Income Communities: An Investigation of Three Bay Area Neighborhoods," California Food Policy Advocates, January 1996; and "Access Denied: An Analysis of Problems Facing East Austin Residents in Their Attempts to Obtain Affordable, Nutritious Food," report, Sustainable Food Center, Austin, Texas.

19. Cook and Rodgers, "Community Food Security."

20. Christopher D. Cook, "Cultivating Locally: Community Gardening for Food Security," *Community Greening Review,* 1997.

21. Federal Document Clearing House, Inc., "Veneman Awards $4.6 Million in Grants to Community Food Projects," press release, October 16, 2003.

22. Brian Skoloff, "Group Pushes for Locally Grown Food in California Schools," Associated Press, September 23, 2003.

23. USDA, Agricultural Marketing Service, "How Local Farmers and School Food Service Buyers Are Building Alliances," report, May 1, 2000.

24. USDA, Agricultural Marketing Service, "Farmers' Market Facts," July 2003.

25. USDA, WIC Farmers' Market Nutrition Program, fact sheet, May 2003.

26. Peter Rosset, interview by the author, Oakland, California, July 17, 2003.

27. Michael Pollan, "Fast Food World: Perils and Promises of the Global Food Chain," a discussion panel at the University of California, Berkeley, November 24, 2003.

28. "Cultivating Locally: Community Gardening for Food Security."

29. For program description and background, see http://www.hartfordfood.org/about/index.html.

30. For more information, see http://www.foodconnect.org/.

31. For program description and background, see http://www.mnfoodassociation.org/.

INDEX

agribusiness, 6–7, 125–52; and agricultural economics, 148–50; and contract farming, 133–35; and corporate consolidation, 7, 132–33, 140–50; effects on rural communities, 126–27, 135–40, 144; and hidden costs, 4–6, 150–52; and hog farming, 125–28, 135–40; and monopolies, 93–96, 141, 150; and new farm crisis, 6, 127–31; and prices, 128–29, 143–46, 150, 152. *See also* alternatives to agribusiness/unsustainable food system; factory farming; subsidies, agricultural; supermarkets

Agricultural Act (1970), 83

Agricultural Adjustment Act (1933), 219

Agricultural Adjustment Administration, 100

Agricultural and Consumer Protection Act (1973), 83

Aid as Obstacle (Food First), 239, 240

air pollution, 155–57, 176

Akplogan, Fatiou, 233

Albertson's, 18, 20, 257

Alegria, Rafael, 232

Alfaki, Adil, 232

algae blooms, 158, 170–71, 176

alternatives to agribusiness/unsustainable food system, 10–11, 243–59; anti-GMO efforts, 246; "community food security" projects, 248, 252–56, 257–58; direct farmer-to-consumer connections, 247, 255–56; efforts to save the family farm, 247–48; fair-trade movements, 247; food safety and consumer health movements, 247; instituting local food policies, 257–58; organic movement, 26, 47–48, 73, 173, 246, 248–52; recognizing the consequences of consumption, 243–45; resistance efforts, 245–48; steps in making the changes, 256–59

Altieri, Miguel A., 173

American Academy of Pediatrics, 54

American Agriculture Movement, 119

American Cancer Society, 54

American Farm Bureau Federation, 43, 102

American Heart Association, 54

American Journal of Epidemiology, 47

American Lung Association, 156

American Meat Institute, 36, 187, 201, 207

American Medical Association, 54

American Rivers, 181

American Stores, 18

Andreas, Dwayne, 3

Andrews, Stanley, 79, 102, 105, 106

antibiotics and meat/dairy production, 64–68

Aposhian, Vas, 30

Archer Daniels Midland (ADM), 7, 133, 142, 143, 146, 226, 257

Arizona Food Policy Council, 258

Arnot, Charlie, 189, 198, 204, 208

Aronowitz, Stanley, 82, 98

assembly-line speeds, 5, 57, 187–88, 195–96, 216

atrazine, 167–68, 191

Austin, Texas, 254

avian flu, 27–28

Azzam, Azzeddine, 17

Babcock, Bruce, 229–30

Bacon, David, 215

bacterial diseases, 48, 54–64, 67–68, 135

Baltimore Sun, 134–35

Barchak, Tim, 212–13, 214

Beef Trust, 77

Beiser, Vince, 41

Bek, Theodore, 60

Belden, Joseph, 113

Bell, Rev. Velda, 205

Benin, 232–33

Berhow, Trent J., 42

Berry, Wendell, 7

Beyond Beef (Rifkin), 47

Bil Mar Foods, 62

Biotechnology Industry Organization (BIO), 163

Blobaum, Roger, 250

Block, John, 111, 115

Blythe, Rudy, 114

Bond, Sen. Christopher S., 13, 15, 16
Boston Globe, 43
Boucher, Douglas H., 241
Bové, Jose, 245
bovine spongiform encephalopathy (BSE), 28–29. *See also* mad cow disease (BSE)
Bracero program, 102–3
Branstad, Gov. Terry, 122, 123
Breimyer, Harold, 116
Brezhnev, Leonid, 79
British Medical Journal, 53
Broken Heartland (Davidson), 84, 110
Browner, Carol, 160
Bush, George W., 33, 34, 230, 233
Butterball Turkey Co., 204
Butz, Earl, 79–83, 84, 109, 124

CAFOs, 175
California: and farm pollution, 155–57, 185; and pesticide-use, 166–70, 190, 191
California Department of Pesticide Regulation, 167
California Farm Bureau, 156, 157
California Food and Justice Coalition, 255
California Food Policy Advocates, 22, 23
California Fruit Growers Exchange, 95
California Public Interest Research Group, 166
Californians for Pesticide Reform, 166, 170, 191
Callicrate, Mike, 125, 145–46, 186
Campylobacter jejuni and *Campylobacter* illnesses, 48, 54–55, 57–58, 68
Cancer Research, 47
Cargill, 7, 133, 140–44, 146–48, 257
Carmen, Diane, 63
Carson, Rachel, 160–62, 167, 173
Carter, Jimmy, 82, 111, 195
Cascadian Farm, 250
Case, David, 179
Case Farms, 208–11
Castillo v. Case Farms (1999), 209
Caterpillar, 226
Catholic Fund for Overseas Development, 238
A Cautionary Tale (Conroy et al.), 241
Center for Food Safety, 253
Center for Rural Affairs, 128, 225
Centers for Disease Control (CDC): on agricultural waste and human health, 181–82; and Creutzfeldt-Jakob disease, 29; and food-borne illnesses, 44, 54–55, 68; and mad cow disease, 31, 32; on overweight and obesity, 46
Central American Free Trade Agreement, 247

Charlestown Gazette, 181
Chavez, Cesar, 190
Chevron, 226
Chicago, Illinois, 22, 90
Chicago Board of Trade, 93
Chicago Tribune, 100
Chile, 233
chlordane, 161–62, 165
chlorpyrifos, 71, 170
Christen, Rolf, 136, 174–75
Citizens Legal Environmental Action Network (CLEAN), 175, 184–85
Civil War, 91, 92
Clean Water Network, 175
Clinton, Bill, 61, 254
Cliver, Dean, 35
Cochrane, Willard W., 91, 93, 102, 103, 222–23
Collins, Joseph, 243
Colombia, 240
Common Cause Magazine, 228, 229
Community Alliance with Family Farmers, 255
Community Food Connections, 258
Community Food Security Act (1995), 254
Community Food Security Coalition, 248, 253
community food security programs, 25, 248, 252–58
Community Supported Agriculture (CSA), 25, 152, 247, 258
ConAgra, 63, 133–34, 144, 146, 199–200, 212, 215, 257
Concerned Citizens of Tillery, 183
Congressional Quarterly Almanac, 112–13
Consumers Union, 176
Continental Grain Co., 81, 140–41, 142, 147, 184
contract farming, 133–35
Cook, Kenneth, 226
Cook, Michael, 180–81
corn industry, 64–66, 100
Cornell University's Institute for Comparative and Environmental Toxicology, 66
The Cotton Industry (Hammond), 96
cotton trade and subsidies, 232–33
Council for Agricultural Science and Technology, 51
Crabtree, John, 128, 129, 135, 136
Creutzfeldt-Jakob disease, 29
CropLife America, 163
Cummins, Ronnie, 251, 252

Daschle, Sen. Tom, 143–44
Davidson, Osha Gray, 84–85, 110, 111

DDT, 69–70, 161, 162, 165

Delmarva Peninsula, 180, 185

Delmarva Poultry Justice Alliance, 210

Denver Post, 63

Depression, Great, 98–99, 119, 219–20

DES (diethylstilbestrol), 66

Des Moines Register, 117

Detroit, Michigan, 21–22

Detroit News, 23

DeWaal, Caroline Smith, 45, 48, 70

diazinon, 170

Diet for a Small Planet (Lappé), 51–52

Dirt Rich, Dirt Poor (Belden), 113

Dominguez, Francisco, 197

Dorgan, Sen. Byron, 141

Drabenstott, Mark, 132

DuPont, 226

Dupont/Pioneer Hi-Bred, 147

Durbin, Sen. Richard, 33, 34

E. coli 0157:H7, 30, 54–58, 63, 135

Eisenhower, Dwight, 104, 105–6

Endocrine Society in the United States and Canada, 69–70

Environmental Defense Fund, 176

Environmental Health Perspectives, 24

Environmental Protection Agency (EPA): and factory farm waste, 175, 180–81, 185; and fish safety, 30; and pesticide residues, 48, 70, 72, 167; and supermarkets, 24

Environmental Working Group, 71, 72, 225, 226

Erie Canal, 90

ETC (Action Group on Erosion, Technology and Concentration), 147

European Journal of Clinical Nutrition, 65

European Union, 66, 230, 231, 233–34, 236

Evert, Jon, 130

Excel Corp., 35, 60, 144, 199–200

exports: and agricultural subsidies, 230–38; and dumping, 236–38; and farm crisis of the 1980s, 112–13; and global market, 131–32; nineteenth century, 90–93. *See also* subsidies, agricultural

Factories in the Field (McWilliams), 190

factory farming: and antibiotic use, 64–68; and bacterial diseases, 56–57, 59–60, 135; and contract farming, 135; emergence of, 109; hog farms, 125–28, 135–40; and meat safety inspections, 38–40, 41–43, 59–60; and workers' health, 56. *See also* hog industry; poultry industry

factory farming and farm waste, 157–58, 174–86; air pollution, 176; citizen lawsuits, 174, 184–85; fish kills, 175–77, 179, 185; hog farm waste, 174–79, 180, 181–85; industry reactions, 183–84; manure spills, 177, 178, 179; poultry industry,177, 180, 181, 185; public health impacts, 181–84; regulation and reform efforts, 184–86; river/stream pollution, 175–79, 180–82; volume of waste, 179–80

fair-trade movement, 247

Farm Bill, 11, 224

Farm Board, 99

Farm Credit System, 122

farm crisis of the 1980s, 84–85, 110–24; causes of, 110–13; and farmers' desperation, 113–16; farmers' incomes and debts, 115–16; farmers' protests/resistance, 118–20; and increasing production costs, 116; liquidations and foreclosures, 117–20, 122; and machinery dealers/manufacturers, 121; and Republican economic policies, 121–24; and rural communities, 120–21

farm policy, history of, 77–78, 79–124; early American, 85–89; nineteenth century, 89–96; and land rush, 89–90; emerging markets and export boom, 90–93; and early agribusiness, 90–96; railroads, 90, 94–95; monopolies, 93–96; farmers' cooperative movements, 94–96; early twentieth century, 96–97; Depression and Dust Bowl, 98–99; Roosevelt and New Deal relief, 81, 99–101, 223; World War II and modern agribusiness, 101–3; creation of subsidy system, 219–20, 222–23, 241–42; early mechanized farming, 101–2; Bracero program, 102–3; mid-1950s and chronic surplus, 103–6, 222–23; mid-twentieth century, 98–109, 219–20, 222–23; convenience culture and food processing, 105–6, 221; Nixon policies of 1970s, 79–84; 1970s and food marketing costs, 106; growing corporate dominance, 107–9; and surpluses, 92–93, 98–101, 103–6, 222–23. *See also* factory farming; farm crisis of the 1980s; subsidies, agricultural

farm-to-retail price spread, 16–18, 23, 144–46, 150, 152, 221

Farmers Home Administration (FmHA), 117–18, 119–20

farmers: *See also* agribusiness; alternatives to agribusiness/unsustainable food system; citizen lawsuits, 174, 184–85; contract farming, 133–35; direct farmer-to-consumer connections, 247, 255–56; effects on rural communities, 126–27, 135–40, 144; efforts to save the family farm, 247–48; farm crisis of the 1980s, 84–85, 110–24; farm-to-retail price spread, 16–18, 23, 144–46, 150, 152, 221; farmers' markets; organic and sustainable agriculture; small farms, productive efficiency of, 149–50; subsidies, agricultural, 78, 217–42; supermarket; surpluses

farmworkers, 190–92

farmers' markets, 25, 152, 246, 247, 255–56

Farmland National Beef, 145–46

Fast Food Nation (Schlosser), 25

FDA. *See* U.S. Food and Drug Administration (FDA)

Federal Register, 35, 195

Federal Surplus Relief Corporation, 101

Financial Times, 116

First Majority, Last Minority (Shover), 12, 80

fish: farm waste and fish kills, 175–77, 179, 185; fish farms, 158; and food safety, 29–30; and pesticides, 30, 168–69

Florida Fruit and Vegetable Association, 17

Food, Shelter, and the American Dream (Aronowitz), 82, 98

food aid programs, 220, 238–41

food-borne illnesses, 5, 30, 44–45, 48, 54–58

"food-chain clusters," 48

Food First, 133, 149, 239, 256–57

Food for Peace program (1954), 84, 161, 239, 242

Food Marketing Institute, 17

Food Politics (Nestle), 44, 46

food prices, 16–18, 23, 82–83, 151, 220–22, 251–52

Food Quality Protection Act (1996), 72

food safety and public health, 44–74; agribusiness and government, 46, 50–51, 73–74; agribusiness interests and nutrition, 46, 48–54; alternatives, 73–74; antibiotics and meat/dairy production, 64–68; and bacterial diseases, 48, 54–64, 68, 135; feedlots and factory farms, 56–57, 59–60, 135; and fish, 29–30; and food-borne illnesses, 5, 30, 44–45, 48, 54–58; health and nutrition issues, 5, 45–54; and mad cow disease, 28–29, 31–43; and meat consumption, 46–48, 51–54; meat inspections, 38–40, 41–43, 58–64; meat recalls, 62–64; and obesity, 45–47; and pesticide residues, 48, 69–72; poultry industry, 27–28, 48, 55, 68; and processing speeds, 56–57; and supermarket disparities, 23–24. *See also* mad cow disease (BSE); pesticides

Foreman, Carol Tucker, 40

Fox, Nicols, 55–56, 58

Fred Meyer, 18

free trade, 230–36, 247

Free Trade Agreement of the Americas, 247

Freedom to Farm Act (1996), 131, 222, 224–25

Fresno Bee, 155–56

Fretwell, Estil, 137

Fry, Randy, 169

Galvan, Michelle, 208–9, 214

Gambone, James, 119

General Accounting Office (GAO), 16, 39, 58–59, 82, 202, 225, 227

General Foods, 108

General Mills, 151–52, 245, 249–50

genetically modified organisms (GMOs), 7–9, 162–63, 241, 246

George, Susan, 239

Georgia-Pacific, 226

Gerberding, Julie, 46

Giampietro, Mario, 158

Gingrich, Rep. Newt, 131

Givens, Holly, 249–50

Glickman, Dan, 61–62, 225

Godfrey, Gary, 126, 136–37, 138, 139

Goodlatte, Rep. Robert, 41, 72

Government Accountability Project, 39, 41, 60

Granger movement, 94–96

Grant, Gary, 183

Grassley, Sen. Charles, 141, 143–44

Green City, Missouri, 200

Green Revolution, 84, 241

Grey, Mark, 192–93, 201–2, 208

The Guardian, 231, 232

Guillain-Barré syndrome, 57–58

Gulf of Mexico, 158, 170–72

Hamilton, Alexander, 88

Hammond, M.B., 96

Hammonds, Tim, 17

Harms, Dennis, 187

Harrison, Alisa, 40

Hart, Sen. Gary, 124
Hartford Food System, 21, 258
Harvest of Shame (Murrow), 190
Hassebrook, Chuck, 225
Hayden, Tom, 236
Hazard Analysis and Critical Control Point
    (HAACP), 59–60
Heffernan, William, 26, 114, 146, 147–48
Heilbroner, Robert, 217
Helmick, Jerry, 208, 212
Heritage Foundation, 227
Higbee, Edward, 98, 101–2, 104
Hightower, Jim, 252
Hindhede, Mikkel, 53
hog industry: and corporate consolidation,
    144; and farm waste, 174–79, 180, 181–84;
    and new farm crisis, 125–28. *See also*
    Premium Standard Farms (PSF)
Holmes, George K., 79
Homestead Act (1862), 89–90
Honduras, 232
Hong Kong, 28
Hoover, Herbert, 99, 219
Horizon, 250
Hormel, 198
Horowitz, Roger, 196, 199, 200
House Agriculture Committee, 41
How the Other Half Dies (George), 239
How to Select Foods (USDA), 50
Humane Society, 248
hunger and the myth of food scarcity, 8–9,
    241–42
Husson, Mark, 12, 19
Huston, Thomas, 121

immigrant labor, 5, 139–40, 198, 200–211,
    216; and company towns, 203–5;
    farmworkers, 190–92; and the INS, 206–7;
    meatpacking industry, 187–89, 192,
    197–98, 200–202; poultry industry, 201,
    202–3; and racism, 205–6; recruiting,
    201–3, 208–11; and union organizing, 209;
    worker turnover and destabilization,
    207–8, 209–11. *See also* labor issues for
    food-processing workers
Immigration and Naturalization Service
    (INS), 206–7
Independent Bakers Association, 15
injuries and illnesses of food-processing
    workers, 188–89, 192–93, 194–98, 216
Institute for Agriculture and Trade Policy,
    129, 233, 238
Insurance Information Institute, 35

International Paper, 226
Iowa: and farm crisis of 1980s, 114, 120, 122;
    hog farming and, 137, 182; pesticide
    residues in, 167; topsoil loss in, 158
Iowa Beef Processors (IBP), 145–46, 199–200,
    202
Iowa Farmers Union, 118
irrigation, large-scale, 158
irrigation subsidies, 228–29
Is Our Food Safe? (Leon and DeWaal), 45
Isom, Roger, 157

Jack in the Box, 58–59
Jackson, Wes, 246
Jefferson, Thomas, 87–88
Jenkins, James Lee, 114
John Deere, 121
John Hancock Mutual Insurance, 226
Johnson, Sen. Tim, 143–44
Johnson (LBJ) administration, 107
Jones, Rep. Ed, 118
Jong-wook, Lee, 27
Journal of Farm Economics, 240
Journal of the American Medical Association,
    53
Jungclaus, Nolan, 144
The Jungle (Sinclair), 45, 192
Justice, Judge William Wayne, 209

Kansas Association of Wheat Growers, 116
Kegley, Susan, 170
Kelly, Oliver Hudson, 94
Kemp, Rep. Jack, 123
Kentucky, 167–68
Kern County Land Company, 107
Kerrey, Bob, 121
Keyes, Chandler, 41
Kiesecker, Joseph, 169
Kraft, 249
Krebs, A.V., 126, 130–31, 142, 143, 151–52
Kroger, 18, 19, 20

LA Weekly, 36
labor issues for food-processing workers,
    187–216; assembly-line speeds, 5, 57,
    187–88, 195–96, 216; company towns and
    worker housing, 203–5; farmworkers'
    labor, 189–92; geographic shifts and plant
    relocations, 199–200; immigrant/migrant
    labor, 5, 139–40, 187–89, 190–92, 197–98,
    200–211, 216; industry changes since mid-
    1980s, 198–200; injuries and illnesses,
    188–89, 190–93, 194–98, 216; and the INS,

labor issues for food-processing workers, (*continued*)
206–7; pesticide poisoning, 190–91; processing, 193–95; recruiting, 201–3, 208–11; unions, 198–99, 209, 214–16; wages, 190; welfare reform and exploitation, 211–14; and worker protection laws, 208–11; worker turnover and destabilization, 207–8, 209–11; workers' lawsuits, 196–98, 208–11, 214. *See also* meatpacking industry; poultry industry

Laborers' International Union of North America, 214

Lancet, 52

Land Act (1800), 89

Land Institute, 246

Land Survey Ordinance of 1785, 85

Lappé, Frances Moore, 51–52, 243

Lee Kyung-hae, 235–36

Leon, Warren, 45, 48, 70

Lewis, Rev. Jim, 210

Linder, Marc, 195

Listeria monocytogenes, 57, 62–63

Living Downstream (Steingraber), 164

Lobb, Richard, 211

Los Angeles, California, 22, 23

Los Angeles Times, 174, 175, 233

Losing Ground (Ulrich), 123–24

Louisville Courier-Journal, 96

Luhan, Regulo, 206

mad cow disease (BSE), 28–29, 31–43; and beef industry, 36–37, 40–43; "downer cows," 33–34, 41; economic fallout of, 34–36; and regulatory systems/inspections, 37–40, 41–43; and rendering process, 31–32

Mad Cow U.S.A. (Rampton and Stauber), 31

Madison, Tom, 178

Majka, Theo J., 94, 96

Martin, Philip, 210

Mathewson, James L., 213

Mayer, Connie, 196–97, 214

McCabe, James Dabney, 94

McDonald's, 74, 149, 216

McKinley, Jeri, 174

McKinley, Lynn, 125–26, 174

McLaughlin, Jennifer, 20

McMichael, Philip, 220, 222

McWilliams, Carey, 109, 190

Meat & Poultry, 60

meat consumption, 46–48, 51–54

meat inspections, 37–40, 41–43, 58–64

meat recalls, 62–64

meatpacking industry: assembly-line speeds, 5, 187–88, 196, 216; and farm-to-retail prices, 150; geographic shifts and plant relocations, 199–200; immigrant/migrant workers, 187–89, 192, 197–98, 200–202; industry changes since mid-1980s, 198–200; injuries and illnesses, 188–89, 192–93, 196–98, 216; market control and economic concentration, 143–44; and unionization, 198–200, 214–16; and worker protection laws, 208–11. *See also* labor issues for food-processing workers

Meese, Edwin, 123

Merchants of Grain (Morgan), 79

Merino, Abel, 197, 214

Messenger, Linda, 213–14

Miami Herald, 233

Micek, Ernest S., 142

Midoux, Albert, 59–60

Milan, Missouri, 187–88, 204, 205–6

Minnesota, 1980s farm crisis in, 113–14, 118, 119–20

Minnesota Food Association, 258

Mississippi Delta Council, 129

Mississippi Farm Bureau, 132

Mississippi River Basin, 171–72

Missouri: "Direct Job Placement" welfare-to-work program in, 212; factory hog farming in, 125–26, 128, 135–40, 174–77, 184; poultry industry and labor issues in, 211–12

Missouri Farm Bureau Federation, 137

Mitchell, Karen Taylor, 34

Mitchell, Robert, 129

Modern Meat (Schell), 66

Monsanto, 8, 142, 147, 148, 162–63, 257

Mooney, Patrick H., 94, 96

Moore, Dale, 41

Moore, David, 15, 17

Morgan, Chip, 129

Morgan, Dan, 79, 81

Morris, Glenn, Jr., 56, 67

Mother Jones, 20

Murphy, Dan, 36

Murphy, Wendell, 179

Murrow, Edward R., 190

The Myth of the Family Farm (Vogeler), 108

NAFTA, 201, 247

National Academy of Sciences, 54

National Cattlemen's Beef Association (NCBA), 34, 36, 40–41, 51, 62

National Chicken Council, 202, 211
National Corn Growers Association, 66
National Corn-Hog Committee of Twenty-Five, 100
National Family Farm Coalition, 247
National Farmers' Union, 114, 117, 247
National Food and Agriculture Policy Project, 15
National Food Processors Association, 62
National Institutes of Health, 24
National Reclamation Act (1902), 228
National Research Council, 59, 71
Natural Resources Defense Council, 175, 191, 228–29
Nature's Valley, 251
Neighborhood Market, 19
neoliberalism, 234
Nestle, Marion, 44, 46, 49–50, 57–59, 65, 67, 68
Nestor, Felicia, 39
New Deal, 81, 99–100, 223
New England Journal of Medicine, 54, 68, 69
New River Foundation, 178
New York Times, 20, 41, 42, 68, 110, 114, 131, 142, 178, 225, 250
Nicholson, Ed, 202
Nixon, Jay, 177
Nixon, Richard, 79–84
North Carolina, factory farm waste in, 176, 177–79, 183–84
North Carolina Pork Council, 183
North Carolina's Neuse River Basin, 177–78
North Dakota, 120
Northwest Missouri Private Industry Council, 136
Norton, Laurence, 210
Novartis, 147, 148
nutrition and health, 45–54; agribusiness interests and, 46, 48–54; meat consumption and, 46–48, 51–54; obesity, 5, 45–47. *See also* food safety and public health

obesity, 5, 45–47
Occidental College's Urban and Environmental Policy Institute, 22
Occupational Safety and Health Administration (OSHA), 215
Ogallala aquifer, 158
Ohio Company, 87, 88
Okun, Melva, 177–78
Omaha Together, One Community, 215
O'Neill, Thomas "Tip," 123

Opie, John, 84, 86, 88, 89
organic and sustainable agriculture: and "community food security" projects, 255; corporations and organic agribusiness, 249–50; and exploitive work conditions, 251; growing popularity of, 246, 248–52; and large-scale monocrop farming, 250–51; limitations of, 249–52; organic foods, 26, 47–48, 73, 246; price issues, 251–52; sales and rates of, 248–49, 250; and supermarkets, 26; transitioning to, 173, 249
Organic Consumers Association, 249, 251–52
Organic Trade Association, 250
Osterholm, Michael, 68
Oxfam, 233

Packaging Corp. of America, 108
The Paradox of Plenty (Boucher, ed.), 239, 241
Parenti, Christian, 236
Patrick, Eugene, 114
Pauley, George J., III, 41
PCBs, 29
People for the Ethical Treatment of Animals, 248
People's Party, 96
Perdue, 133–34
Pesticide Action Network, Asia and Pacific branch, 163
Pesticide Action Network of North America (PANNA), 166, 170, 190
pesticides, 5, 157, 160–73; air currents and pesticide drift, 169–70, 190; and algae blooms, 158, 170–71, 176; alternatives to, 172–73; biotechnology and GM crops, 162–63; bird deaths, 161–62, 166; chemical fertilizers, 170–72; continuing environmental presence of, 165–70; farmworkers and pesticide poisoning, 190–91; in fish/aquatic creatures, 168–69; and groundwater contamination, 162, 167; and industry-agriculture dependence, 164, 173; mid-century proliferation of, 160–62, 163–64; and pest resistance, 164–65; pesticide residues, 48, 69–72; in rivers and streams, 162, 167–68
Pfiesteria piscicida, 179, 185
Physicians Committee for Responsible Medicine, 33
Pilgrims Pride Corp., 226
Pimentel, David, 5, 158, 228, 252
The Politics of Food (Solkoff), 80
Pollan, Michael, 11, 64–66, 181, 250, 257

pollution, agricultural, 4, 155–59. *See also* factory farming and farm waste
Poppendieck, Janet, 99, 100–101, 219
Potash and Phosphate Institute, 171–72
Potomac River, South Branch, 181
poultry industry: and assembly-line speeds, 5, 57, 195–96; and avian flu, 27–28; and contract farming, 133–35; execution devices, 193–94; farm waste, 177, 180, 181, 185; and food safety crisis, 27–28, 48, 55, 68; labor issues, 193–96, 201, 202–3, 205, 208–11, 214–15; and worker protection laws, 208–11; workers' injuries and illnesses, 194–96. *See also* labor issues for food-processing workers
Premium Standard Farms (PSF): and corporate consolidation, 142, 144; exploitation of cheap labor force, 212; and farm waste, 136, 174–77, 184; immigrant/migrant workers, 139–40, 187–89, 200–201, 204–5, 208; and labor environments, 187–89, 196–98, 204–5; lawsuits against, 174, 184; in Missouri, 125–26, 128, 135–40, 174–77, 184
Price Waterhouse Coopers LLC, 23
prices: and agribusiness, 128–29, 143–46, 150, 152; and farm-to-retail price spread, 16–18, 23, 144–46, 150, 152, 221; food, 16–18, 23, 82–83, 151, 220–22, 251–52; and organics, 251–52; and subsidies, 220–22; and supermarkets, 16–18, 23
Probst, Ed and Georgia, 134
Proceedings of the National Academy of Sciences, 169
processed foods, 9–10, 45, 106
Proctor, Brenda, 213
Producers Rice Mill Inc., 226
Proposition 187 (California), 192
protectionism, 233–35
Prusiner, Stanley, 43
Public Citizen, 41, 60–61, 234–35, 247
public health: and costs of food-borne illness, 57–58; and impacts of farm waste/pollution, 181–84. *See also* food safety and public health
Purina Mills Inc., 38
Pyle, Robert N., 15

Rachleff, Peter, 198
Ralph's/Food 4 Less Warehouse Stores, 15, 23
Rampton, Sheldon, 31–32, 42
Ranchers-Cattlemen Action Legal Fund, 144–45

Rascón, Olivia, 197–98
Reagan, Ronald, 121–22, 195, 199, 215
Recreational Fishing Alliance of Northern California, 169
Rengam, Sarojeni V., 163
Riceland Foods Inc., 226
Rifkin, Jeremy, 47, 51, 52, 53, 54
Ritchie, Mark, 129
Rivera, Sergio, 188–89, 200–201
Robbins, John, 50, 53, 66, 69
Robbins, Robyn, 192
Roenigk, Bill, 202
Rogers, Arkansas, 206
Roosevelt, Franklin Delano, 81, 219
Rosset, Peter, 133, 135, 142, 149–50, 256–57
Roundup Ready, 8, 163
Rudolph, Lauren, 58
Rural Life Outreach of Northwest Minnesota, 130
Ruthton, Minnesota, 113–14

Safe Tables Our Priority, 34
Safeway, 7, 20, 257
Salmonella, 30, 54, 55, 57, 68
Sampier, John, 206
Sam's Club, 19
San Francisco, California, 23
San Joaquin Valley, 155–56
Sara Lee, 62
Schell, Orville, 66
Schlosser, Eric, 25, 40–41, 63, 243
Schuh, G. Edward, 117
Schultz, Floyd, 142
Schumacher, Herman, 144–45
Scott, Jenny, 62
Seattle Post-Intelligencer, 38
Sedalia, Missouri, 213
seed industry, 132–33, 146–47, 148
Senate Agriculture Committee, 144, 179–80
Senate Small Business Committee, 12, 16
Service Employees International Union, 213, 214
Sheets, Larry, 114
Shover, John L., 12, 80, 82, 106
Shuman, Charles W., 119
Sierra Club, 178–79
Silent Spring (Carson), 160–61, 163–64, 173
Simplot, J.R., 229
Sinclair, Upton, 45, 192
slotting fees, 13, 14–17
"slow foods" movement, 74
small farms, productive efficiency of, 149–50

Smith, Adam, 150
Snyder, Cliff, 171–72
Solis, Selena, 211
Solkoff, Joel, 80
Solomon, Steven, 34
South Korea, 235–36, 240
Soviet Union, 79–81, 111
Spence, Terry, 138, 140
Spoiled (Fox), 55
St. Louis-Post Dispatch, 137
St. Paul Pioneer Press, 129
Stallman, Bob, 43
Stanley, Elaine, 180–81
Stauber, John, 31–32, 42
Steingraber, Sandra, 69, 164–65
Stenholm, Rep. Charles, 41
Stenzel, Thomas E., 15
Stern, Nicholas, 234
Stevenson, Shawn, 129
Stockman, David, 122–23
Strawberry Fields (Wells), 102
Stuart, Michael J., 17
subsidies, agricultural, 78, 217–42;
    alternatives to current system, 242, 257;
    and corporate welfare, 225–28; and
    export dumping, 236–38; and exports,
    230–38; and food aid programs, 220,
    238–41; and food prices, 220–22; and
    Freedom to Farm Act, 224–25; history of,
    219–20, 241–42; increases since mid-
    1990s, 224–25; inequities in, 224–30;
    and myth of food scarcity, 241; and
    pesticides, 173; and protectionism, 233–35;
    and surpluses, 173, 218–20, 222–24,
    236–38, 241–42; for water/irrigation,
    228–29
Supermarket News, 19
supermarkets, 12–26; alternatives to
    corporate monopoly of, 25; and food
    prices, 16–18, 23; processed foods and food
    advertising, 106; and retail consolidation,
    7, 13–14, 18–20; and slotting fees, 13,
    14–17; threats to small food
    manufacturers, 12–16; unequal
    distribution of, 20–22; in urban/poor
    neighborhoods, 20–24, 253–54
surpluses: and agricultural subsidies, 173,
    218–20, 222–24, 236–38, 241–42; and
    Depression era subsidy system, 219–20,
    241–42; and export dumping, 236–38; and
    history of farm policy, 92–93, 98–101,
    103–6, 219–20, 222–23, 241–42; of mid-
    1950s, 103–6, 222–23, 242

Swain, Kenny, 249
Swift & Co., 35–36
Symmes, John Cleves, 87

Tauxe, Robert, 54, 56
Taylor, C. Robert, 150
Teamsters, 214
Tenneco, 107, 108
Texas Rural Legal Aid, 211
Thomas, Karrie Stevens, 255
Thu, Kendall, 182
Thurow, Lester, 217
topsoil, 158
Trading the Future (Wessel), 218
transportation costs and food system, 5,
    252–56
Treat, Payson Jackson, 86, 87, 89
Trevino, Israel, 211
Trimble, William, 92–93
Tyson Foods: and contract farming, 134; and
    corporate consolidation, 7, 257; and labor
    issues, 202–3, 206, 211–14; and mad cow
    disease, 36; pollution and legal
    responsibility, 185

Ulrich, Hugh, 123–24
UN Food and Agriculture Organization, 8,
    52, 163
Union of Concerned Scientists, 8, 64
unions, 198–99, 206, 214–16, 248
Unionville, Missouri, 125, 135–40, 174,
    196–97
United Farm Workers, 190
United Food and Commercial Workers
    International Union (UFCW), 192, 205,
    208, 214, 215
United Fresh Fruit and Vegetable Association,
    15
United Packinghouse Workers of America,
    199–200
United Press International, 38
University of Connecticut's Food Marketing
    Policy Center, 21
University of Missouri, 14, 20–21, 26, 138
"The Urban Grocery Store Gap," 22
U.S. Agency for International Development
    (USAID), 240
U.S. Congress: and agribusiness
    consolidation, 141, 143–44; and
    community food security projects, 254–55;
    and farm crisis of 1980s, 118, 122–23; and
    farm subsidies, 224–25; and farm waste
    crisis, 179–80

U.S. Department of Agriculture (USDA): and agribusiness consolidation, 143, 145; and assembly-line speeds, 57, 195–96; and BSE, 29, 32–34, 38–42; Commission on Small Farms, 143, 152; and community food security projects, 254–56; Economic Research Service, 18, 21; and factory farm waste, 181; and farm subsidies and surpluses, 224, 237; and farmworkers' labor, 190; food pyramid, 46, 50–51; on food-related illnesses and public health costs, 57; food safety inspections, 38–39, 41–42, 59–63, 195; and new farm crisis, 126, 131; nutritional advice and agribusiness interests, 46, 50–51; and pesticides, 163; and productive efficiency of small farms, 149–50; and supermarket slotting fees, 16

U.S. Fish and Wildlife Service, 165

U.S. Food and Drug Administration (FDA), 8; and antibiotic resistance, 67; and BSE-related monitoring, 37–40; Center for Veterinary Medicine, 37; Food Advisory Committee, 30; and pesticide residues, 48, 70–71

U.S. Geological Survey, 165, 167, 168, 169, 171, 180

U.S. News & World Report, 251

"The Value of Herbicides in U.S. Crop Production" (Gianessi and Sankula), 163

Veneman, Ann, 33, 34, 36, 40–41, 42, 163

Vern's Moses Lake Meats, 38

Via Campesina, 232

Vietnam, 27–28, 80

Vogeler, Ingolf, 108

Volcker, Paul, 110–11, 123

Waide, David, 132

Wal-Mart, 19–20, 250, 252, 257

Wall Street Journal, 19–20, 147, 202

Walters, Charles, Jr., 217

Washington Post, 32–33, 111, 119, 203–4

Washington state, 28, 33, 37–38

waste. *See* factory farming and farm waste; pollution

water: drinking water, 181–82; farm waste and pollution of, 175–79, 180–82; irrigation, 158, 228–29; pesticide contamination, 162, 167–68; and subsidies, 228–29

welfare reform, 211–14

Wells, Miriam J., 102

Wellstone, Sen. Paul, 141

Wessel, James, 218

Western Growers Association, 15, 17

Whitman, Christine Todd, 175

Whole Foods grocery chain, 248–49

Wilson, Duff, 172

Winesburg, Ohio, 208–9, 211

Winfrey, Oprah, 40

Wing, Steve, 182–84

Winne, Mark, 21

Wolf, Susanne, 183

Wolfe, Crystal, 214

Wolfe, Jason, 202

Womack, Steve, 206

Women, Infants and Children Farmers' Market Nutrition Program (WIC), 256

World Bank, 172, 233–34

World Health Organization (WHO), 27

World Trade Organization (WTO), 222, 230–36, 234–36

World War I, 96–97

World War II, 52–53, 101–3, 220, 222, 239

Worldwatch Institute, 252

Wright, Jerry, 119

Writers Block, 235–36

X-Cel Feeds Inc., 37–38, 39

Yersinia enterocolitica and *Yersinia* infections, 56

Yost, Mike, 142

Zinn, Ryan, 251, 252